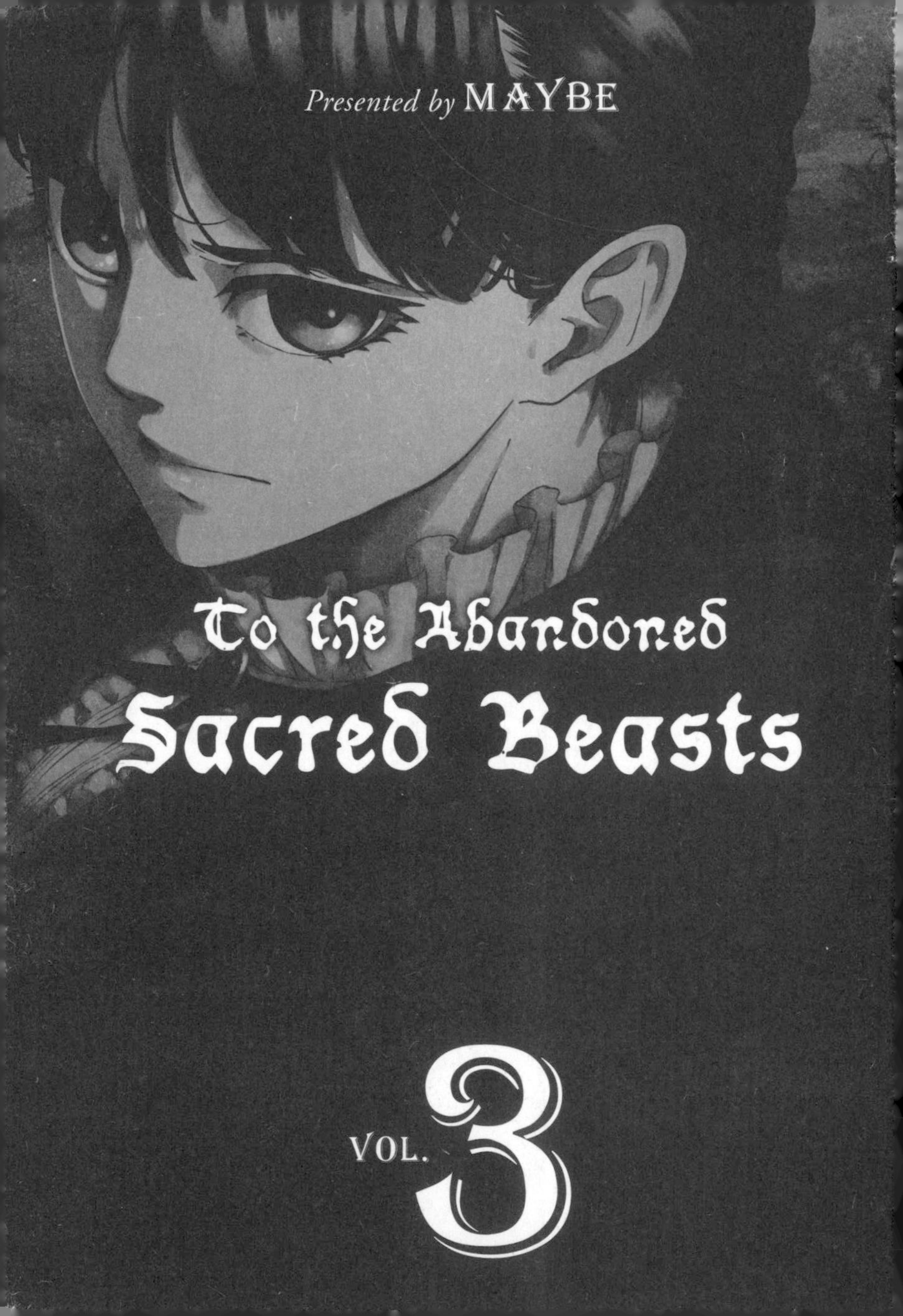
Presented by MAYBE
To the Abandoned
Sacred Beasts
VOL. 3

CONTENTS

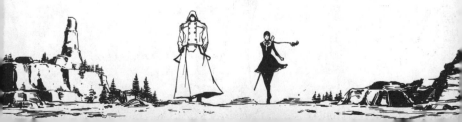

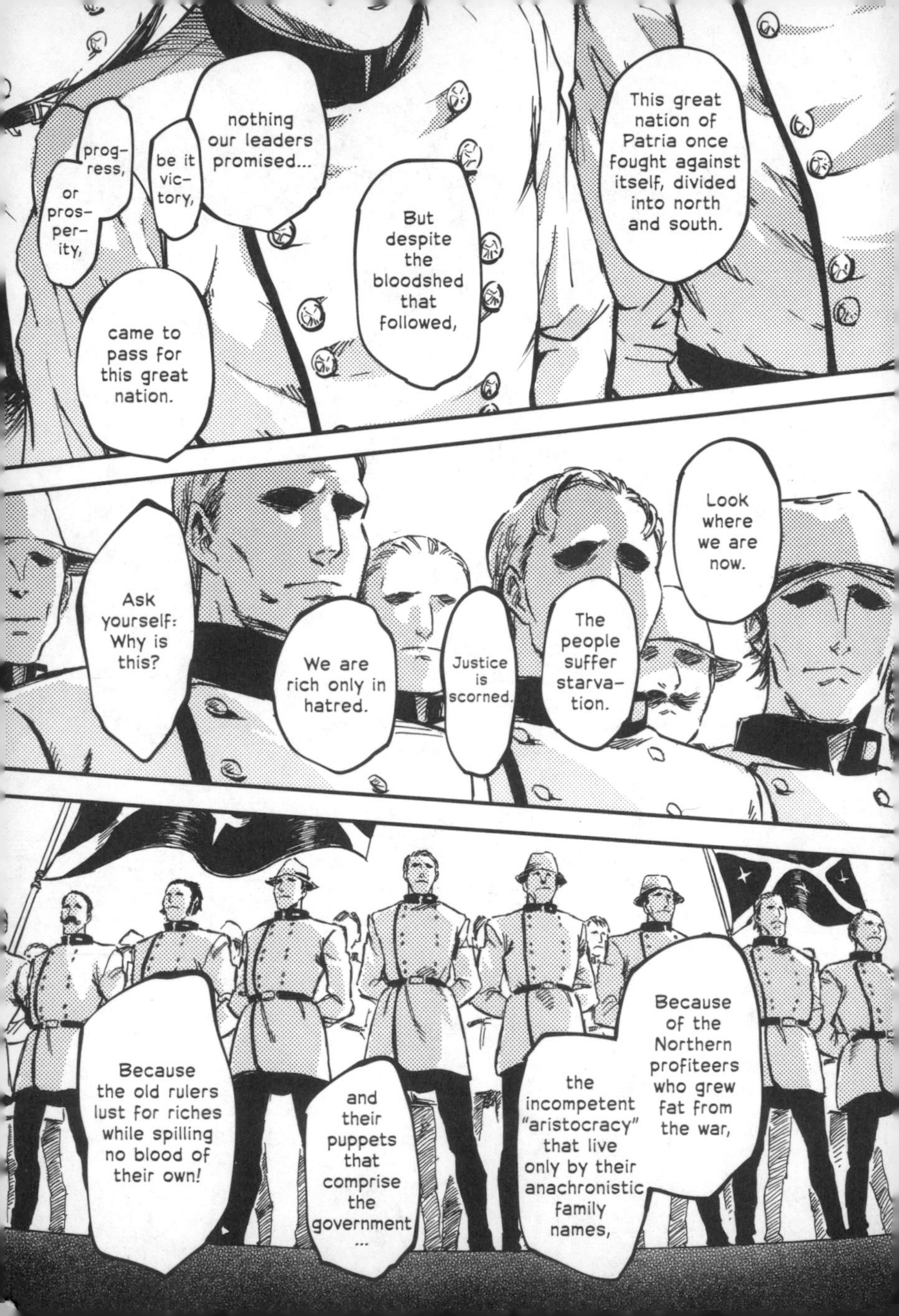
This great nation of Patria once fought against itself, divided into north and south.
But despite the bloodshed that followed,
nothing our leaders promised...
be it victory,
progress,
or prosperity,
came to pass for this great nation.
Look where we are now.
The people suffer starvation.
Justice is scorned.
We are rich only in hatred.
Ask yourself: Why is this?
Because of the Northern profiteers who grew fat from the war,
the incompetent "aristocracy" that live only by their anachronistic family names,
and their puppets that comprise the government...
Because the old rulers lust for riches while spilling no blood of their own!

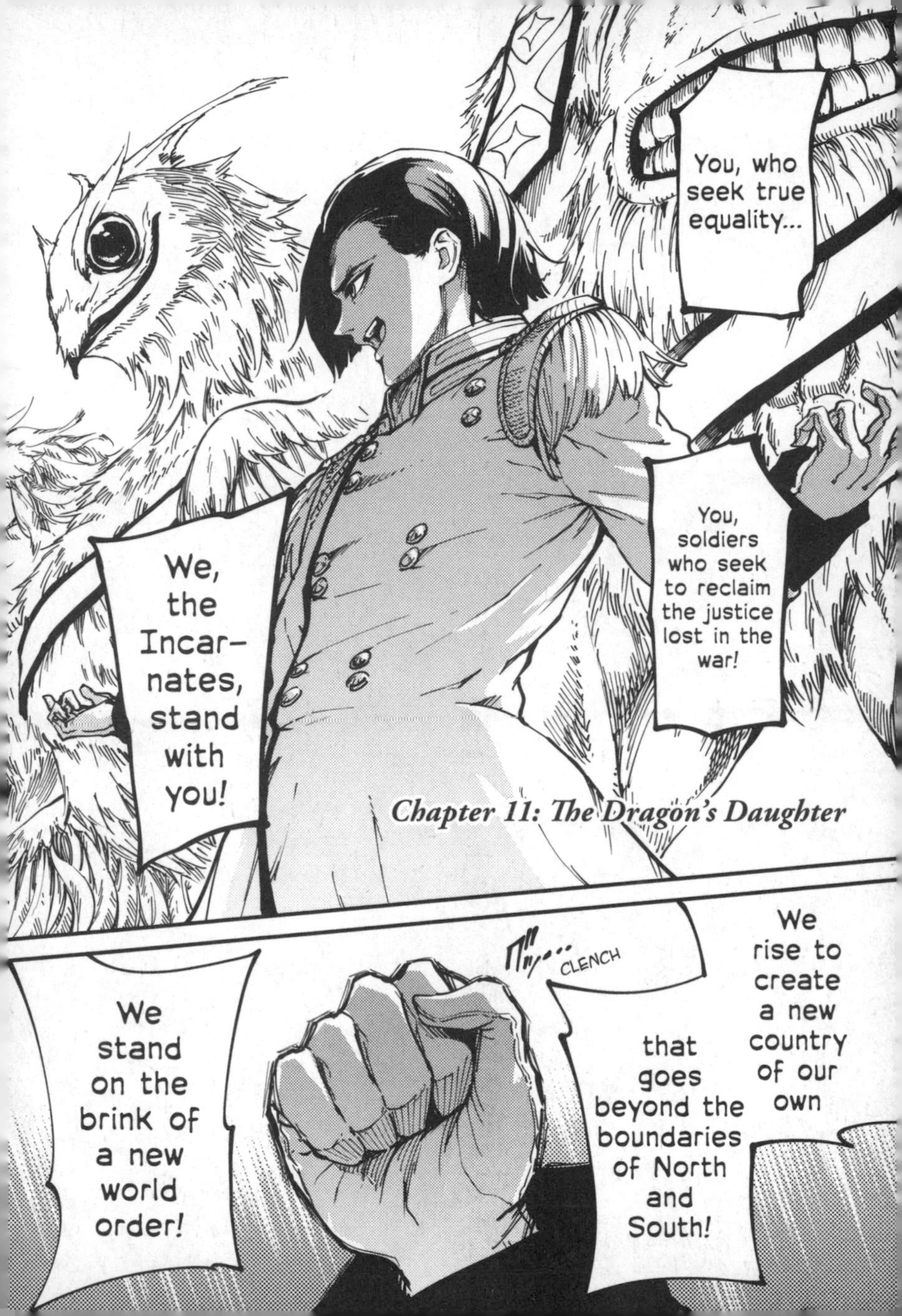
You, who seek true equality...
You, soldiers who seek to reclaim the justice lost in the war!
We, the Incar-nates, stand with you!
Chapter 11: The Dragon's Daughter
We rise to create a new country of our own
that goes beyond the boundaries of North and South!
CLENCH
We stand on the brink of a new world order!

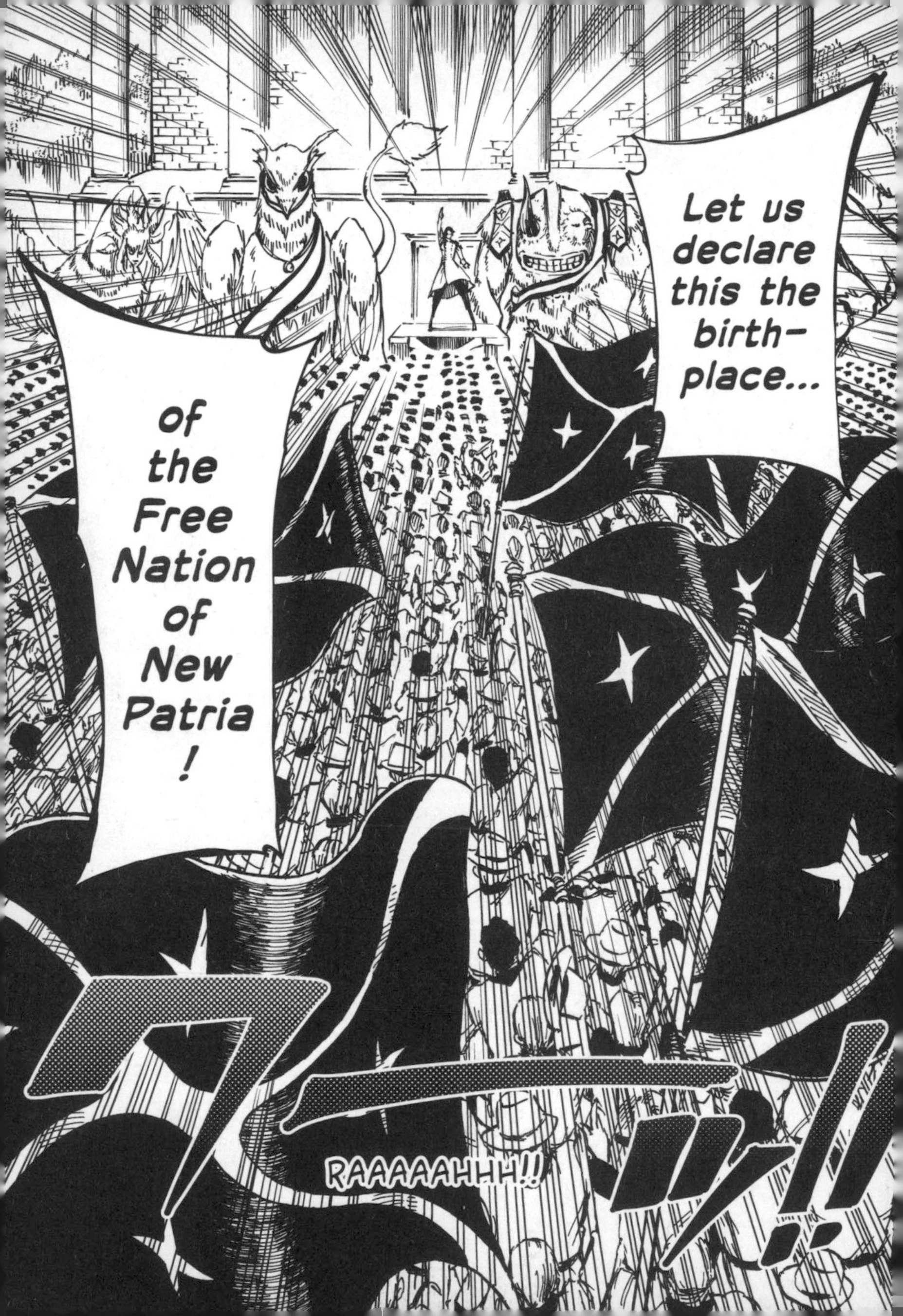
Let us declare this the birth-place...
of the Free Nation of New Patria!
RAAAAAHHH!!

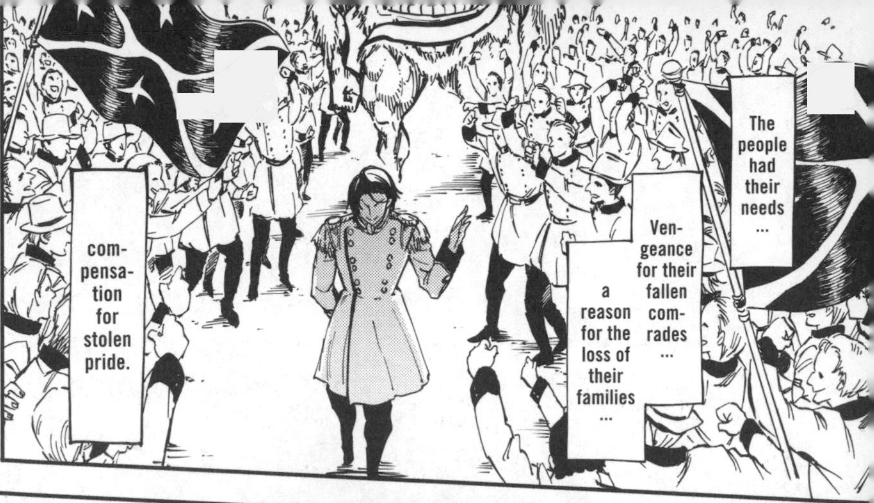
The people had their needs...
Vengeance for their fallen comrades...
a reason for the loss of their families...
compensation for stolen pride.

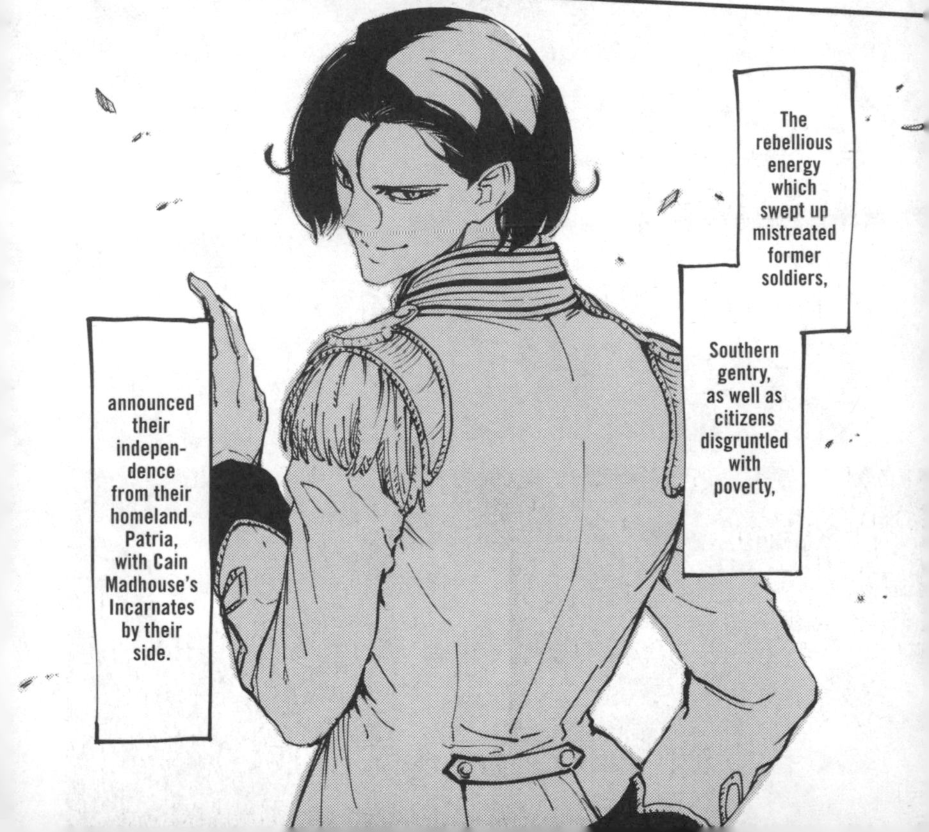
The rebellious energy which swept up mistreated former soldiers,
Southern gentry, as well as citizens disgruntled with poverty,
announced their independence from their homeland, Patria, with Cain Madhouse's Incarnates by their side.

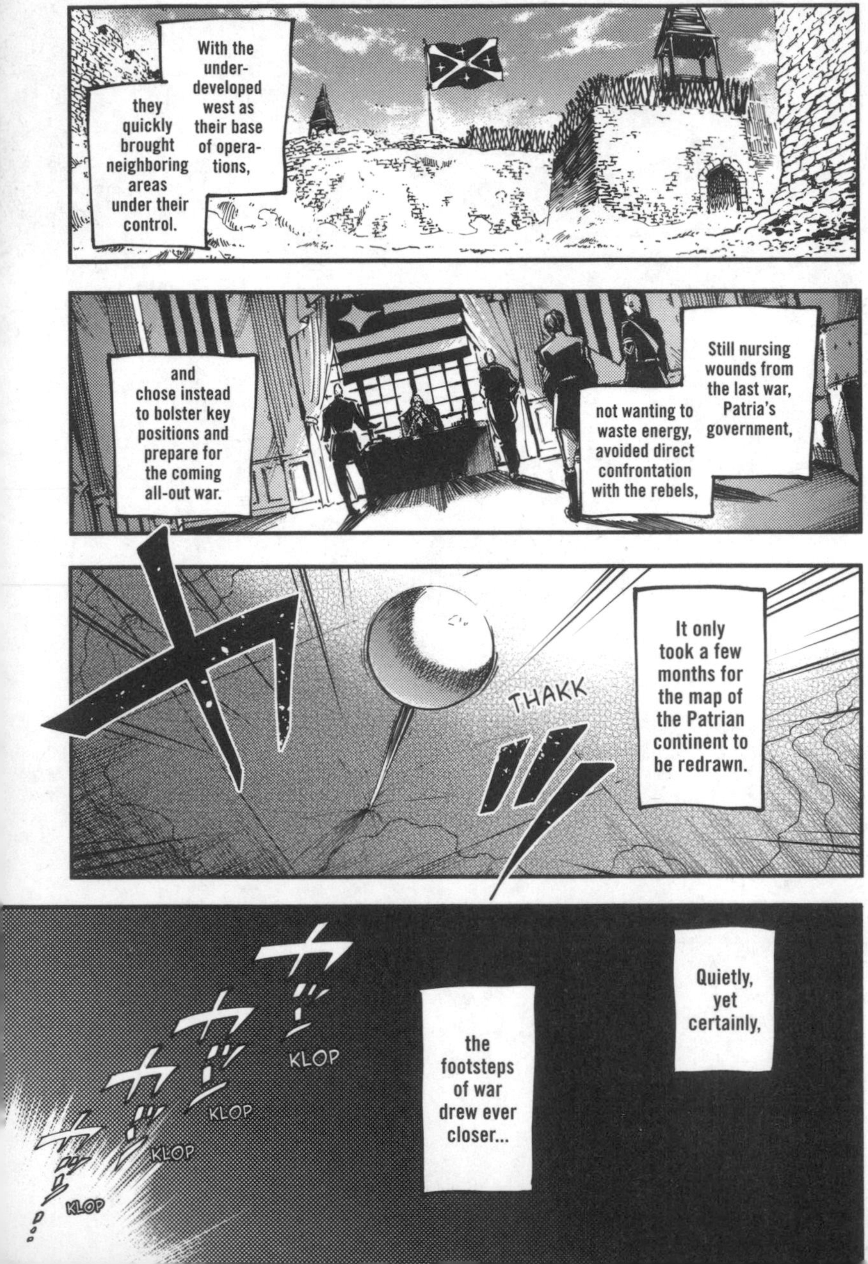
With the under-developed west as their base of operations,
they quickly brought neighboring areas under their control.
Still nursing wounds from the last war, Patria's government,
not wanting to waste energy, avoided direct confrontation with the rebels,
and chose instead to bolster key positions and prepare for the coming all-out war.
It only took a few months for the map of the Patrian continent to be redrawn.
THAKK
Quietly, yet certainly,
the footsteps of war drew ever closer...
KLOP
KLOP
KLOP
KLOP

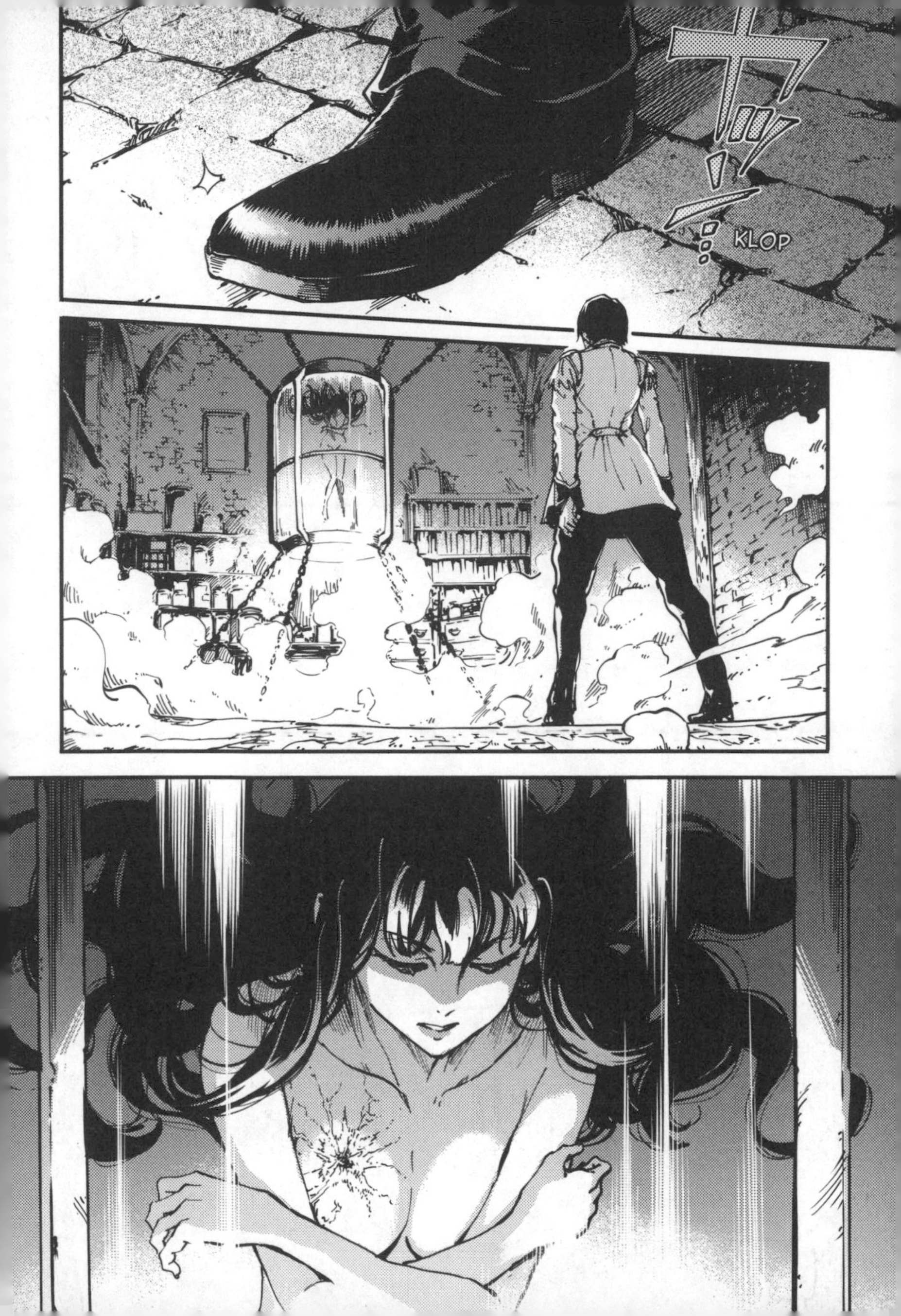
KLOP

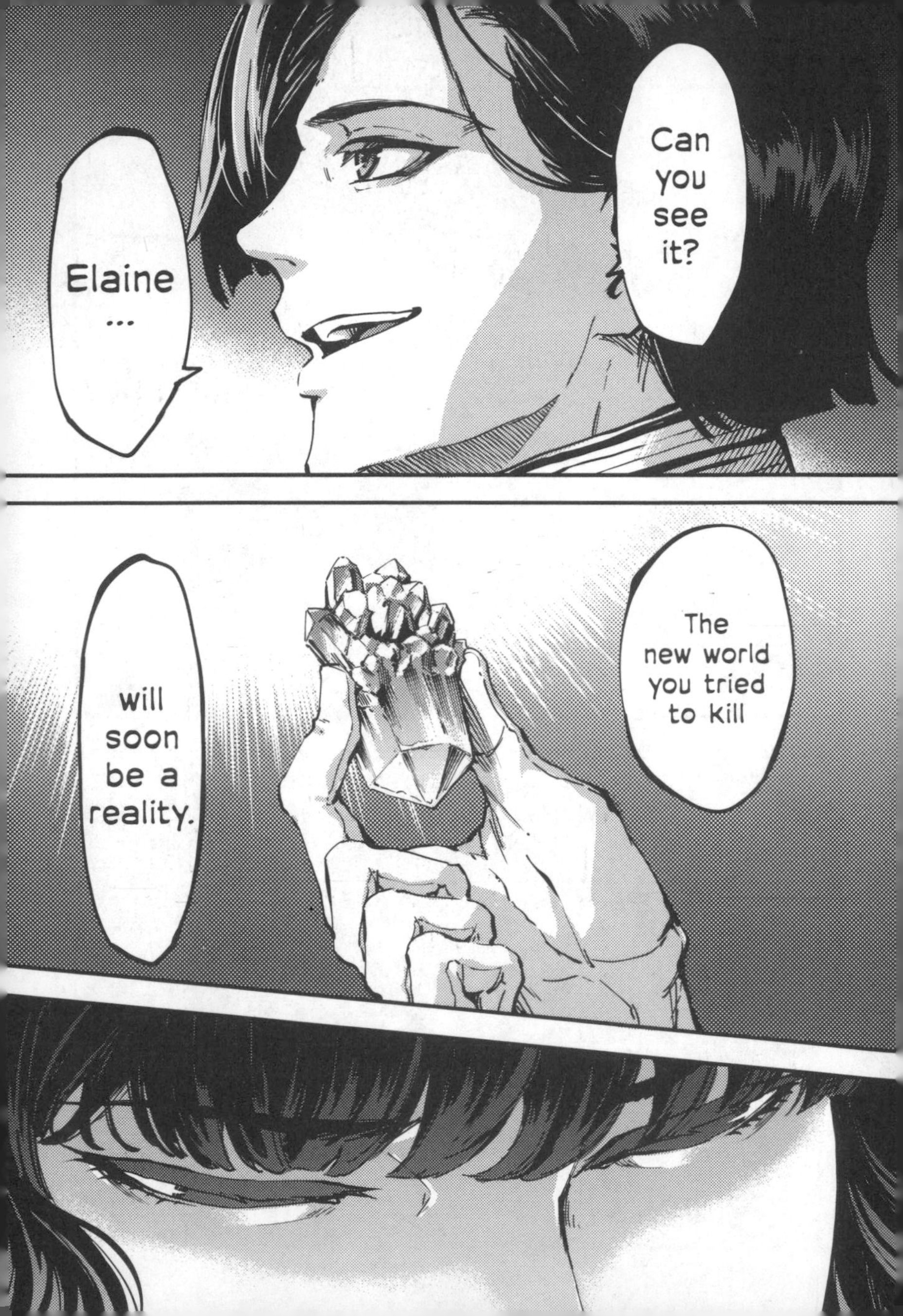
Can you see it?
Elaine...
The new world you tried to kill
will soon be a reality.

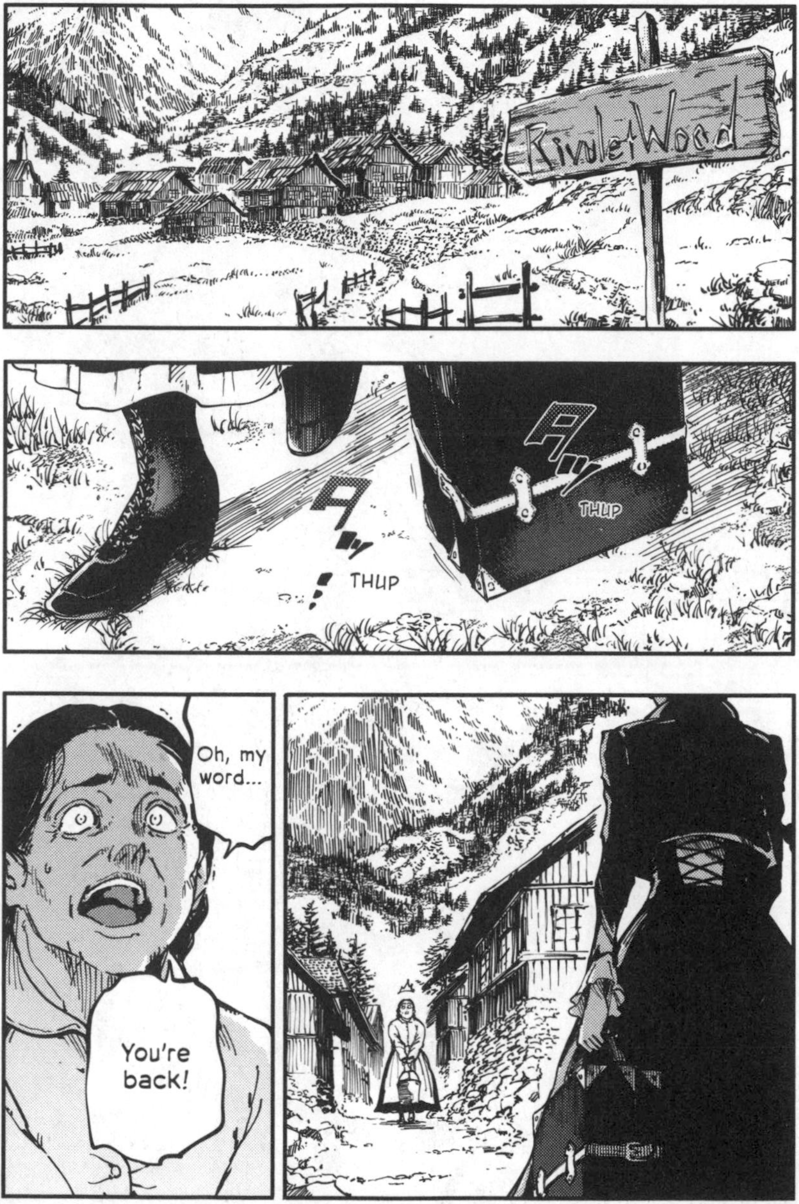
RivuletWood
THUP
THUP
Oh, my word...
You're back!

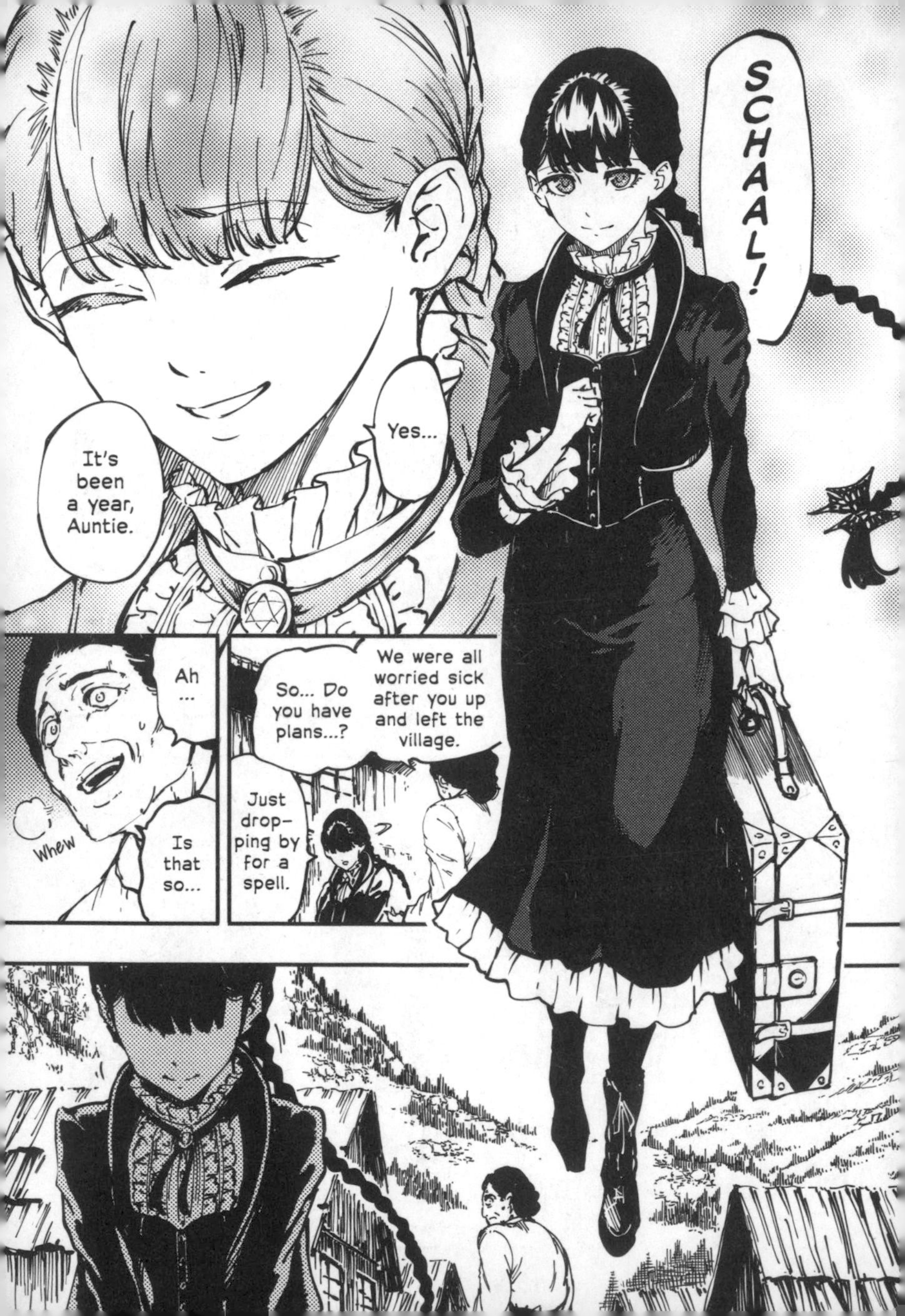
SCHAAL!
Yes...
It's been a year, Auntie.
We were all worried sick after you up and left the village.
So... Do you have plans...?
Just drop-ping by for a spell.
Ah ...
Whew
Is that so...

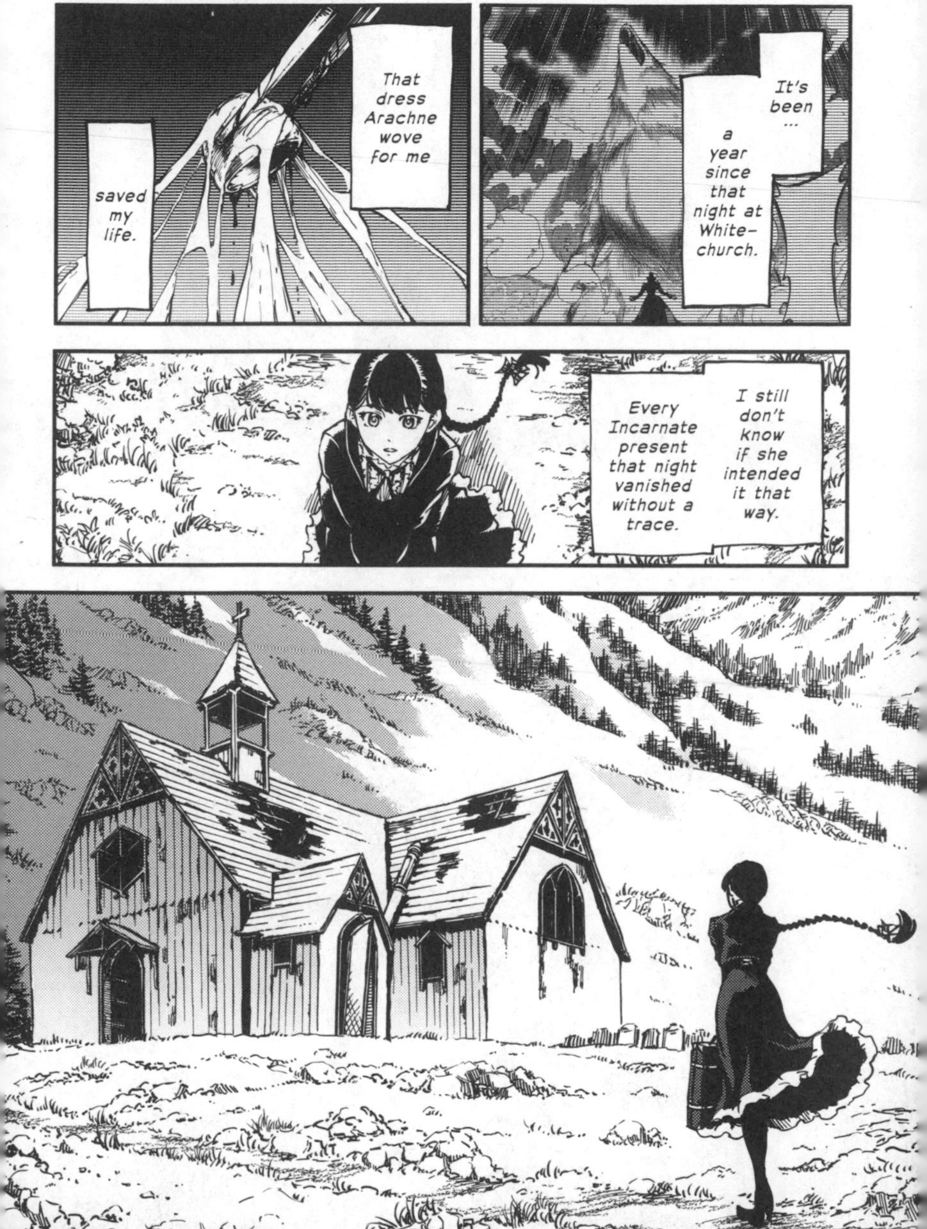
It's been ...
a year since that night at White-church.
That dress Arachne wove for me
saved my life.
I still don't know if she intended it that way.
Every Incarnate present that night vanished without a trace.

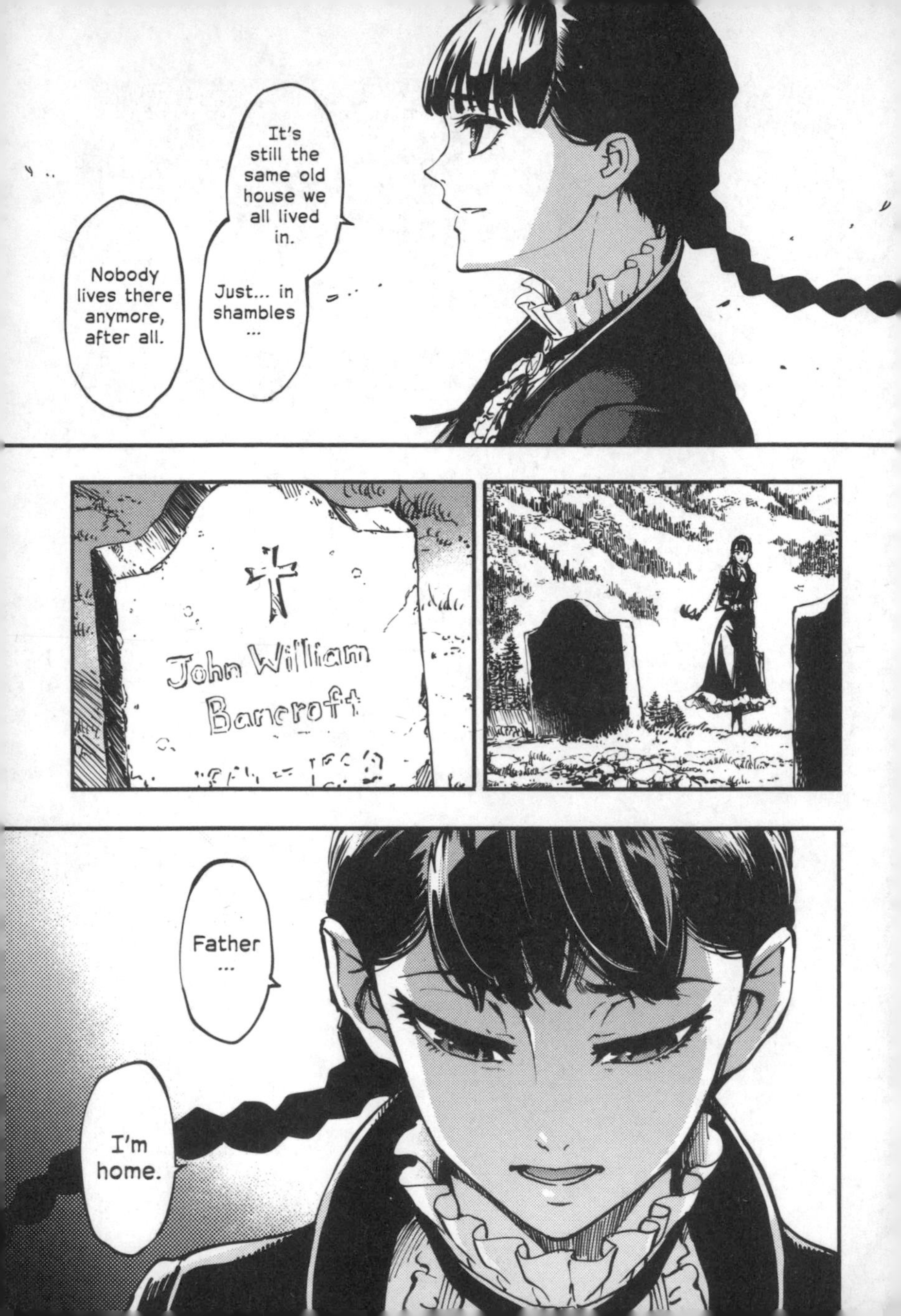
It's still the same old house we all lived in.
Just... in shambles...
Nobody lives there anymore, after all.
John William Bancroft
Father...
I'm home.

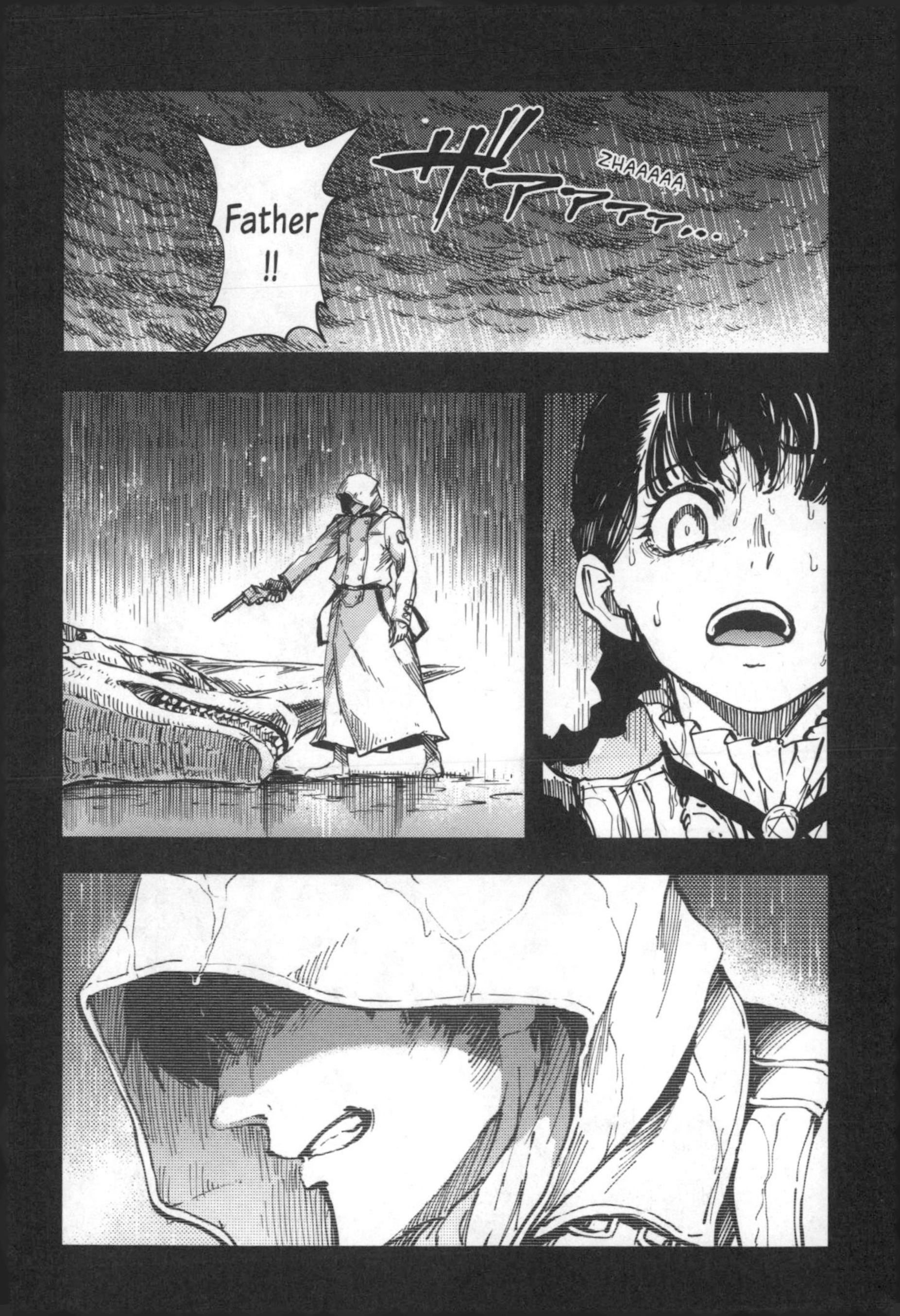
ザァァァァァ..
ZHAAAAAA
Father !!

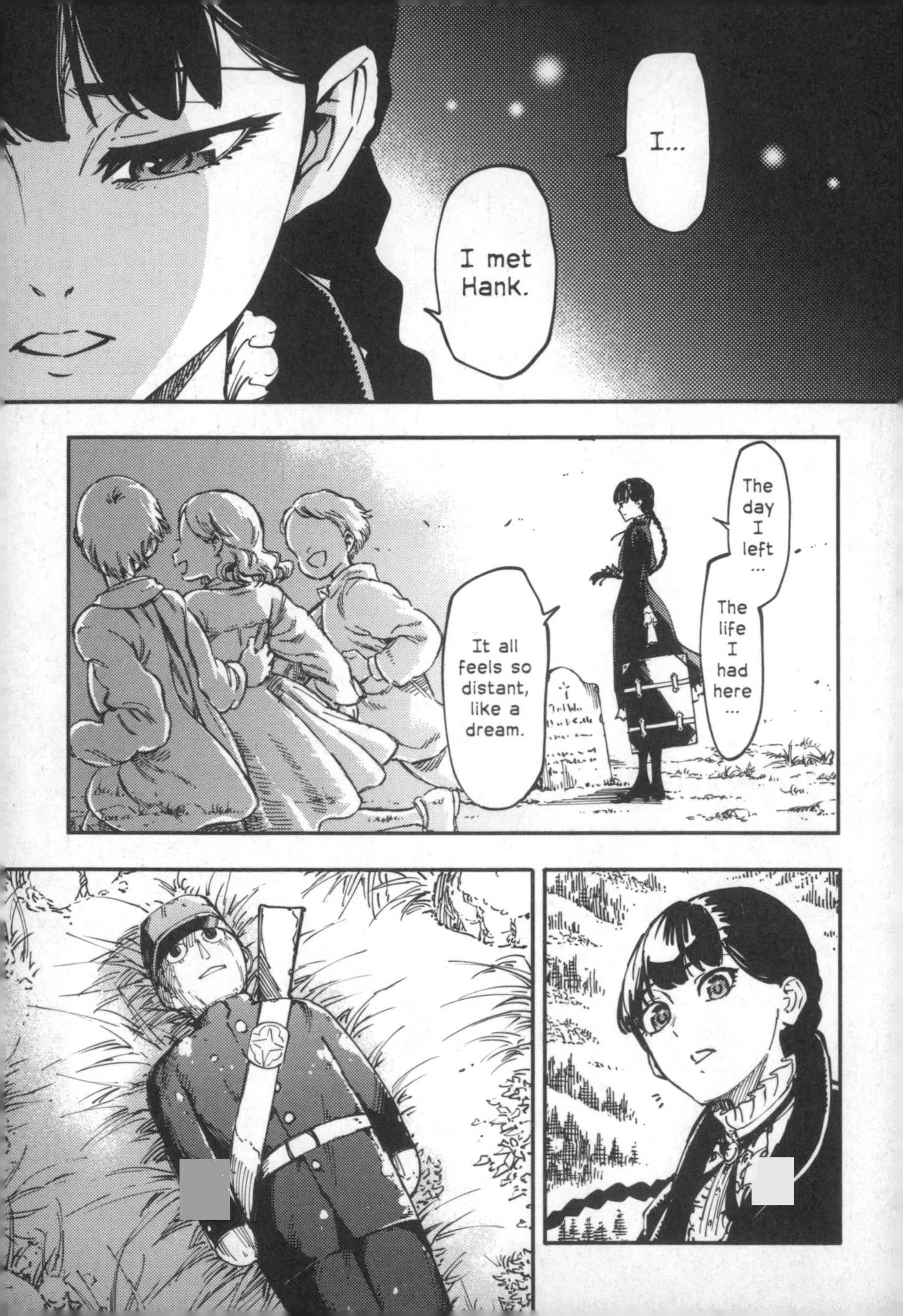
I...
I met Hank.
The day I left...
The life I had here...
It all feels so distant, like a dream.

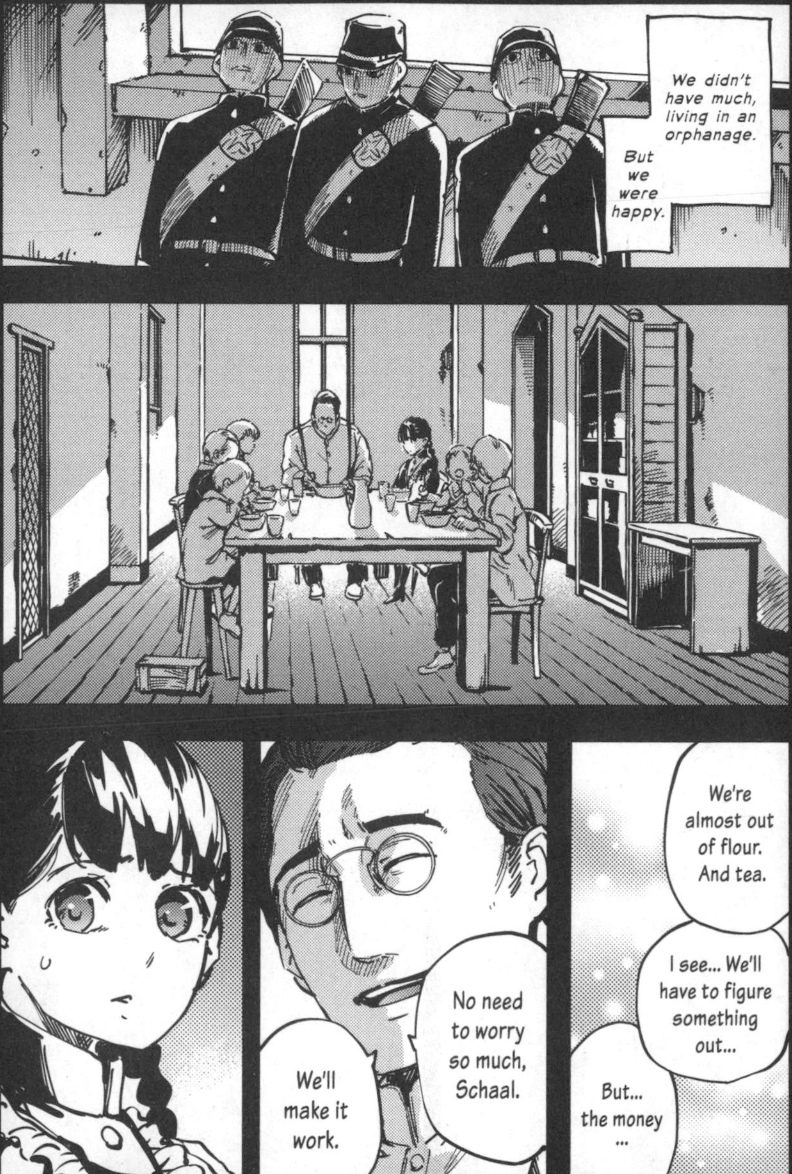
We didn't have much, living in an orphanage.
But we were happy.
We're almost out of flour. And tea.
I see... We'll have to figure something out...
But... the money ...
No need to worry so much, Schaal.
We'll make it work.

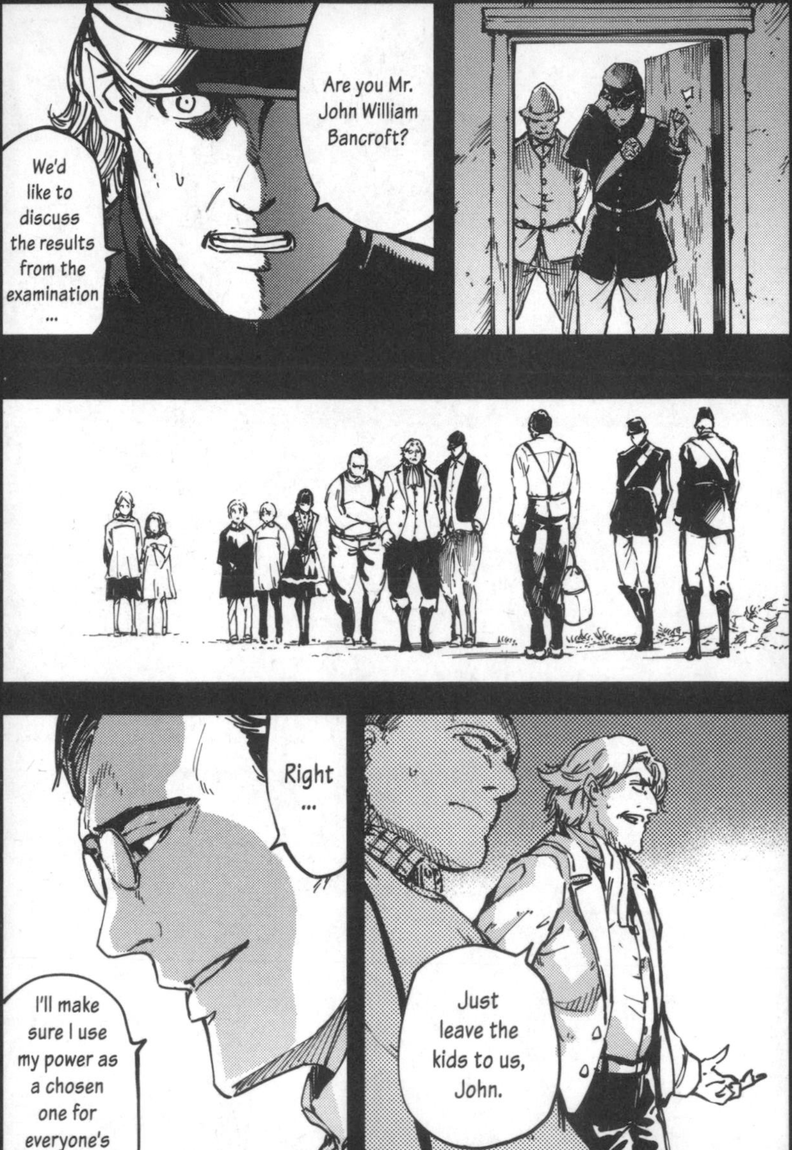
Are you Mr. John William Bancroft?
We'd like to discuss the results from the examination ...
Just leave the kids to us, John.
Right ...
I'll make sure I use my power as a chosen one for everyone's benefit.

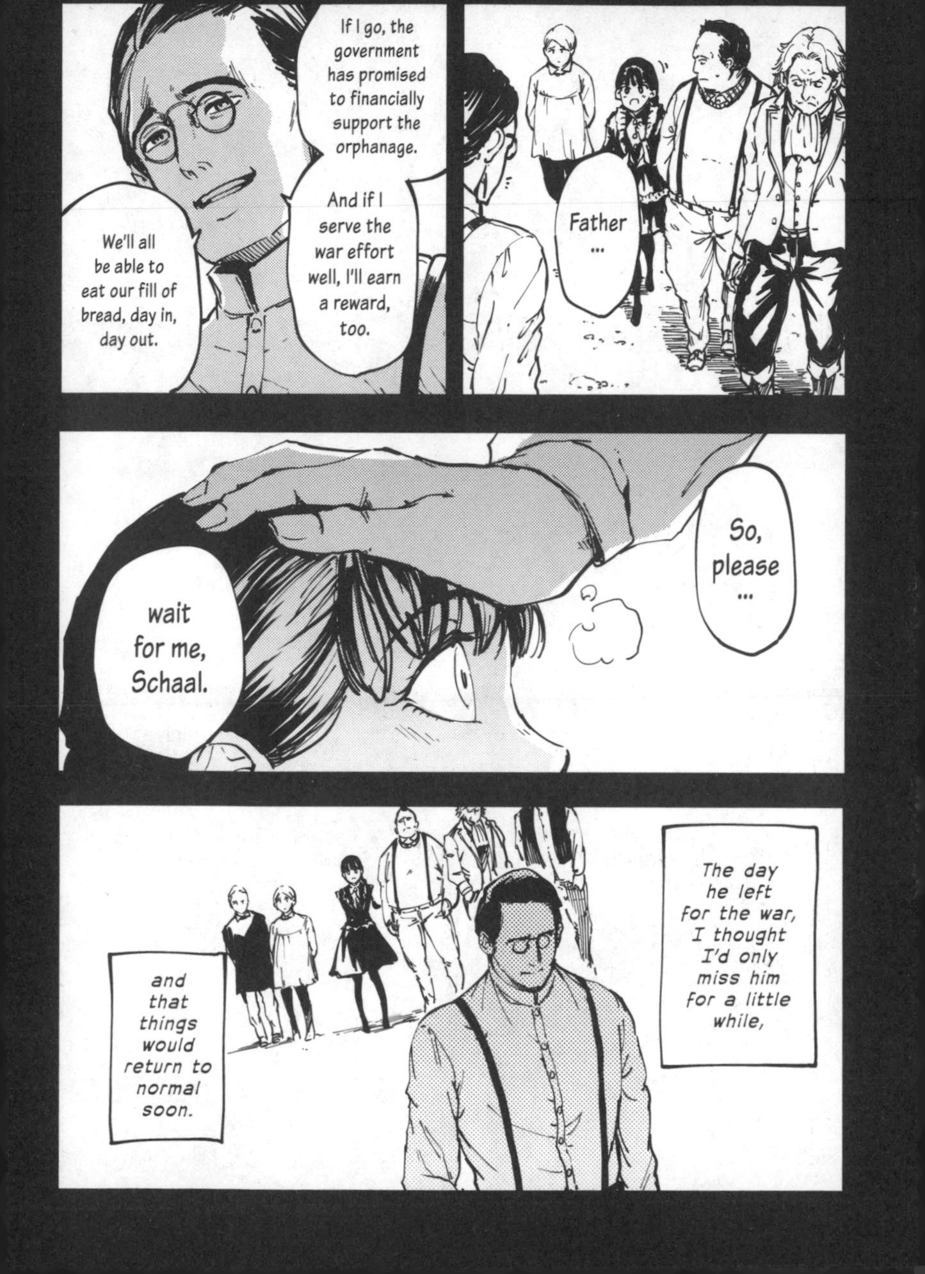
Father...
If I go, the government has promised to financially support the orphanage.
And if I serve the war effort well, I'll earn a reward, too.
We'll all be able to eat our fill of bread, day in, day out.
So, please...
wait for me, Schaal.
The day he left for the war, I thought I'd only miss him for a little while,
and that things would return to normal soon.

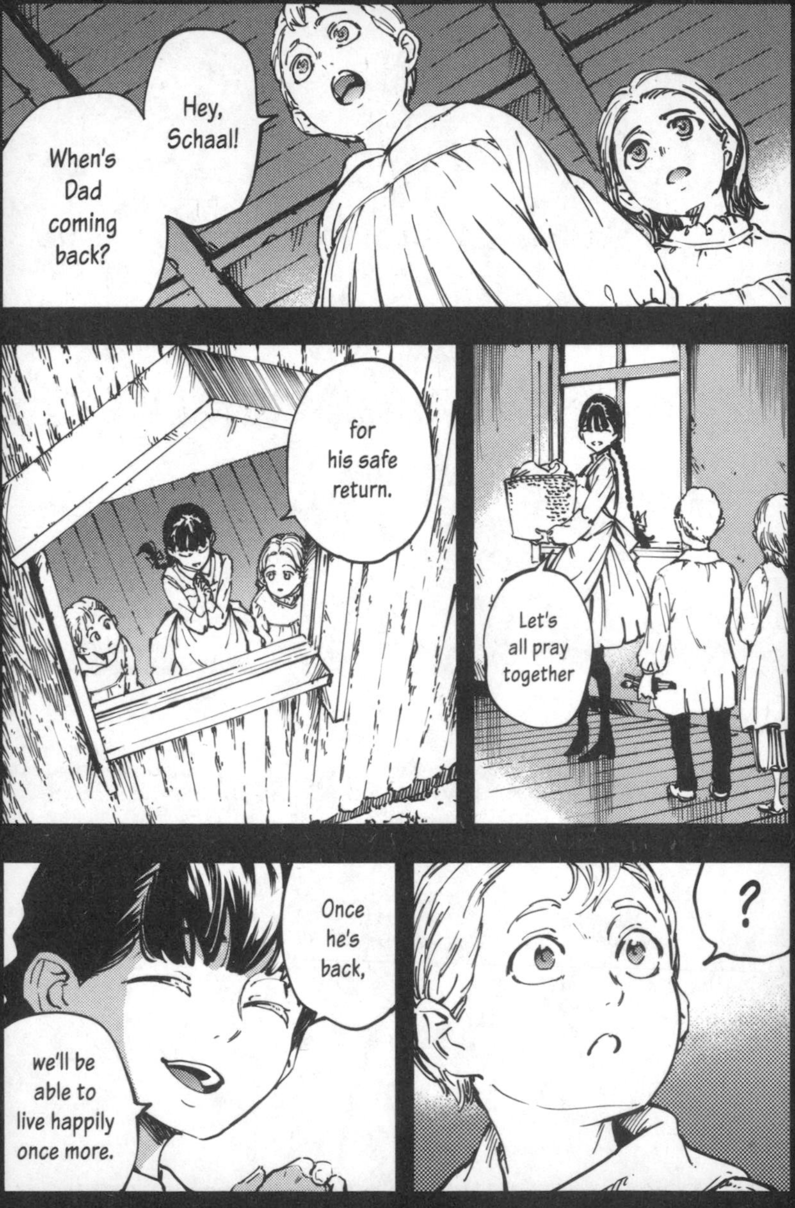
Hey, Schaal!
When's Dad coming back?
Let's all pray together
for his safe return.
?
Once he's back,
we'll be able to live happily once more.

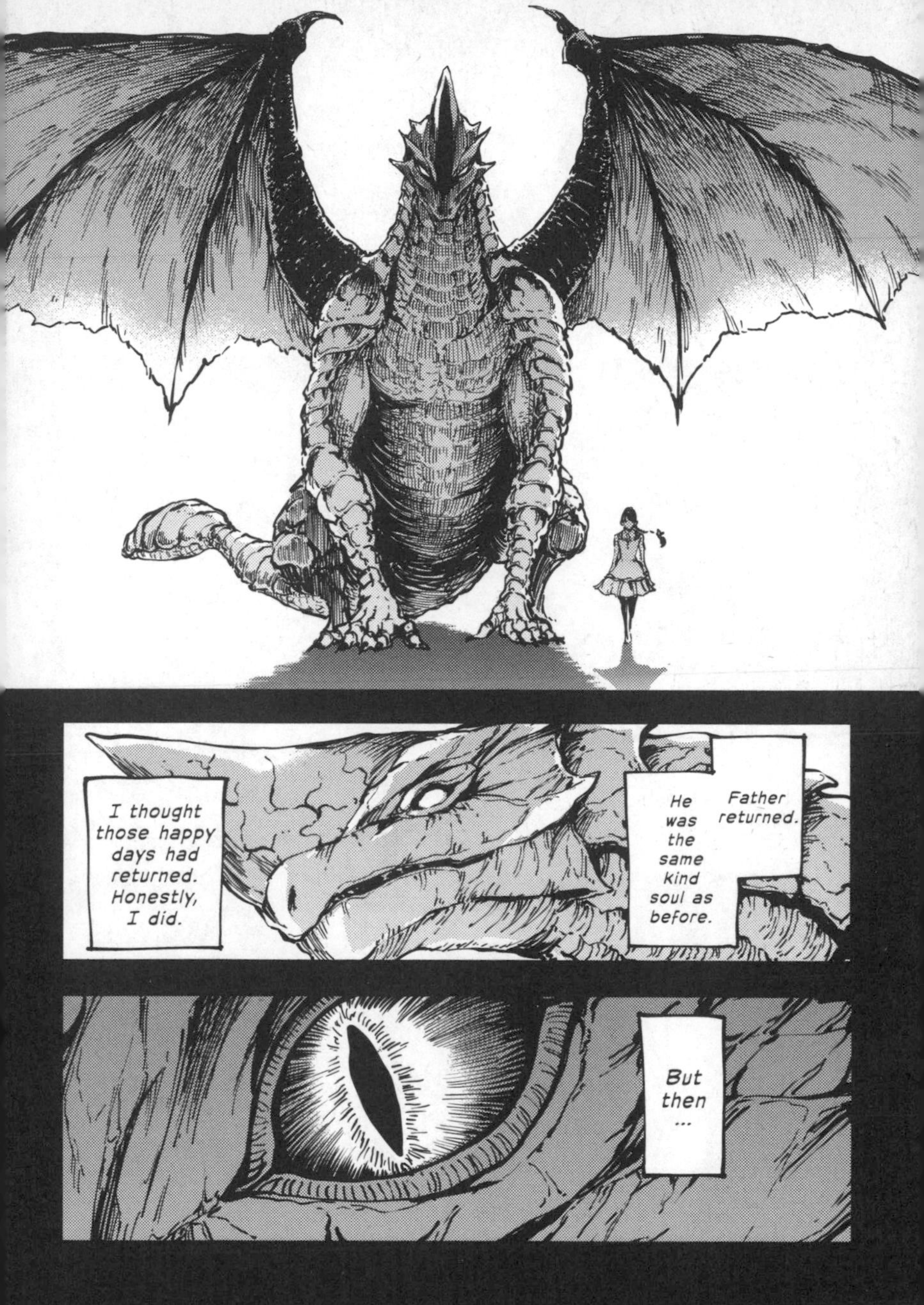
Father returned.
He was the same kind soul as before.
I thought those happy days had returned. Honestly, I did.
But then ...

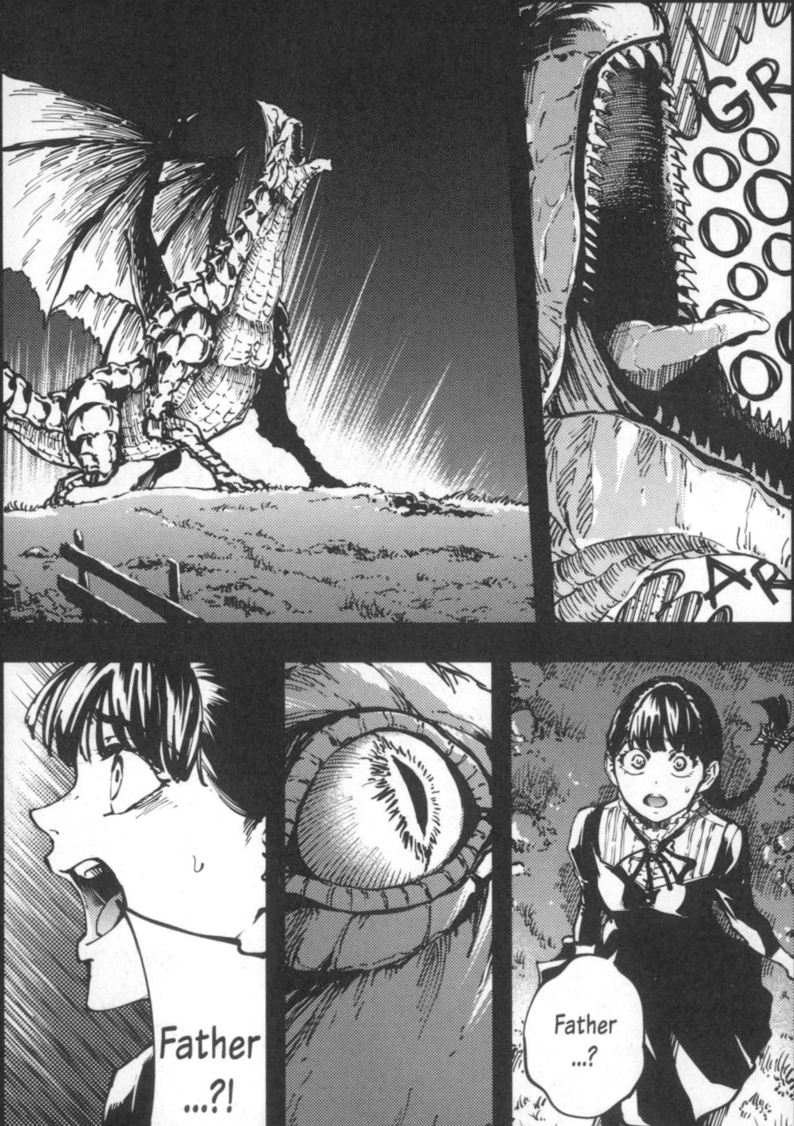
GROOOOOOOOOAR
Father ...?
Father ...?!

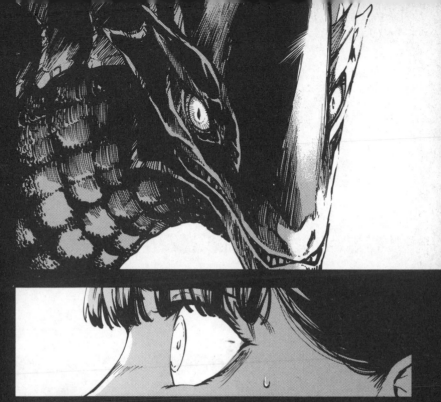

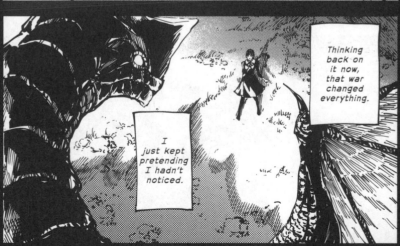

Thinking back on it now, that war changed everything.

I just kept pretending I hadn't noticed.

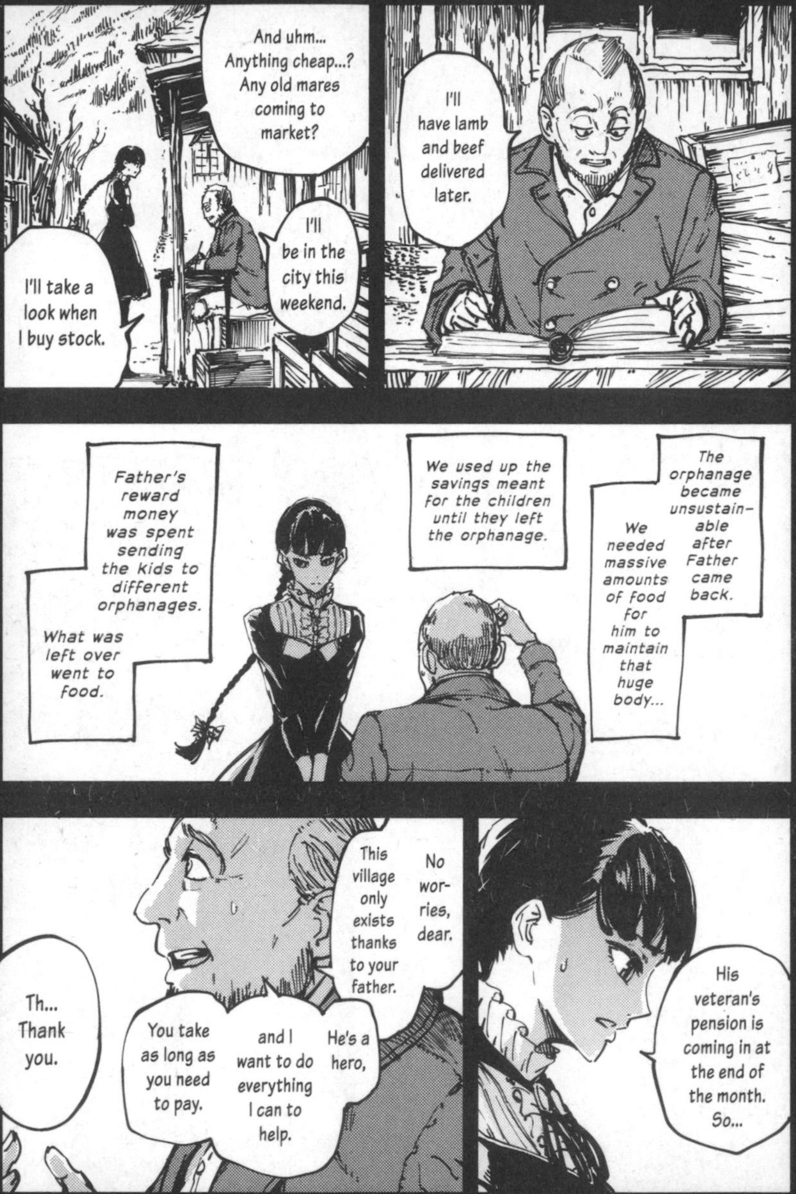
I'll have lamb and beef delivered later.
And uhm... Anything cheap...? Any old mares coming to market?
I'll be in the city this weekend.
I'll take a look when I buy stock.
The orphanage became unsustainable after Father came back.
We needed massive amounts of food for him to maintain that huge body...
We used up the savings meant for the children until they left the orphanage.
Father's reward money was spent sending the kids to different orphanages.
What was left over went to food.
His veteran's pension is coming in at the end of the month. So...
No worries, dear.
This village only exists thanks to your father.
He's a hero,
and I want to do everything I can to help.
You take as long as you need to pay.
Th... Thank you.

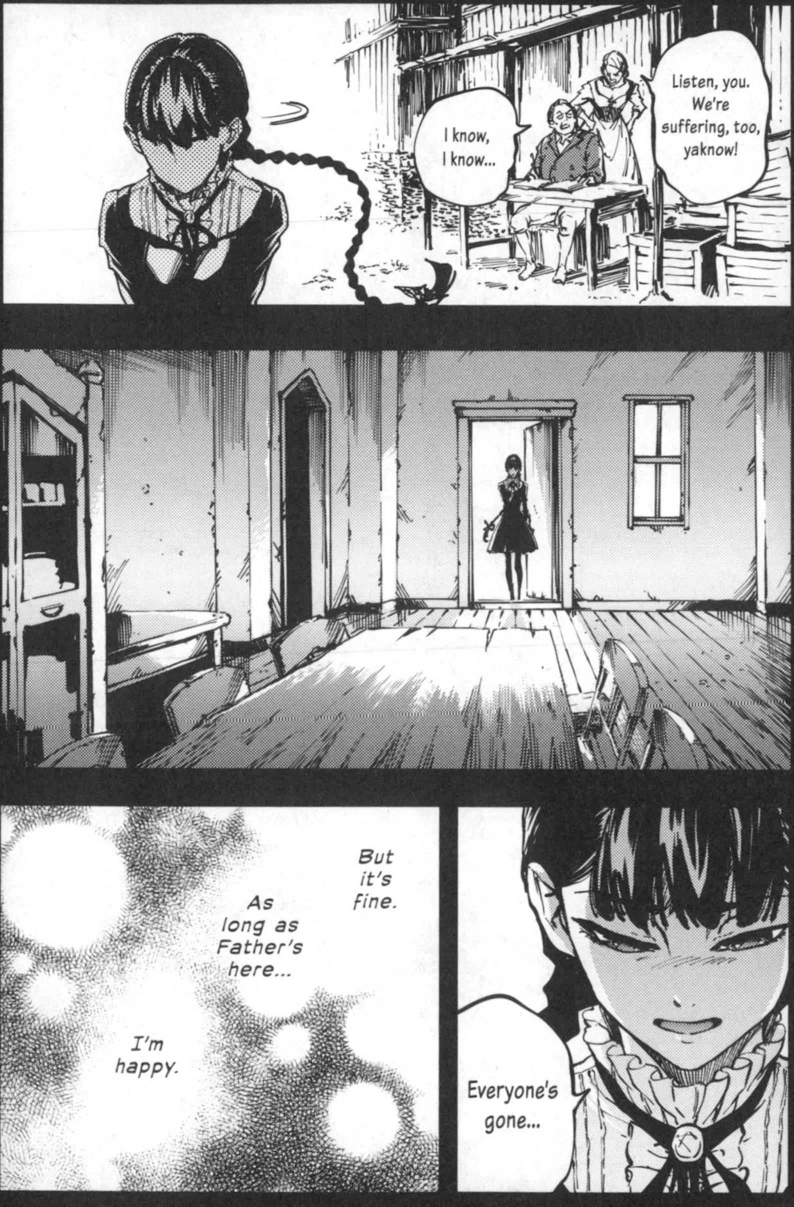
Listen, you. We're suffering, too, yaknow!
I know, I know...
Everyone's gone...
But it's fine.
As long as Father's here...
I'm happy.

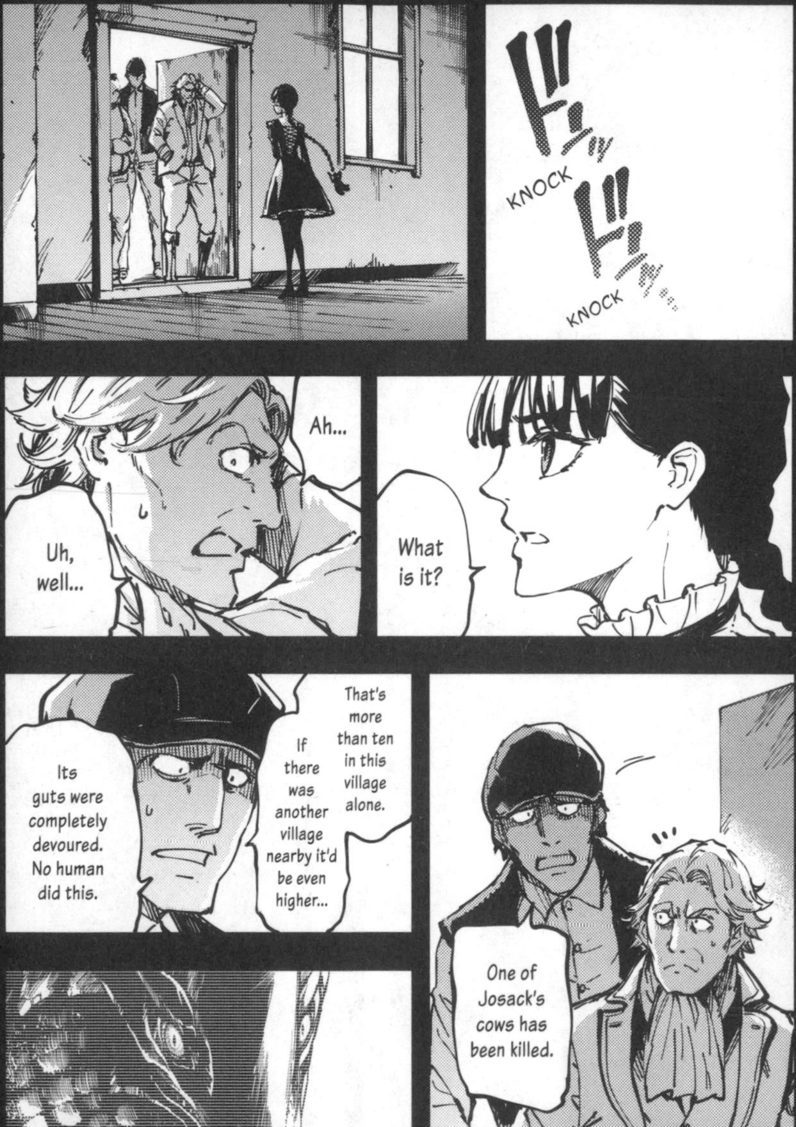
KNOCK
KNOCK
What is it?
Ah...
Uh, well...
One of Josack's cows has been killed.
That's more than ten in this village alone.
If there was another village nearby it'd be even higher...
Its guts were completely devoured. No human did this.

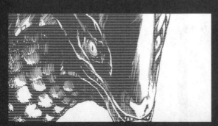

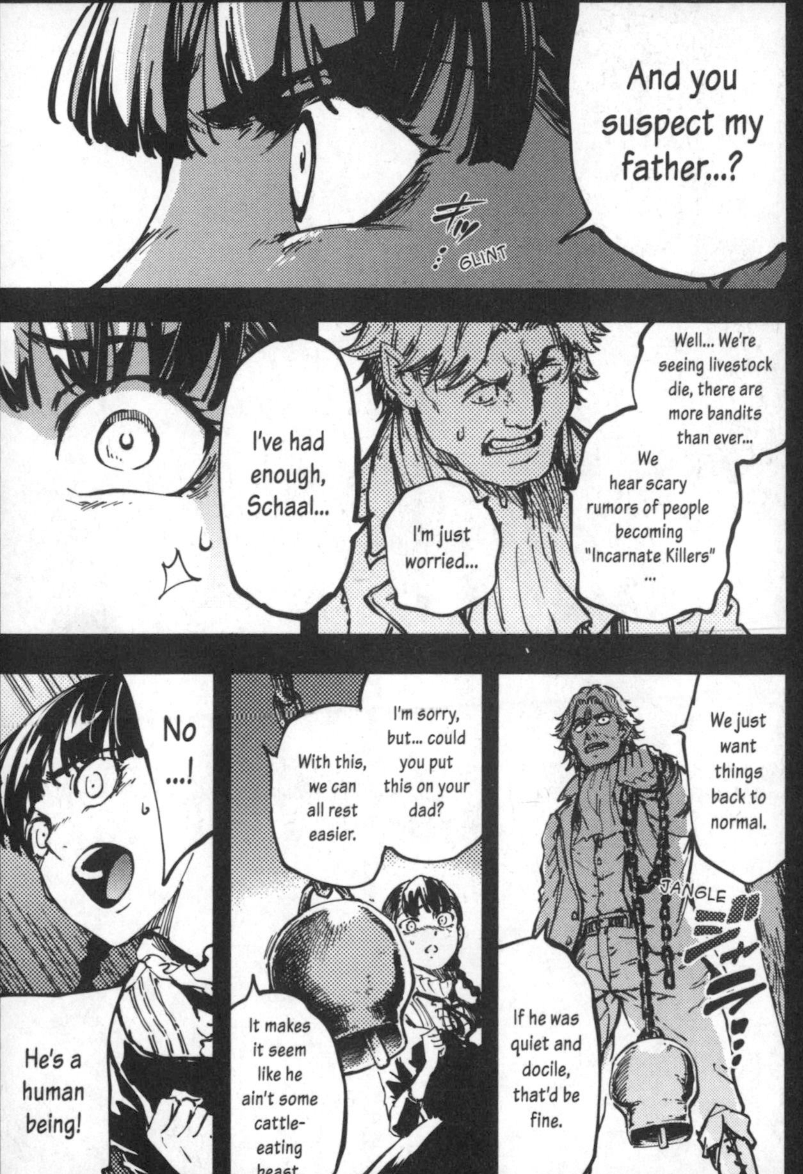
And you suspect my father...?
GLINT
Well... We're seeing livestock die, there are more bandits than ever...
We hear scary rumors of people becoming "Incarnate Killers" ...
I'm just worried...
I've had enough, Schaal...
We just want things back to normal.
JANGLE
If he was quiet and docile, that'd be fine.
I'm sorry, but... could you put this on your dad?
With this, we can all rest easier.
It makes it seem like he ain't some cattle-eating beast.
No ...!
He's a human being!

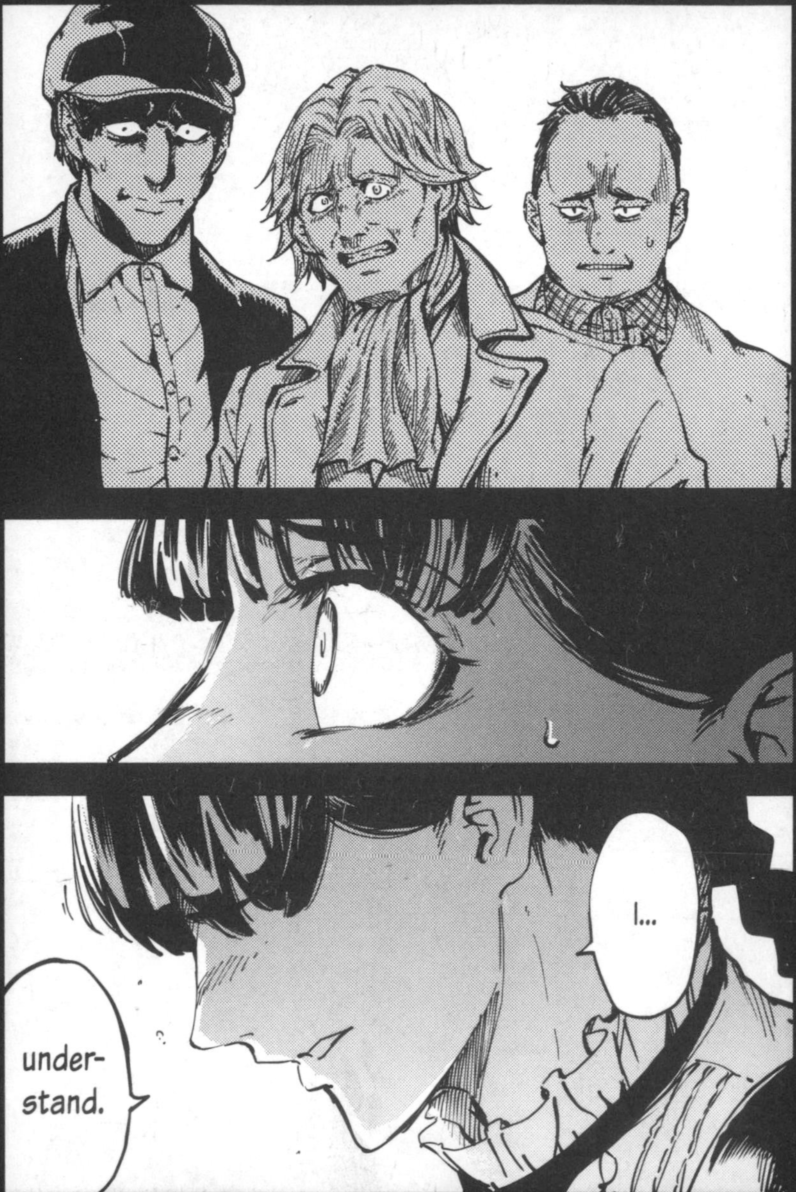
I...
under-stand.

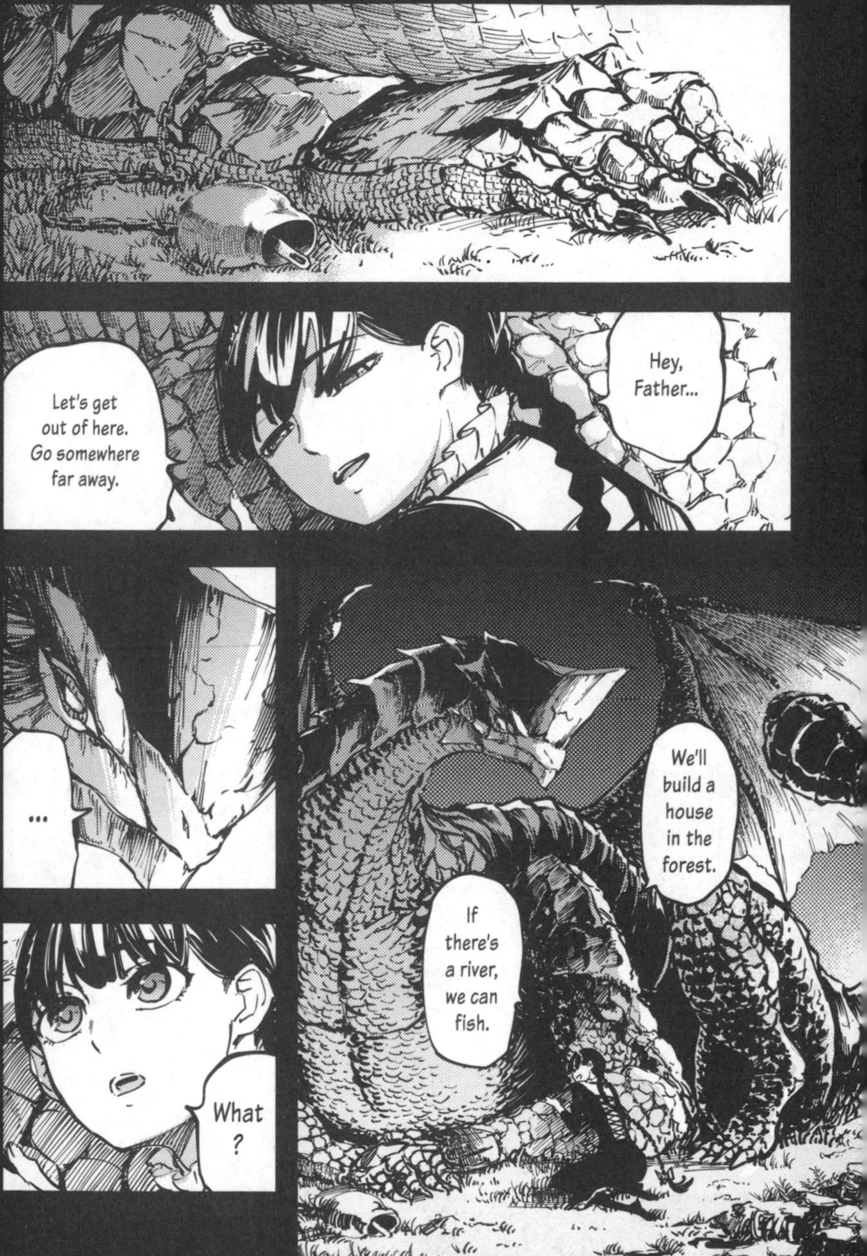
Hey, Father...
Let's get out of here. Go somewhere far away.
We'll build a house in the forest.
If there's a river, we can fish.
...
What?

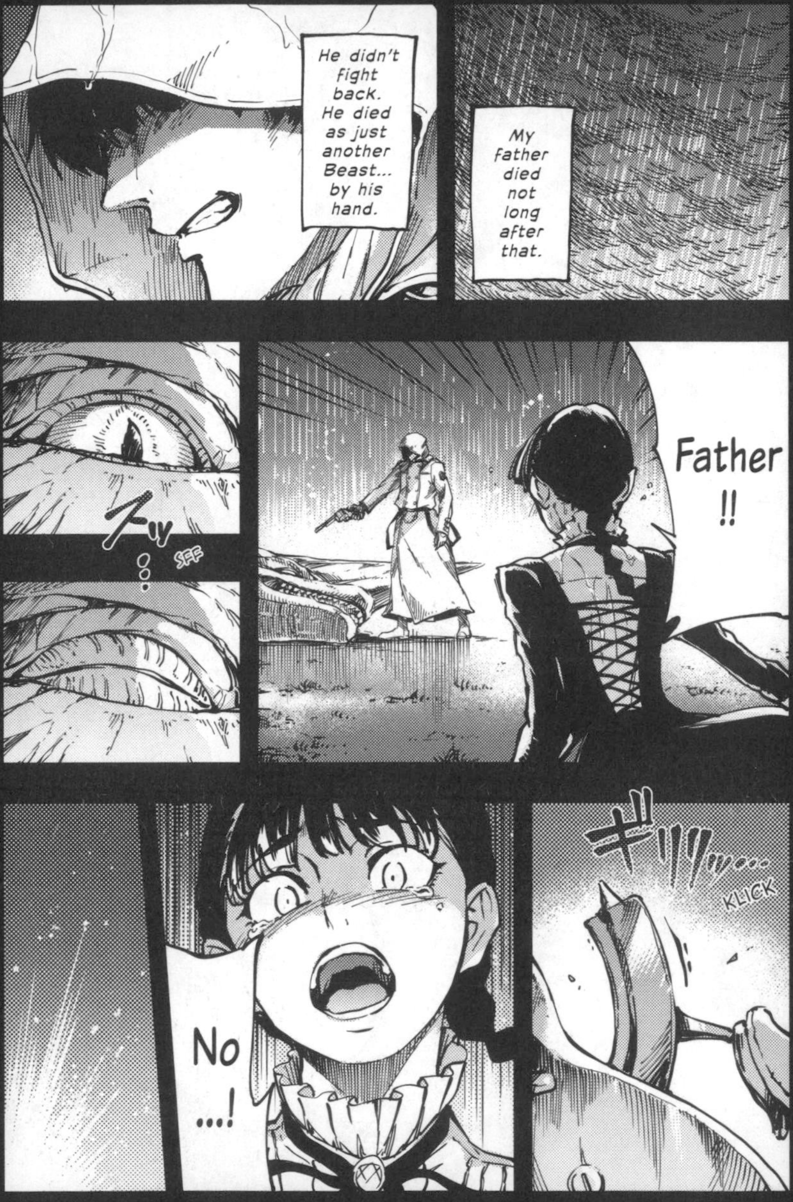
My father died not long after that.
He didn't fight back. He died as just another Beast... by his hand.
Father !!
SFF
KLICK
No ...!

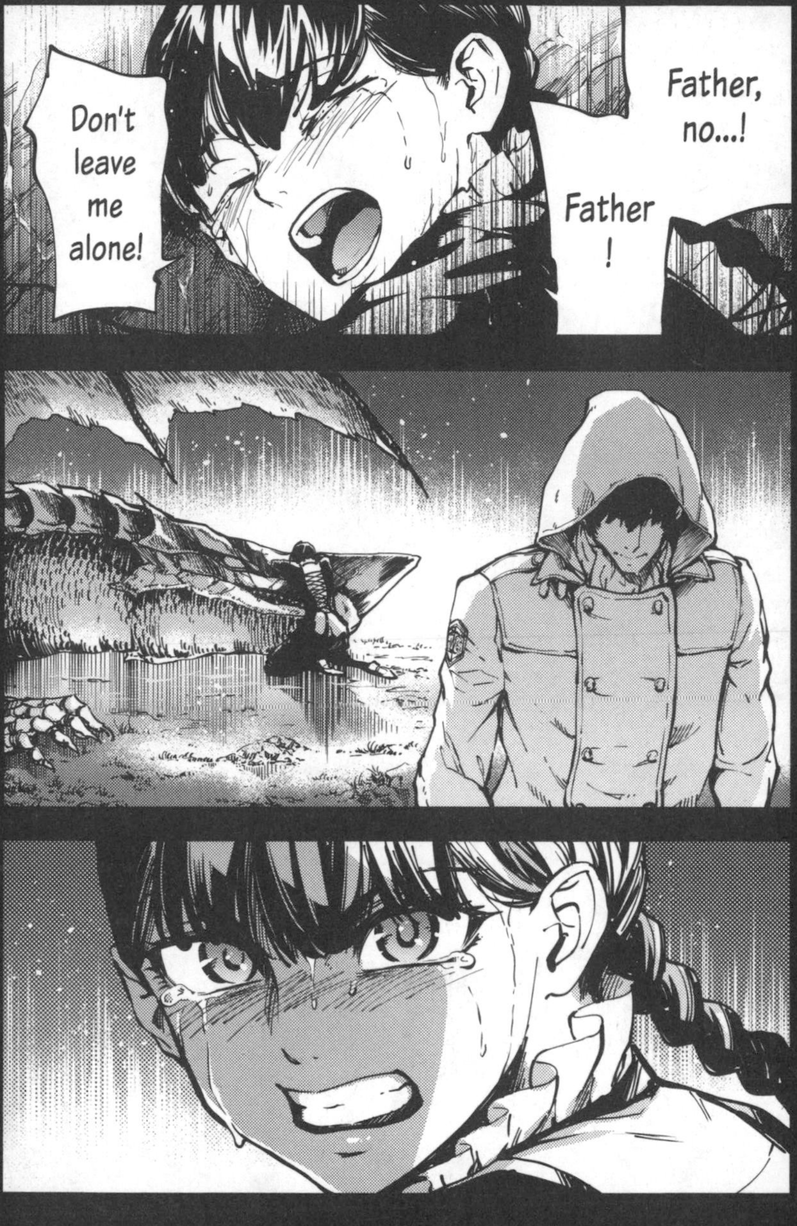
Father, no...!
Father!
Don't leave me alone!

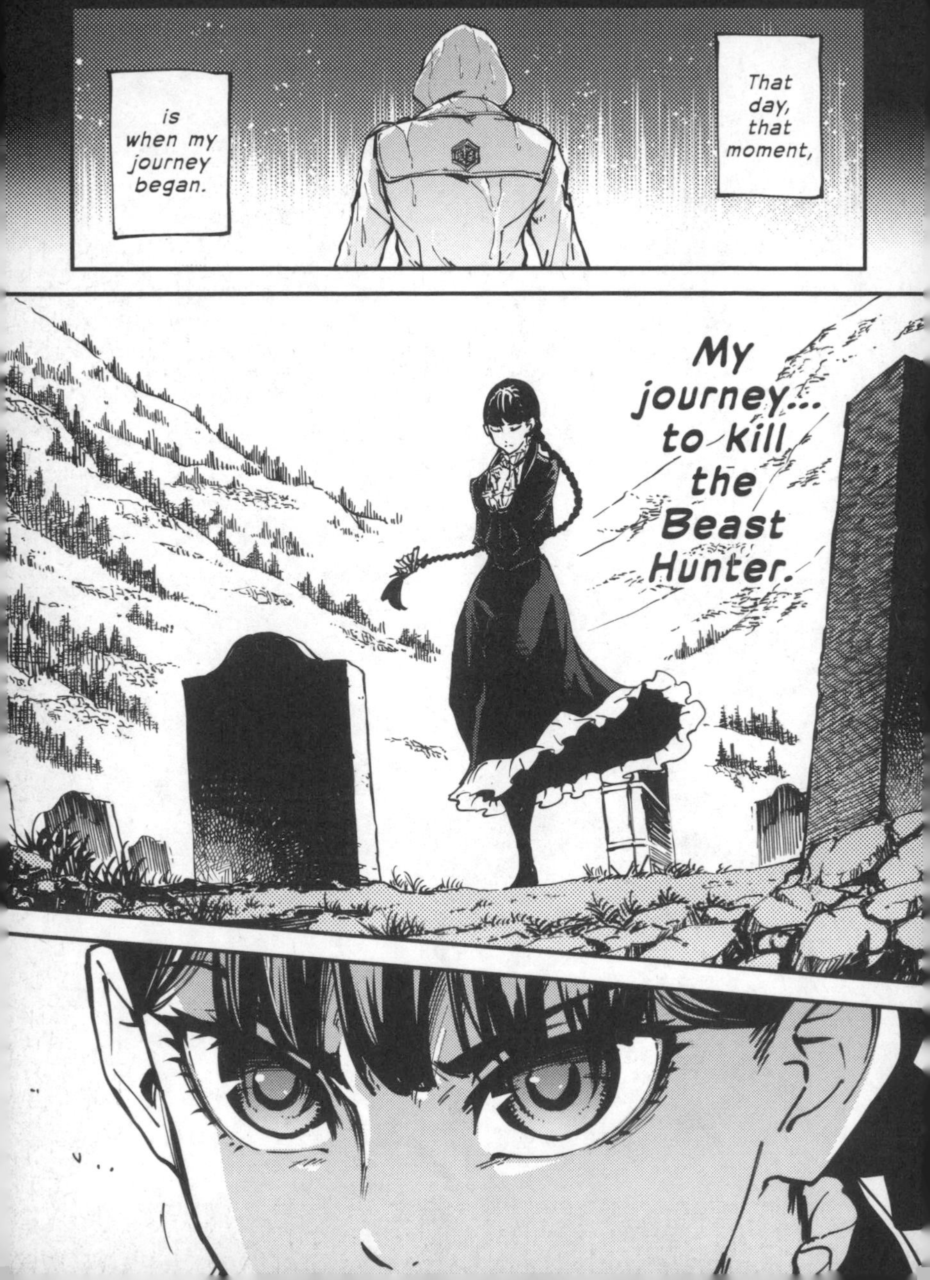
That day, that moment,
is when my journey began.
My journey... to kill the Beast Hunter.

To the Abandoned

Sacred Beasts

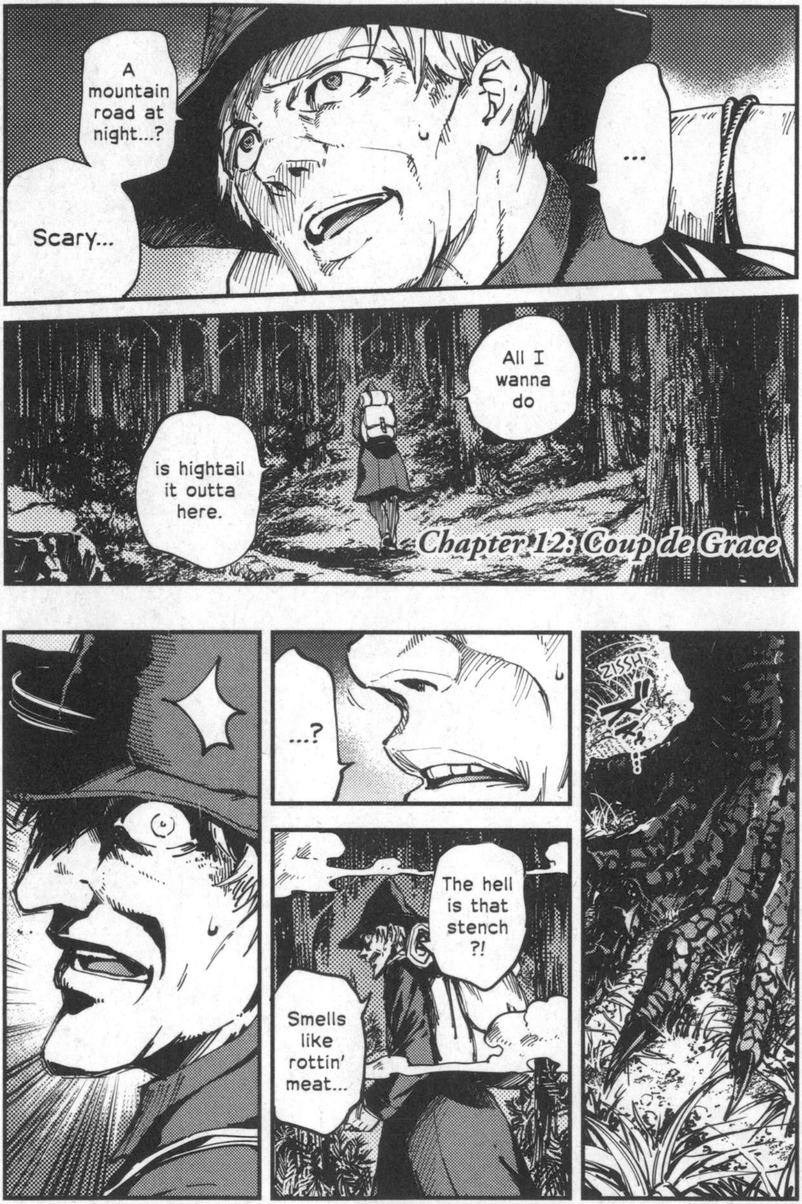
...
A mountain road at night...?
Scary...
All I wanna do
is hightail it outta here.
Chapter 12: Coup de Grace
ZISSH
...?
The hell is that stench ?!
Smells like rottin' meat...

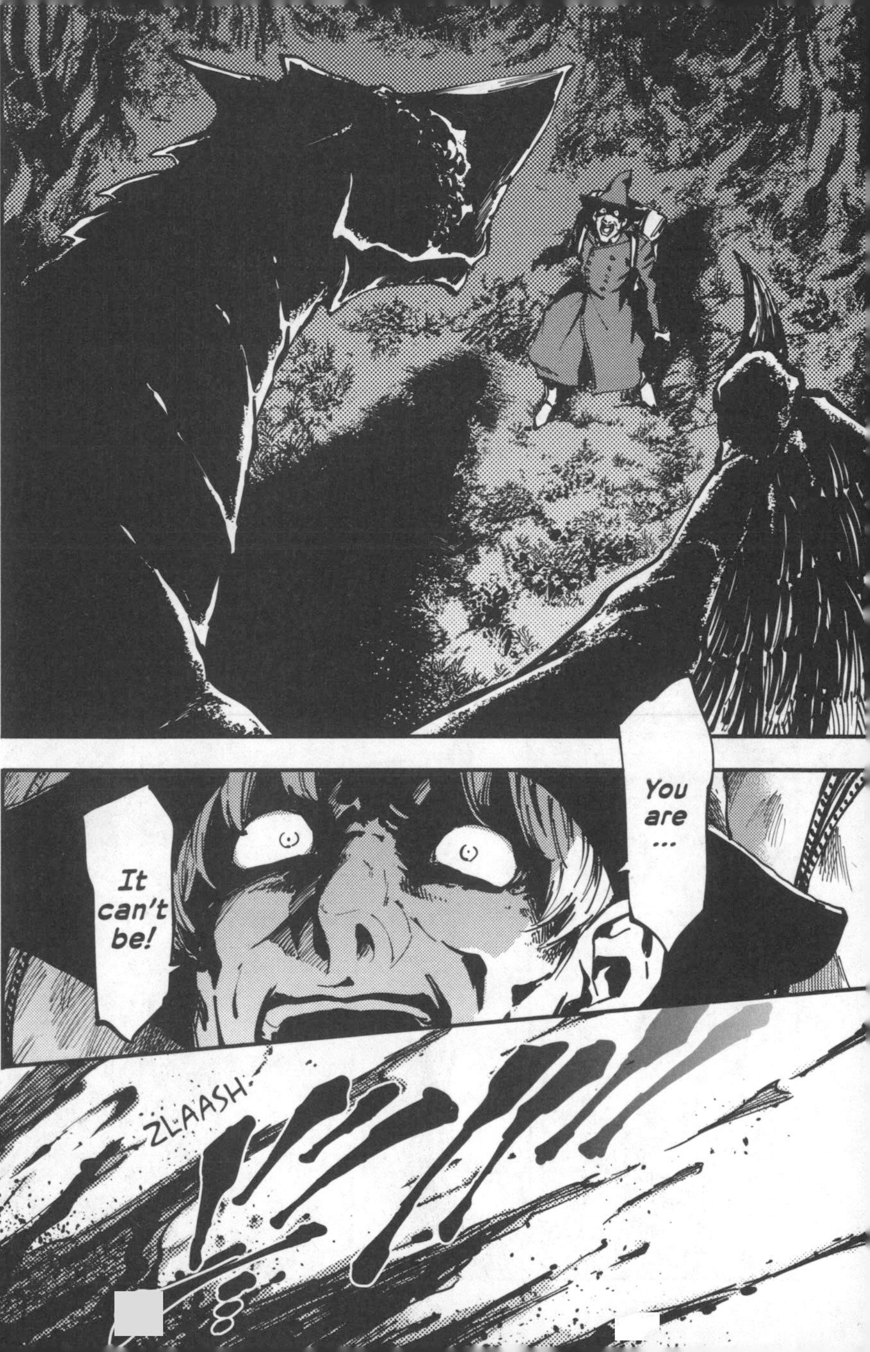
You are ...
It can't be!
ZLAASH

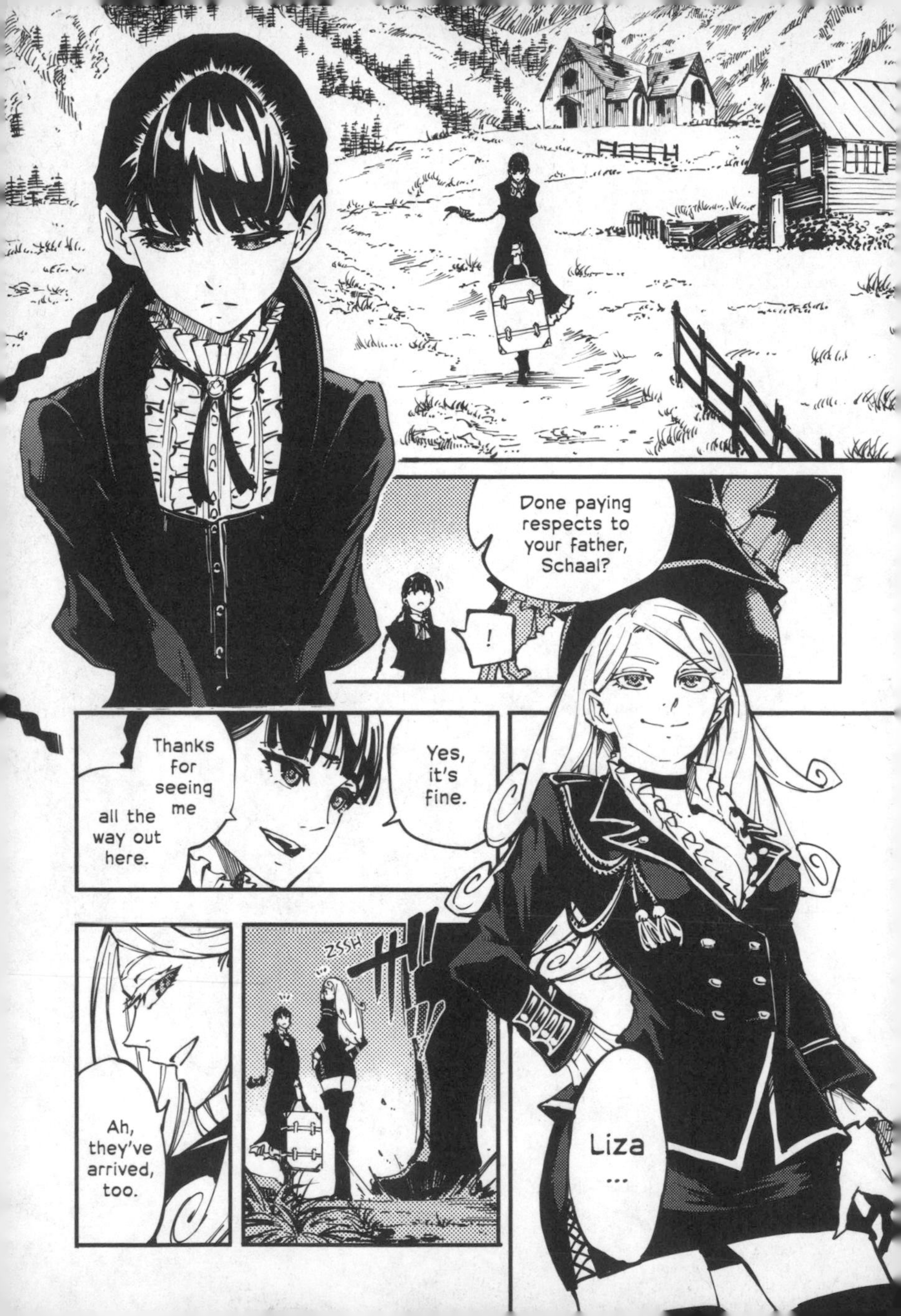
Done paying respects to your father, Schaal?
!
Liza ...
Yes, it's fine.
Thanks for seeing me all the way out here.
ZSSH
Ah, they've arrived, too.

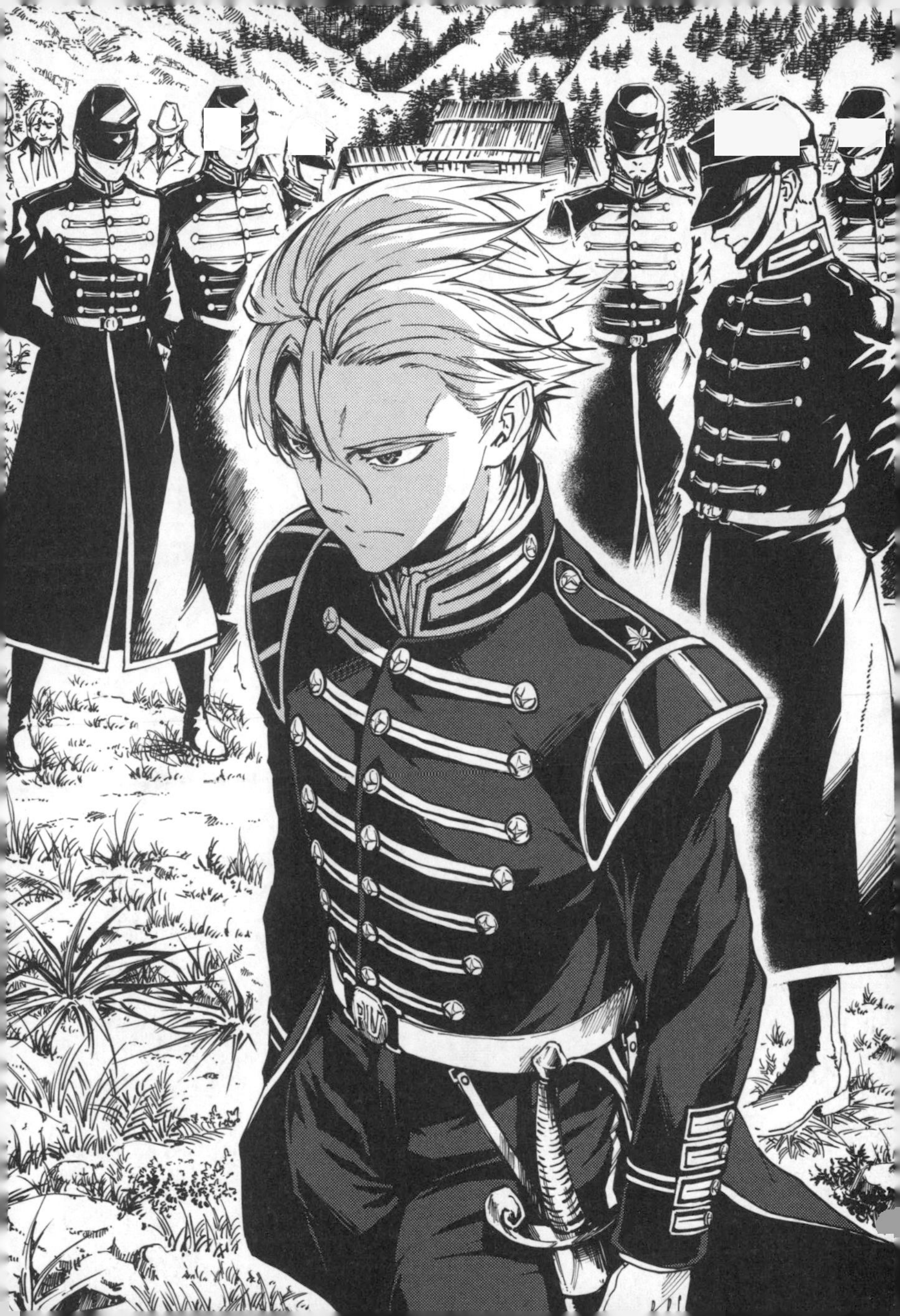

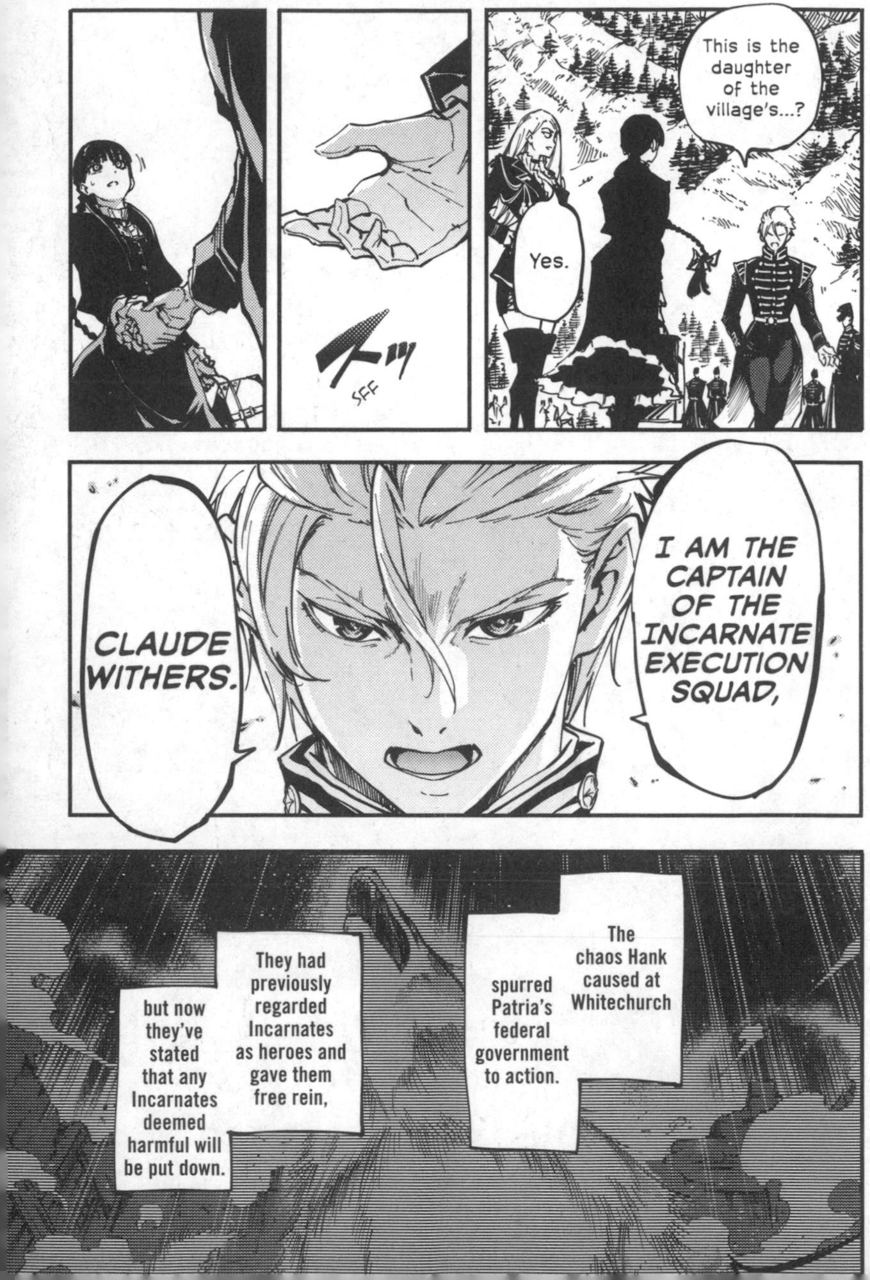
This is the daughter of the village's...?
Yes.
SFF
I AM THE CAPTAIN OF THE INCARNATE EXECUTION SQUAD,
CLAUDE WITHERS.
The chaos Hank caused at Whitechurch
spurred Patria's federal government to action.
They had previously regarded Incarnates as heroes and gave them free rein,
but now they've stated that any Incarnates deemed harmful will be put down.

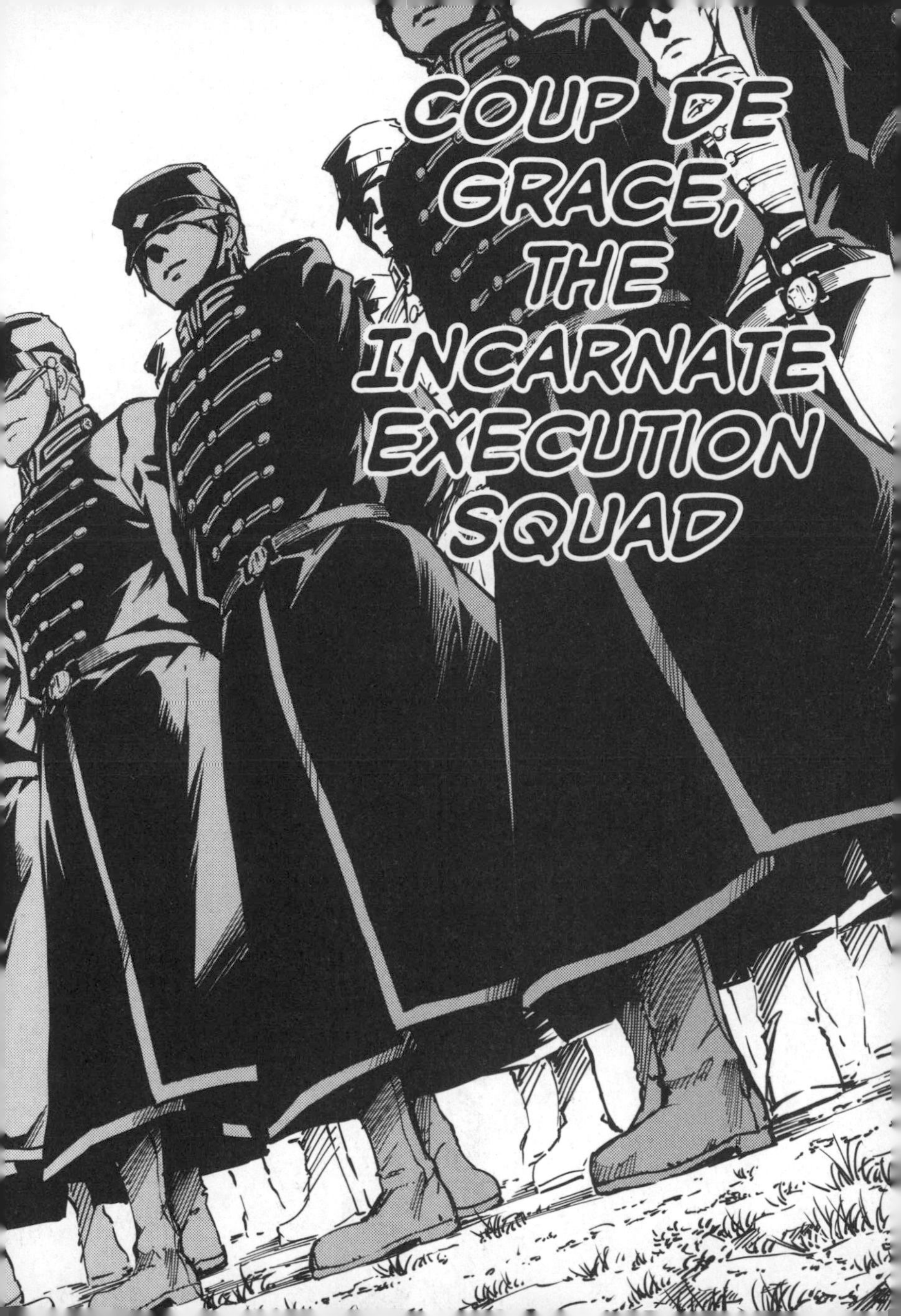
COUP DE GRACE, THE INCARNATE EXECUTION SQUAD

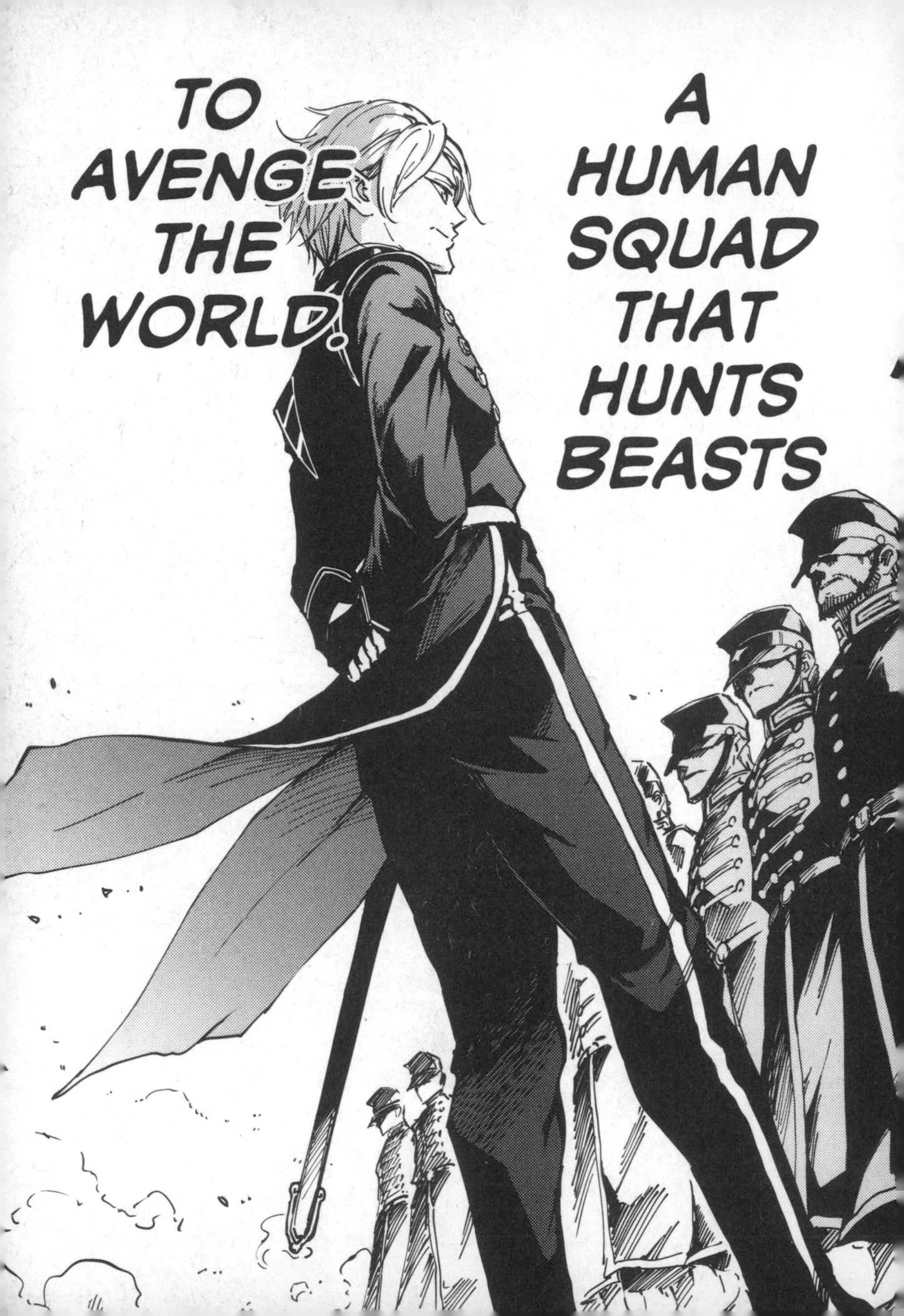
A HUMAN SQUAD THAT HUNTS BEASTS
TO AVENGE THE WORLD.

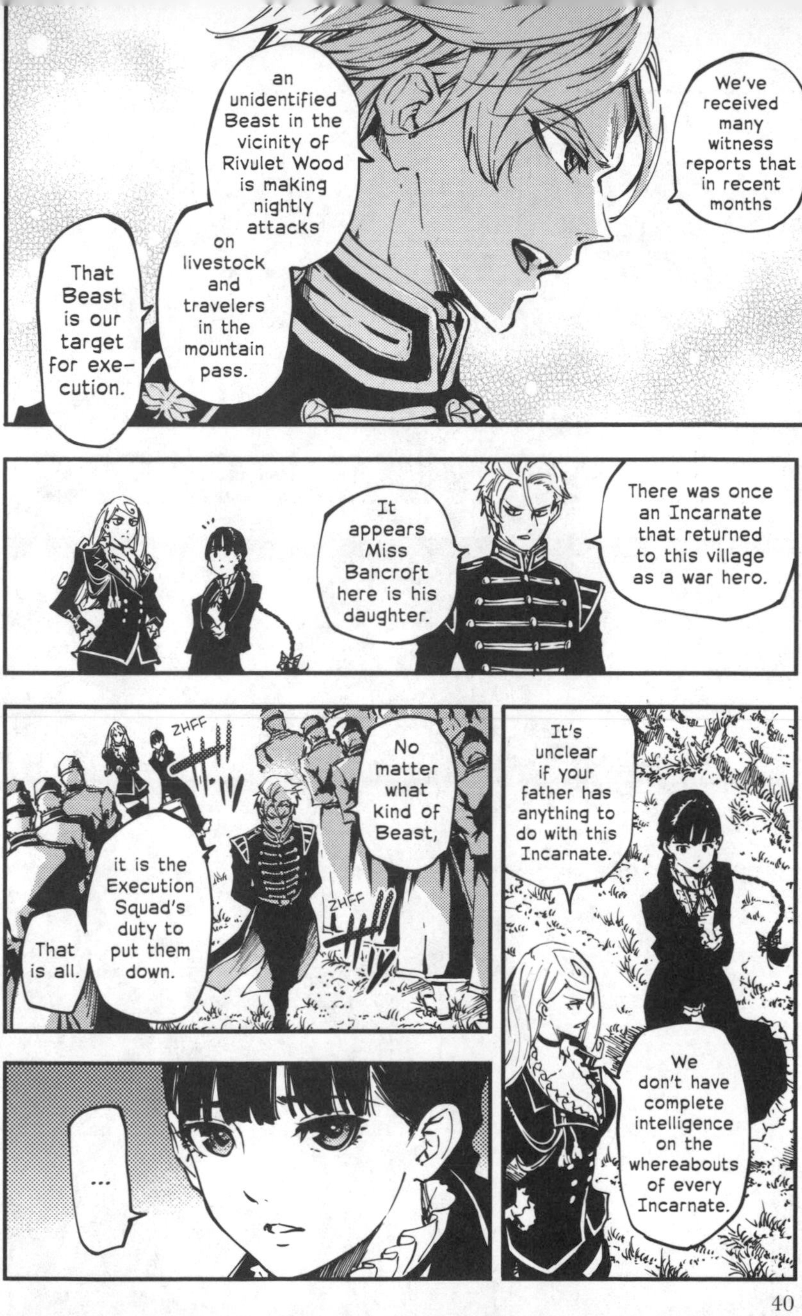
We've received many witness reports that in recent months
an unidentified Beast in the vicinity of Rivulet Wood is making nightly attacks
on livestock and travelers in the mountain pass.
That Beast is our target for execution.
There was once an Incarnate that returned to this village as a war hero.
It appears Miss Bancroft here is his daughter.
It's unclear if your father has anything to do with this Incarnate.
We don't have complete intelligence on the whereabouts of every Incarnate.
No matter what kind of Beast,
it is the Execution Squad's duty to put them down.
That is all.
ZHFF
ZHFF
...

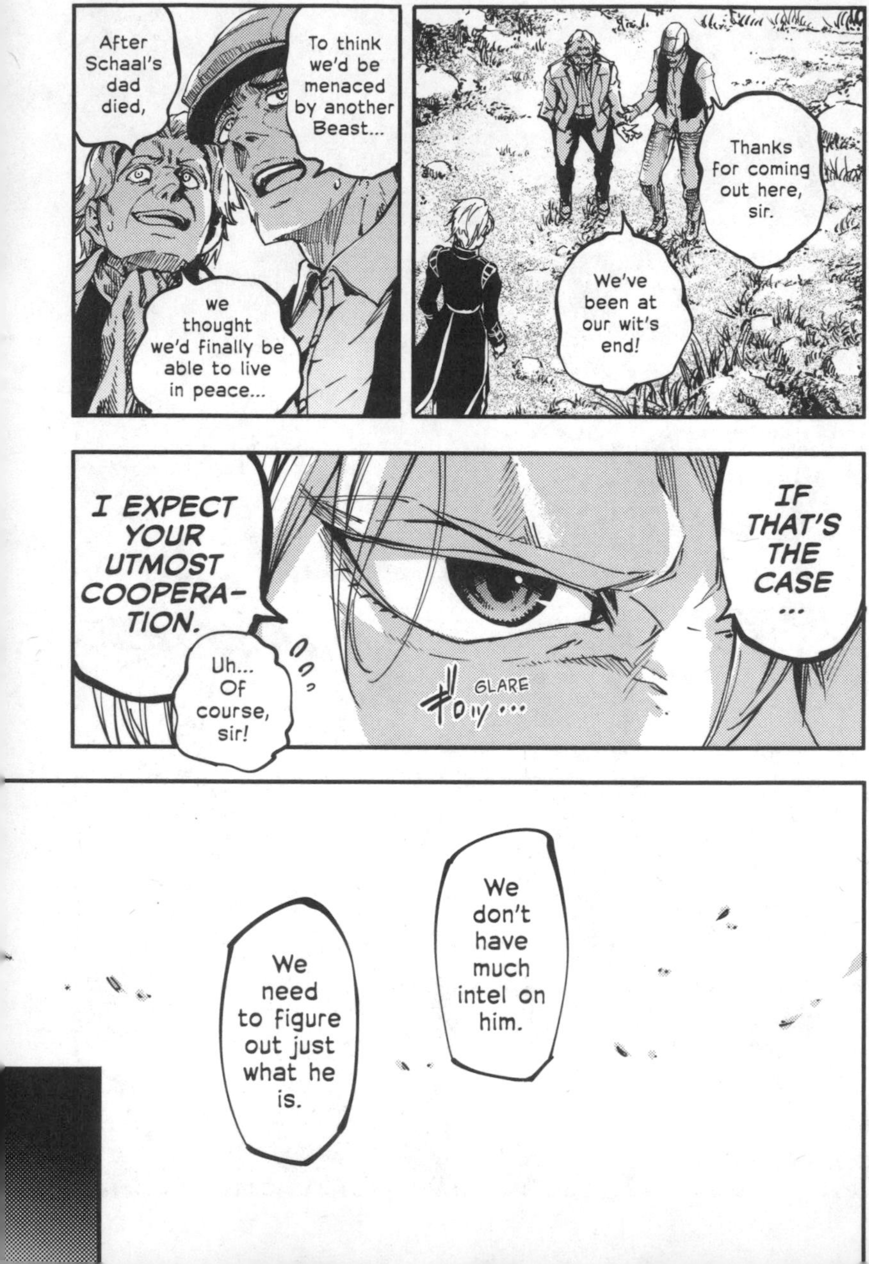
Thanks for coming out here, sir.
We've been at our wit's end!
To think we'd be menaced by another Beast...
After Schaal's dad died,
we thought we'd finally be able to live in peace...
IF THAT'S THE CASE...
GLARE
I EXPECT YOUR UTMOST COOPERATION.
Uh... Of course, sir!
We don't have much intel on him.
We need to figure out just what he is.

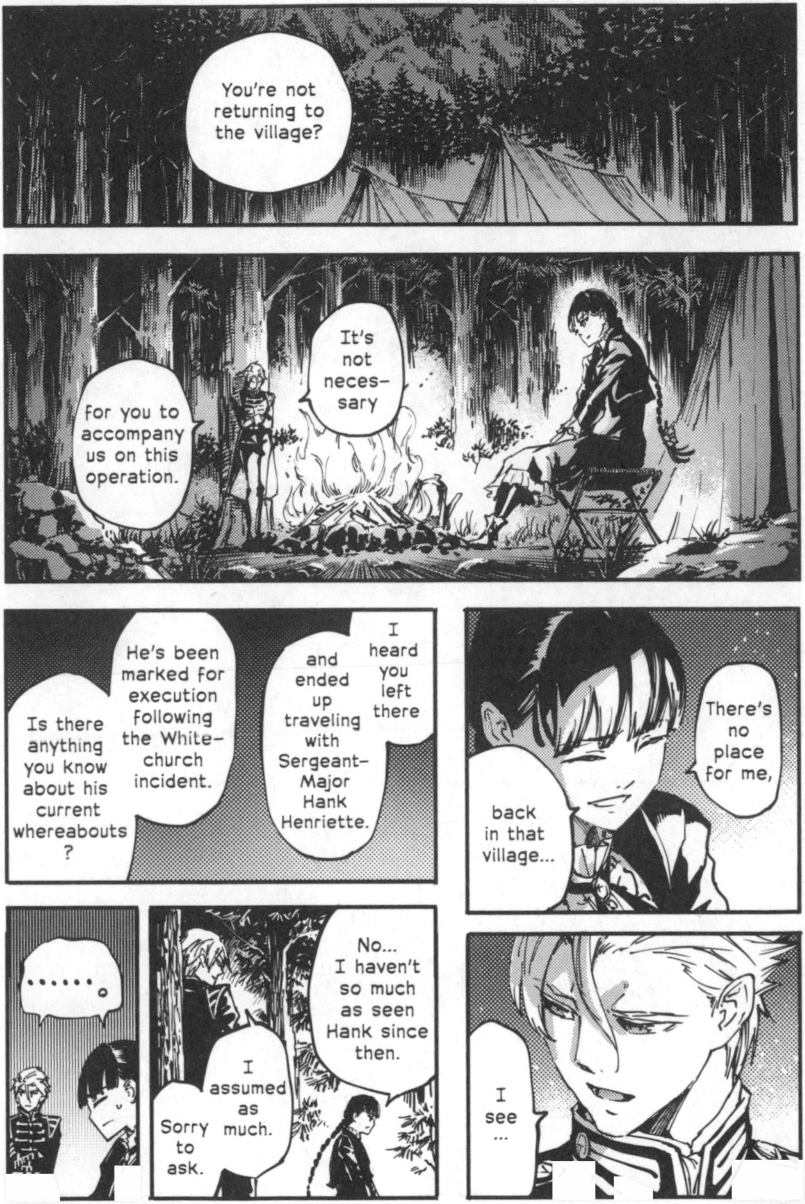
You're not returning to the village?
It's not neces-sary
for you to accompany us on this operation.
There's no place for me,
back in that village...
I heard you left there
and ended up traveling with Sergeant-Major Hank Henriette.
He's been marked for execution following the White-church incident.
Is there anything you know about his current whereabouts?
I see...
No... I haven't so much as seen Hank since then.
I assumed as much.
Sorry to ask.
......。

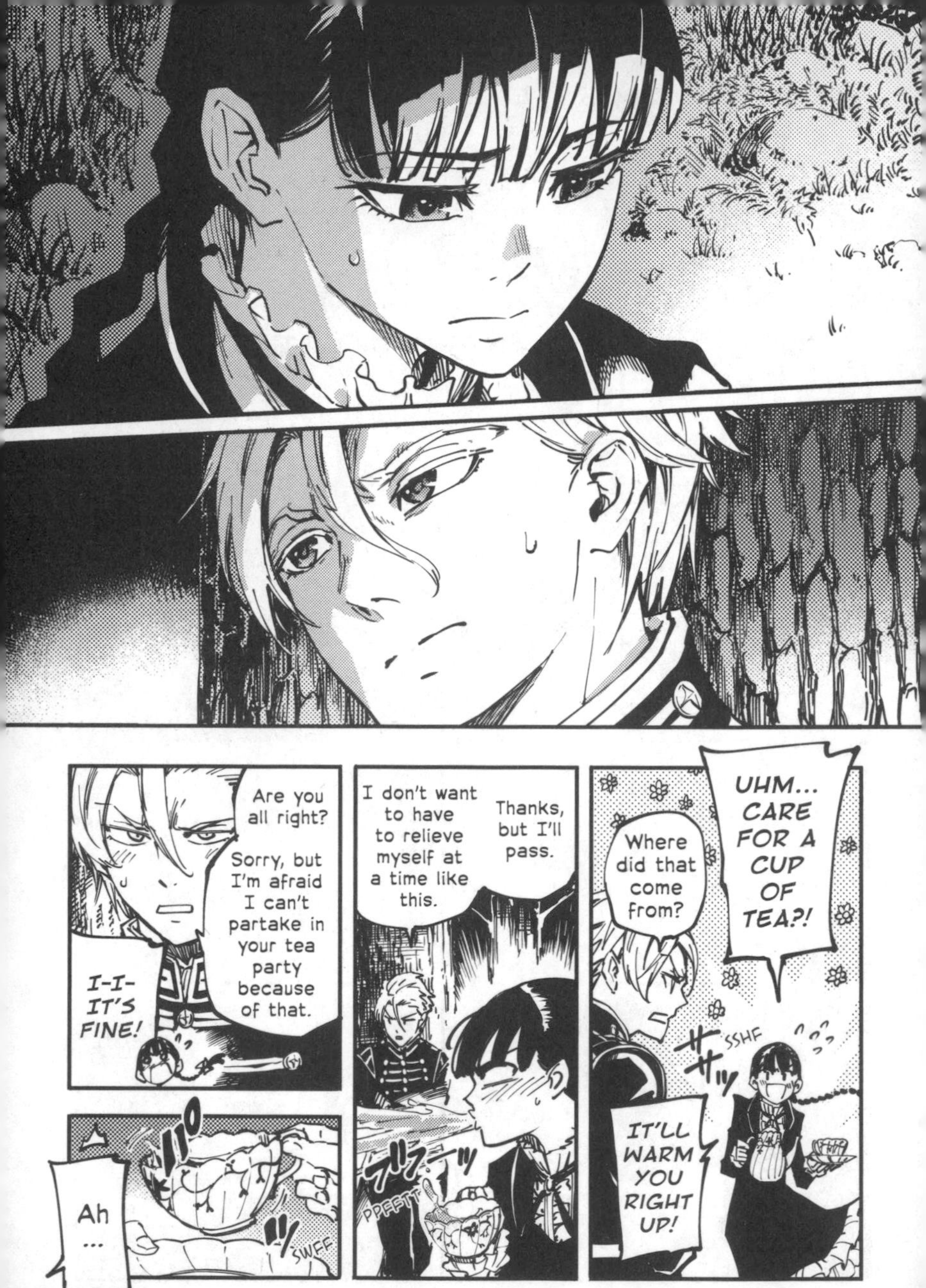

UHM... CARE FOR A CUP OF TEA?!
Where did that come from?
SSHF
IT'LL WARM YOU RIGHT UP!
Thanks, but I'll pass.
I don't want to have to relieve myself at a time like this.
PPFFTT
Are you all right?
Sorry, but I'm afraid I can't partake in your tea party because of that.
I-I-IT'S FINE!
Ah ...
SWFF

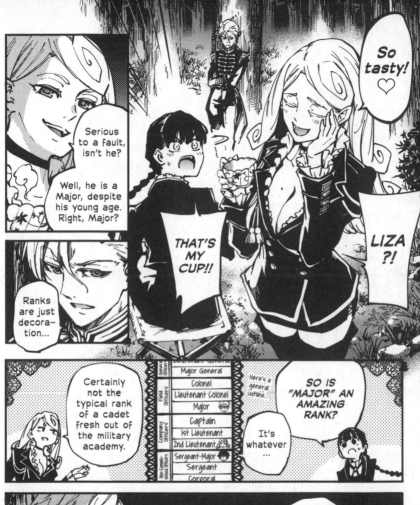

So tasty! ♡

Serious to a fault, isn't he?

Well, he is a Major, despite his young age. Right, Major?

THAT'S MY CUP!!

LIZA ?!

Ranks are just decora— tion...

Certainly not the typical rank of a cadet fresh out of the military academy.

Here's a general outline

SO IS "MAJOR" AN AMAZING RANK?

It's whatever...

	Rank
General Officers	Major General
Field Officers	Colonel
	Lieutenant Colonel
	Major
Company Officers	Captain
	1st Lieutenant
	2nd Lieutenant
Non-commissioned Officers	Sergeant-Major
	Sergeant
	Corporal

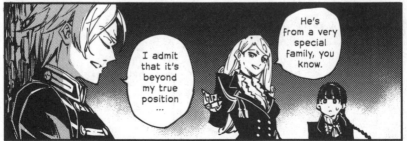

I admit that it's beyond my true position ...

He's from a very special family, you know.

44

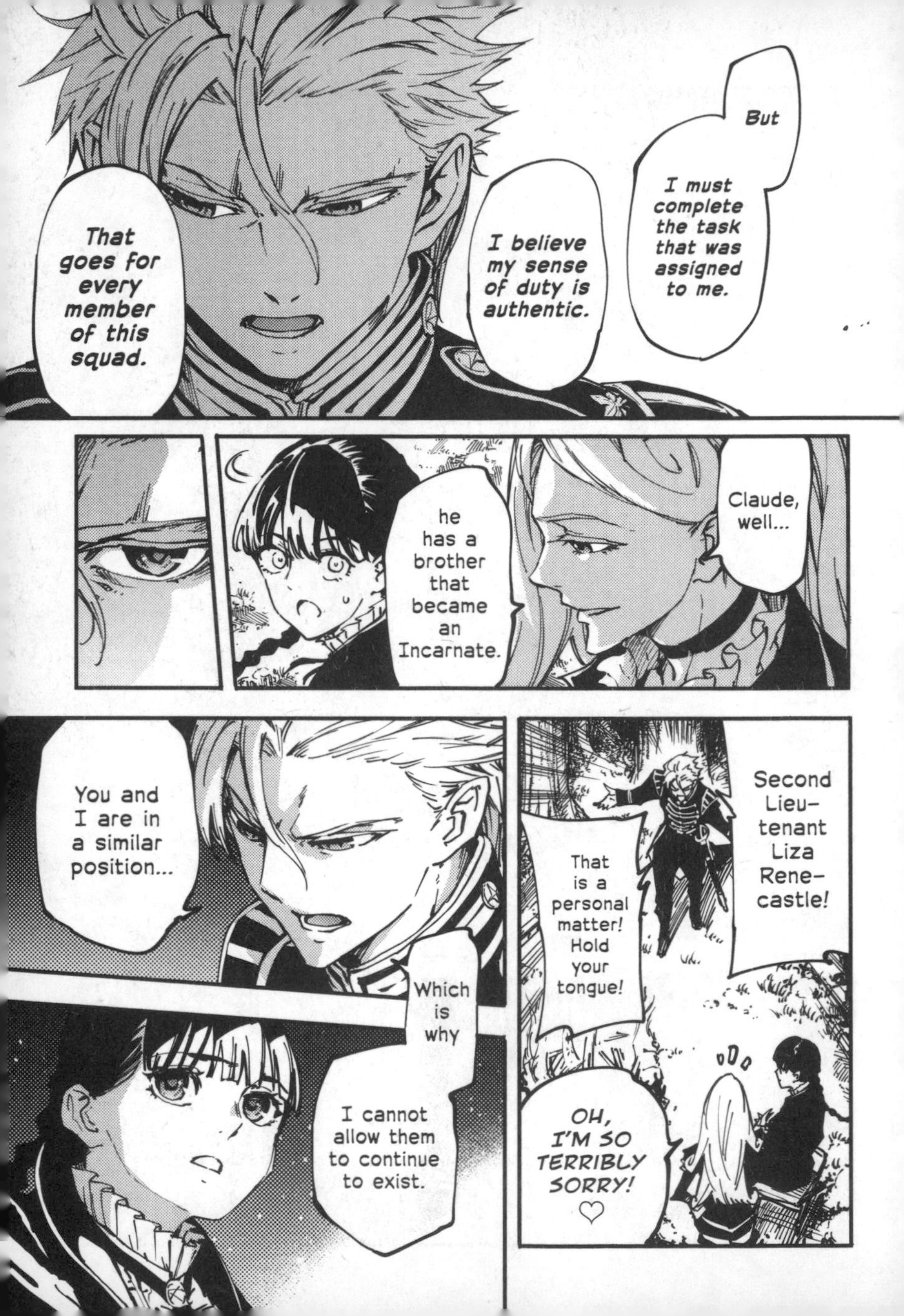
But
I must complete the task that was assigned to me.
I believe my sense of duty is authentic.
That goes for every member of this squad.
Claude, well...
he has a brother that became an Incarnate.
Second Lieu-tenant Liza Rene-castle!
That is a personal matter! Hold your tongue!
OH, I'M SO TERRIBLY SORRY! ♡
You and I are in a similar position...
Which is why
I cannot allow them to continue to exist.

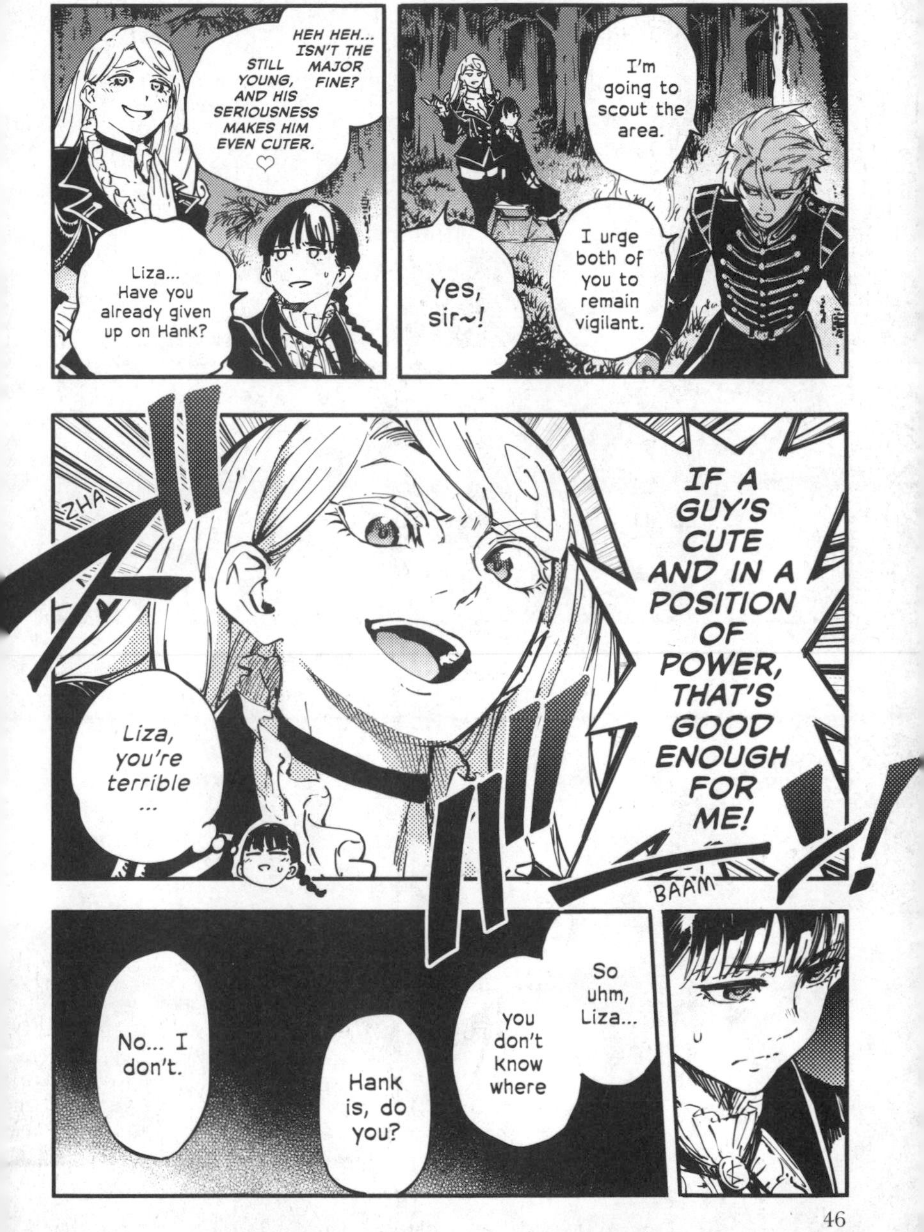
I'm going to scout the area.
I urge both of you to remain vigilant.
Yes, sir~!
HEH HEH... ISN'T THE MAJOR FINE? STILL YOUNG, AND HIS SERIOUSNESS MAKES HIM EVEN CUTER. ♡
Liza... Have you already given up on Hank?
ZHA
IF A GUY'S CUTE AND IN A POSITION OF POWER, THAT'S GOOD ENOUGH FOR ME!
Liza, you're terrible ...
BAAM
So uhm, Liza...
you don't know where
Hank is, do you?
No... I don't.

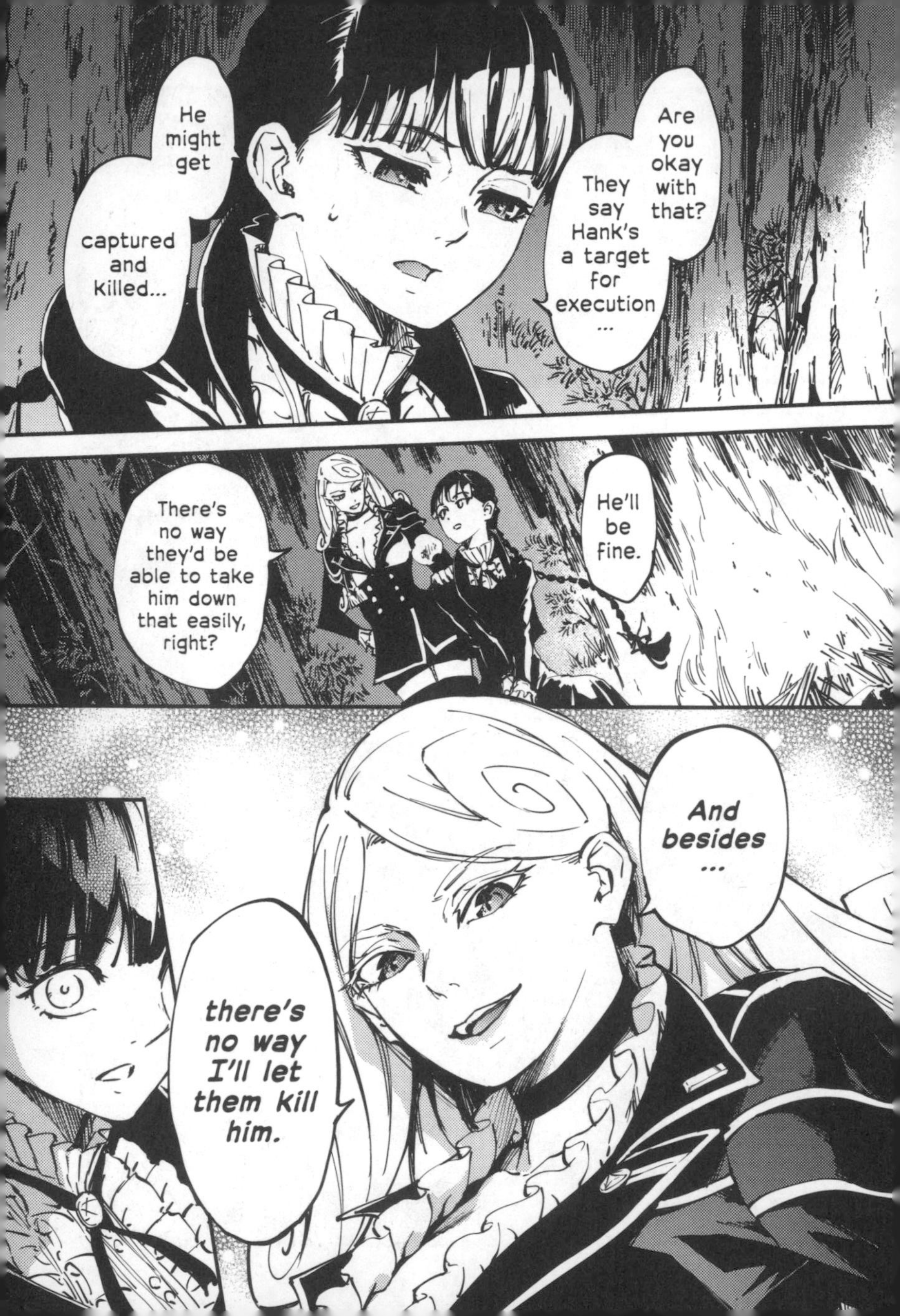
Are you okay with that?
They say Hank's a target for execution ...
He might get
captured and killed...
He'll be fine.
There's no way they'd be able to take him down that easily, right?
And besides ...
there's no way I'll let them kill him.

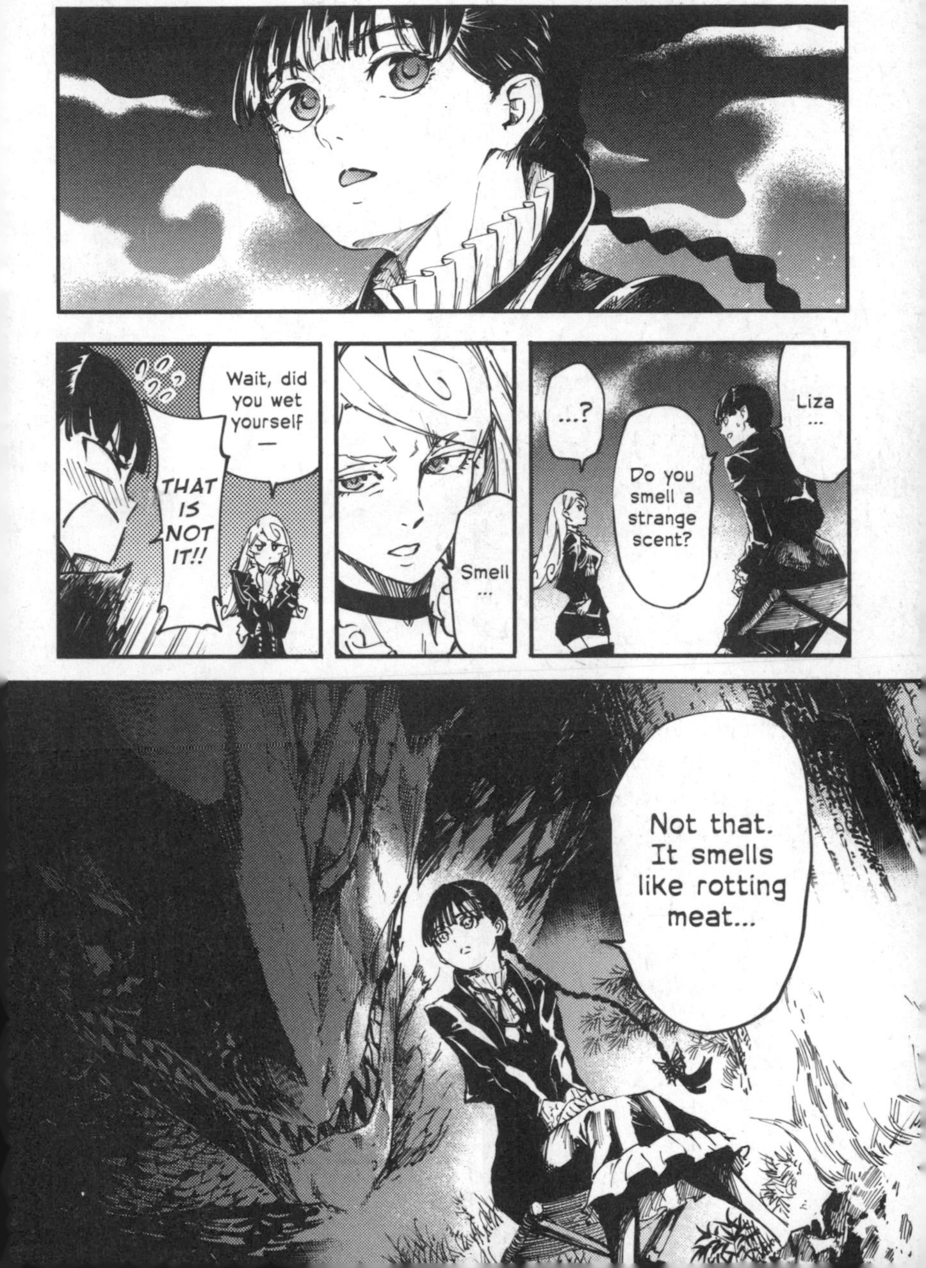
Liza ...
...?
Do you smell a strange scent?
Smell ...
Wait, did you wet yourself —
THAT IS NOT IT!!
Not that. It smells like rotting meat...

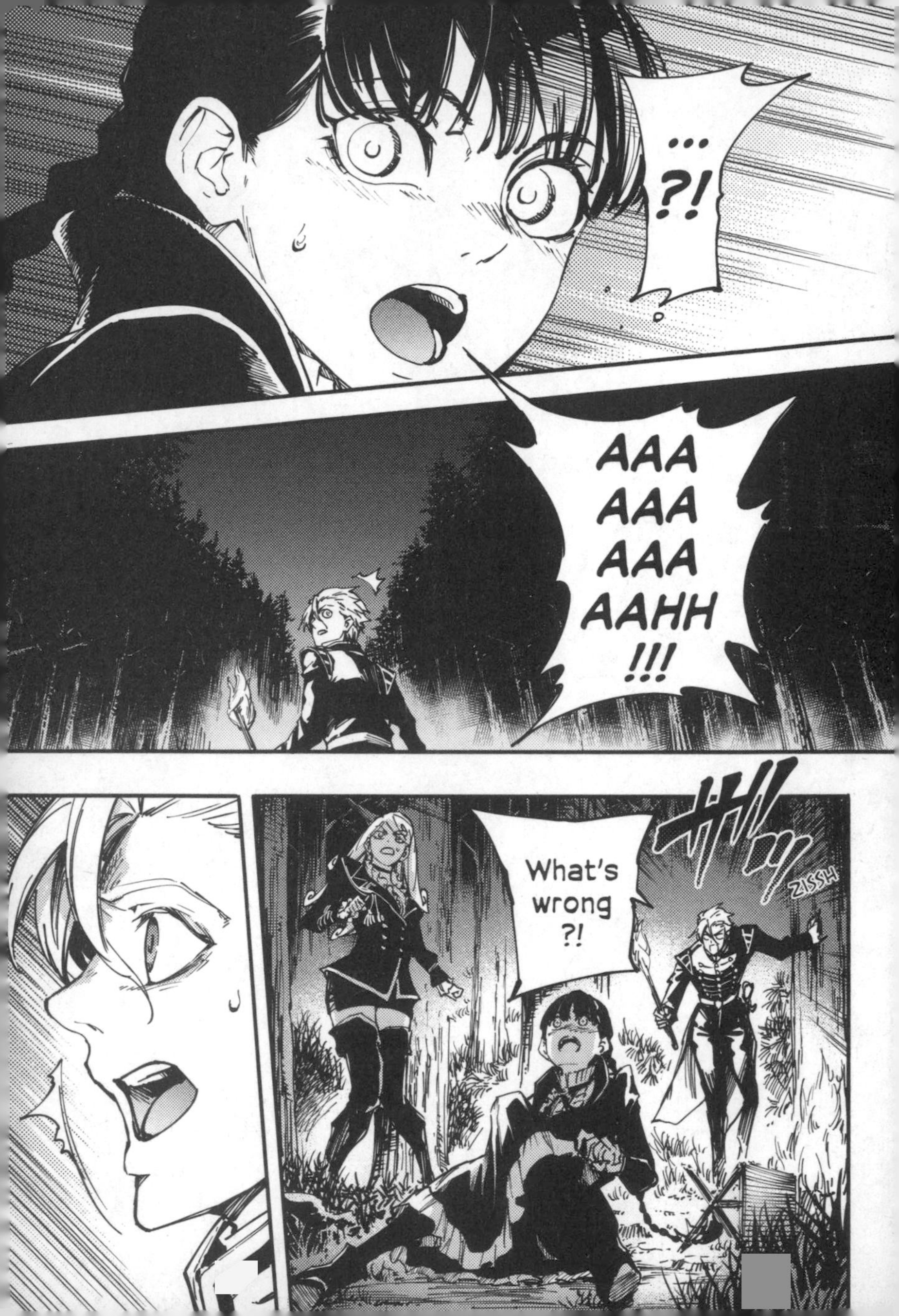
...
?!
AAA AAA AAA AAHH !!!
ZISSH
What's wrong ?!

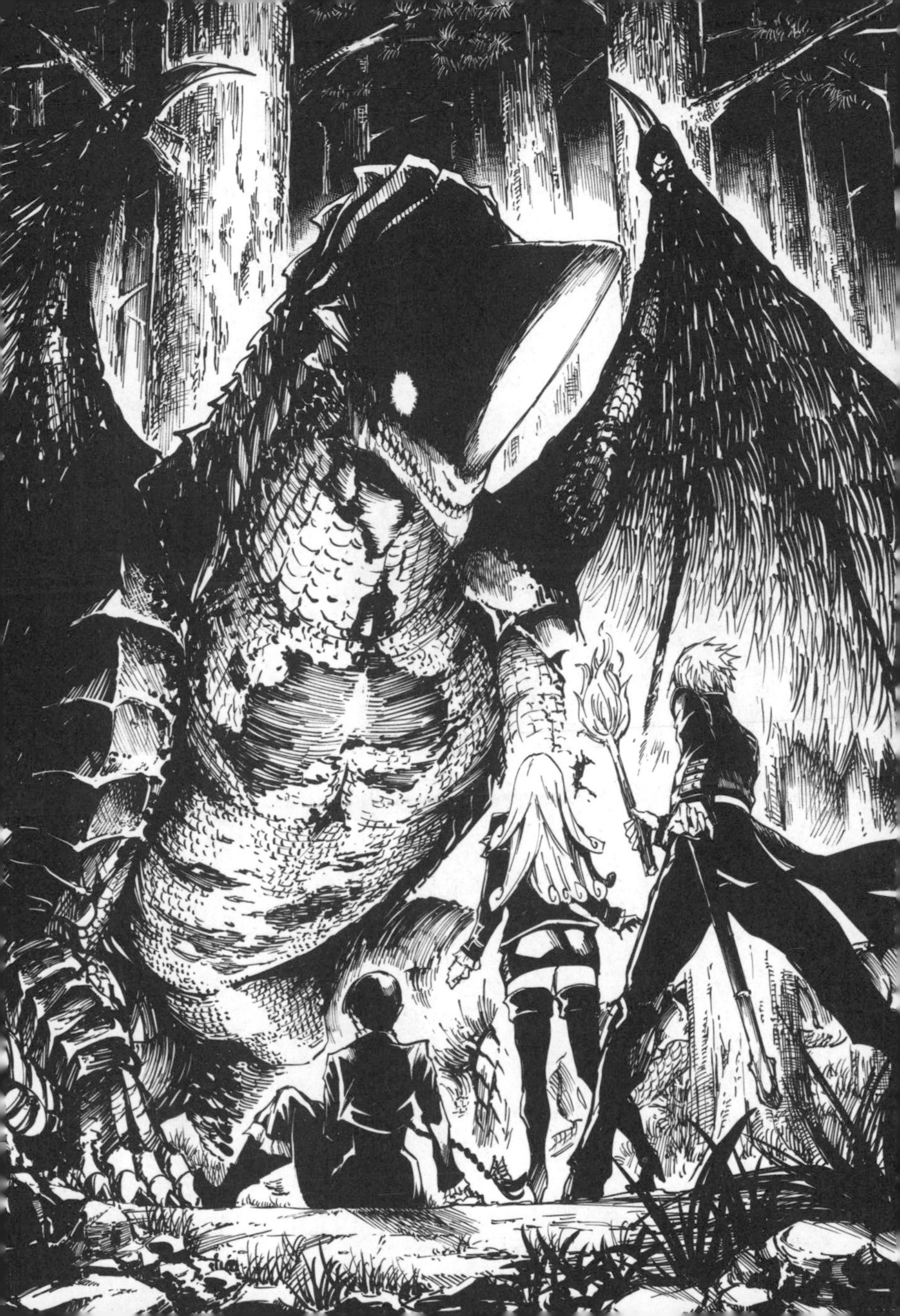

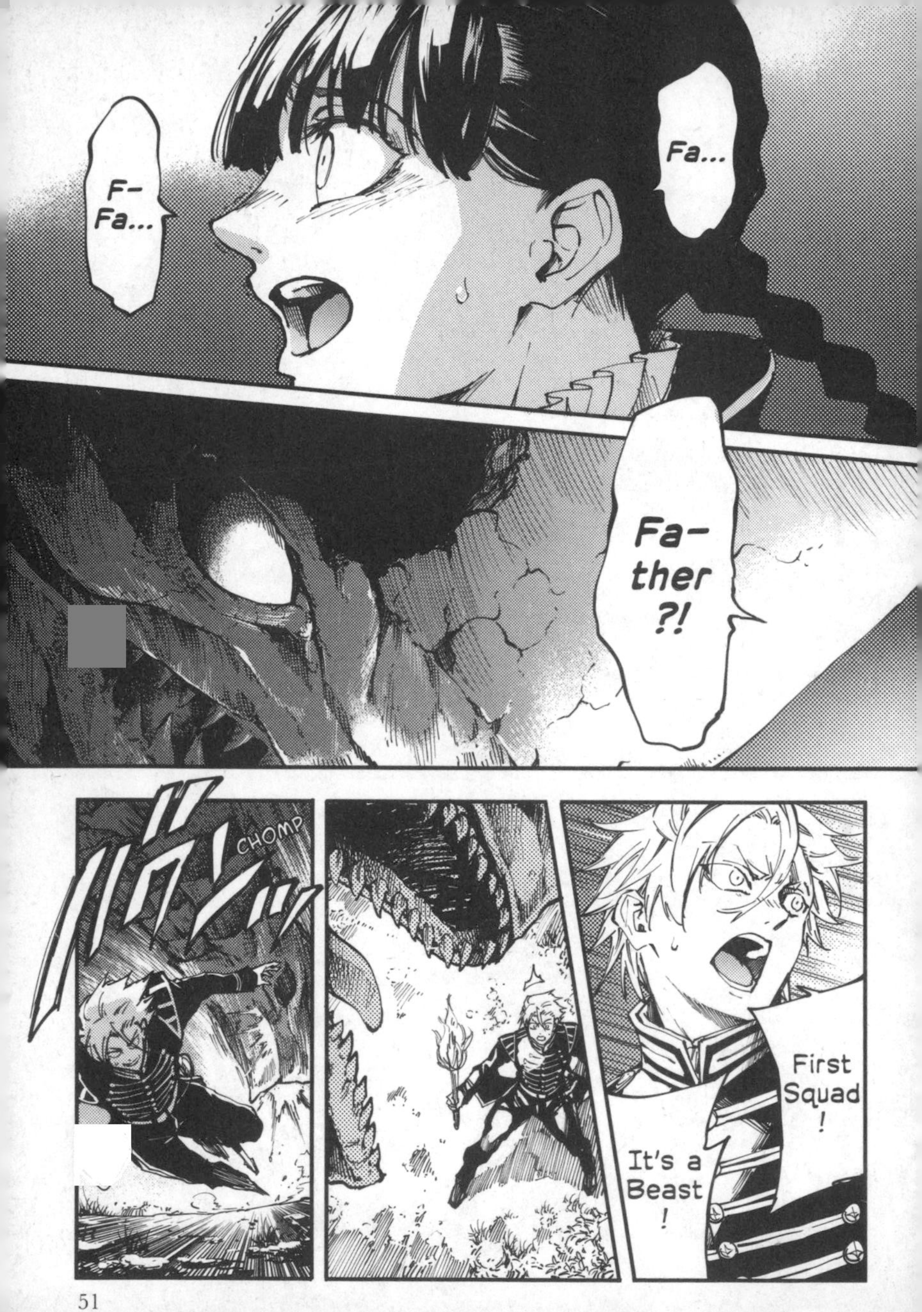
Fa...
F- Fa...
Fa- ther ?!
First Squad !
It's a Beast !
CHOMP

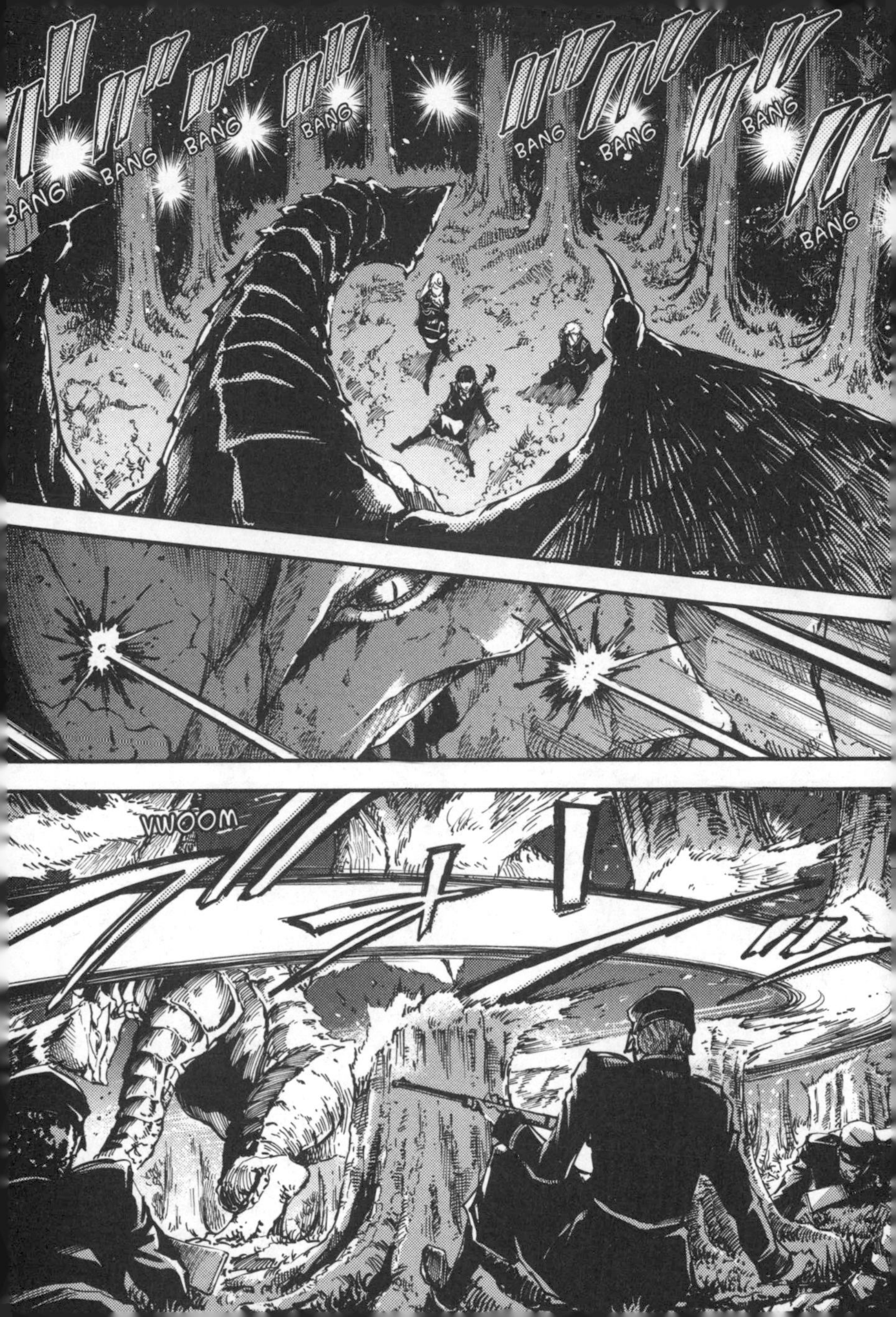
BANG
BANG
BANG
BANG
BANG
BANG
BANG
BANG
VWOOM

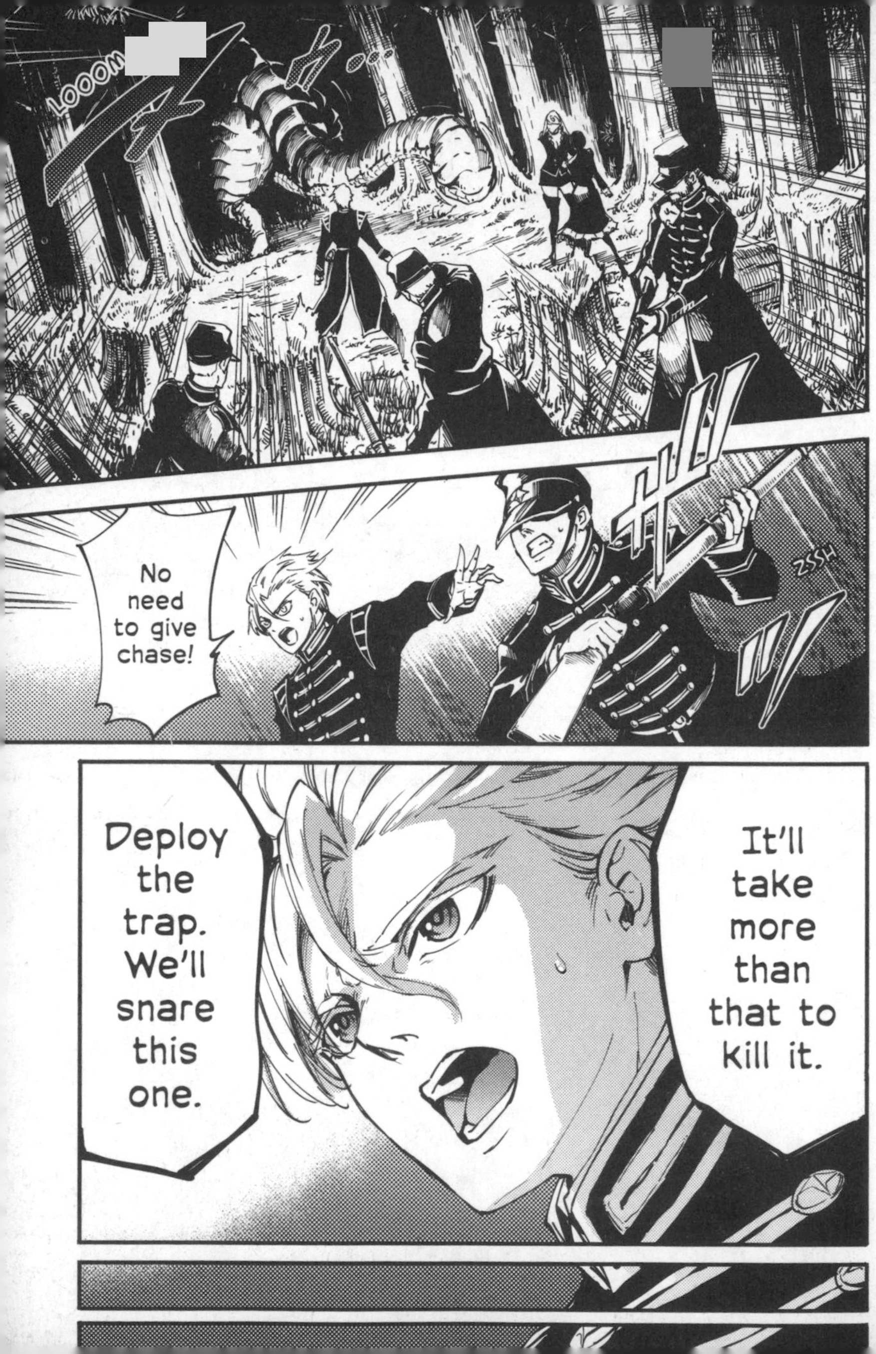
LOOOM
No need to give chase!
ZSSH
It'll take more than that to kill it.
Deploy the trap. We'll snare this one.

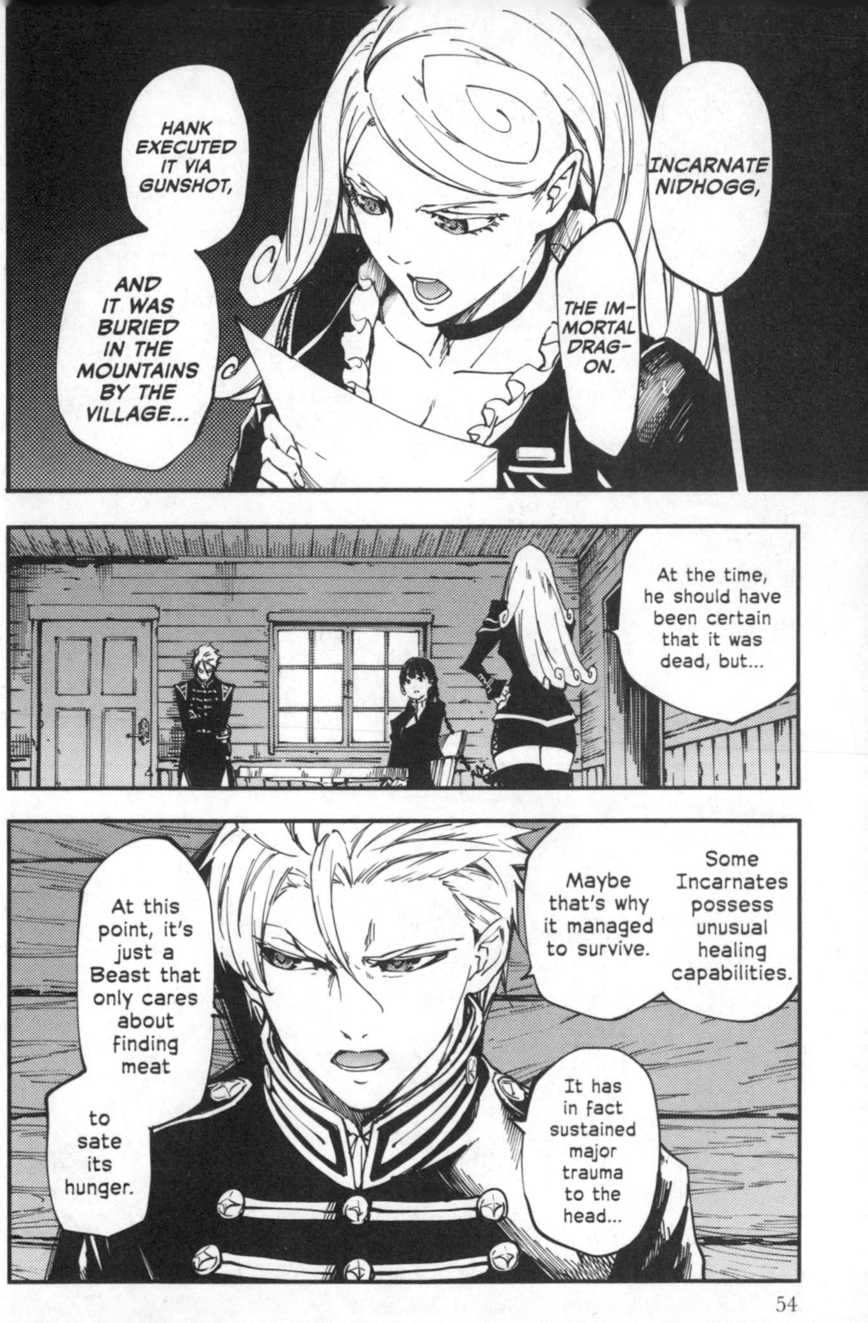
INCARNATE NIDHOGG,
THE IM-MORTAL DRAG-ON.
HANK EXECUTED IT VIA GUNSHOT,
AND IT WAS BURIED IN THE MOUNTAINS BY THE VILLAGE...
At the time, he should have been certain that it was dead, but...
Some Incarnates possess unusual healing capabilities.
Maybe that's why it managed to survive.
It has in fact sustained major trauma to the head...
At this point, it's just a Beast that only cares about finding meat
to sate its hunger.

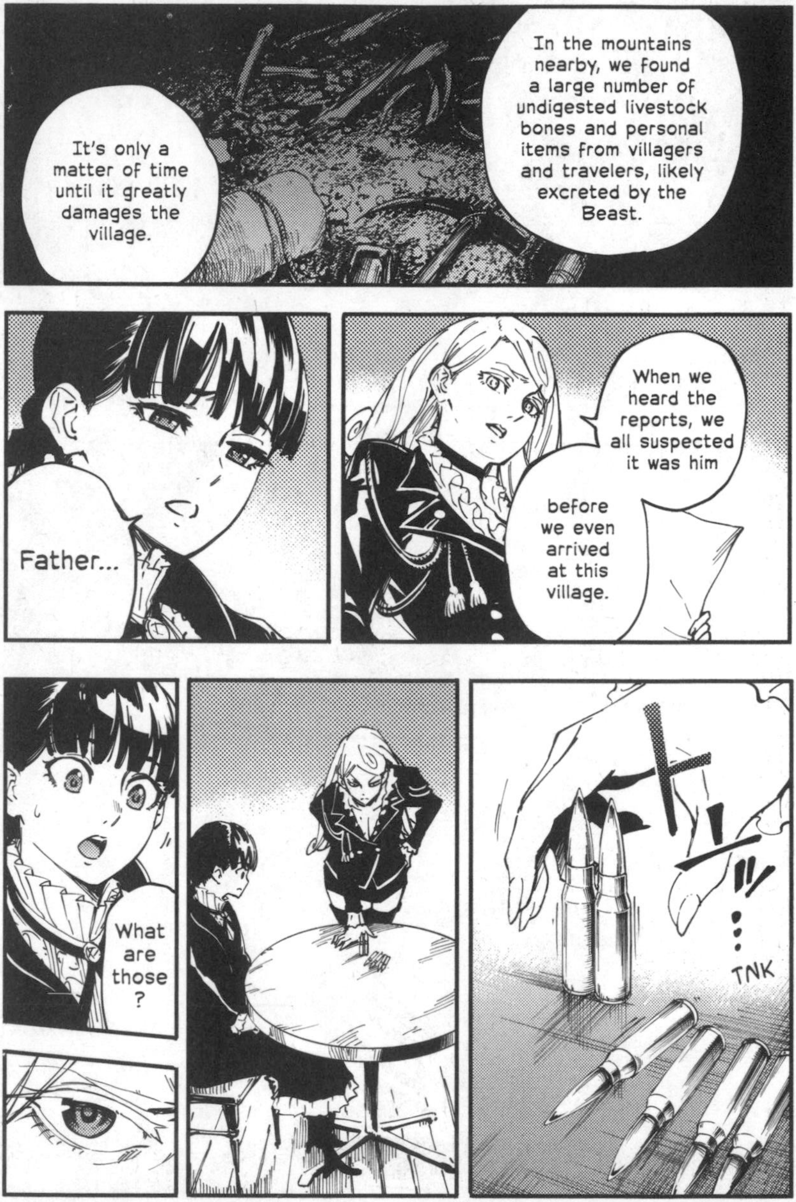

In the mountains nearby, we found a large number of undigested livestock bones and personal items from villagers and travelers, likely excreted by the Beast.
It's only a matter of time until it greatly damages the village.
When we heard the reports, we all suspected it was him
before we even arrived at this village.
Father...
TNK
What are those ?

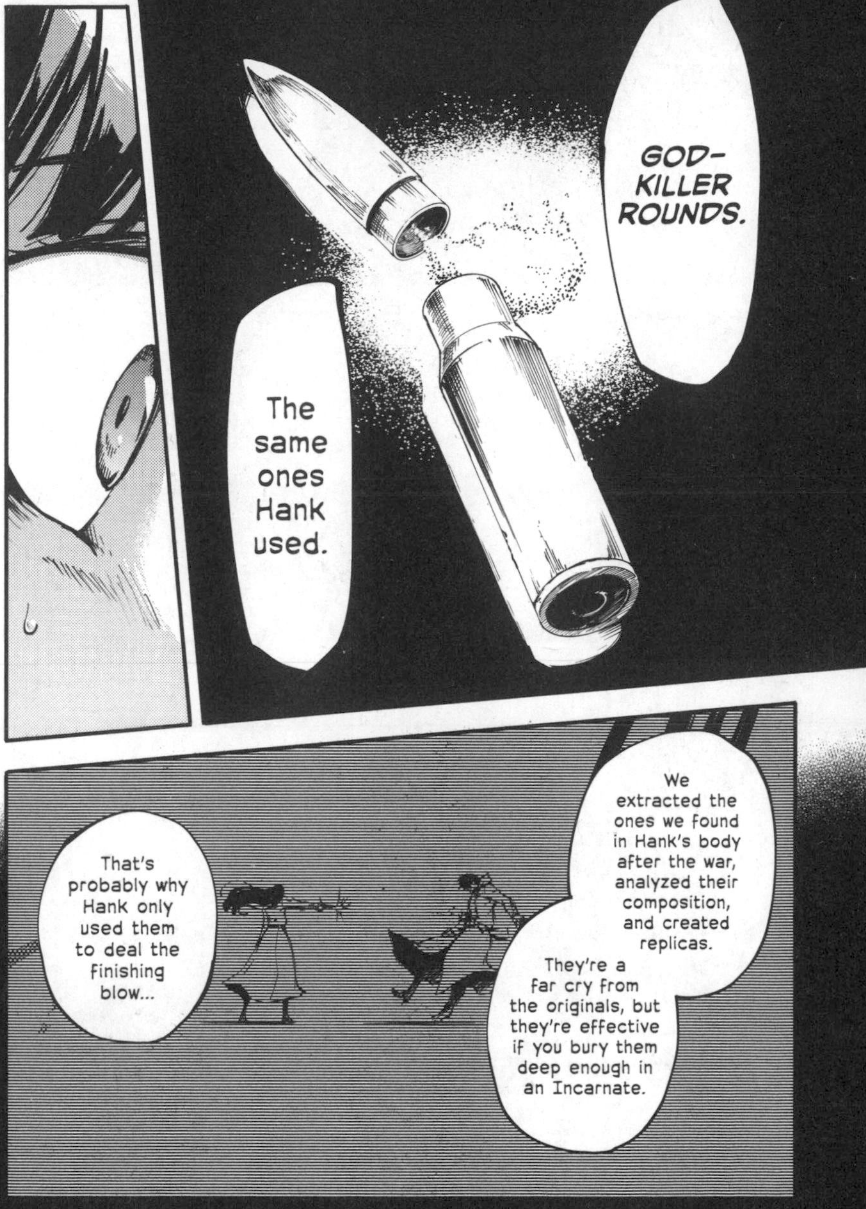
GOD-KILLER ROUNDS.
The same ones Hank used.
We extracted the ones we found in Hank's body after the war, analyzed their composition, and created replicas.
They're a far cry from the originals, but they're effective if you bury them deep enough in an Incarnate.
That's probably why Hank only used them to deal the finishing blow...

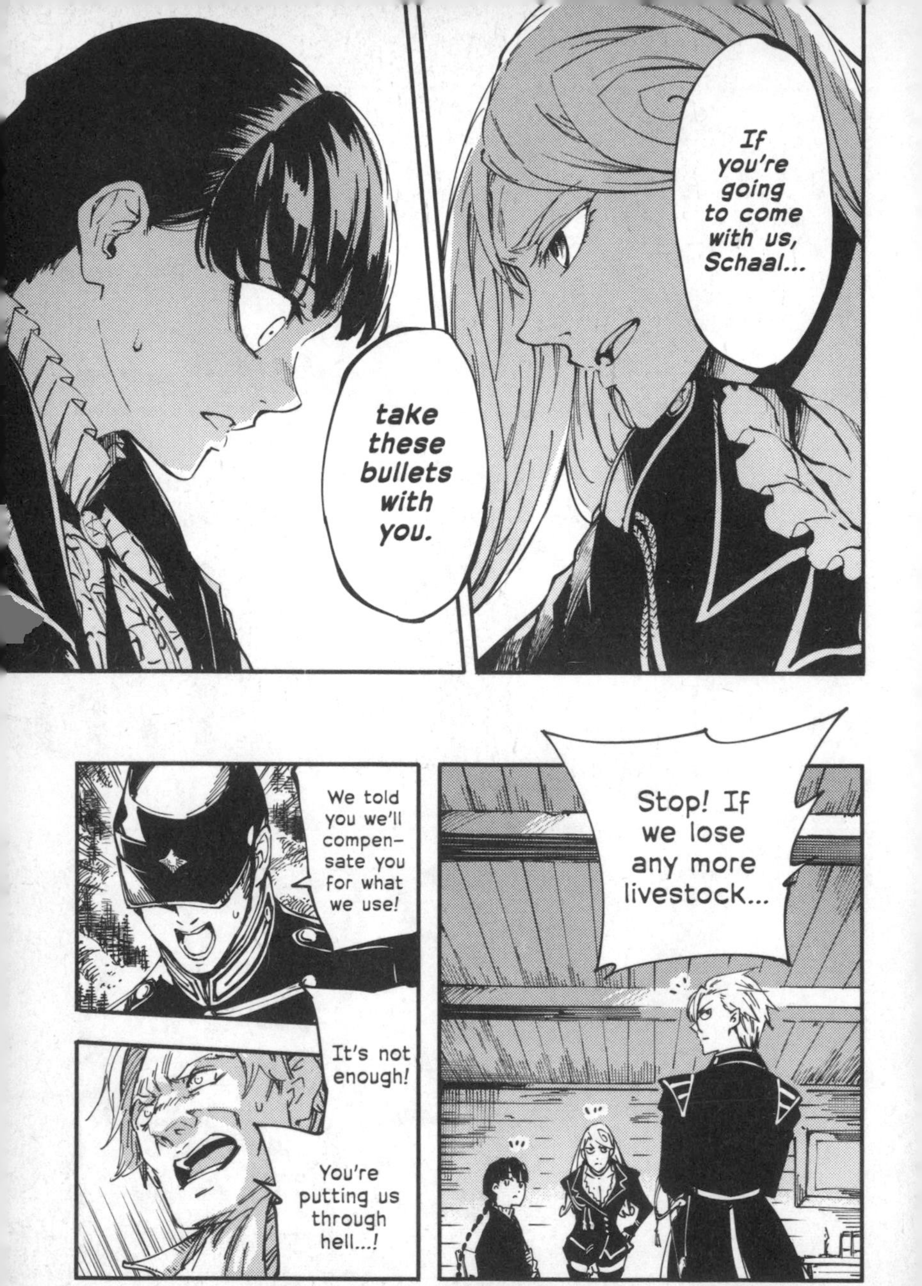
If you're going to come with us, Schaal...
take these bullets with you.
Stop! If we lose any more livestock...
We told you we'll compen-sate you for what we use!
It's not enough!
You're putting us through hell...!

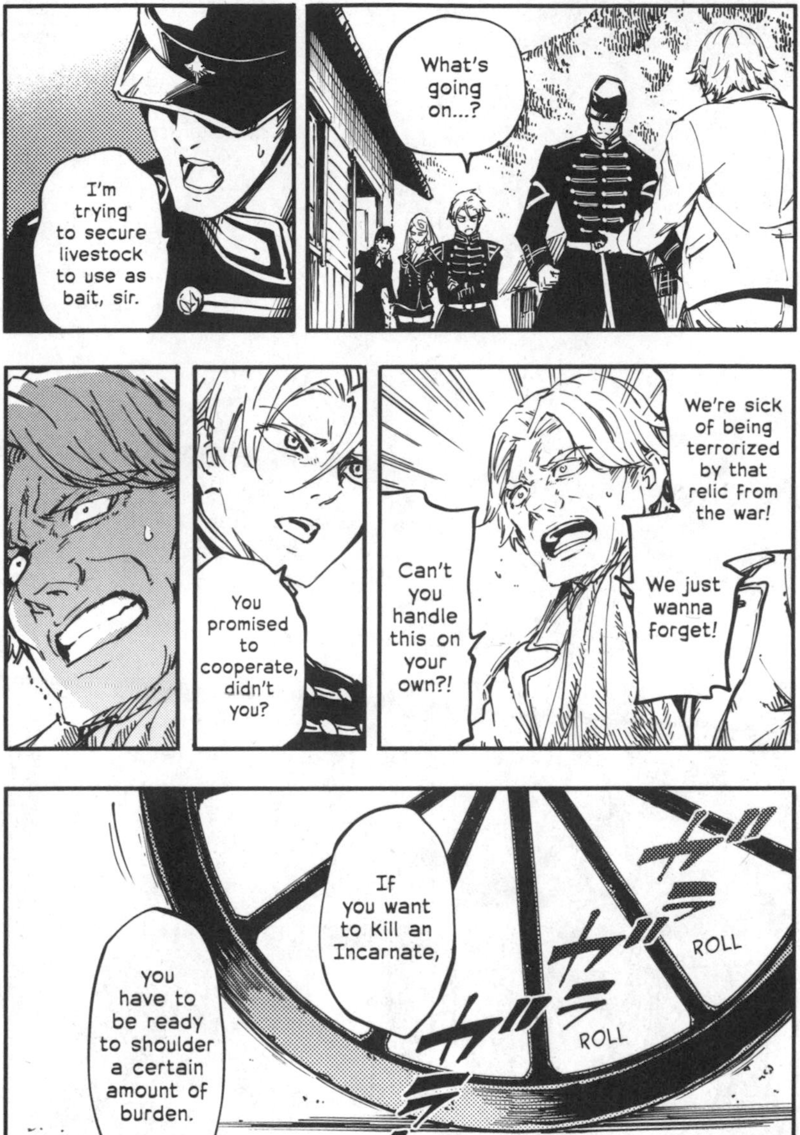
What's going on...?
I'm trying to secure livestock to use as bait, sir.
We're sick of being terrorized by that relic from the war!
We just wanna forget!
Can't you handle this on your own?!
You promised to cooperate, didn't you?
ROLL
If you want to kill an Incarnate,
ROLL
you have to be ready to shoulder a certain amount of burden.
ROLL

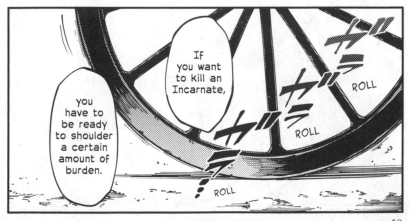

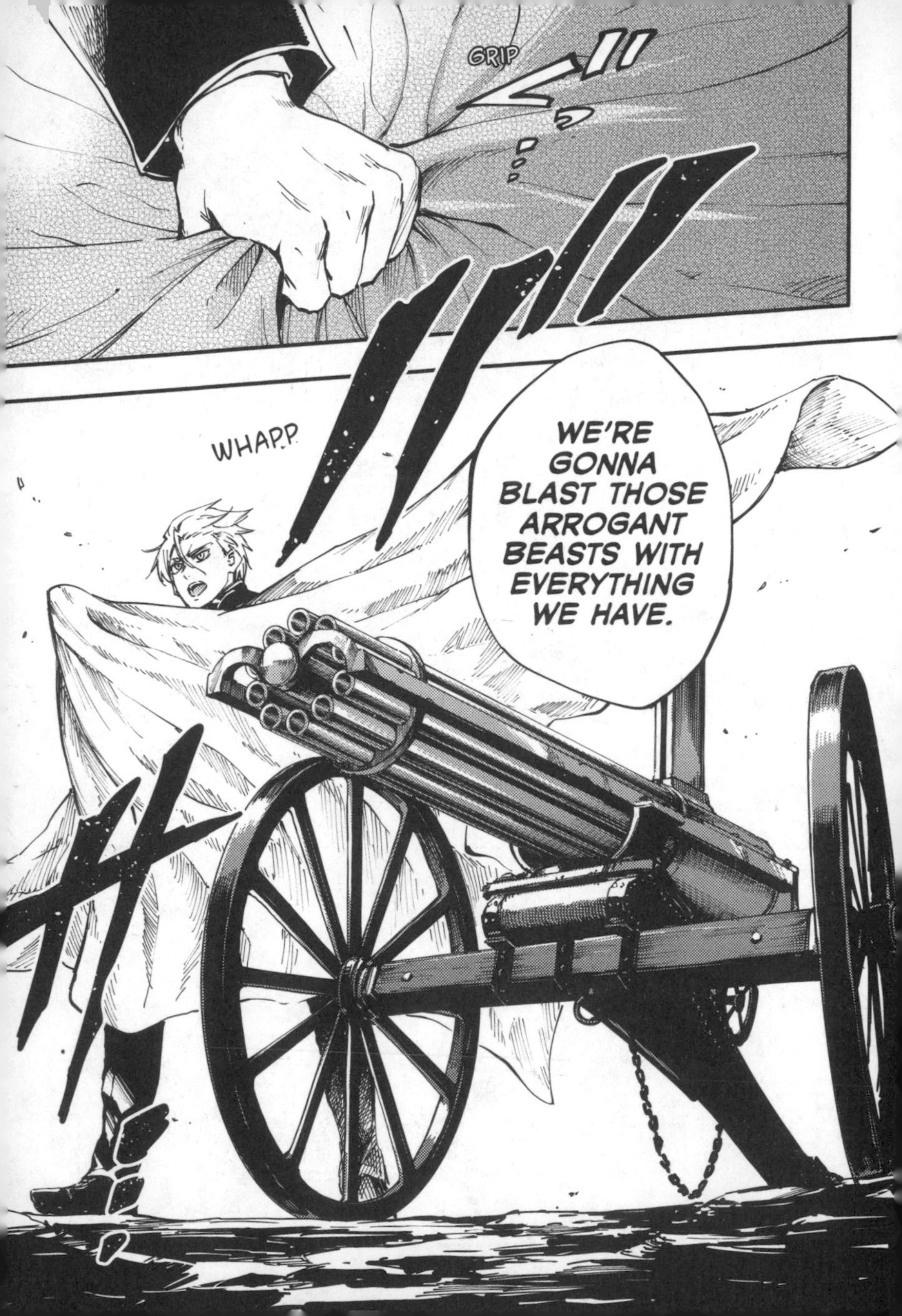
GRIP
WHAPP
WE'RE GONNA BLAST THOSE ARROGANT BEASTS WITH EVERYTHING WE HAVE.

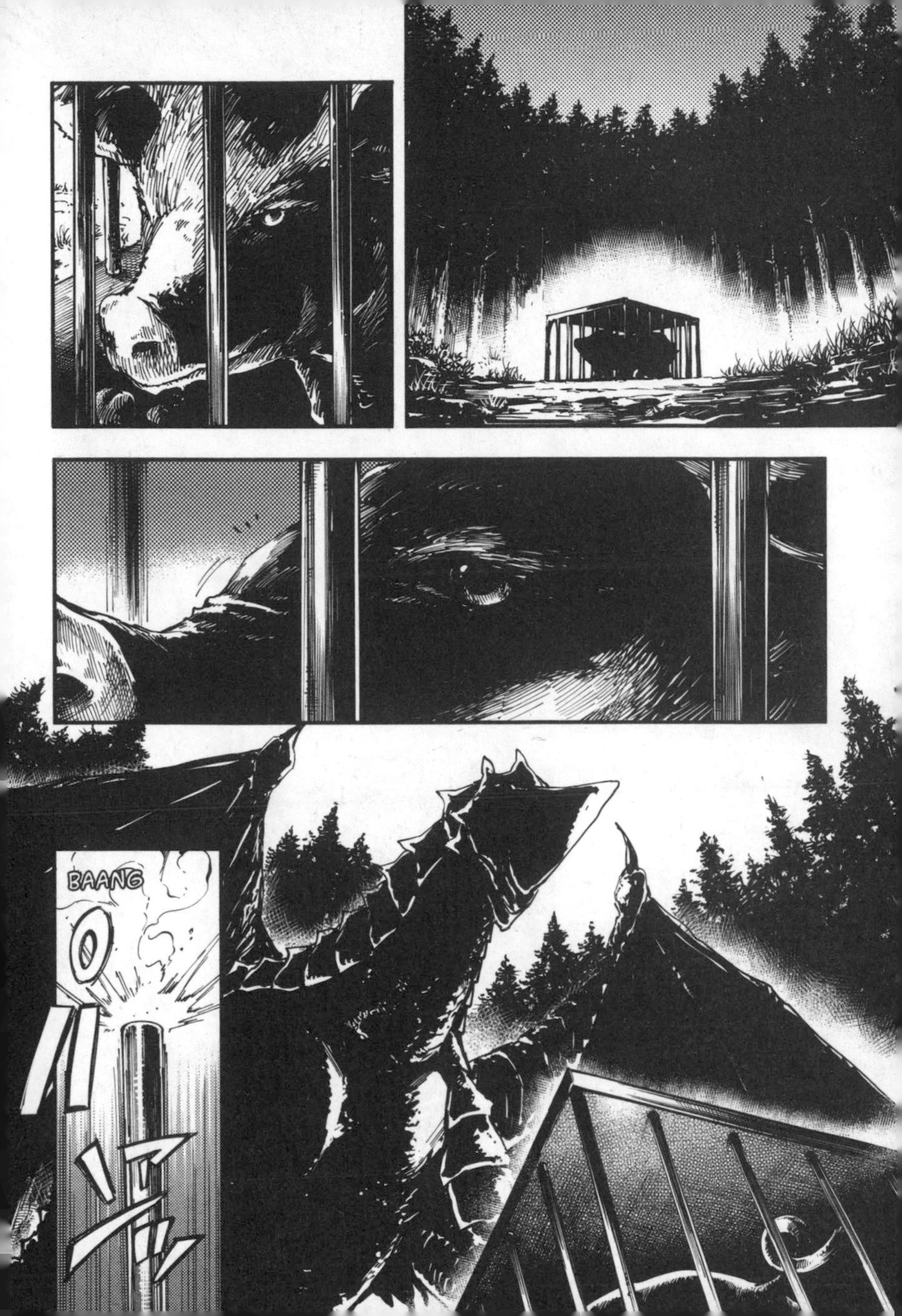
BAANG

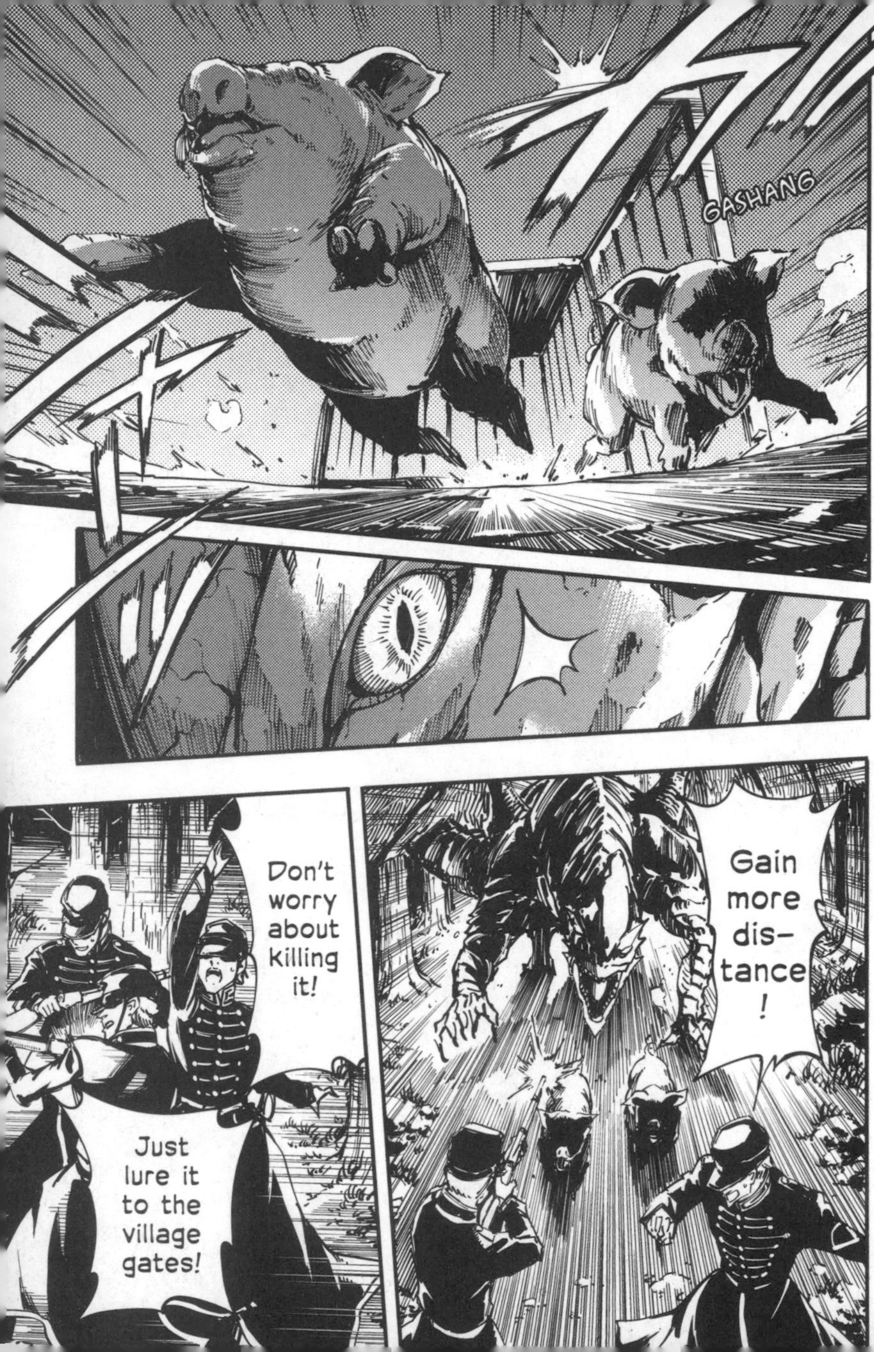
GASHANG
Gain more dis-tance!
Don't worry about killing it!
Just lure it to the village gates!

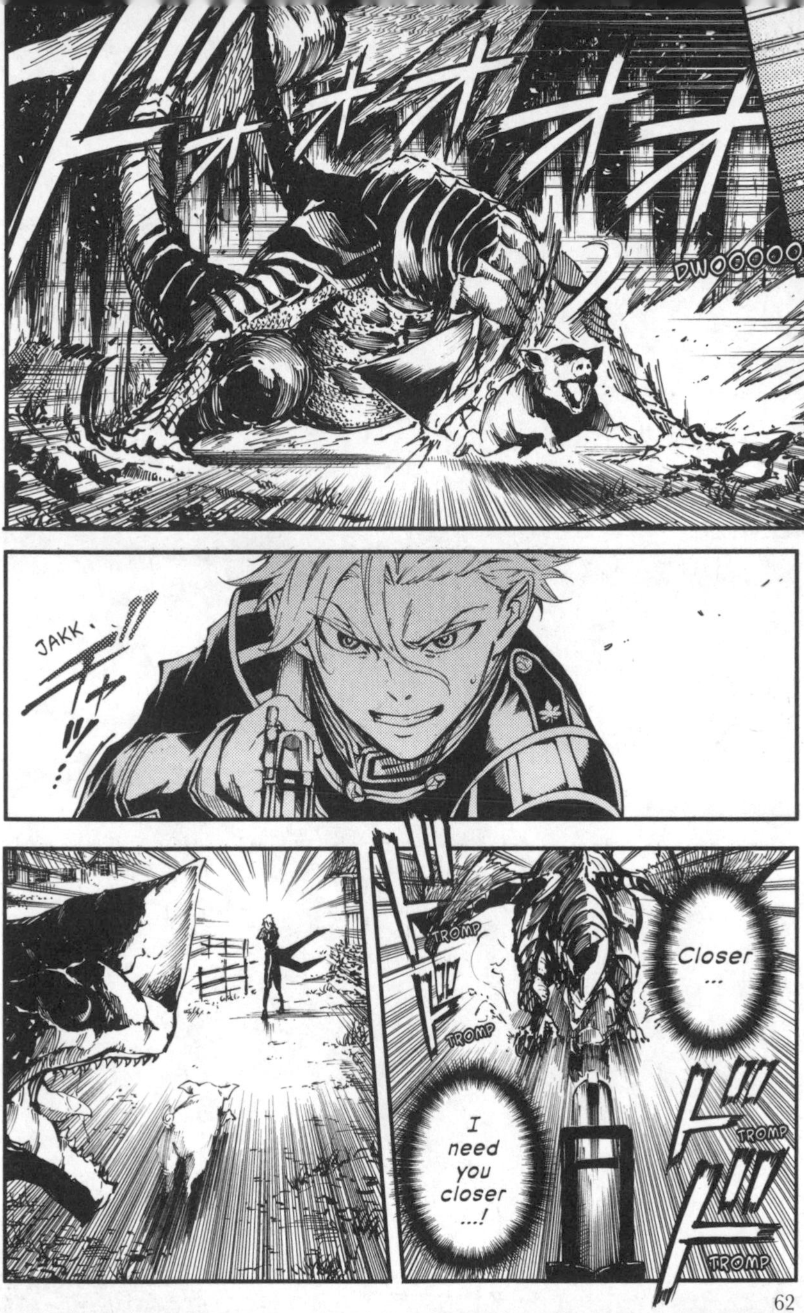
DWOOOOOM
JAKK
Closer ...
TROMP
TROMP
I need you closer ...!
TROMP
TROMP

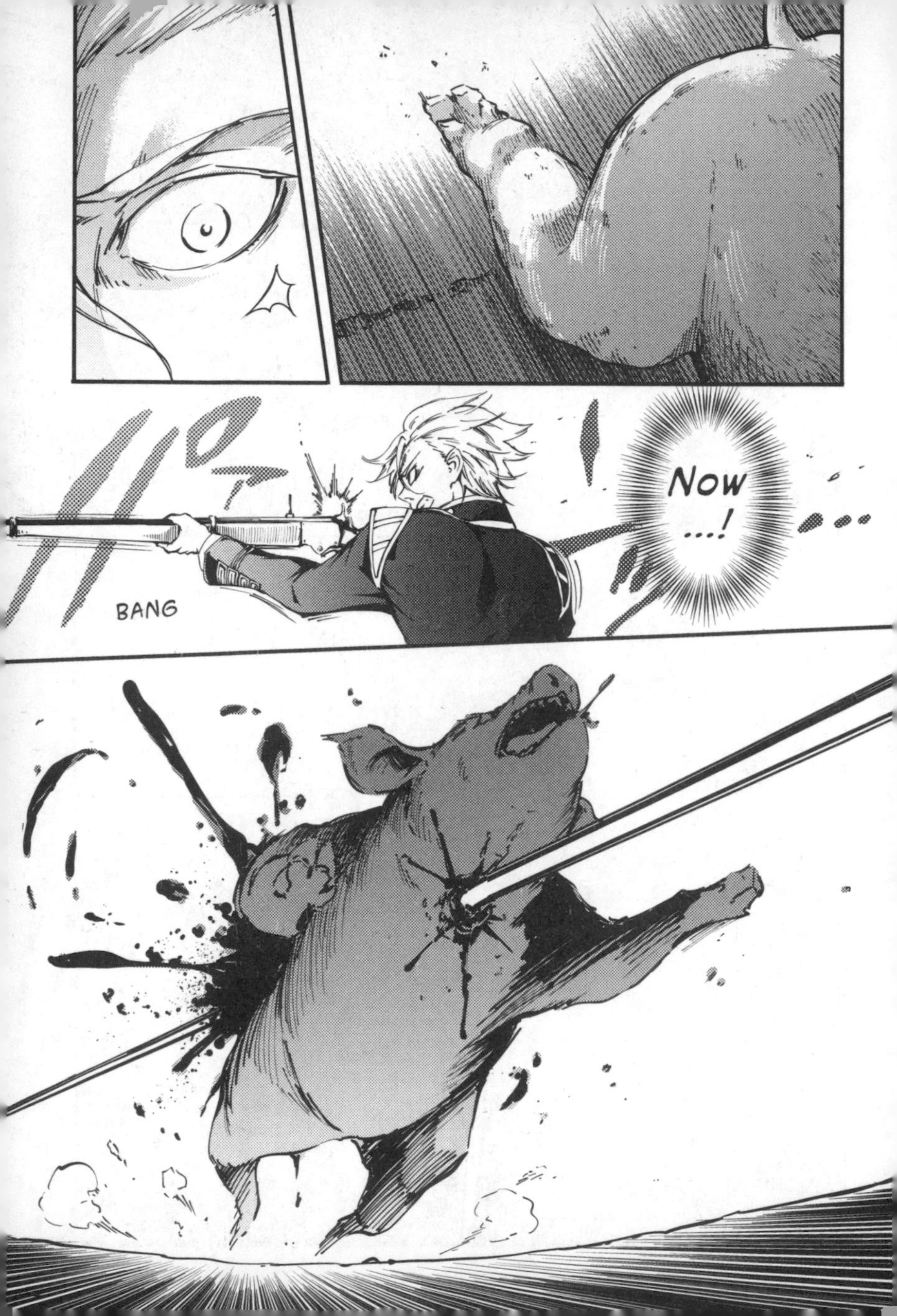
Now ....!
BANG

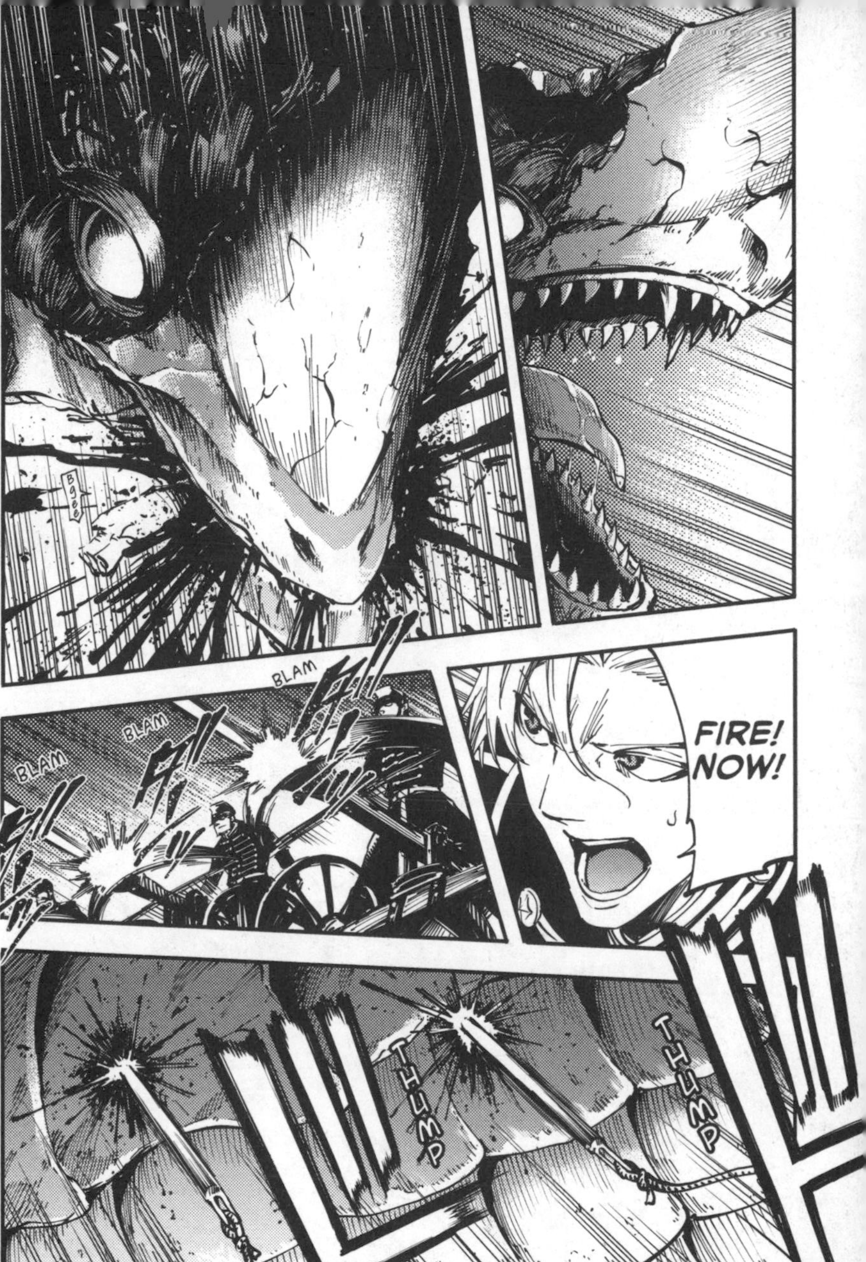
Bgee
FIRE! NOW!
BLAM
BLAM
BLAM
THUMP
THUMP

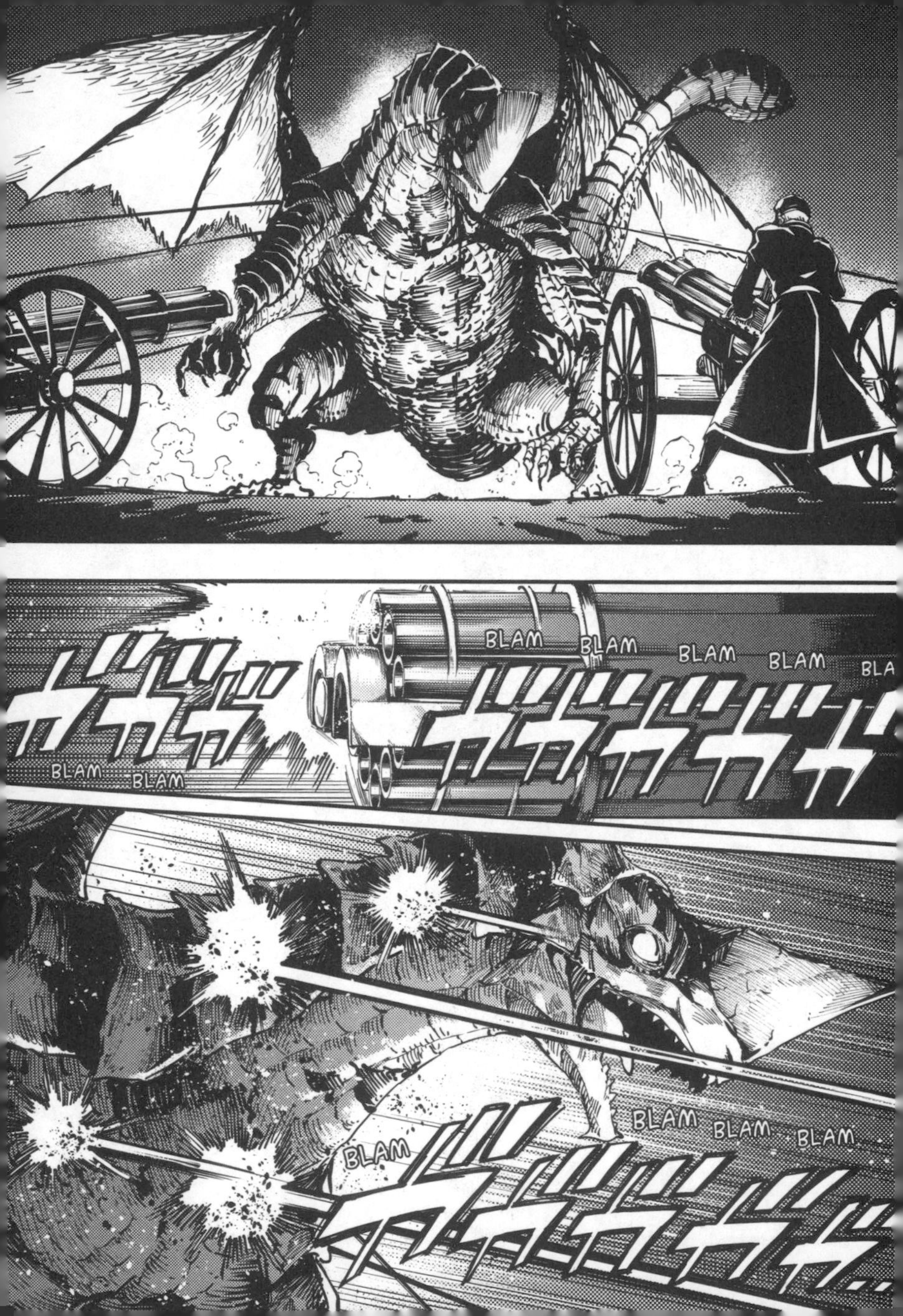
BLA
BLAM
BLAM
BLAM
BLAM
BLAM
BLAM
BLAM
BLAM
BLAM
BLAM

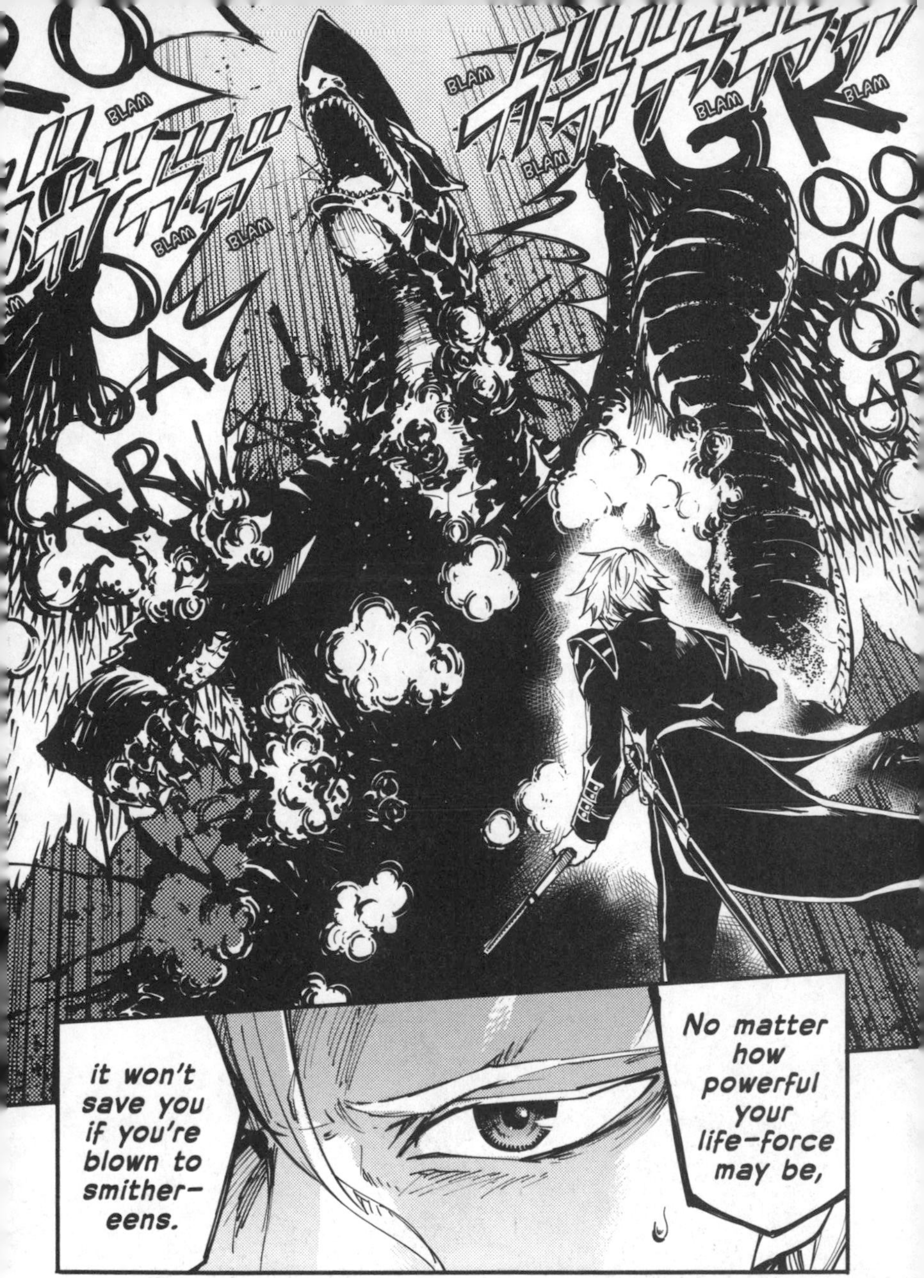
BLAM
BLAM
BLAM
BLAM
BLAM
BLAM
BLAM
BLAM
No matter how powerful your life-force may be,
it won't save you if you're blown to smither-eens.

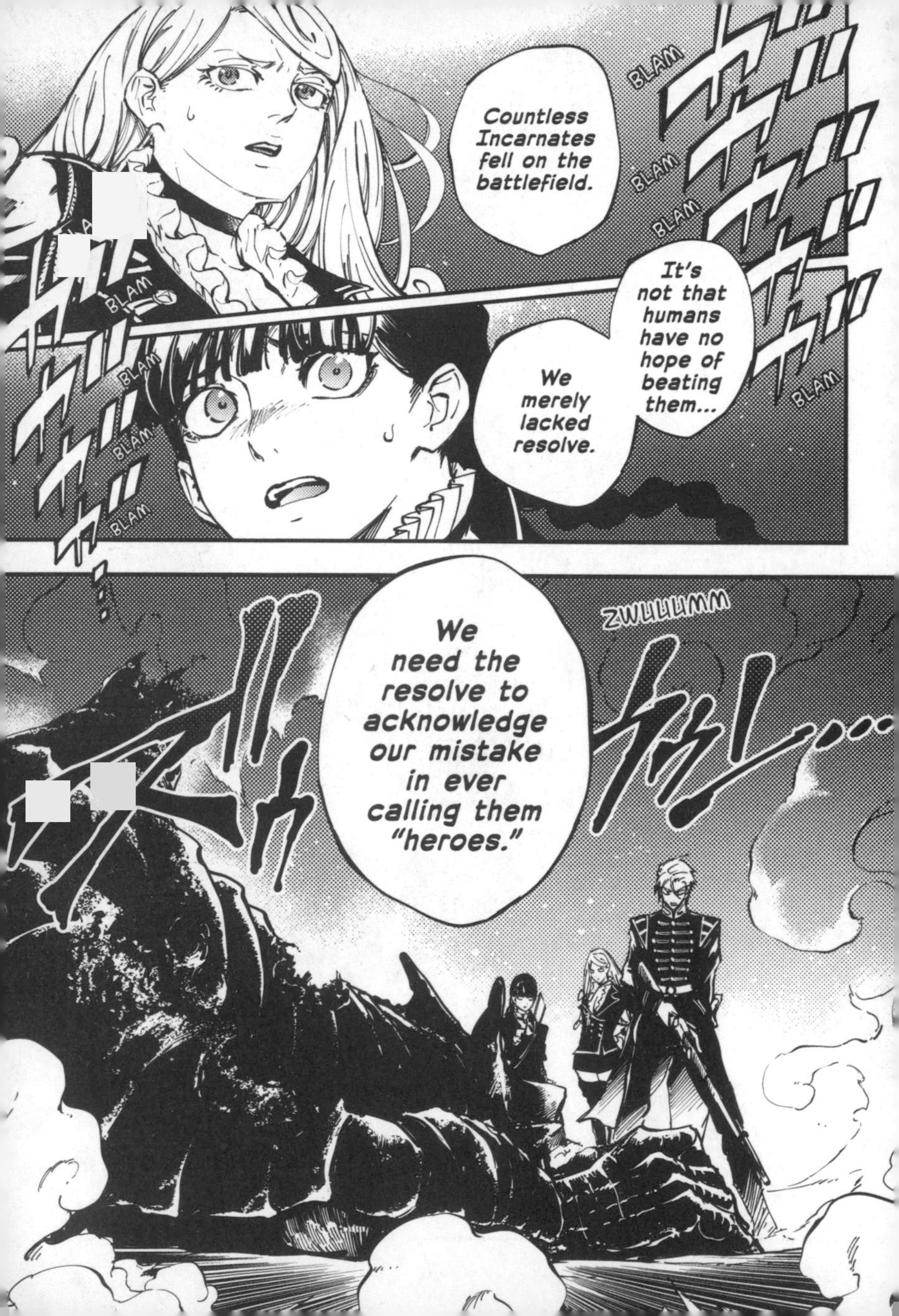
BLAM
BLAM
BLAM
Countless Incarnates fell on the battlefield.
It's not that humans have no hope of beating them...
We merely lacked resolve.
BLAM
BLAM
BLAM
BLAM
BLAM
ZWULULUMM
We need the resolve to acknowledge our mistake in ever calling them "heroes."

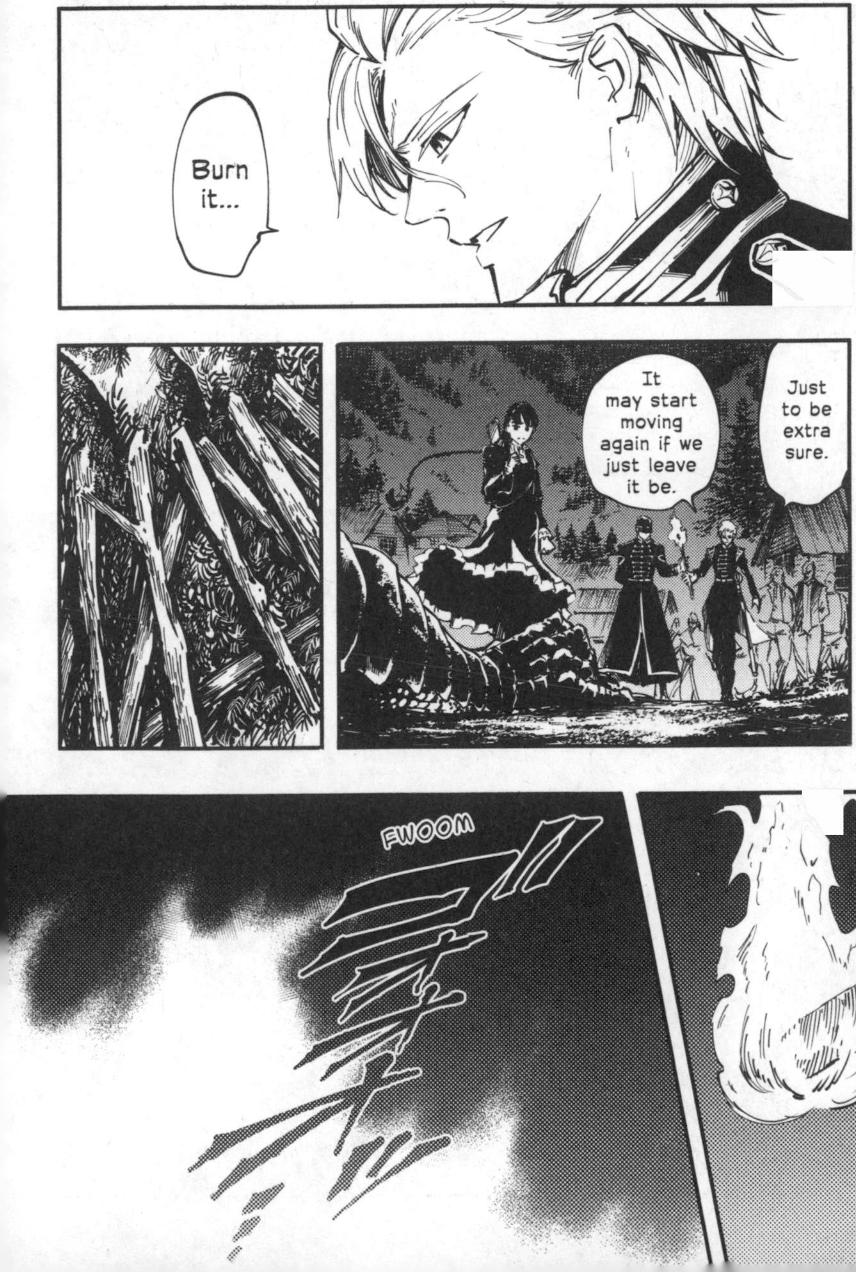
Burn it...
Just to be extra sure.
It may start moving again if we just leave it be.
FWOOM

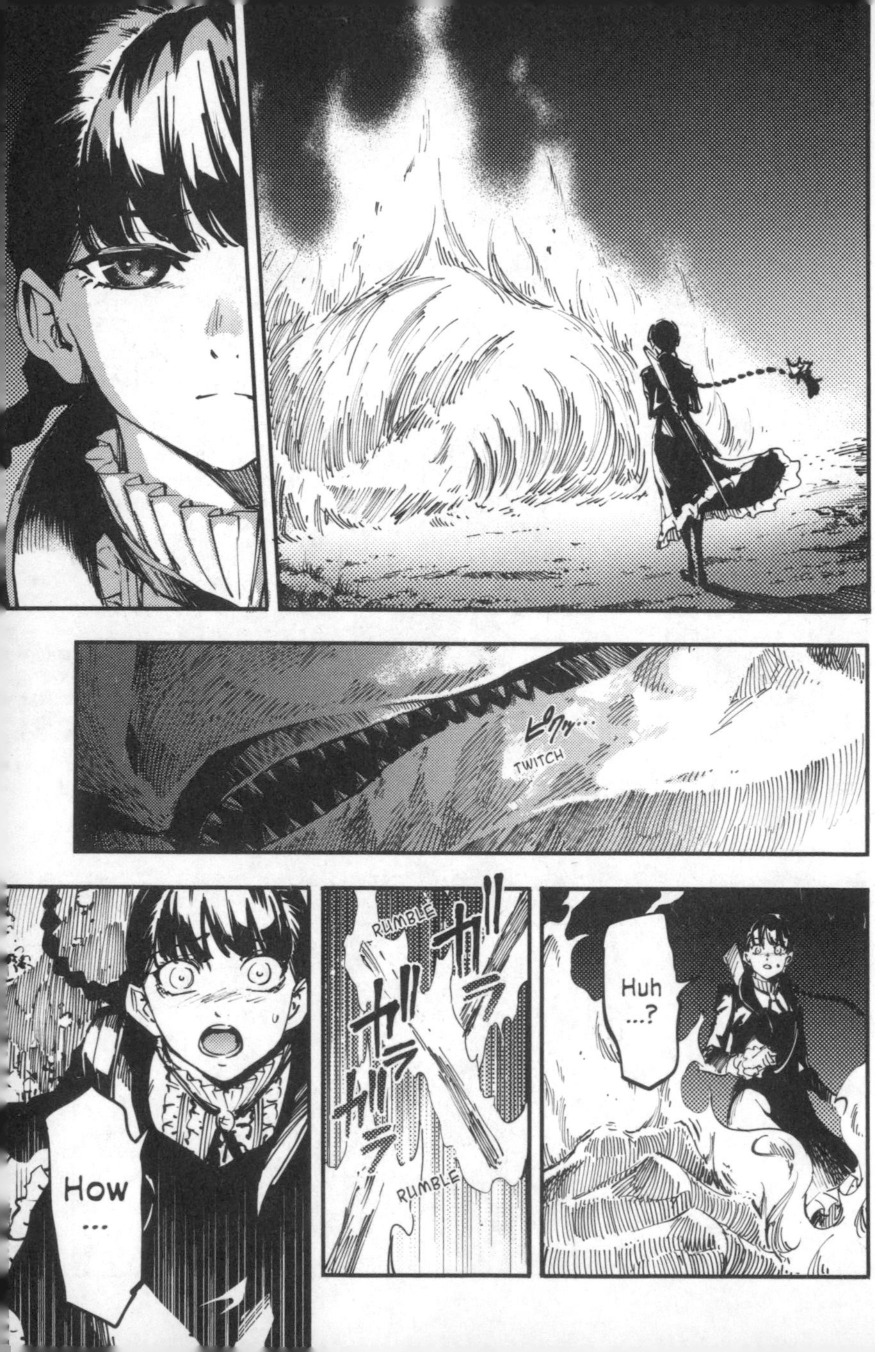
ピクッ…
TWITCH
Huh ...?
RUMBLE
ガラ
ガラ
ガラ
RUMBLE
How ...

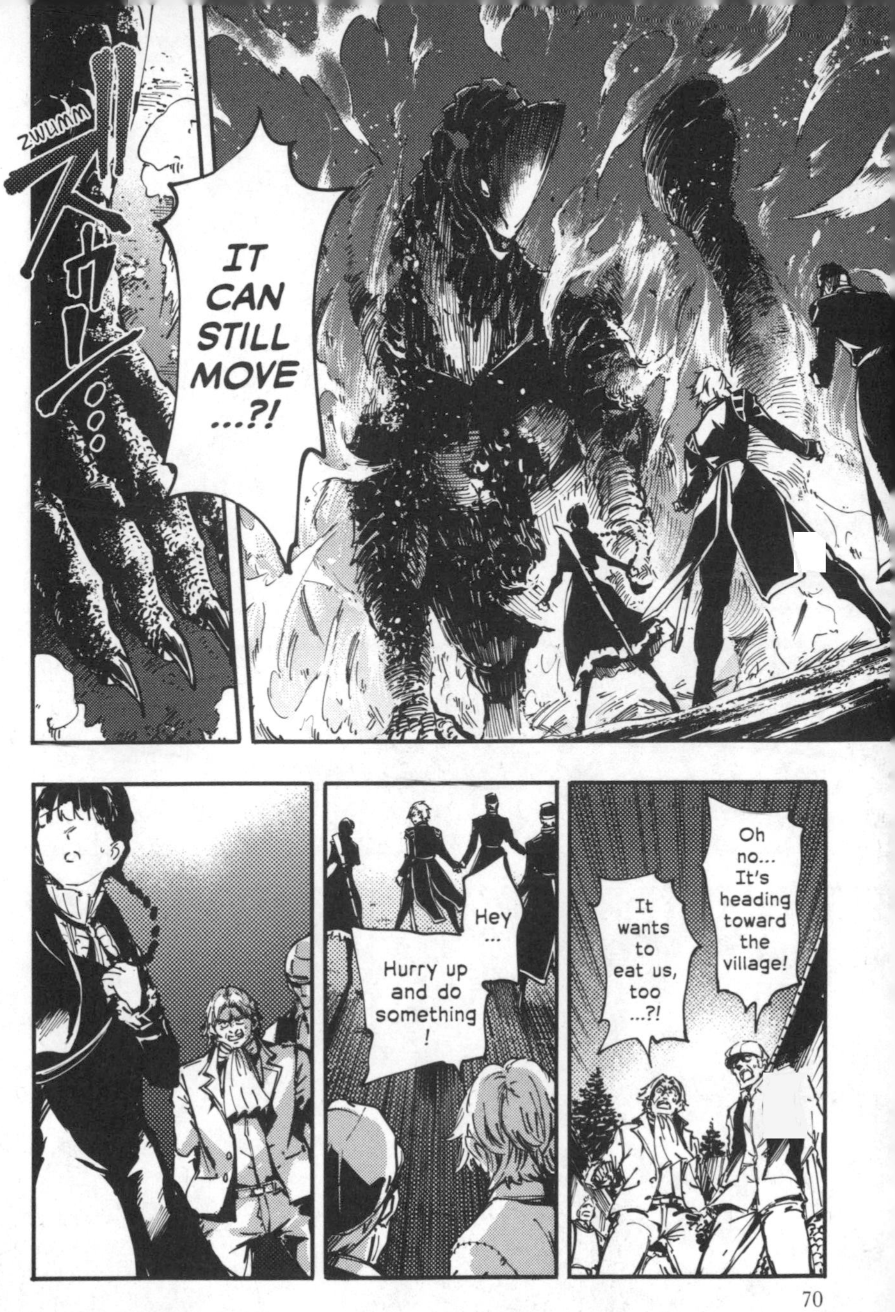
IT CAN STILL MOVE ...?!
ZWUMM
Oh no... It's heading toward the village!
It wants to eat us, too ...?!
Hey ...
Hurry up and do something!

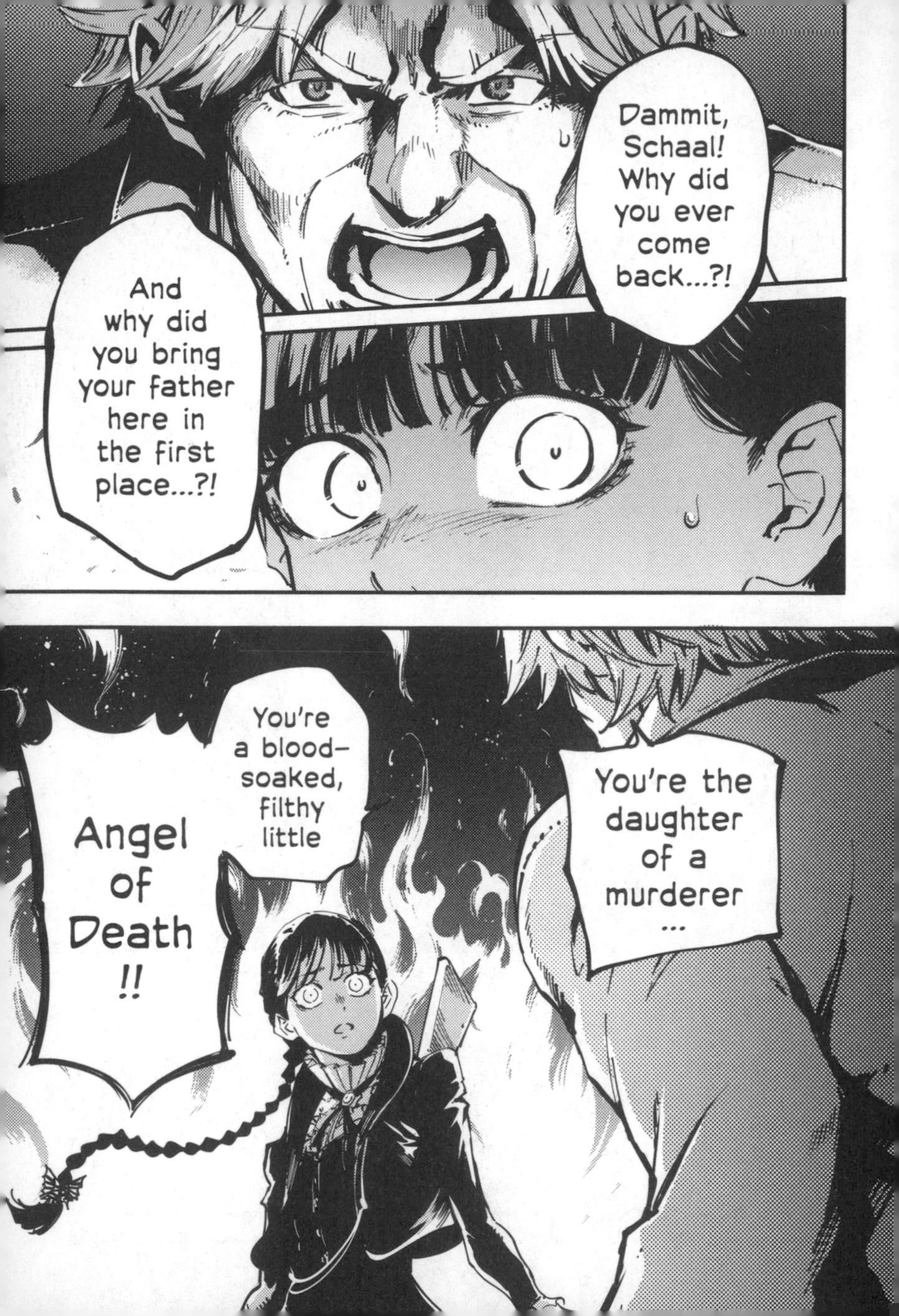
Dammit, Schaal! Why did you ever come back...?!
And why did you bring your father here in the first place...?!
You're the daughter of a murderer ...
You're a blood-soaked, filthy little
Angel of Death !!

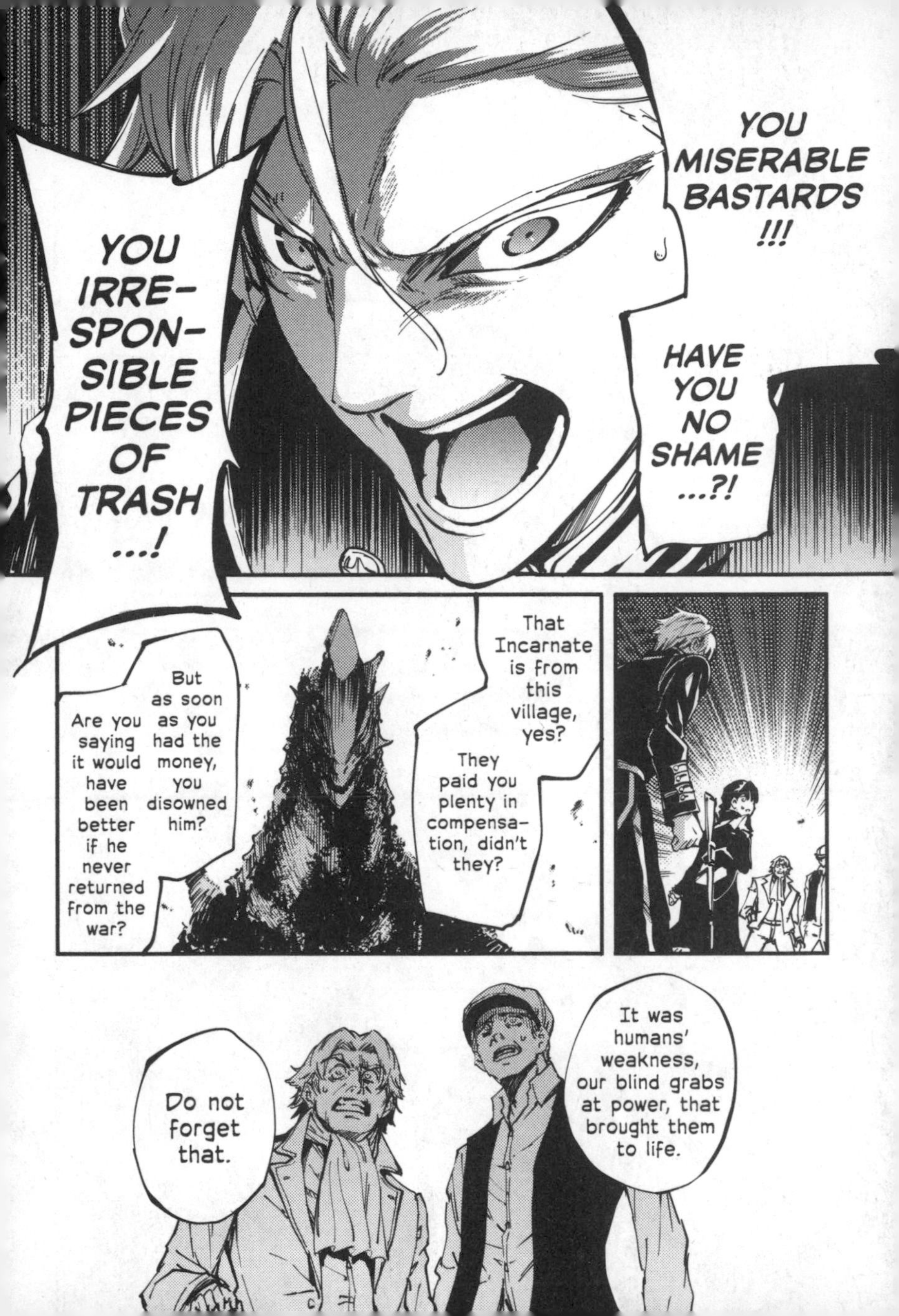
YOU MISERABLE BASTARDS !!!
HAVE YOU NO SHAME ...?!
YOU IRRE-SPON-SIBLE PIECES OF TRASH ...!
That Incarnate is from this village, yes?
They paid you plenty in compensa-tion, didn't they?
But as soon as you had the money, you disowned him?
Are you saying it would have been better if he never returned from the war?
It was humans' weakness, our blind grabs at power, that brought them to life.
Do not forget that.

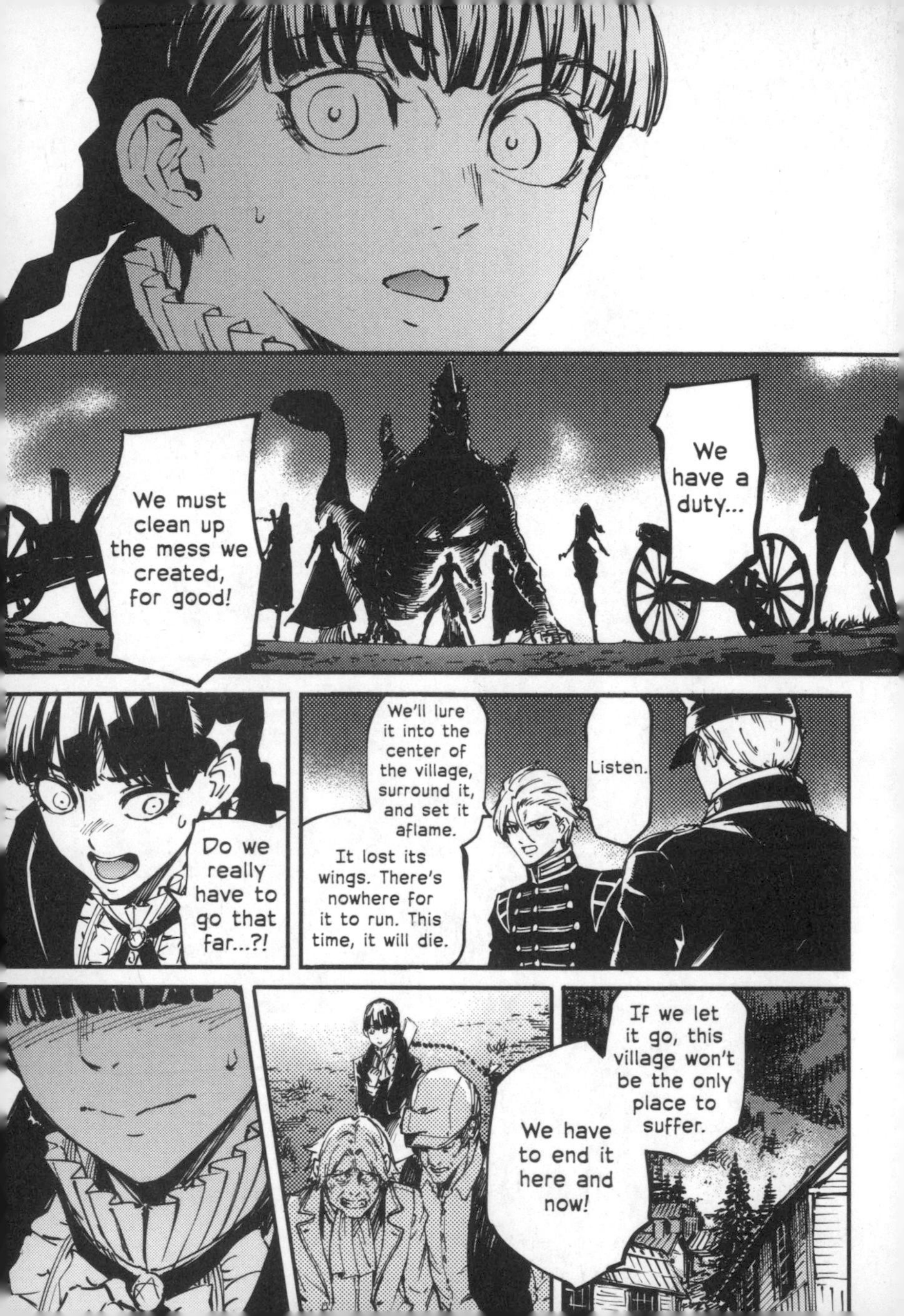
We have a duty...
We must clean up the mess we created, for good!
Listen.
We'll lure it into the center of the village, surround it, and set it aflame.
It lost its wings. There's nowhere for it to run. This time, it will die.
Do we really have to go that far...?!
If we let it go, this village won't be the only place to suffer.
We have to end it here and now!

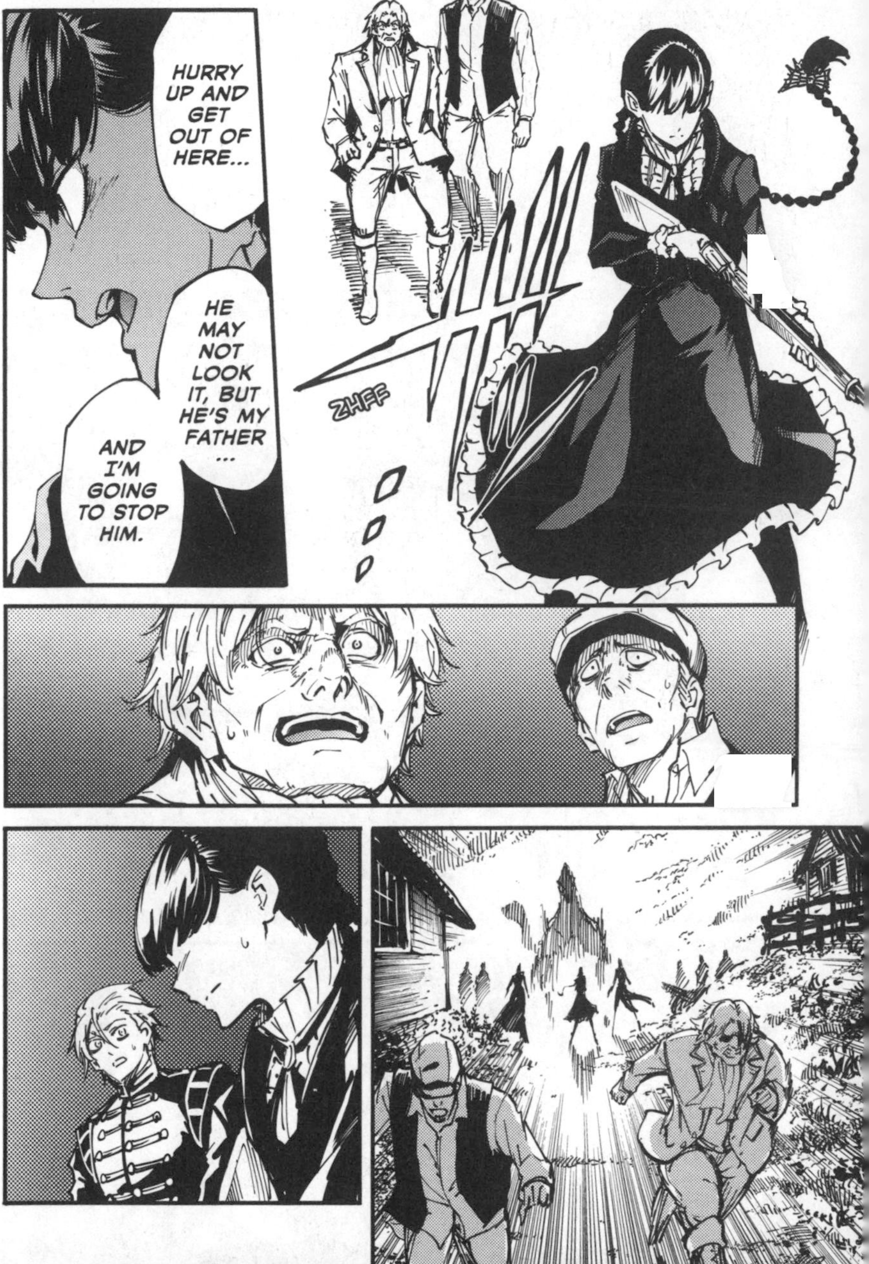
ZHFF
HURRY UP AND GET OUT OF HERE...
HE MAY NOT LOOK IT, BUT HE'S MY FATHER ...
AND I'M GOING TO STOP HIM.

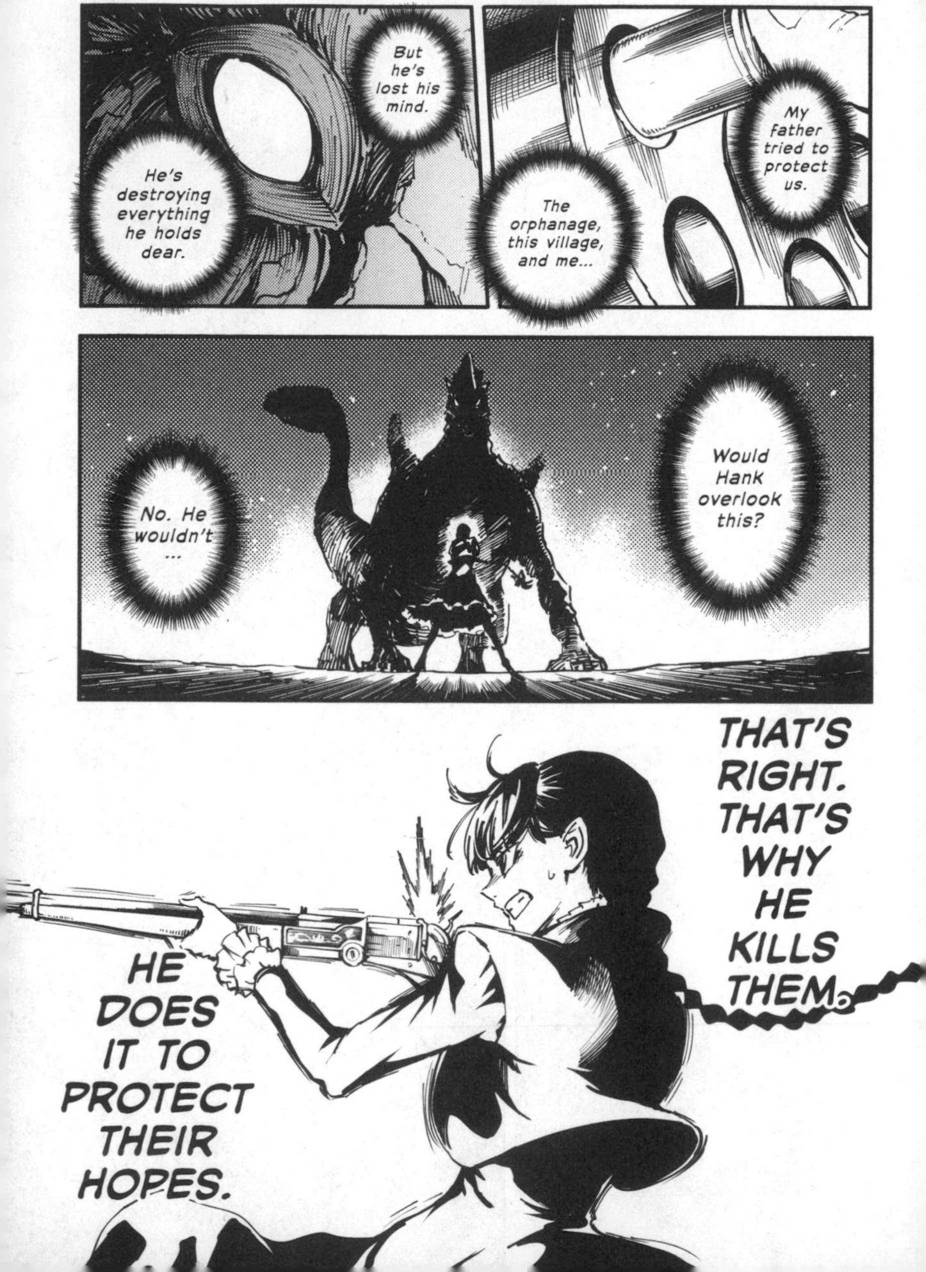
My father tried to protect us.
The orphanage, this village, and me...
But he's lost his mind.
He's destroying everything he holds dear.
Would Hank overlook this?
No. He wouldn't ...
THAT'S RIGHT. THAT'S WHY HE KILLS THEM.
HE DOES IT TO PROTECT THEIR HOPES.

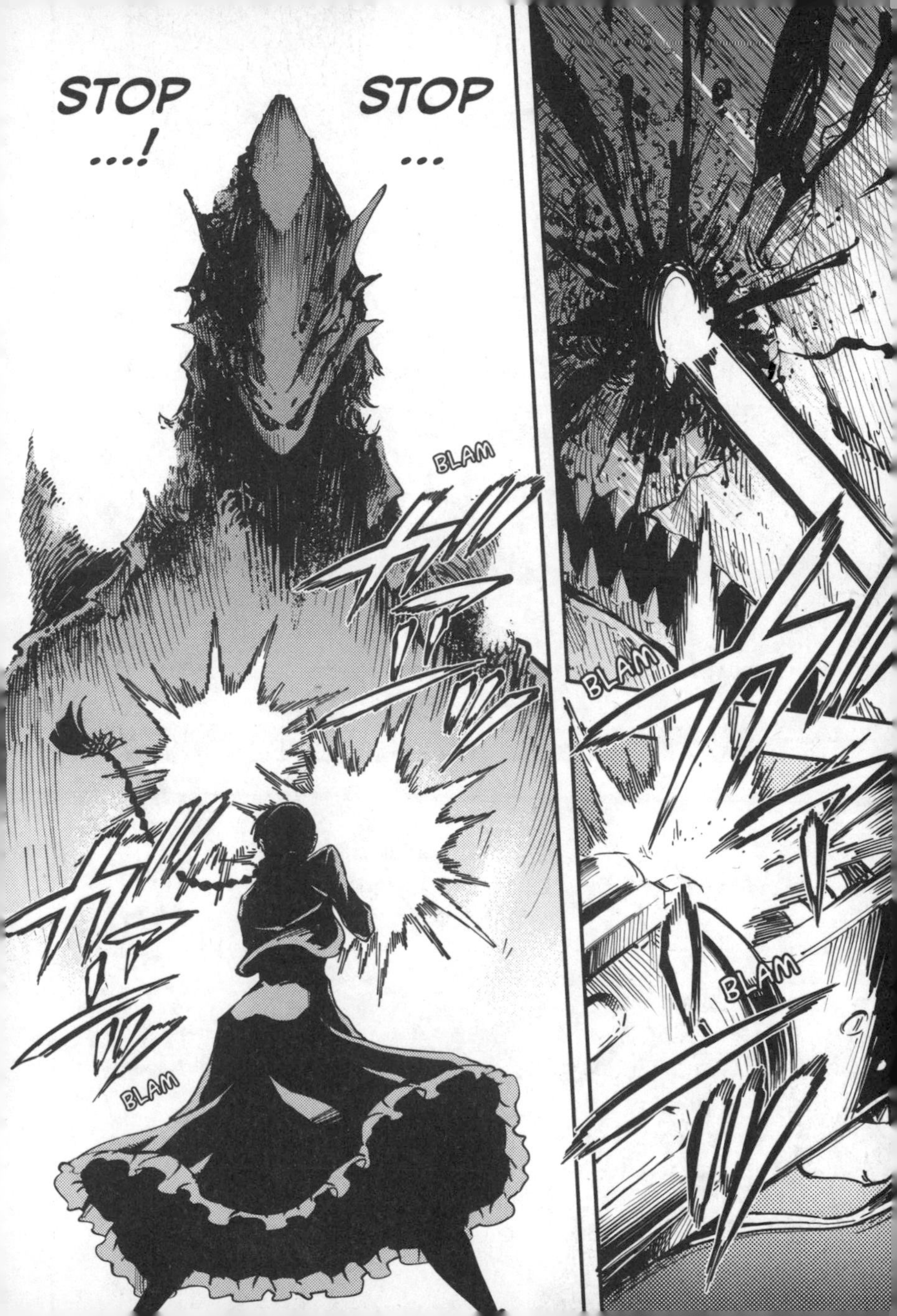
BLAM
BLAM
STOP ...
STOP ...!
BLAM
BLAM

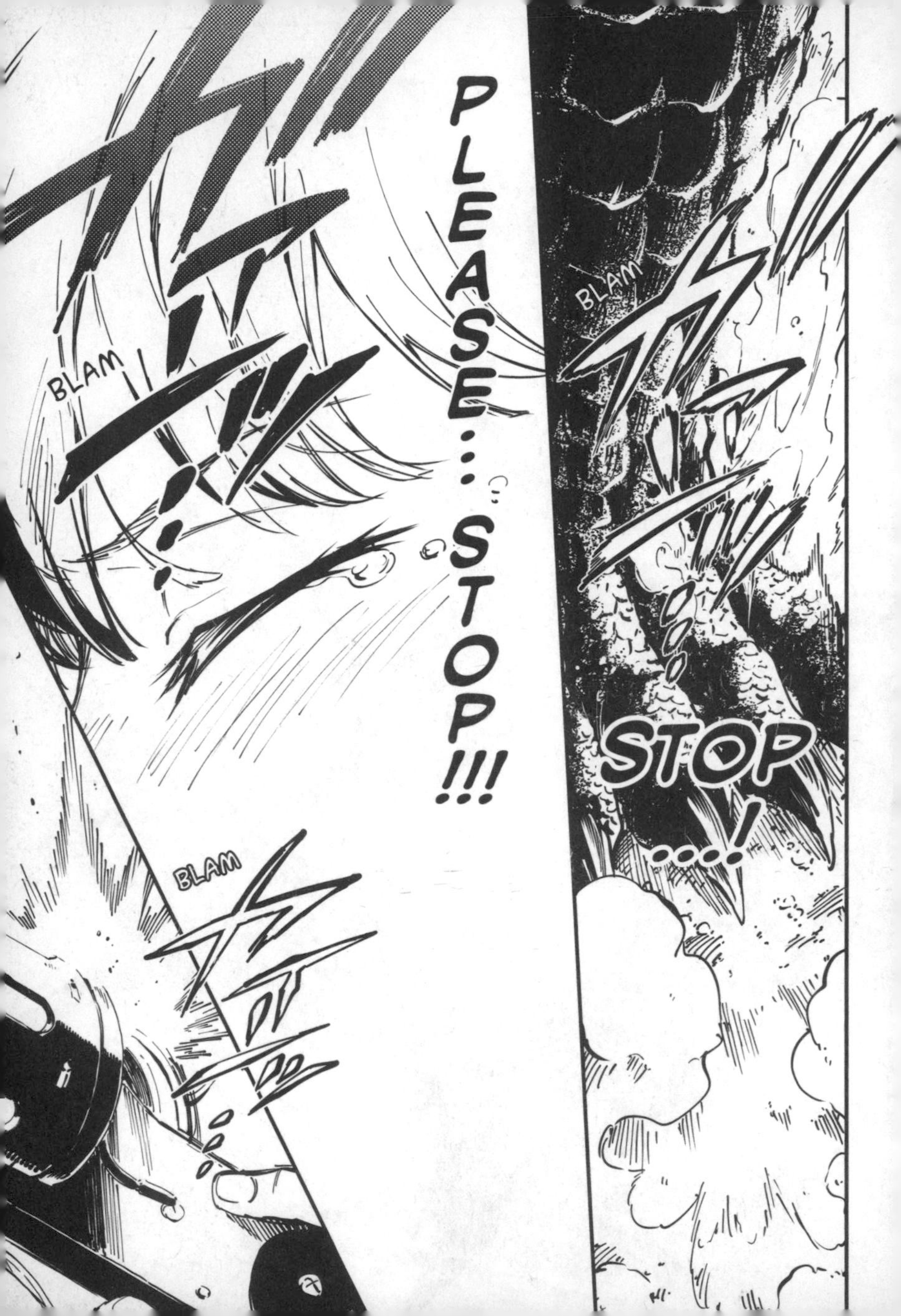
BLAM
STOP...!
PLEASE... STOP!!!
BLAM
BLAM

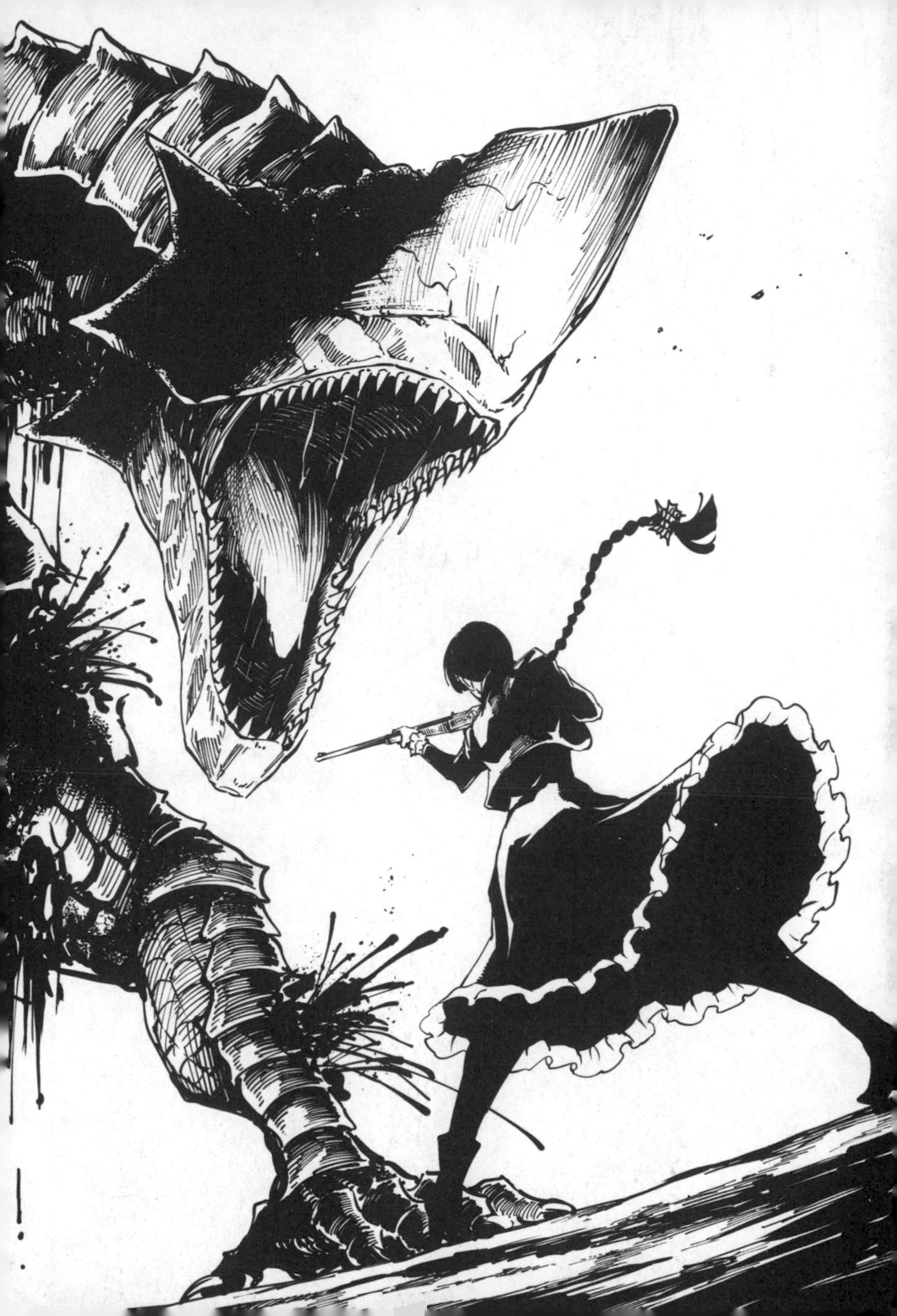

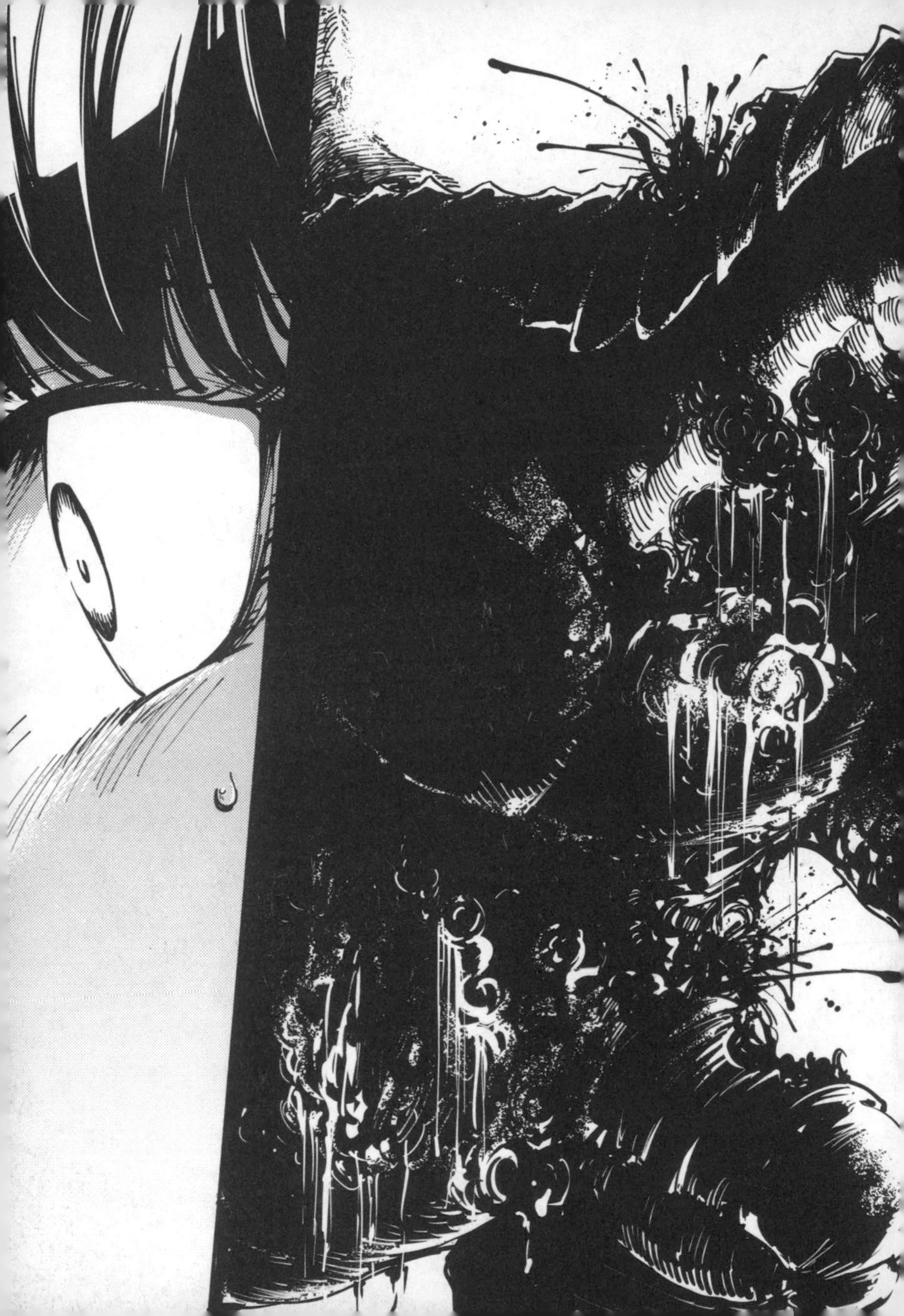

To the Abandoned
Sacred Beasts

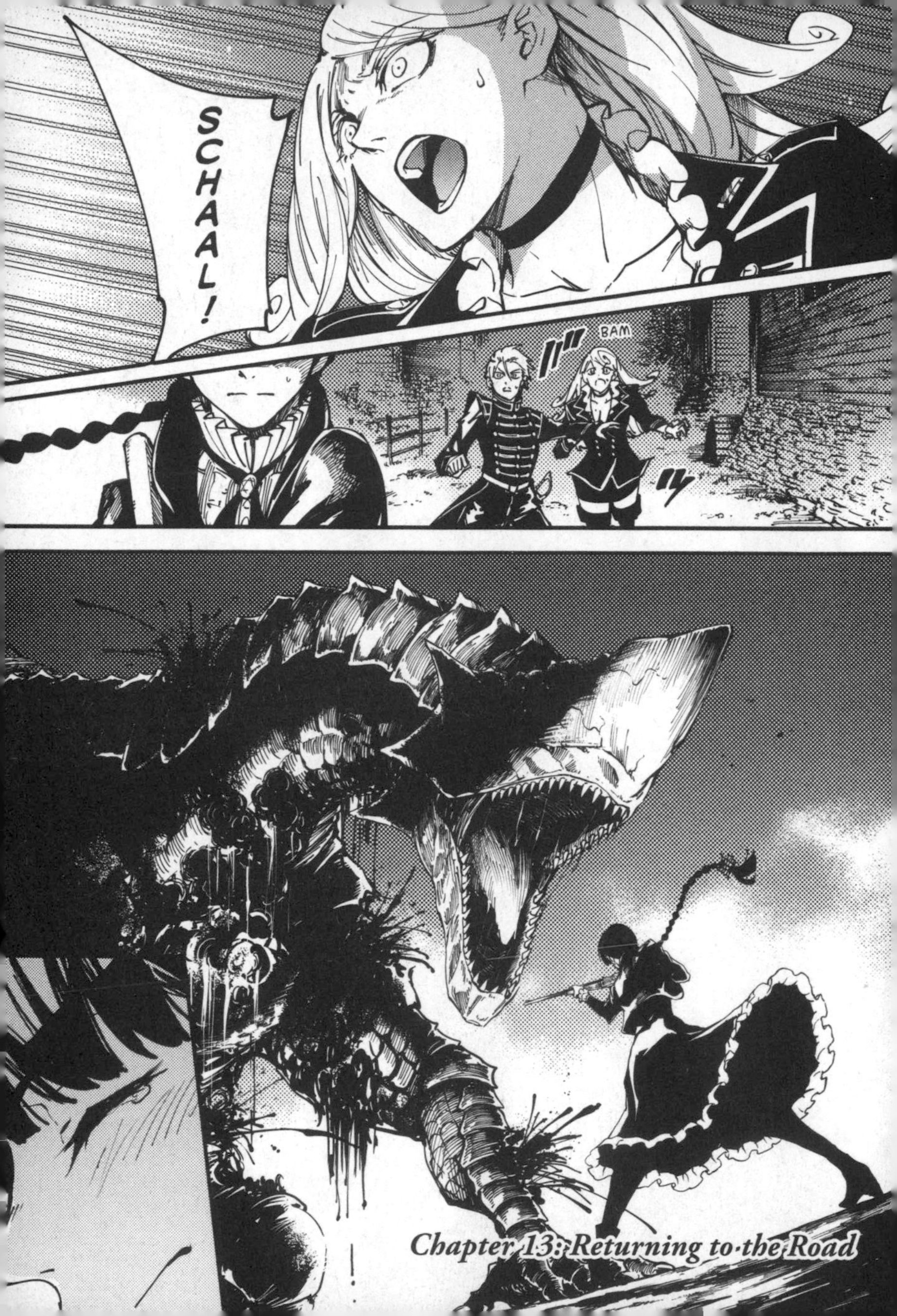
SCHAAL!
BAM
!

Chapter 13: Returning to the Road

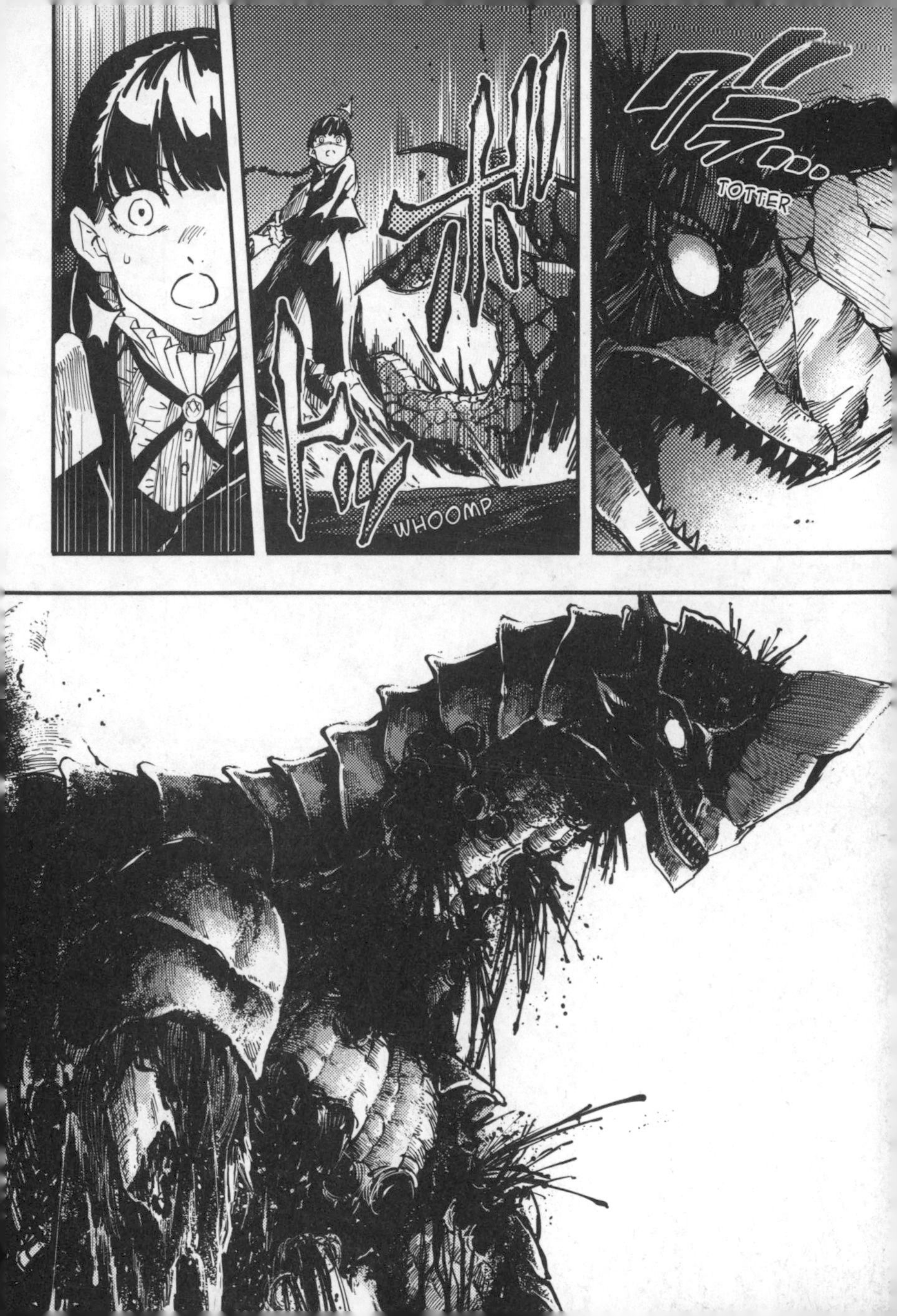
TOTTER
WHOOMP

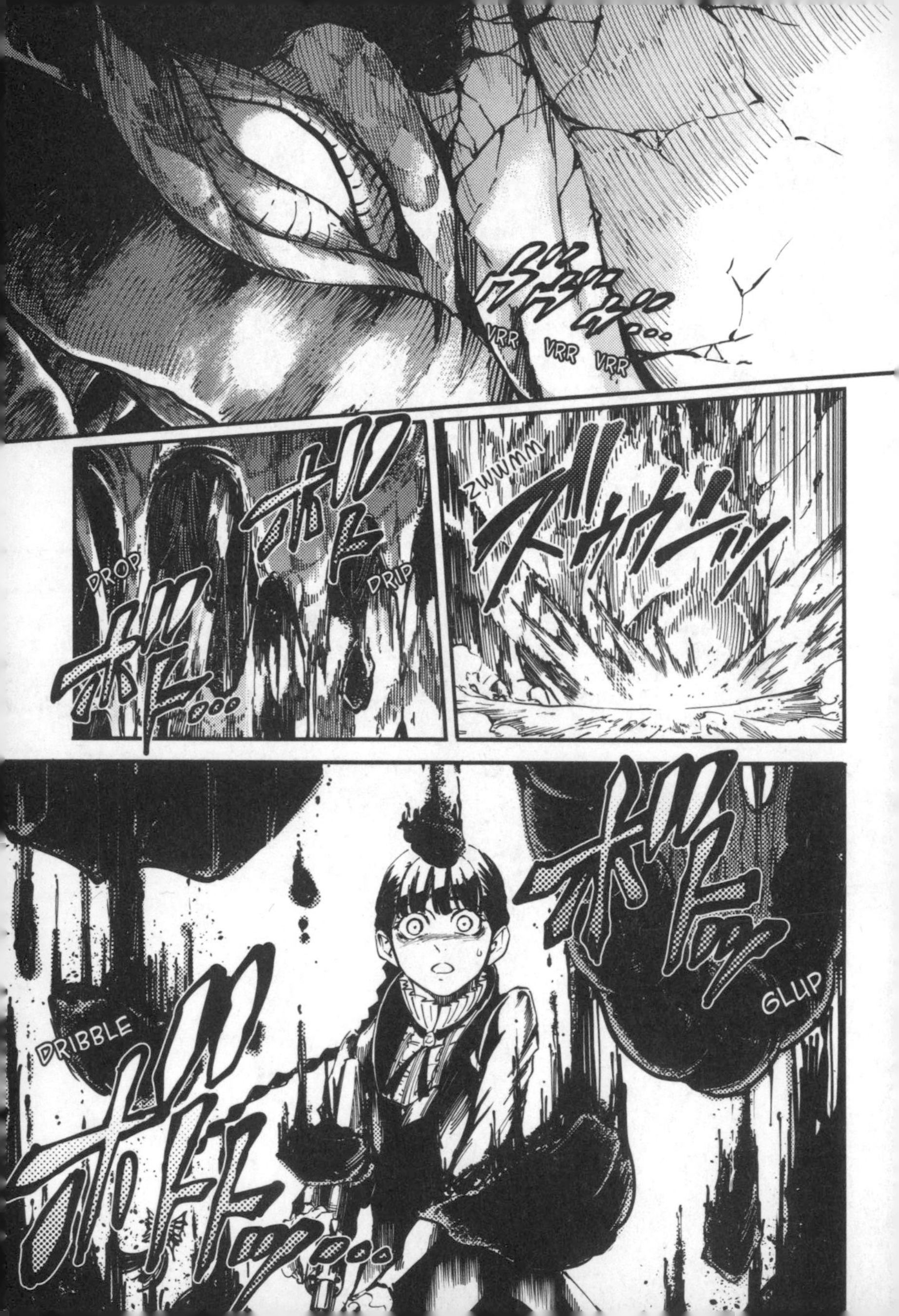
VRR
VRR
VRR
ZWWMM
DRIP
DROP
GLUP
DRIBBLE

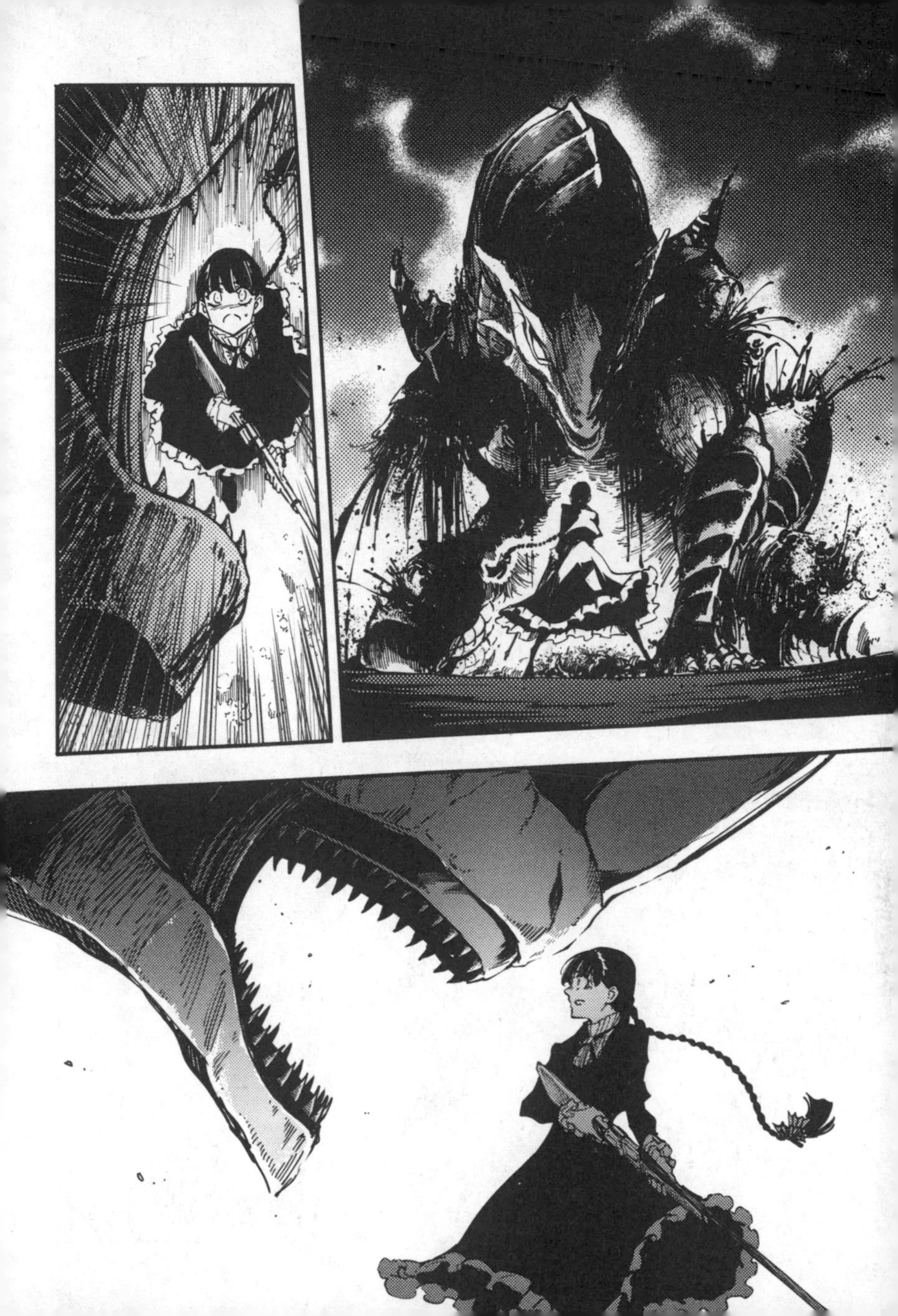

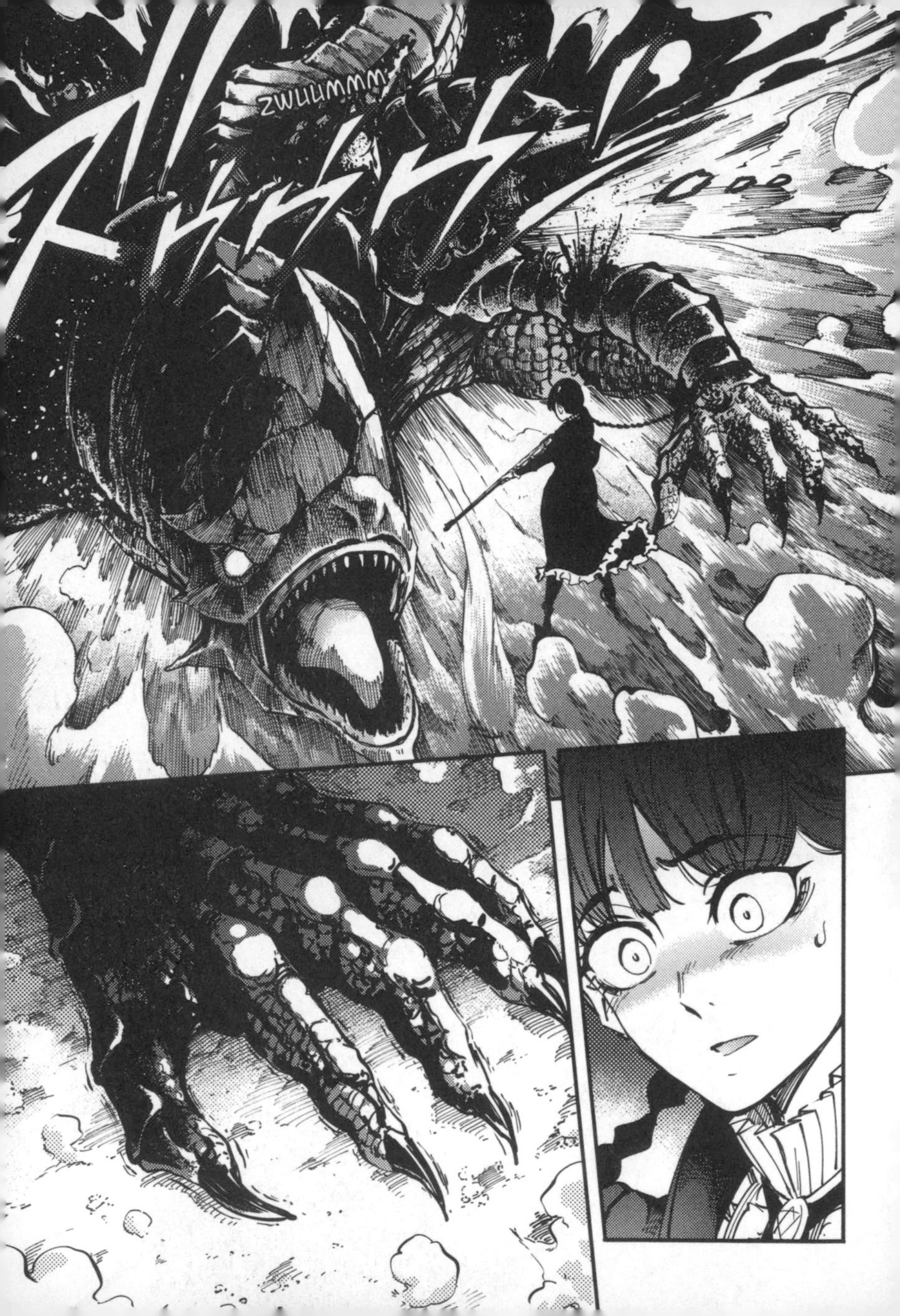
ZWUUMMMM

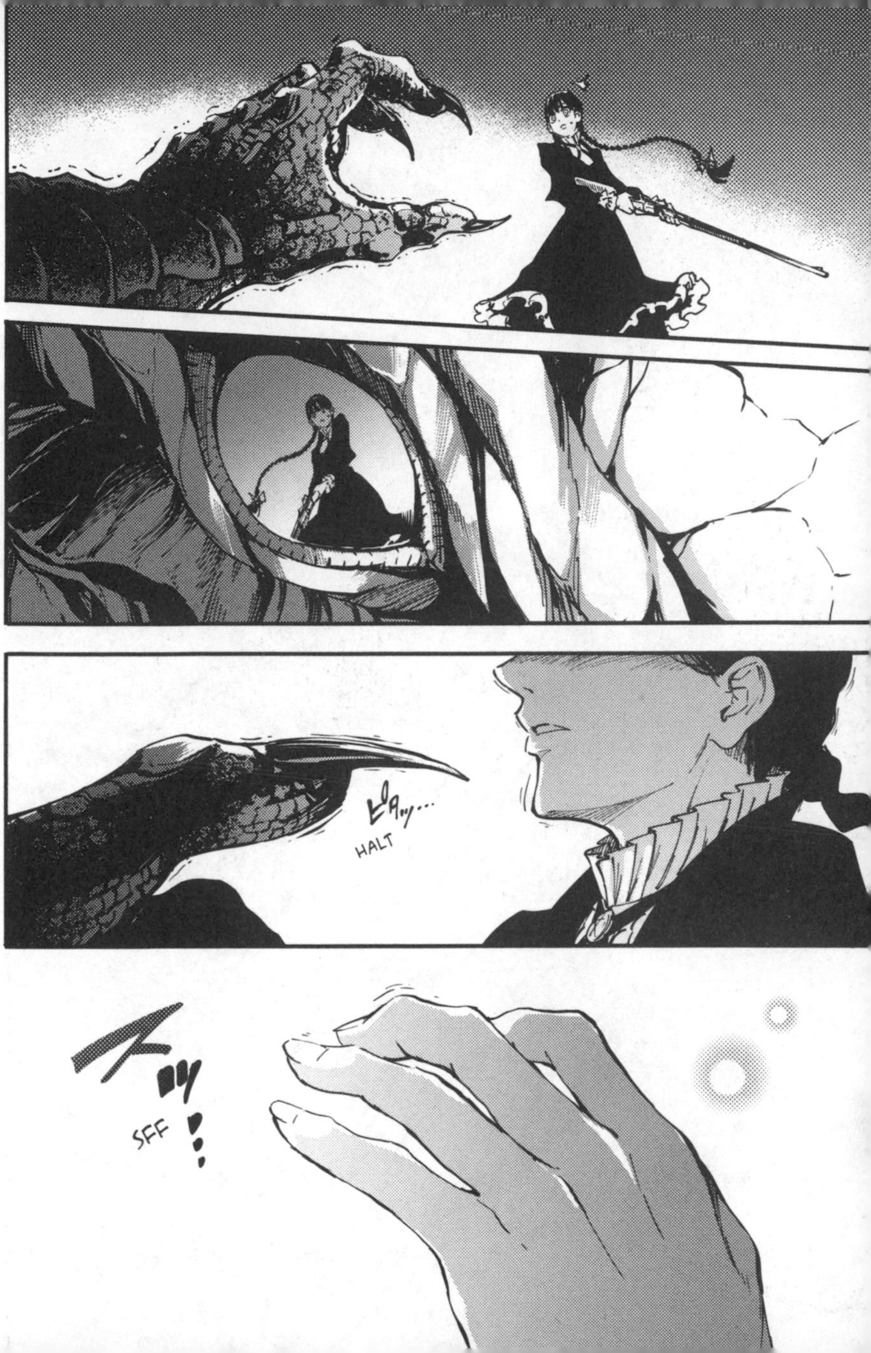
ピタッ…
HALT
スッ…
SFF

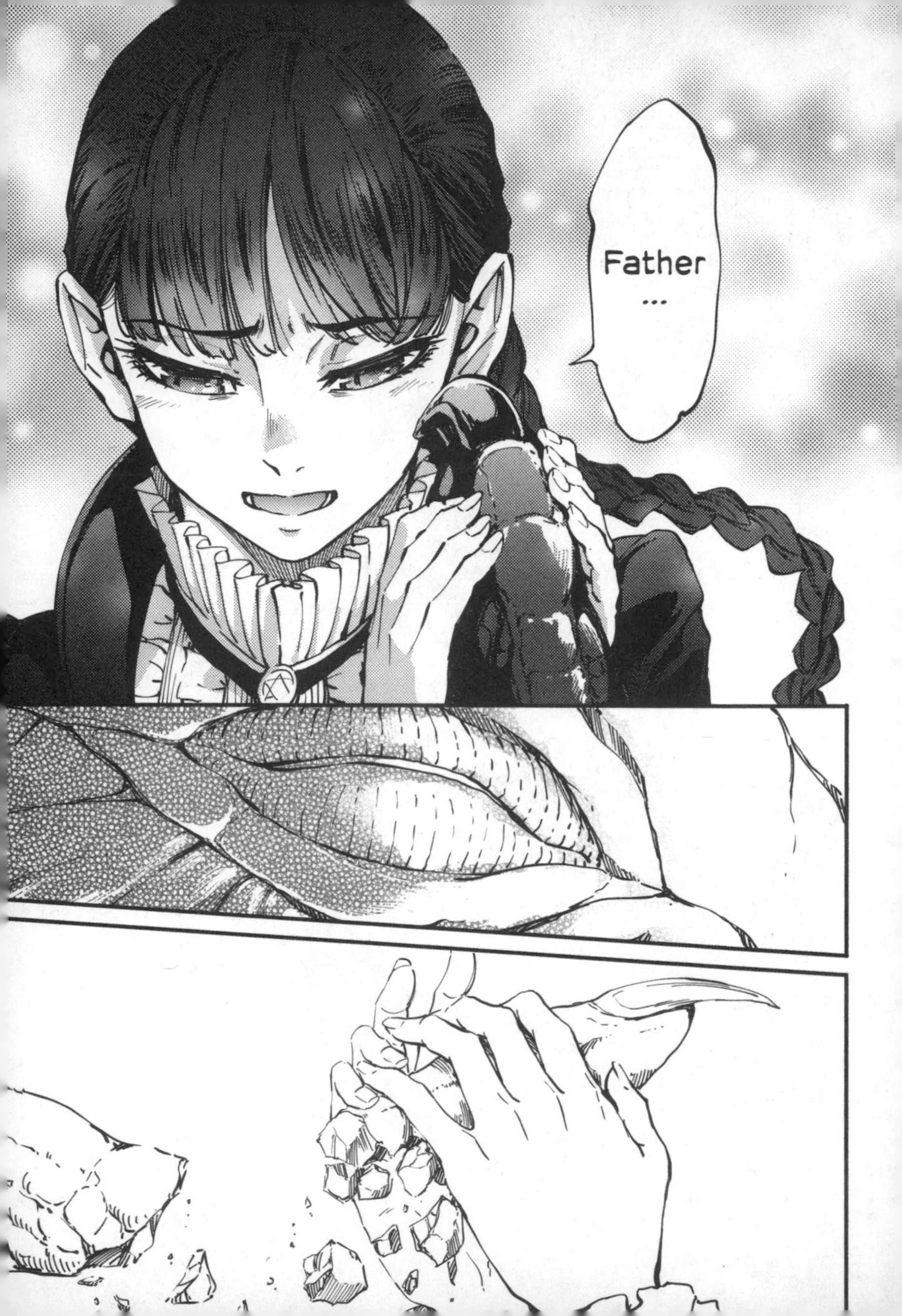
Father
...

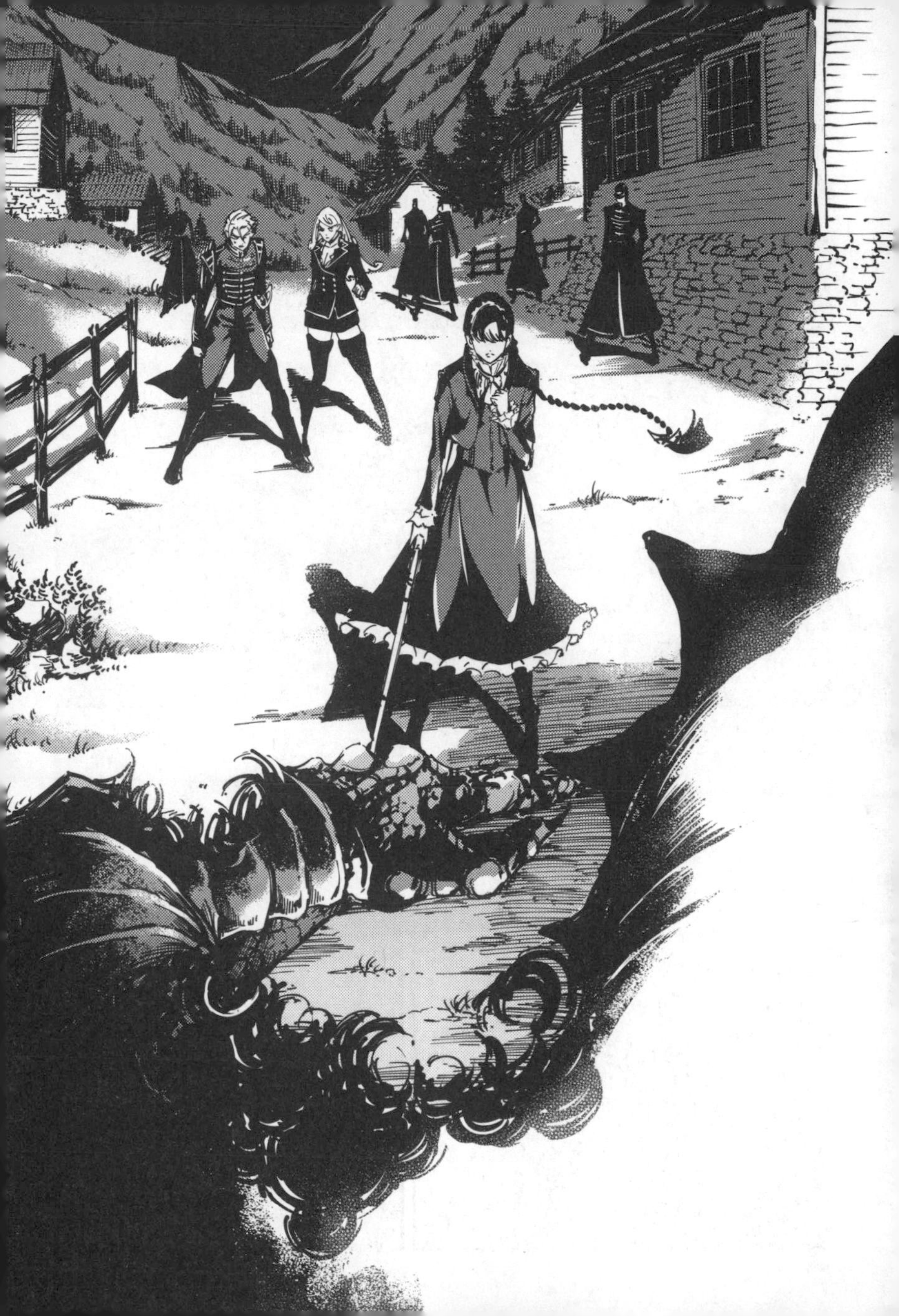

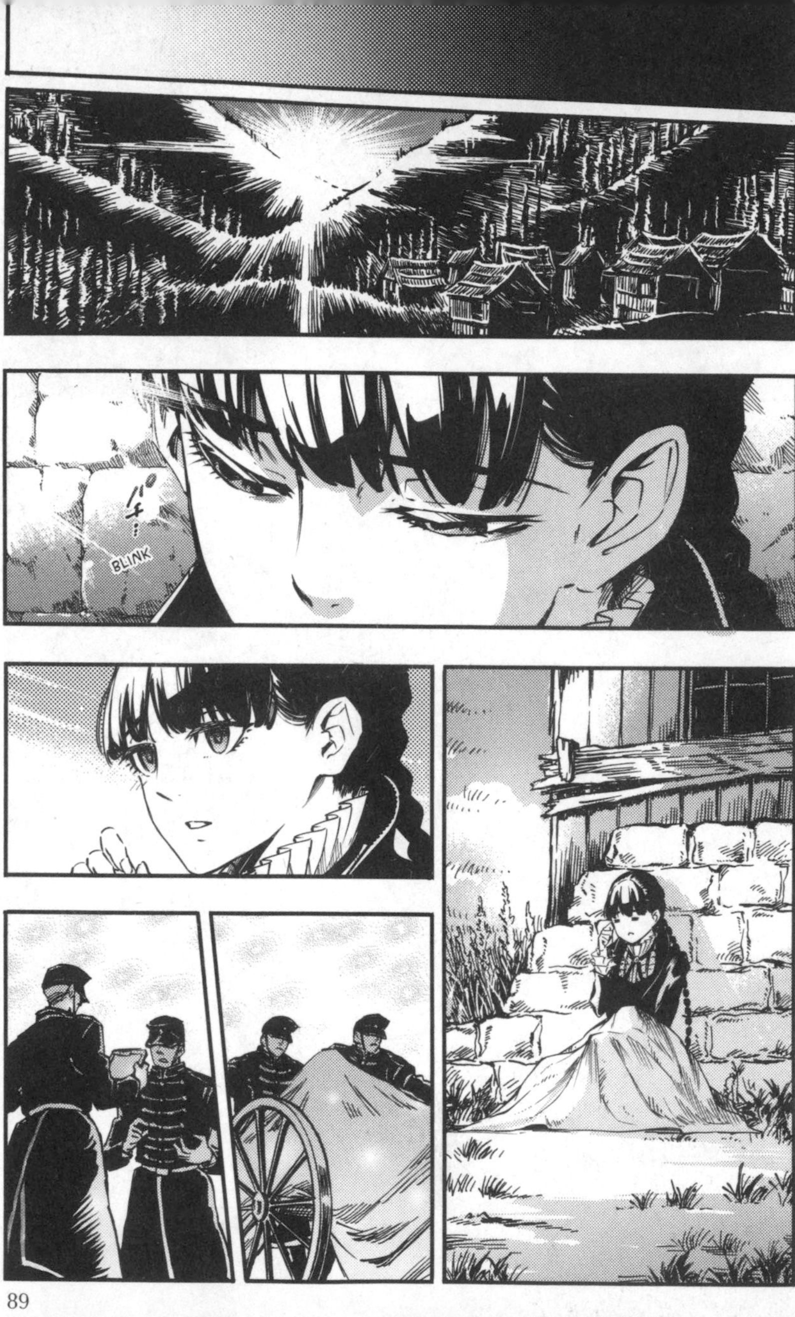
パチ…
BLINK

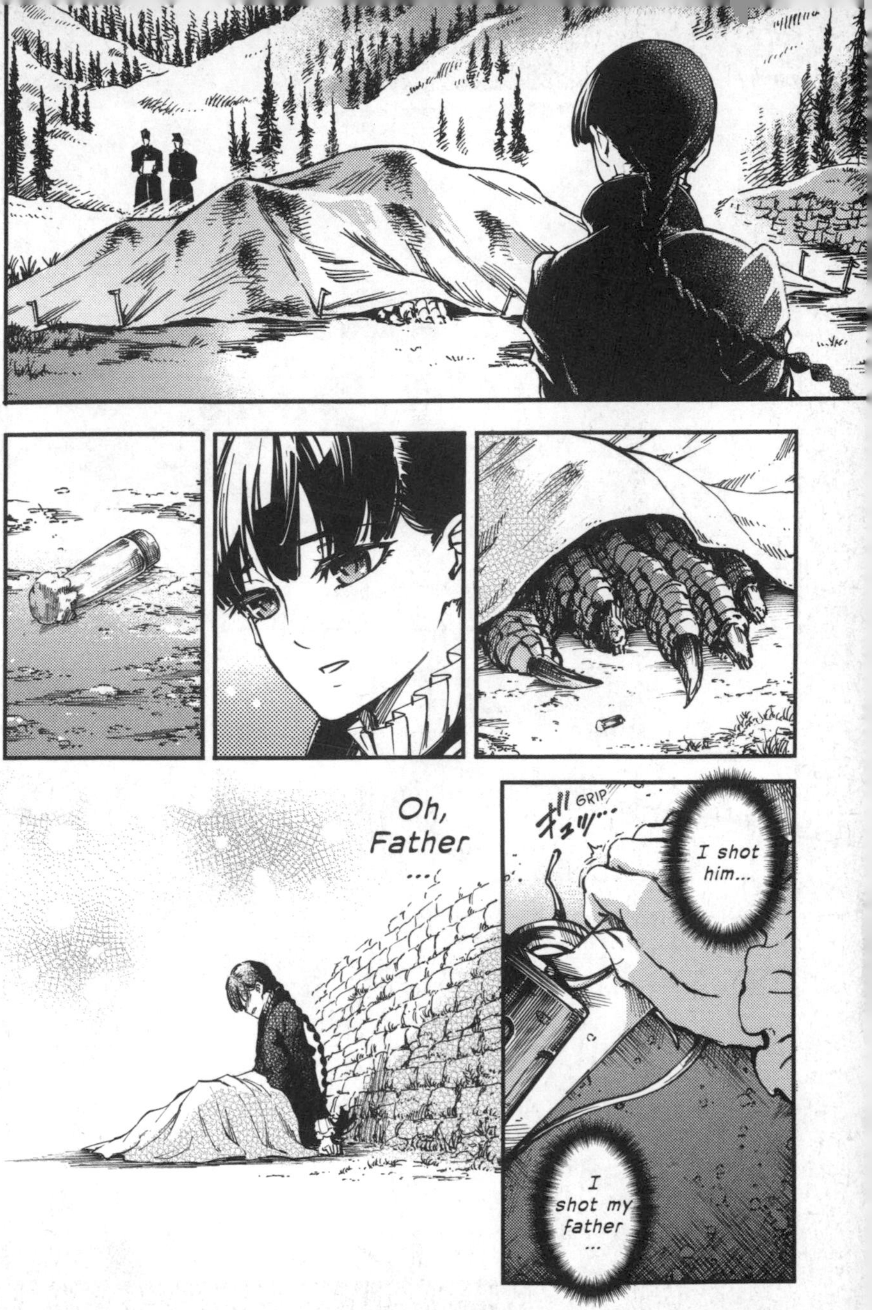
GRIP
ギュッ…
I shot him...
I shot my father ...
Oh, Father ...

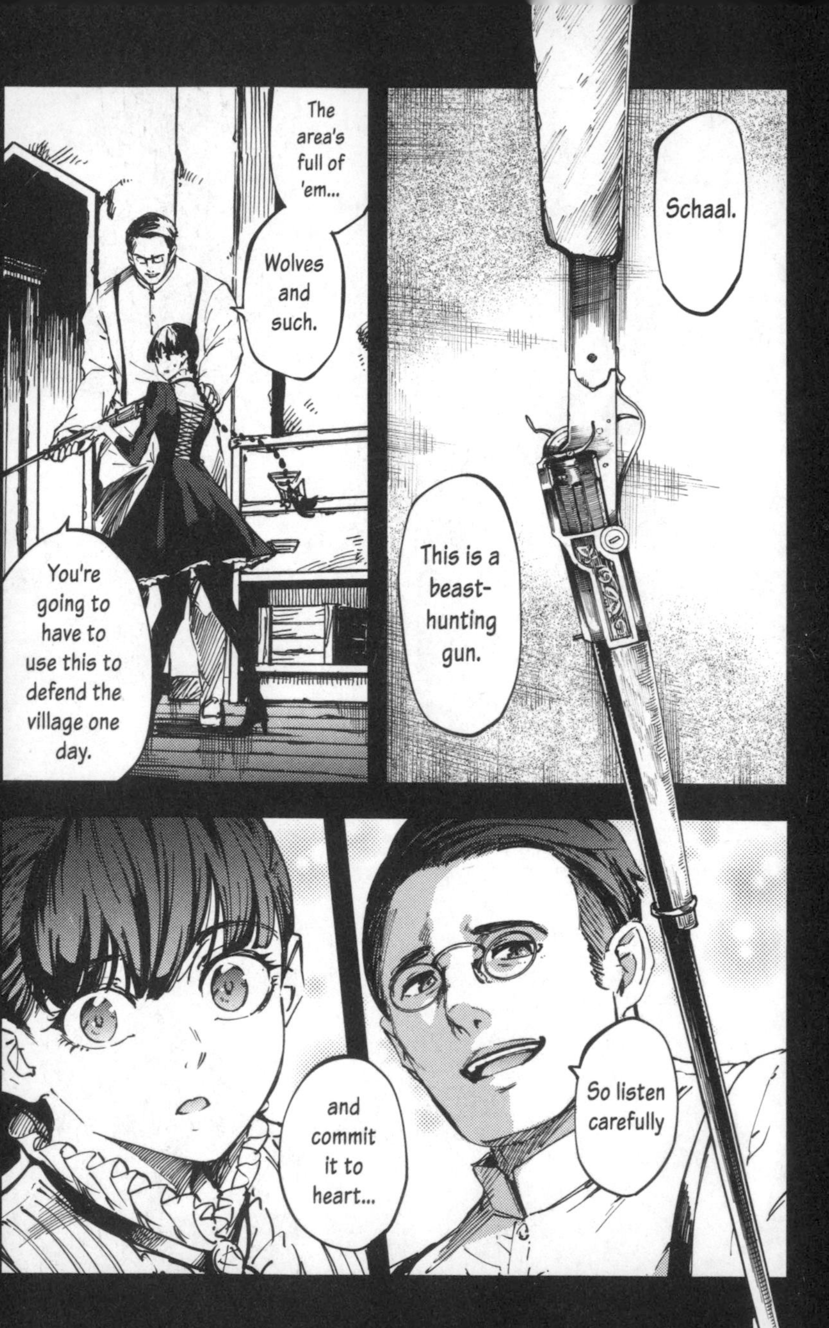
Schaal.
This is a beast-hunting gun.
The area's full of 'em...
Wolves and such.
You're going to have to use this to defend the village one day.
So listen carefully
and commit it to heart...

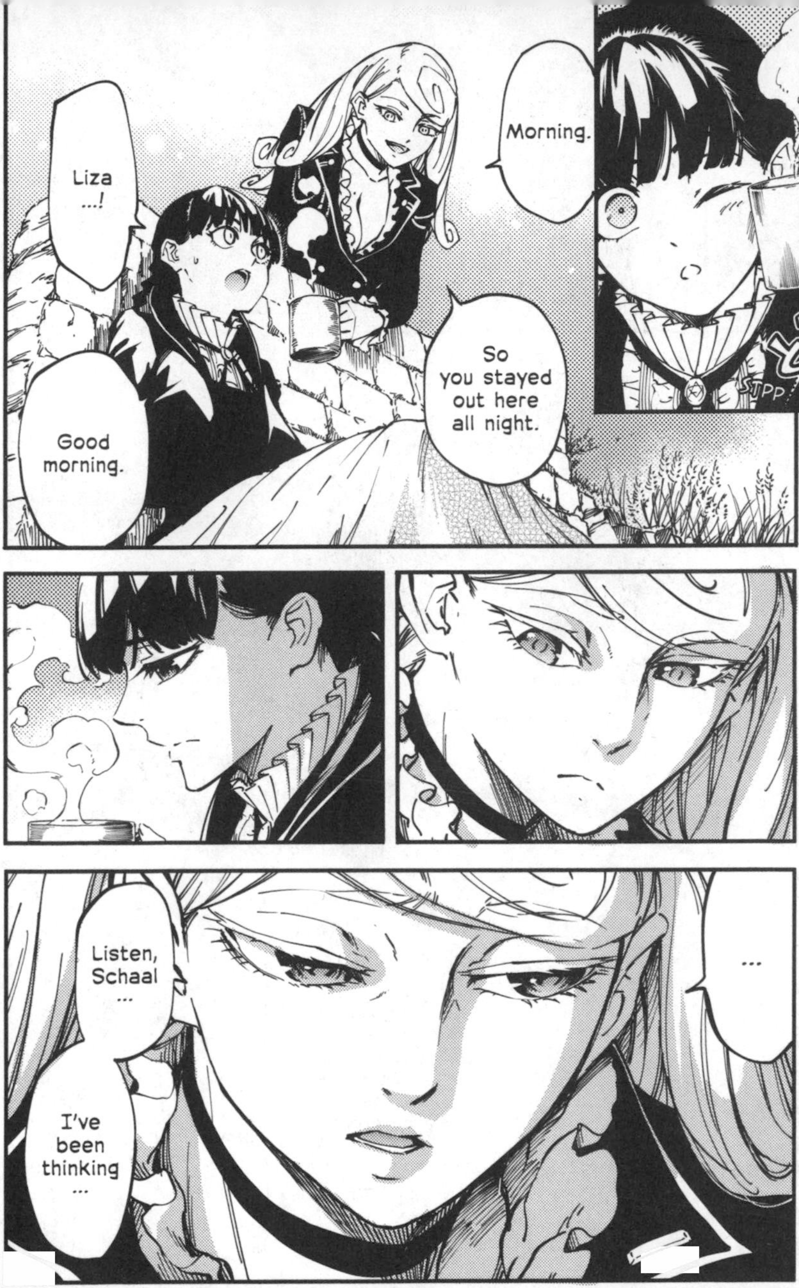
STPP
Morning.
Liza ...!
So you stayed out here all night.
Good morning.
...
Listen, Schaal ...
I've been thinking ...

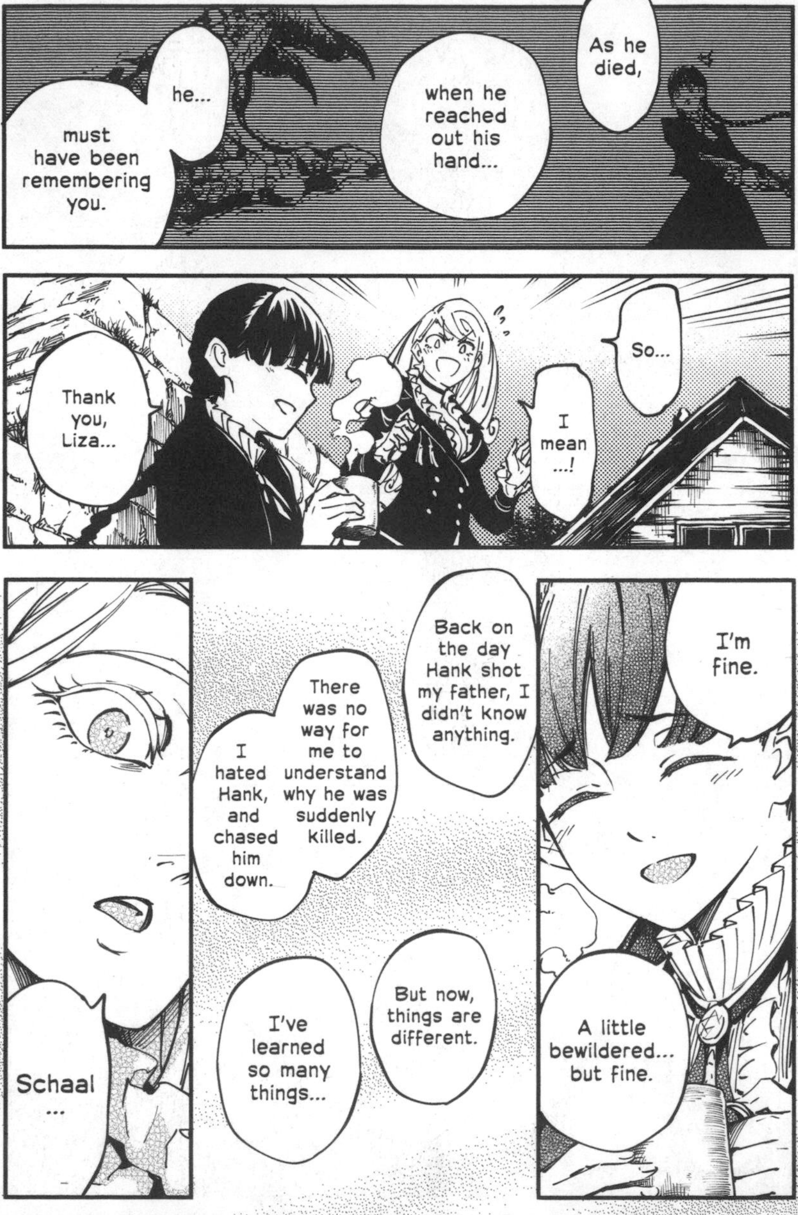
As he died,
when he reached out his hand...
he...
must have been remembering you.
So...
I mean ...!
Thank you, Liza...
I'm fine.
A little bewildered... but fine.
Back on the day Hank shot my father, I didn't know anything.
There was no way for me to understand why he was suddenly killed.
I hated Hank, and chased him down.
But now, things are different.
I've learned so many things...
Schaal ...

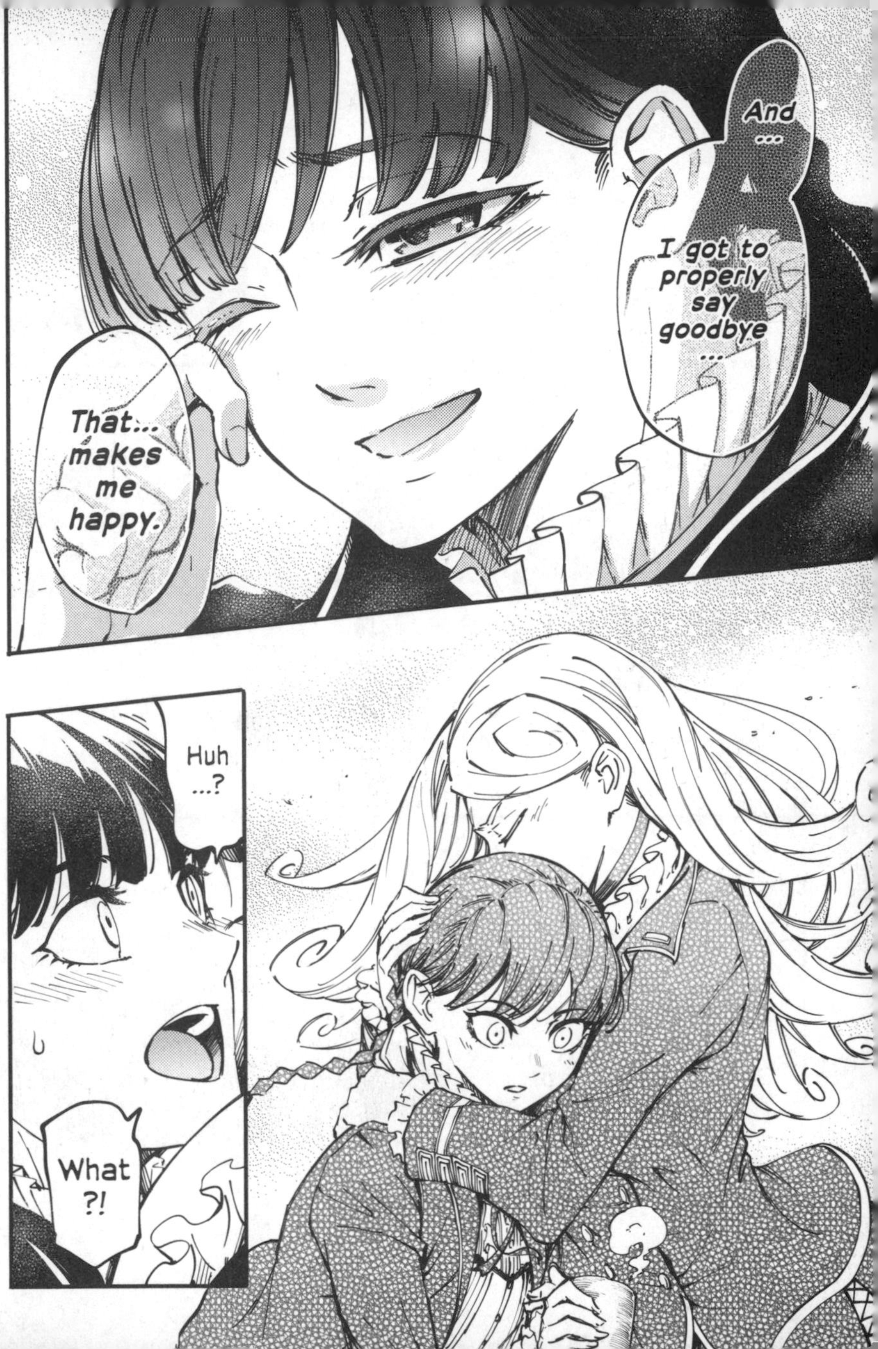
And ... I got to properly say goodbye ...
That... makes me happy.
Huh ...?
What ?!

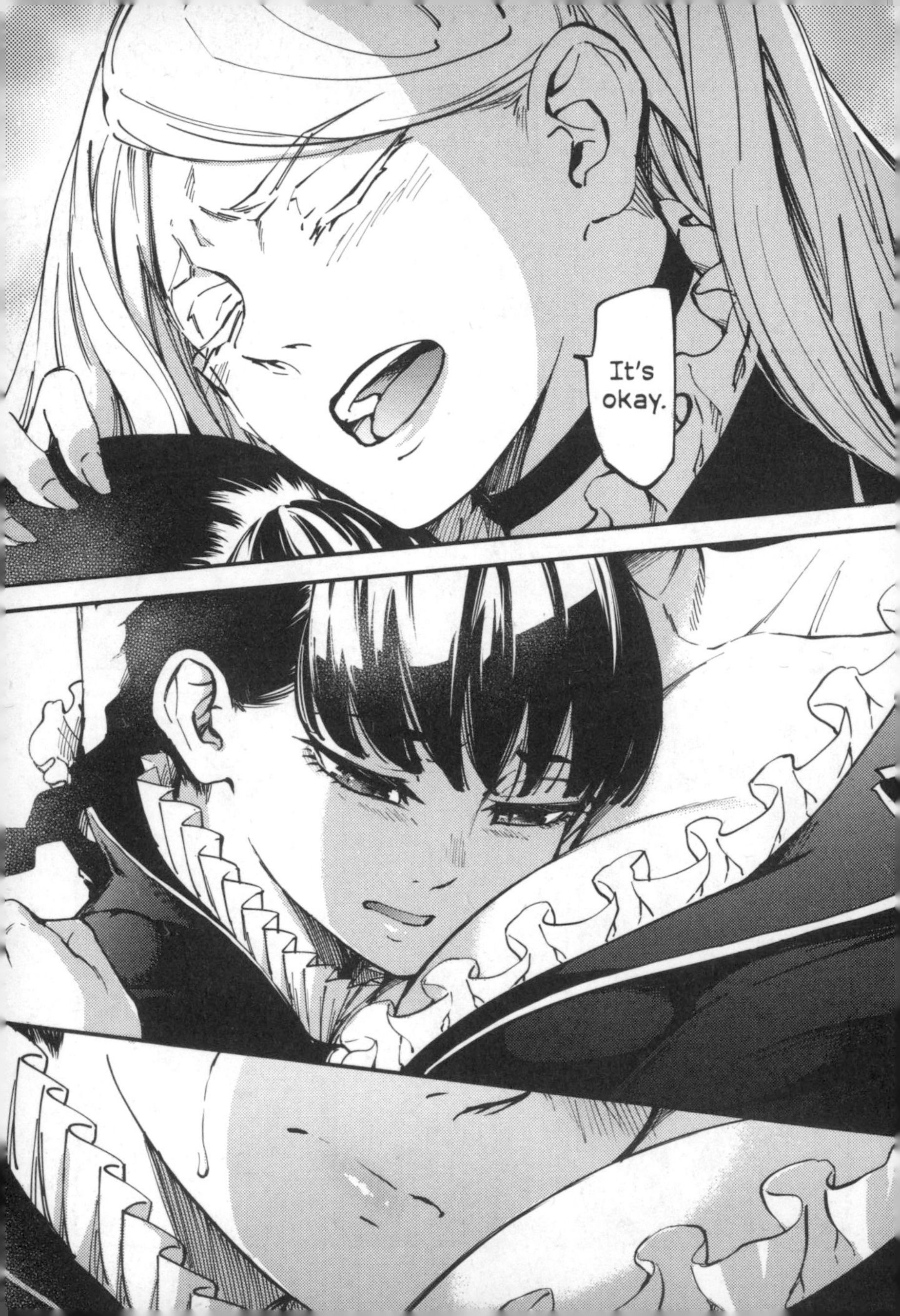
It's okay.

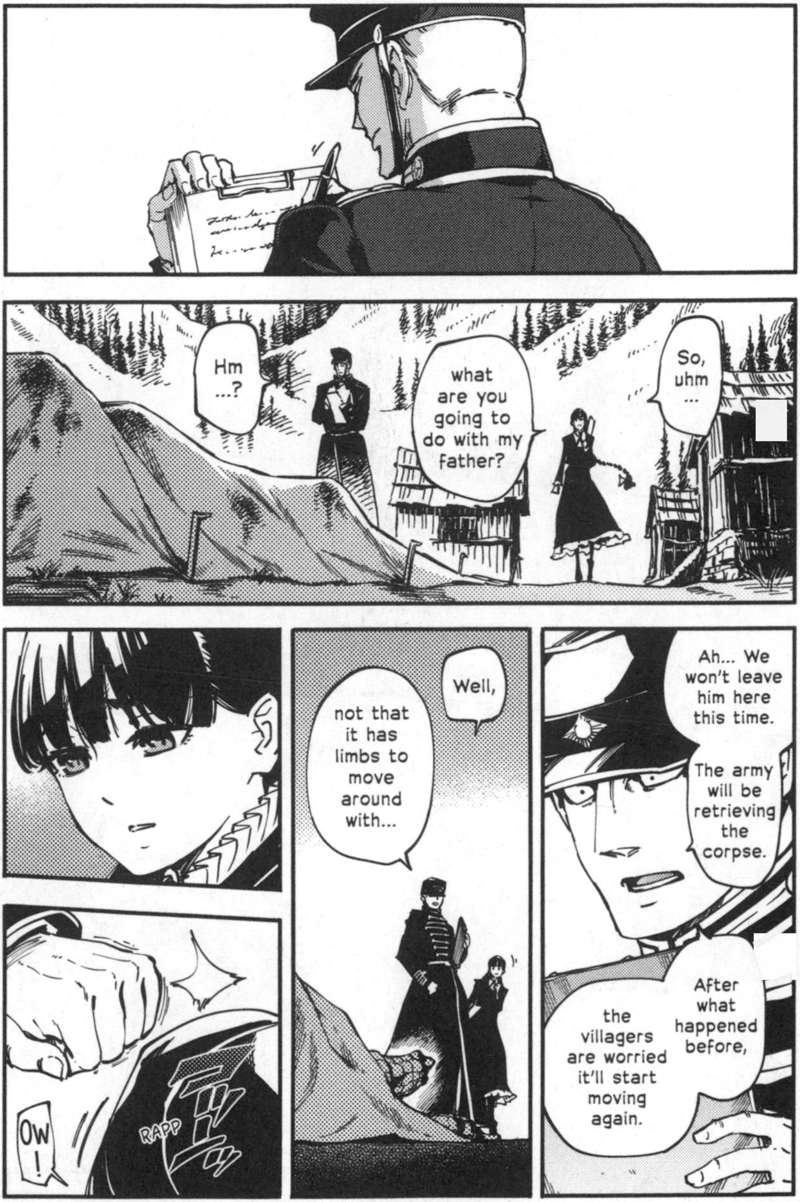
So, uhm ...
what are you going to do with my father?
Hm ...?
Ah... We won't leave him here this time.
The army will be retrieving the corpse.
After what happened before,
the villagers are worried it'll start moving again.
Well,
not that it has limbs to move around with...
RAPP
OW!

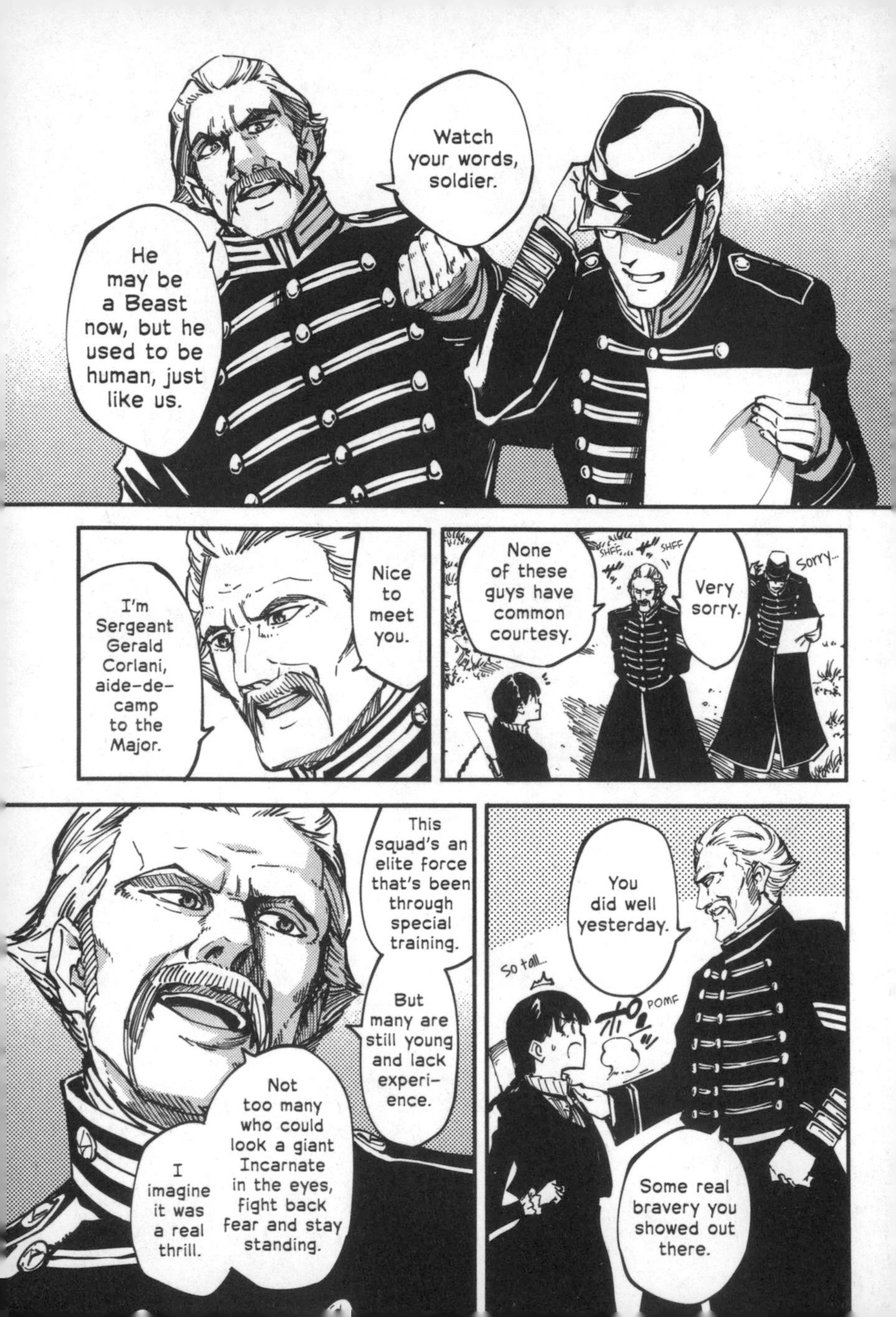
Watch your words, soldier.
He may be a Beast now, but he used to be human, just like us.
Sorry...
Very sorry.
SHFF SHFF
None of these guys have common courtesy.
Nice to meet you.
I'm Sergeant Gerald Corlani, aide-de-camp to the Major.
You did well yesterday.
So tall...
POMF
Some real bravery you showed out there.
This squad's an elite force that's been through special training.
But many are still young and lack experi-ence.
Not too many who could look a giant Incarnate in the eyes, fight back fear and stay standing.
I imagine it was a real thrill.

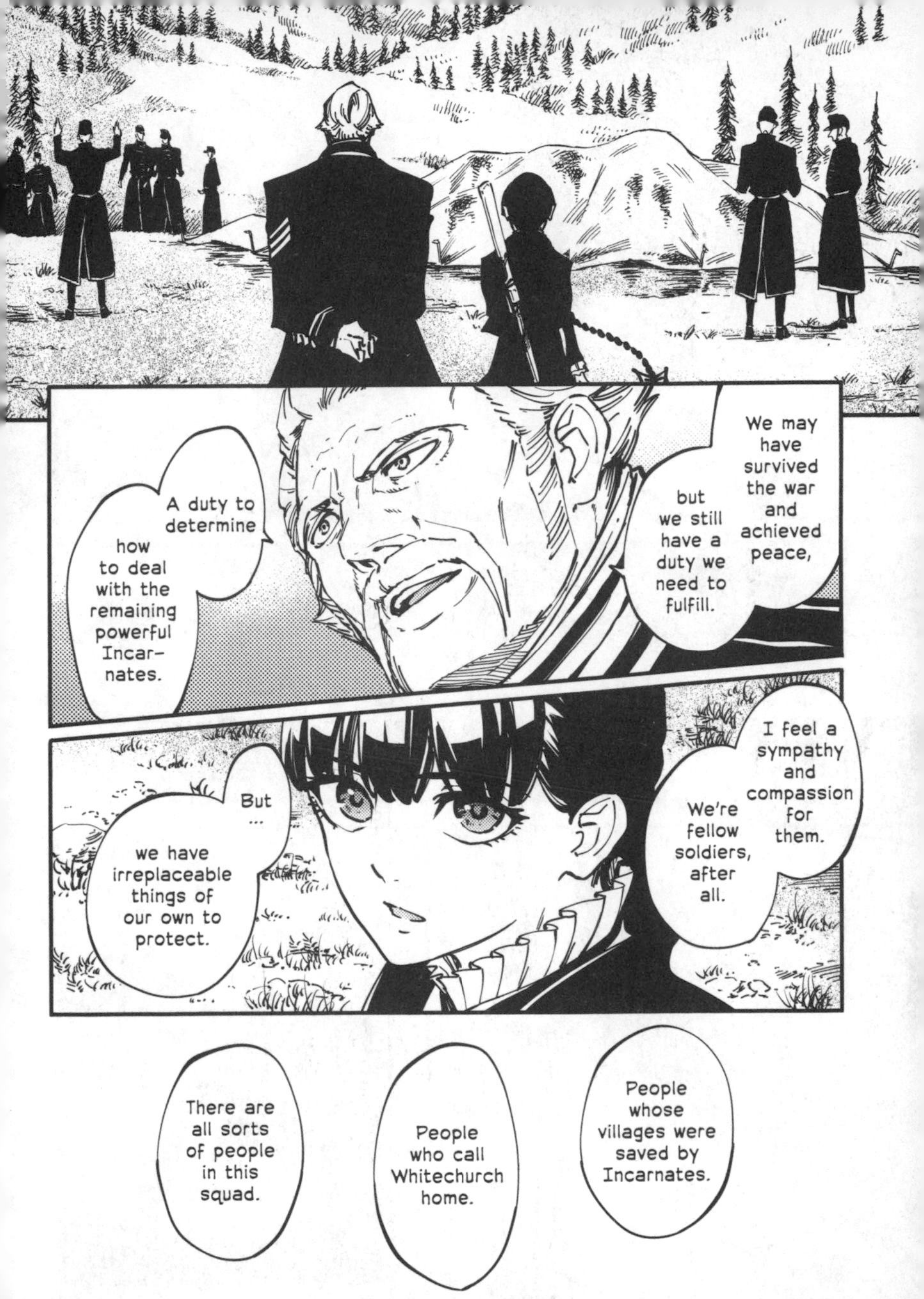
We may have survived the war and achieved peace,
but we still have a duty we need to fulfill.
A duty to determine how to deal with the remaining powerful Incarnates.
I feel a sympathy and compassion for them.
We're fellow soldiers, after all.
But... we have irreplaceable things of our own to protect.
People whose villages were saved by Incarnates.
People who call Whitechurch home.
There are all sorts of people in this squad.

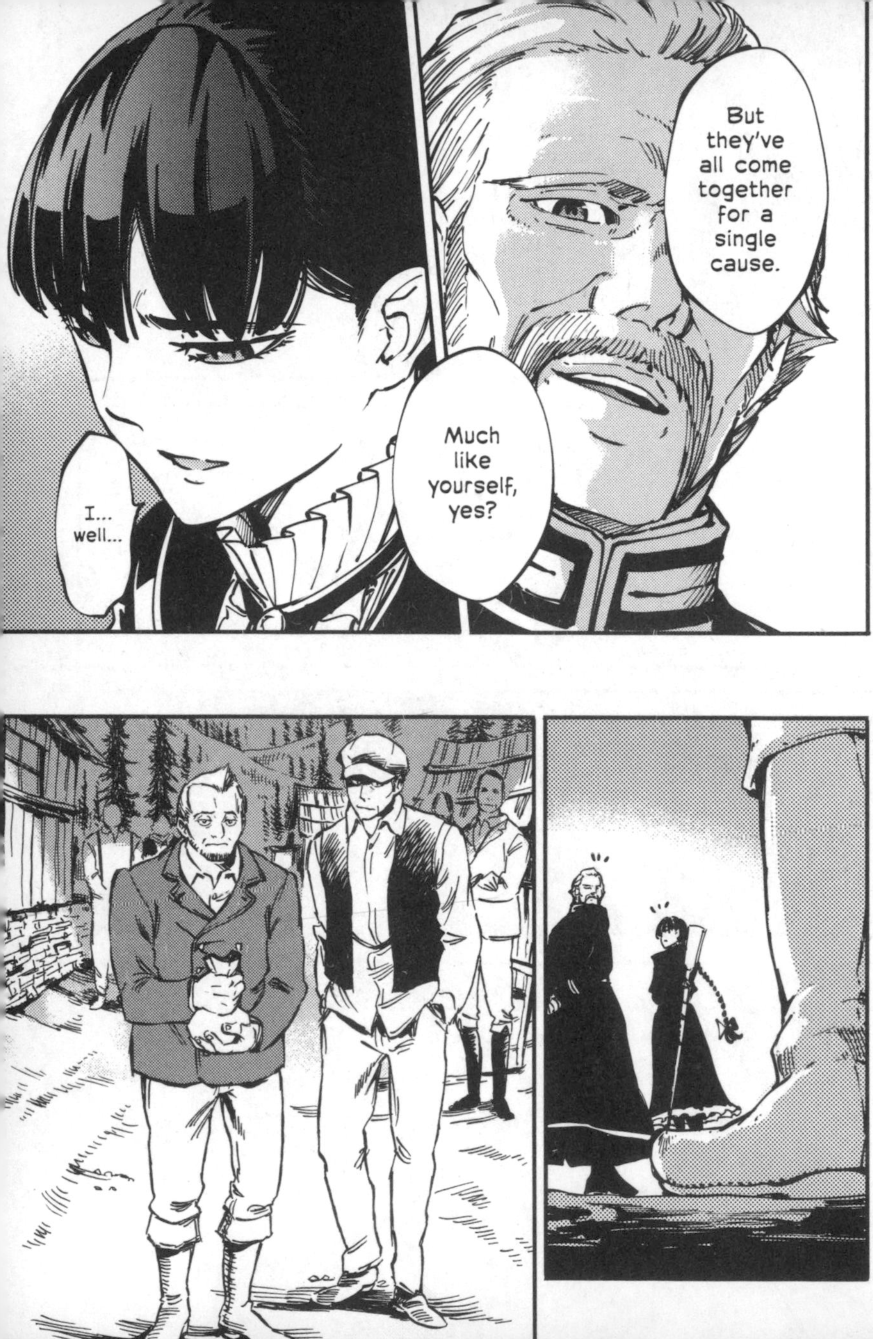
But they've all come together for a single cause.
Much like yourself, yes?
I... well...

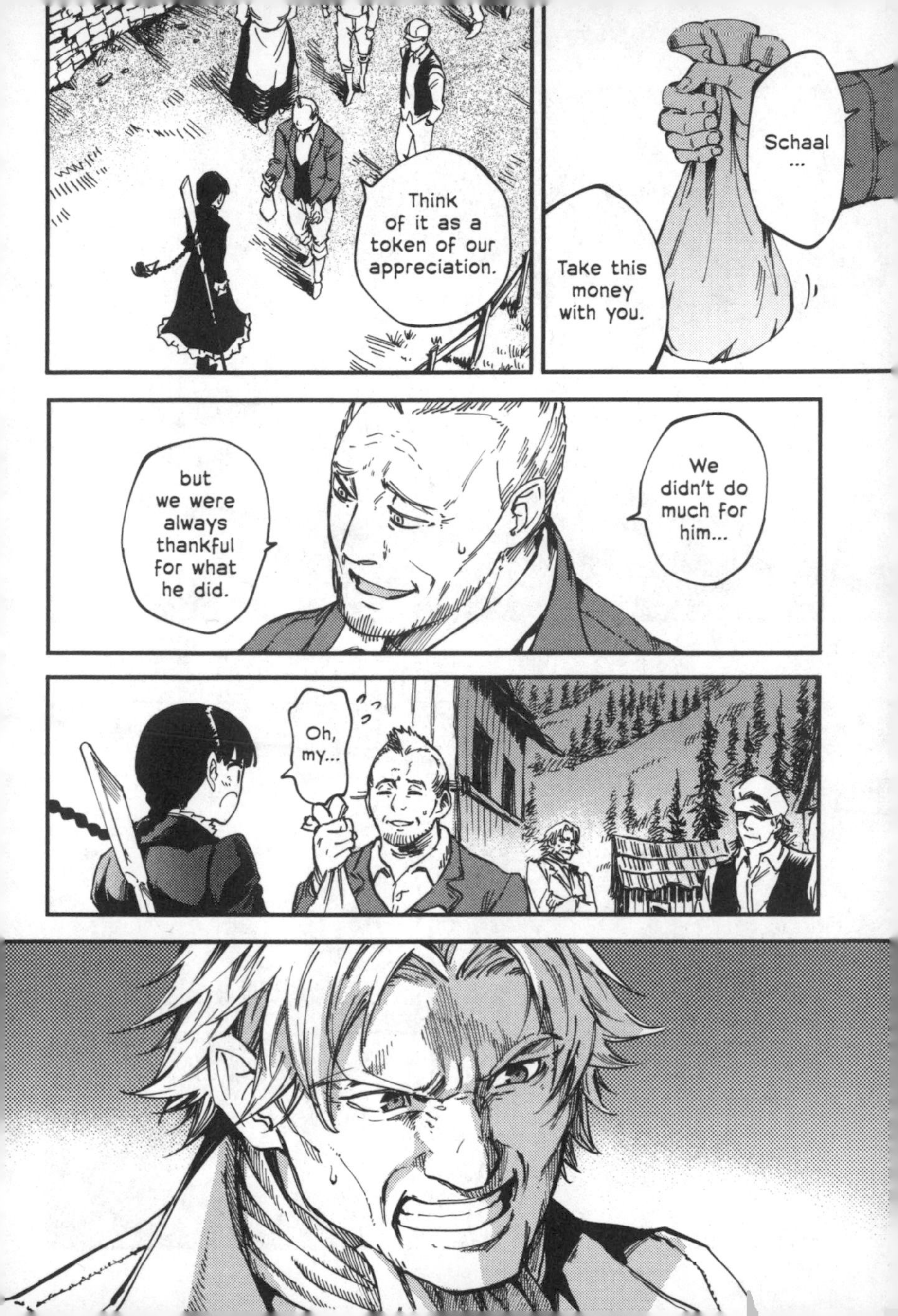
Schaal...
Take this money with you.
Think of it as a token of our appreciation.
We didn't do much for him...
but we were always thankful for what he did.
Oh, my...

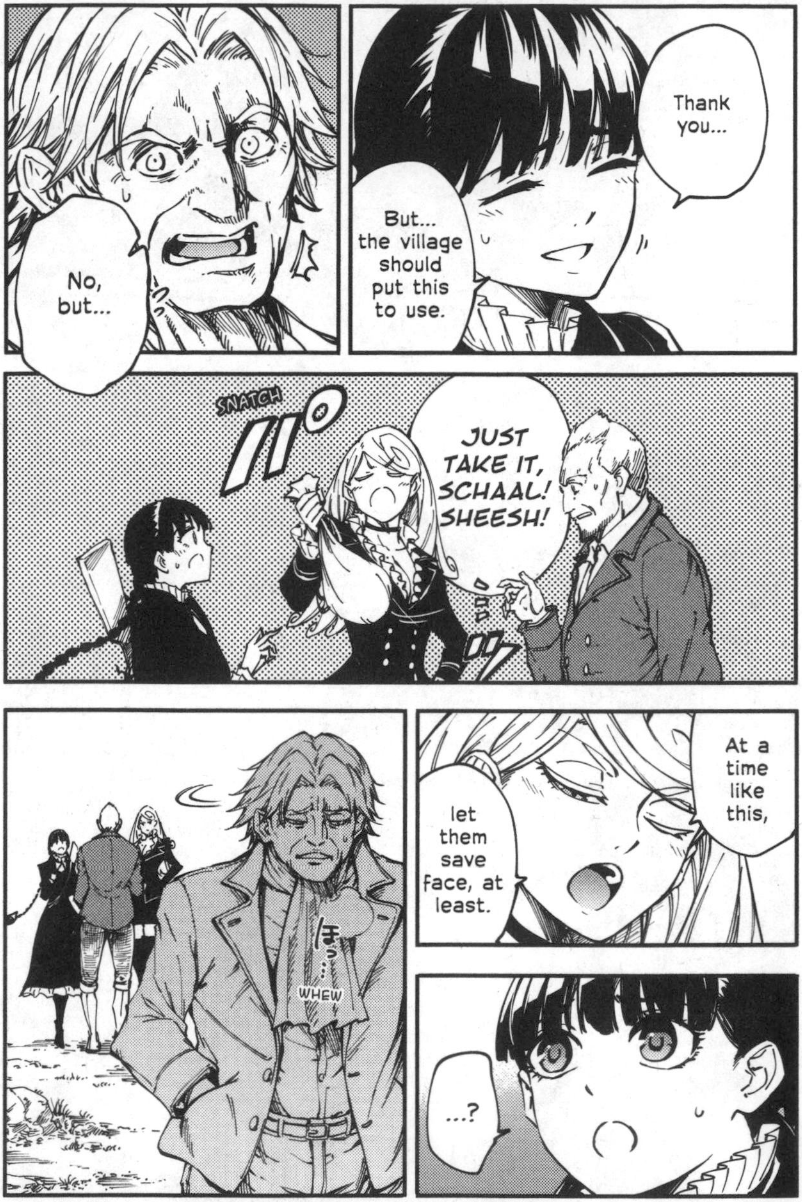
Thank you...
But... the village should put this to use.
No, but...
SNATCH
JUST TAKE IT, SCHAAL! SHEESH!
At a time like this,
let them save face, at least.
...?
ほっ…
WHEW

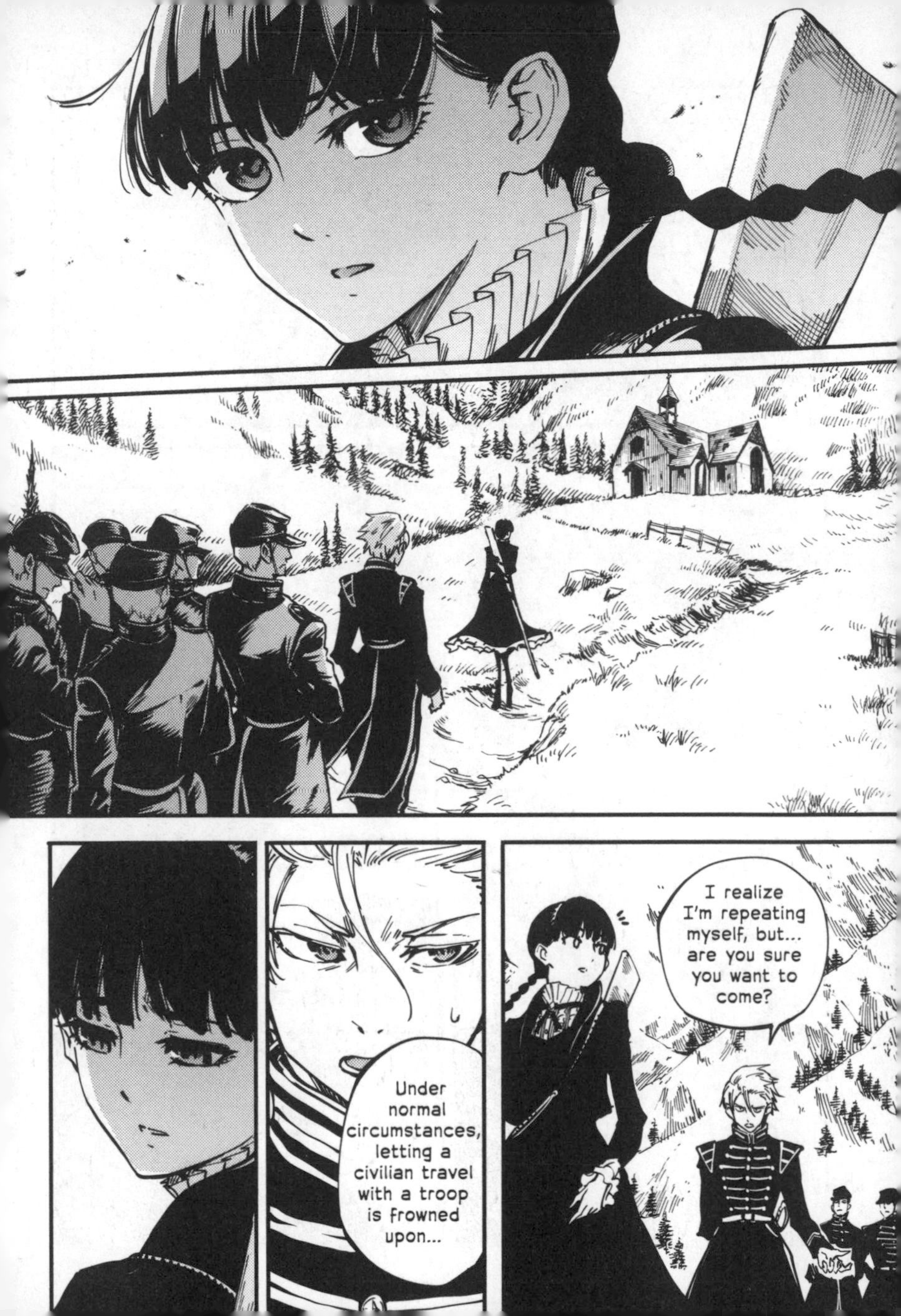
I realize I'm repeating myself, but... are you sure you want to come?
Under normal circumstances, letting a civilian travel with a troop is frowned upon...

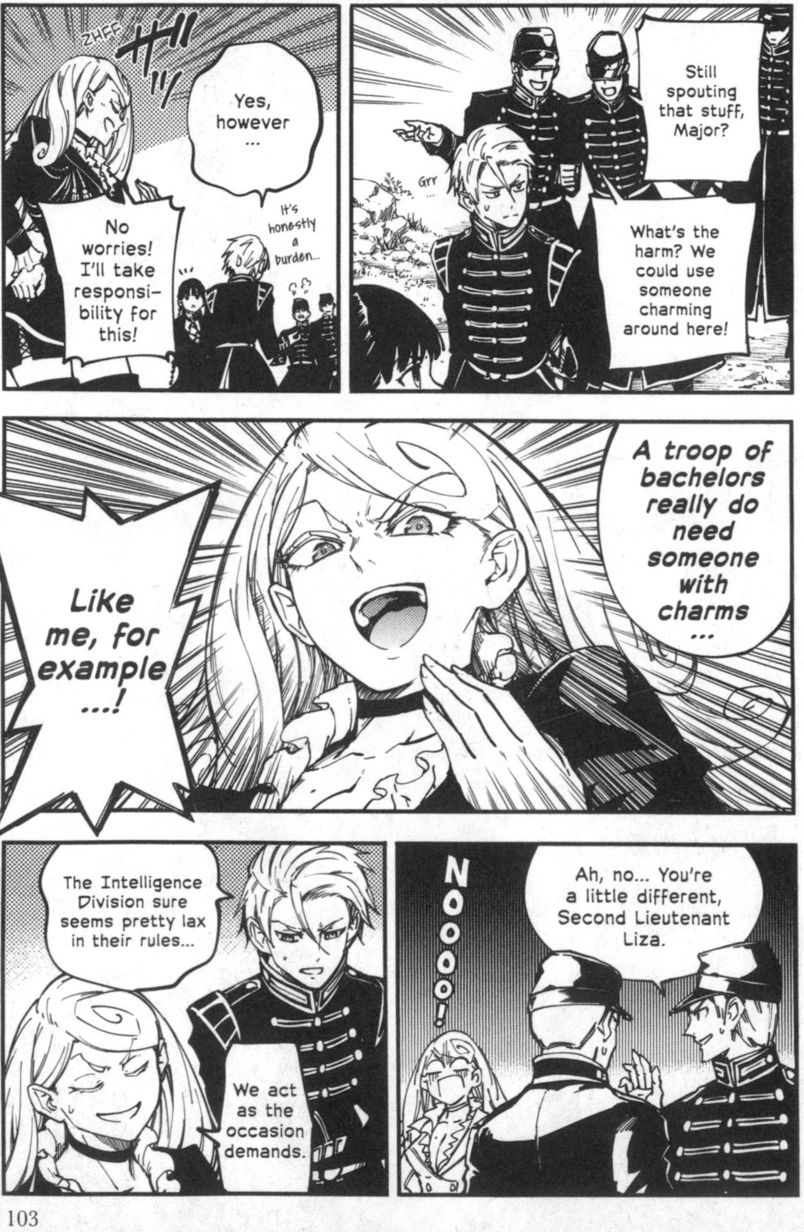
Still spouting that stuff, Major?
Grr...
What's the harm? We could use someone charming around here!
ZHFF
Yes, however ...
No worries! I'll take responsi-bility for this!
It's honestly a burden...
A troop of bachelors really do need someone with charms ...
Like me, for example ...!
Ah, no... You're a little different, Second Lieutenant Liza.
NOOOOO!
The Intelligence Division sure seems pretty lax in their rules...
We act as the occasion demands.

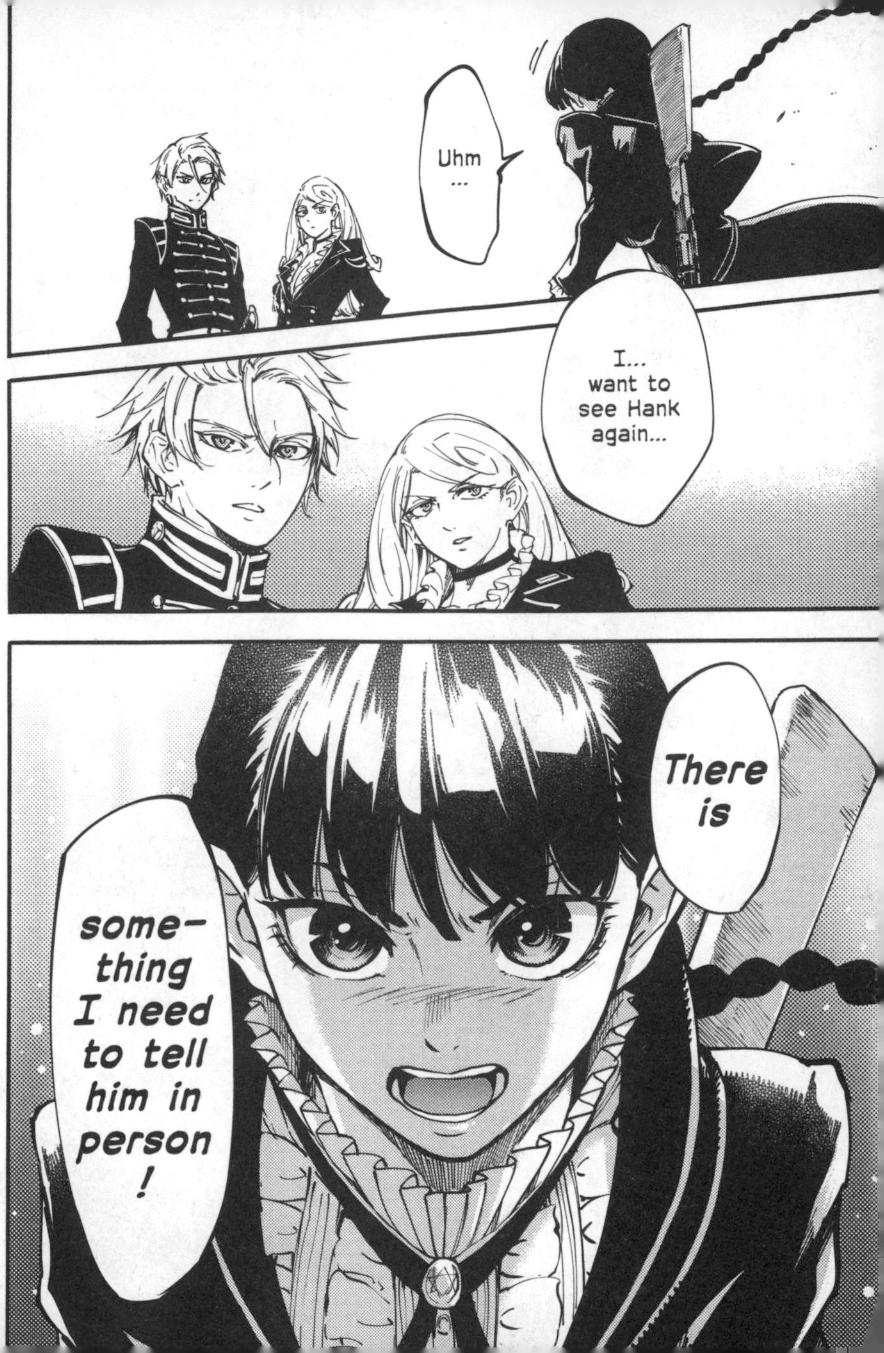
Uhm ...
I... want to see Hank again...
There is
something I need to tell him in person!

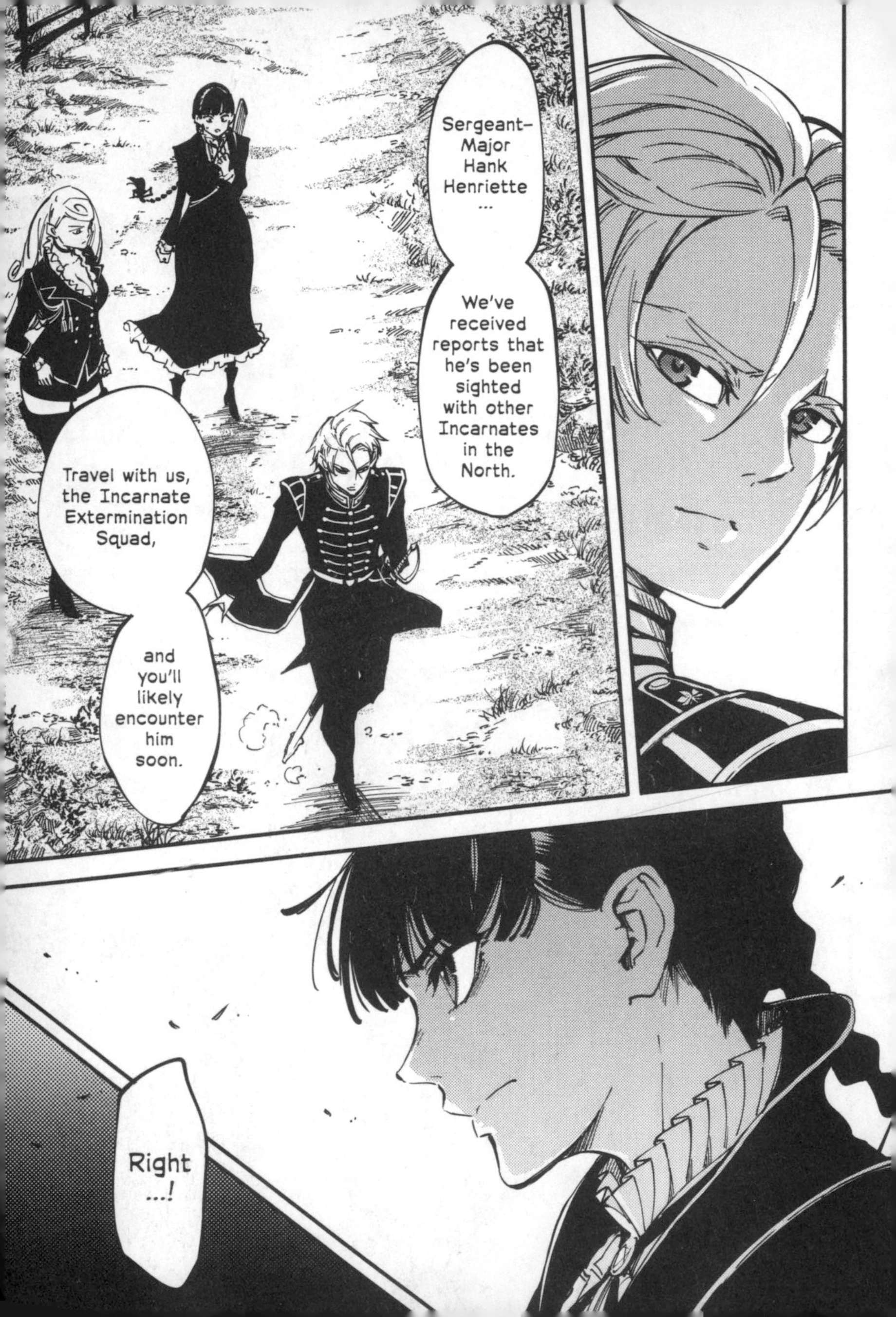
Sergeant-Major Hank Henriette ...
We've received reports that he's been sighted with other Incarnates in the North.
Travel with us, the Incarnate Extermination Squad,
and you'll likely encounter him soon.
Right ...!

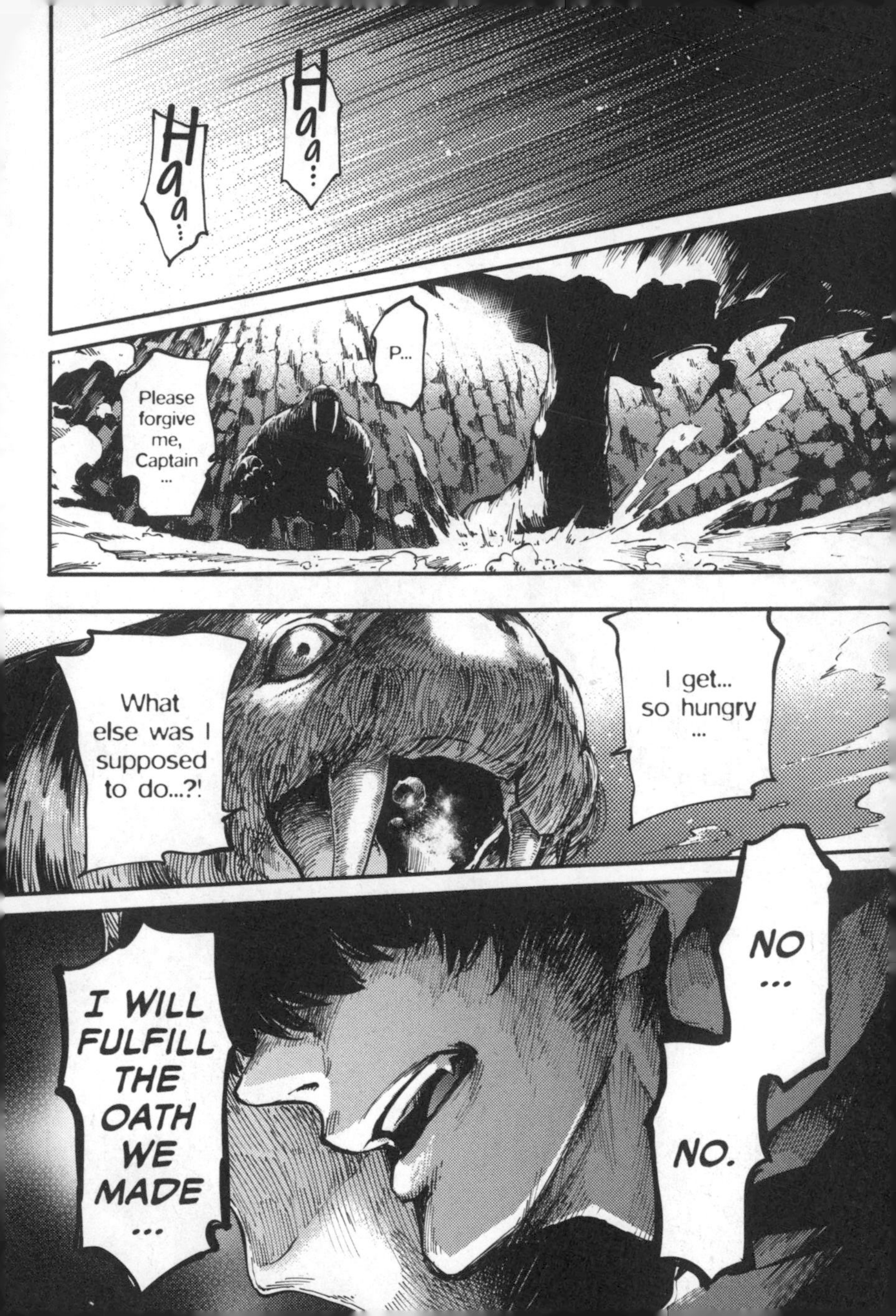
Haa...
Haa...
P...
Please forgive me, Captain...
I get... so hungry...
What else was I supposed to do...?!
NO...
NO.
I WILL FULFILL THE OATH WE MADE...

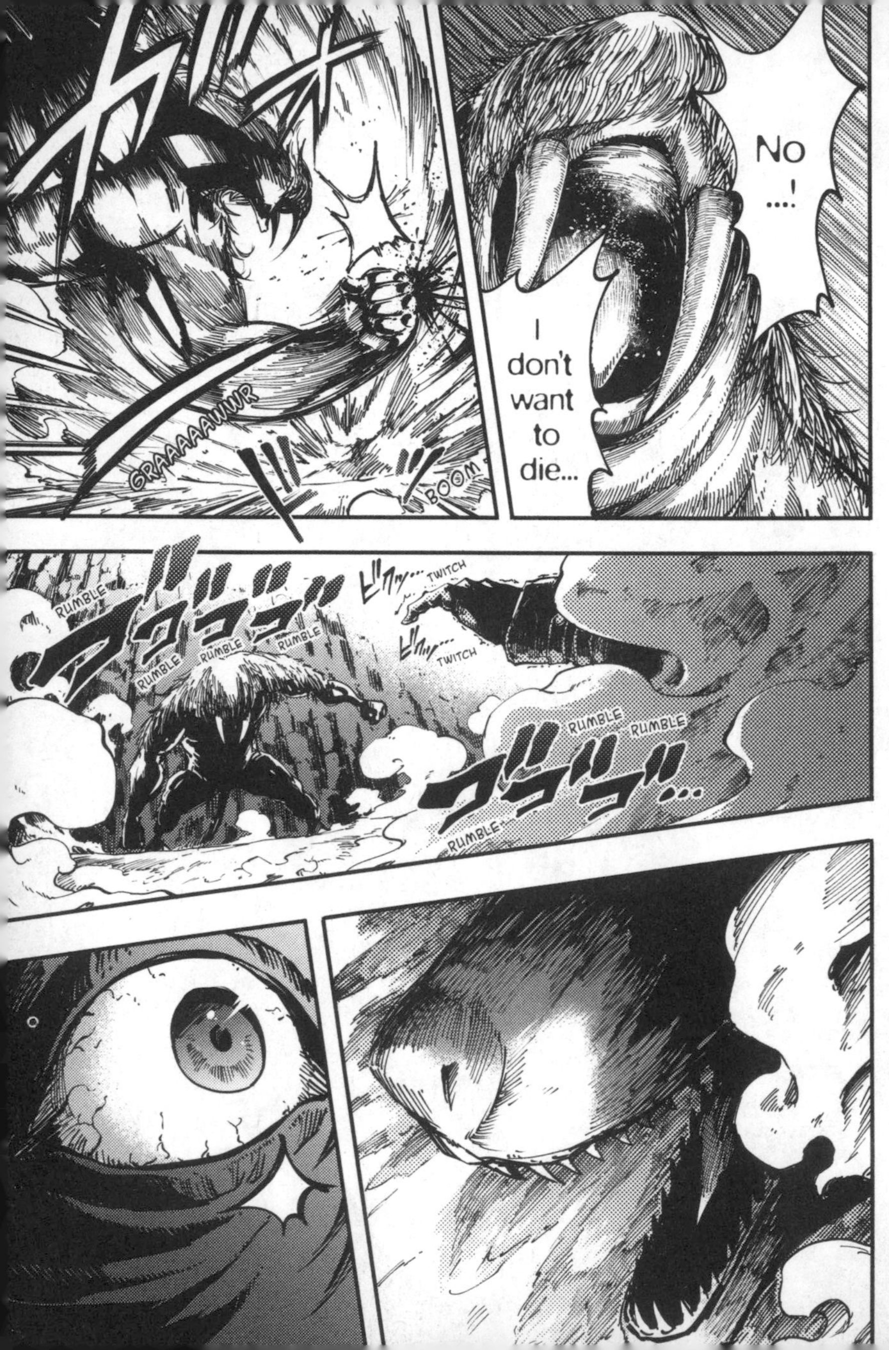
No ...!
I don't want to die...
GRAAAAAWWR
BOOM
TWITCH
TWITCH
RUMBLE
RUMBLE
RUMBLE
RUMBLE
RUMBLE
RUMBLE
RUMBLE

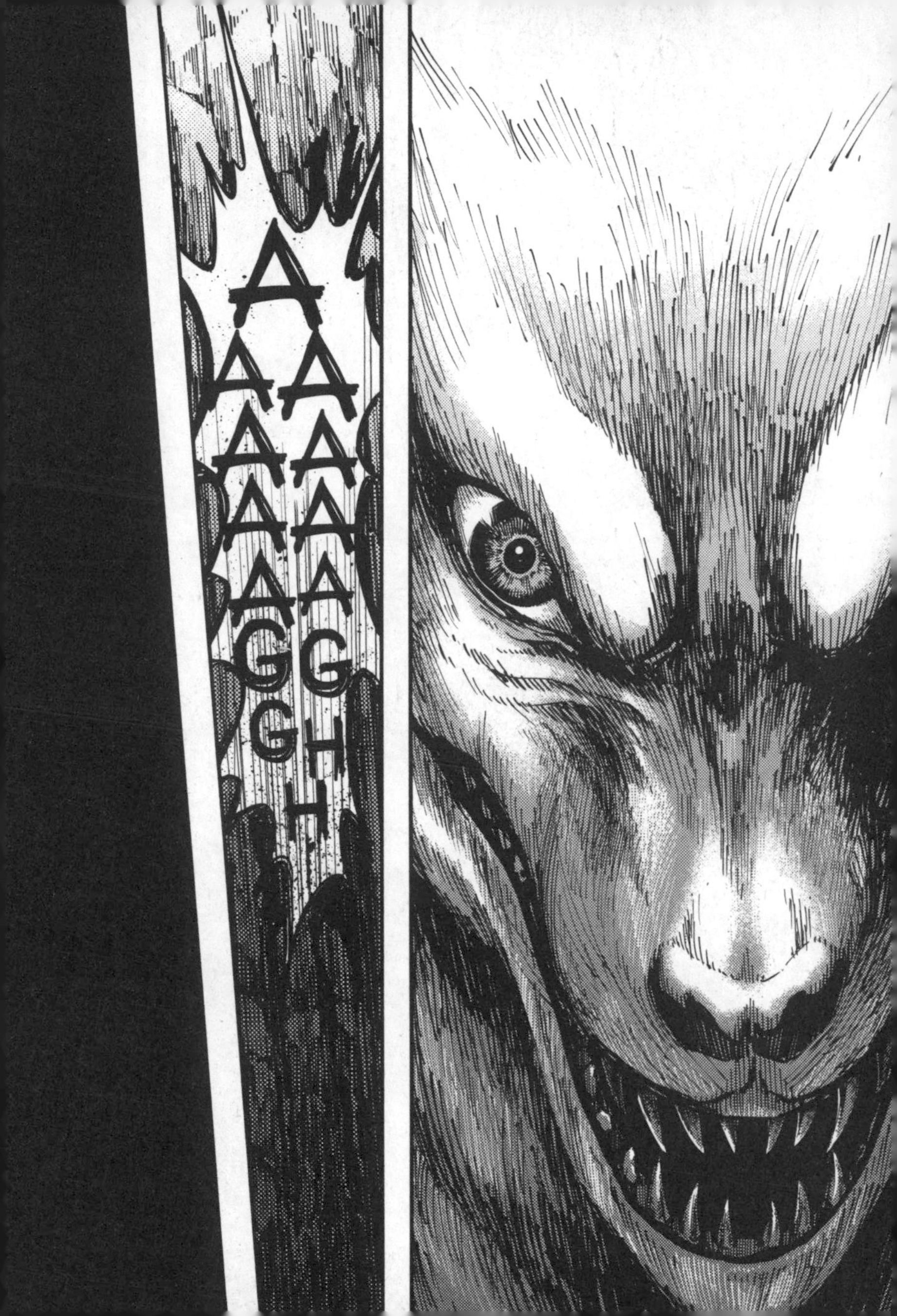
AAAAAAAAAGGGHH

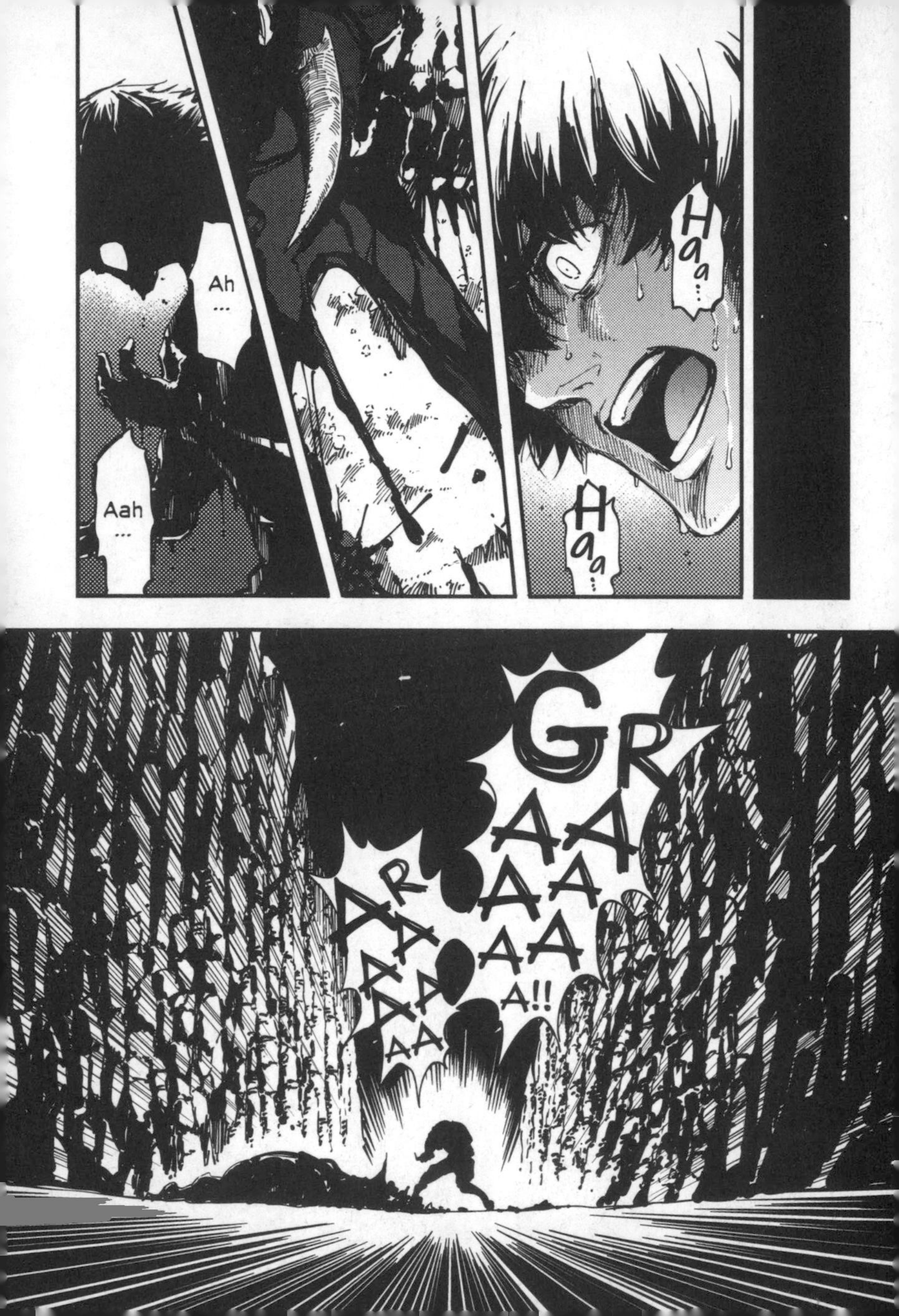
Haa...
Haa...
Ah...
Aah...
GRAAAAAAA!!
ARAAAAAA

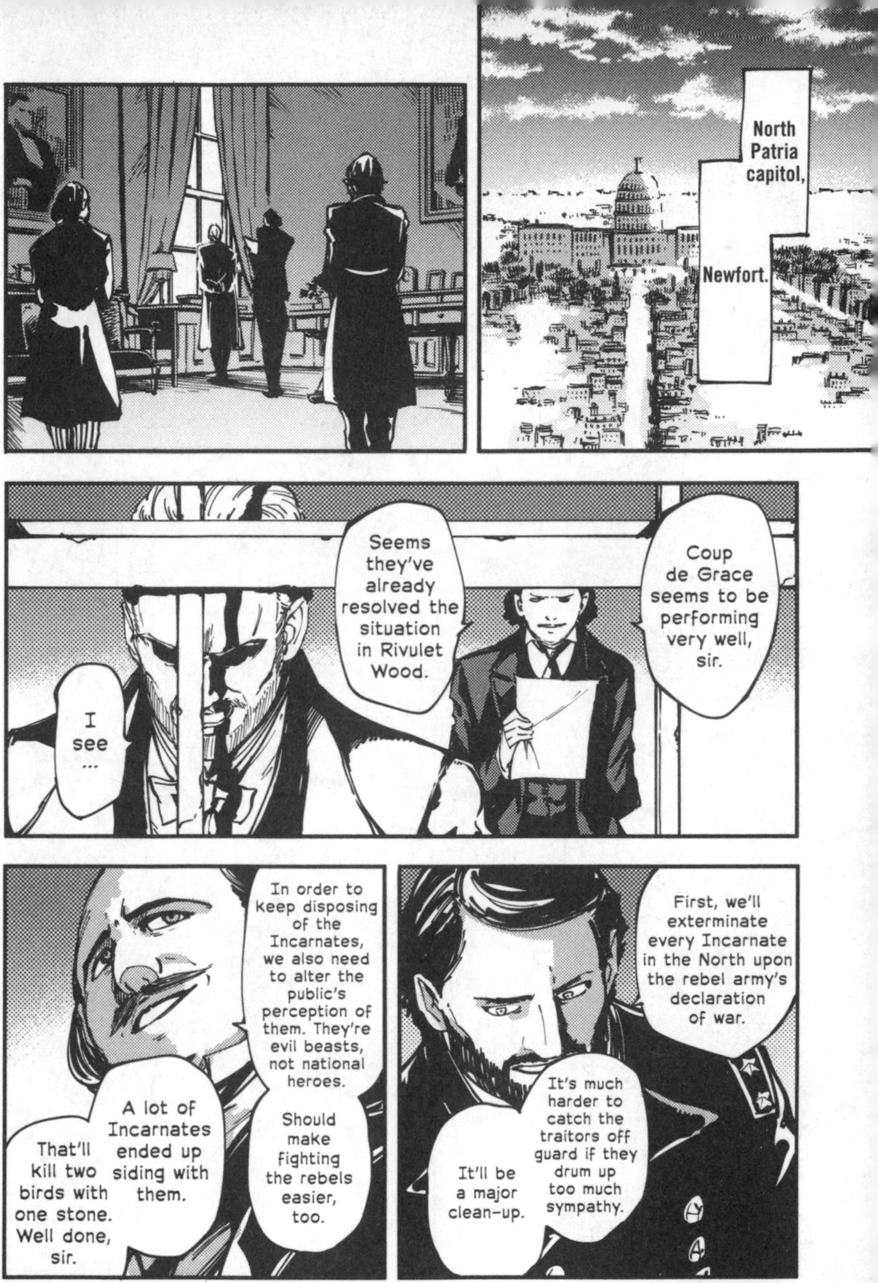
North Patria capitol,
Newfort.
Coup de Grace seems to be performing very well, sir.
Seems they've already resolved the situation in Rivulet Wood.
I see...
First, we'll exterminate every Incarnate in the North upon the rebel army's declaration of war.
It's much harder to catch the traitors off guard if they drum up too much sympathy.
It'll be a major clean-up.
In order to keep disposing of the Incarnates, we also need to alter the public's perception of them. They're evil beasts, not national heroes.
Should make fighting the rebels easier, too.
A lot of Incarnates ended up siding with them.
That'll kill two birds with one stone. Well done, sir.

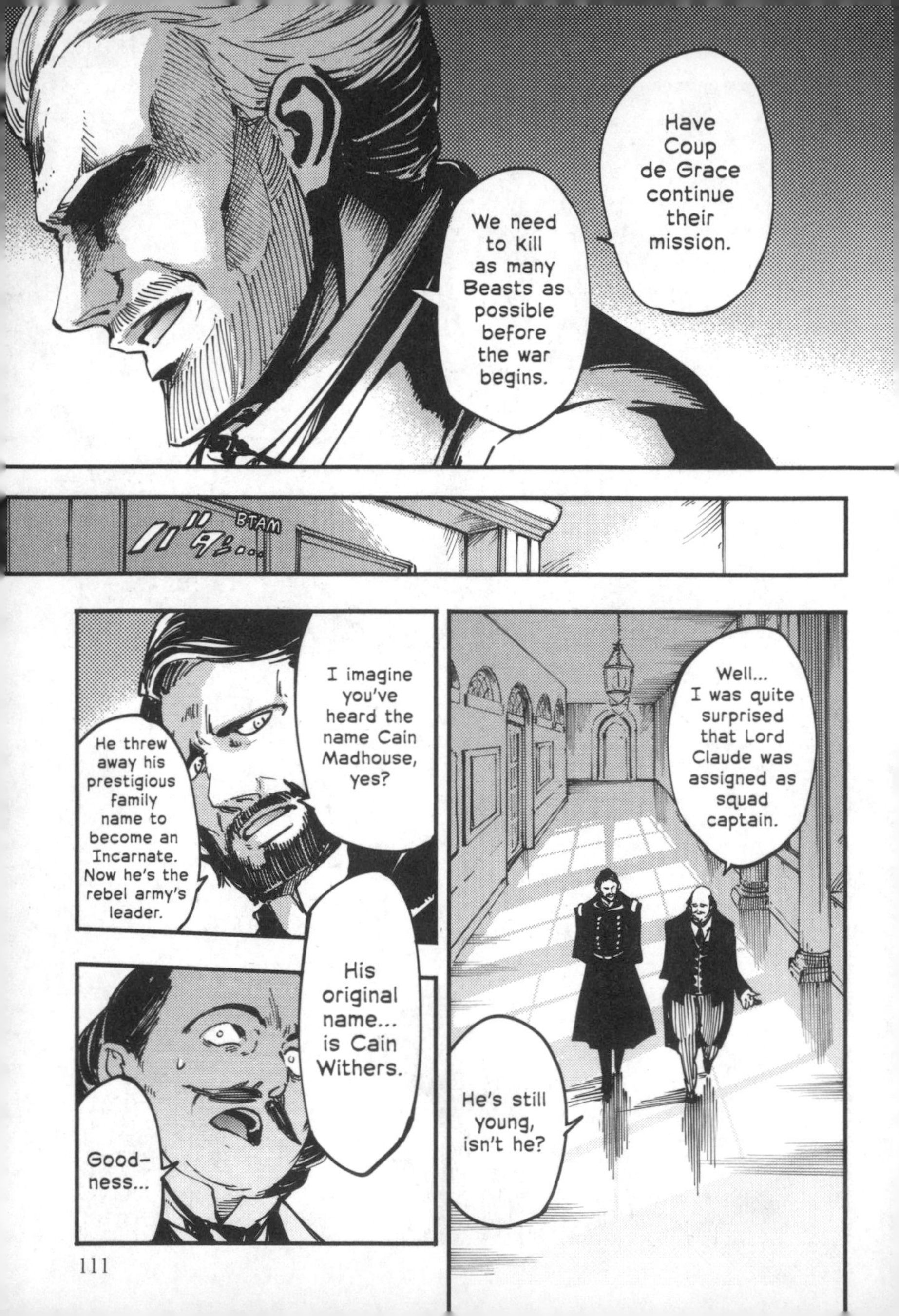
Have Coup de Grace continue their mission.
We need to kill as many Beasts as possible before the war begins.
BTAM
Well... I was quite surprised that Lord Claude was assigned as squad captain.
He's still young, isn't he?
I imagine you've heard the name Cain Madhouse, yes?
He threw away his prestigious family name to become an Incarnate. Now he's the rebel army's leader.
His original name... is Cain Withers.
Goodness...

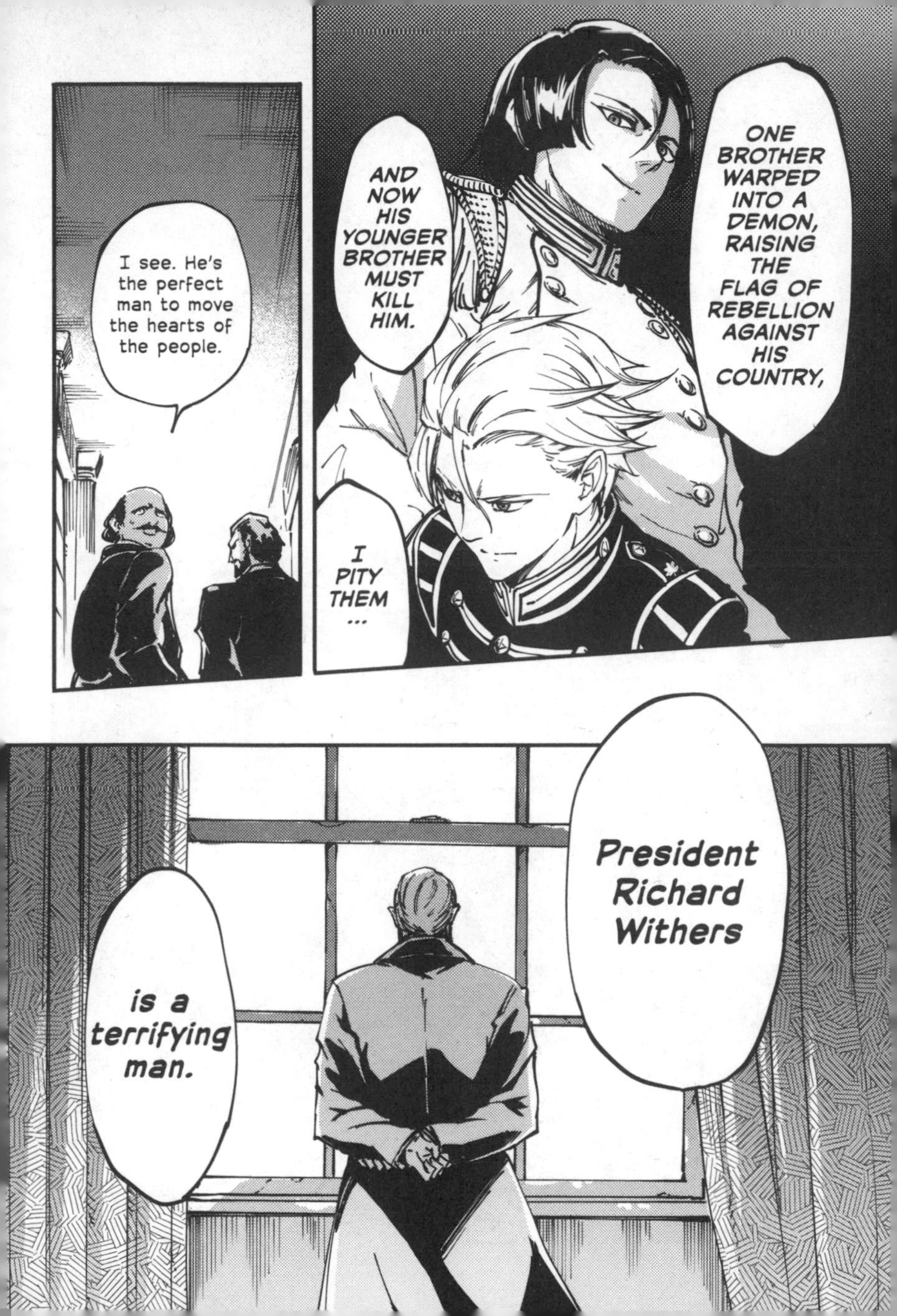
ONE BROTHER WARPED INTO A DEMON, RAISING THE FLAG OF REBELLION AGAINST HIS COUNTRY,
AND NOW HIS YOUNGER BROTHER MUST KILL HIM.
I PITY THEM...
I see. He's the perfect man to move the hearts of the people.
President Richard Withers
is a terrifying man.

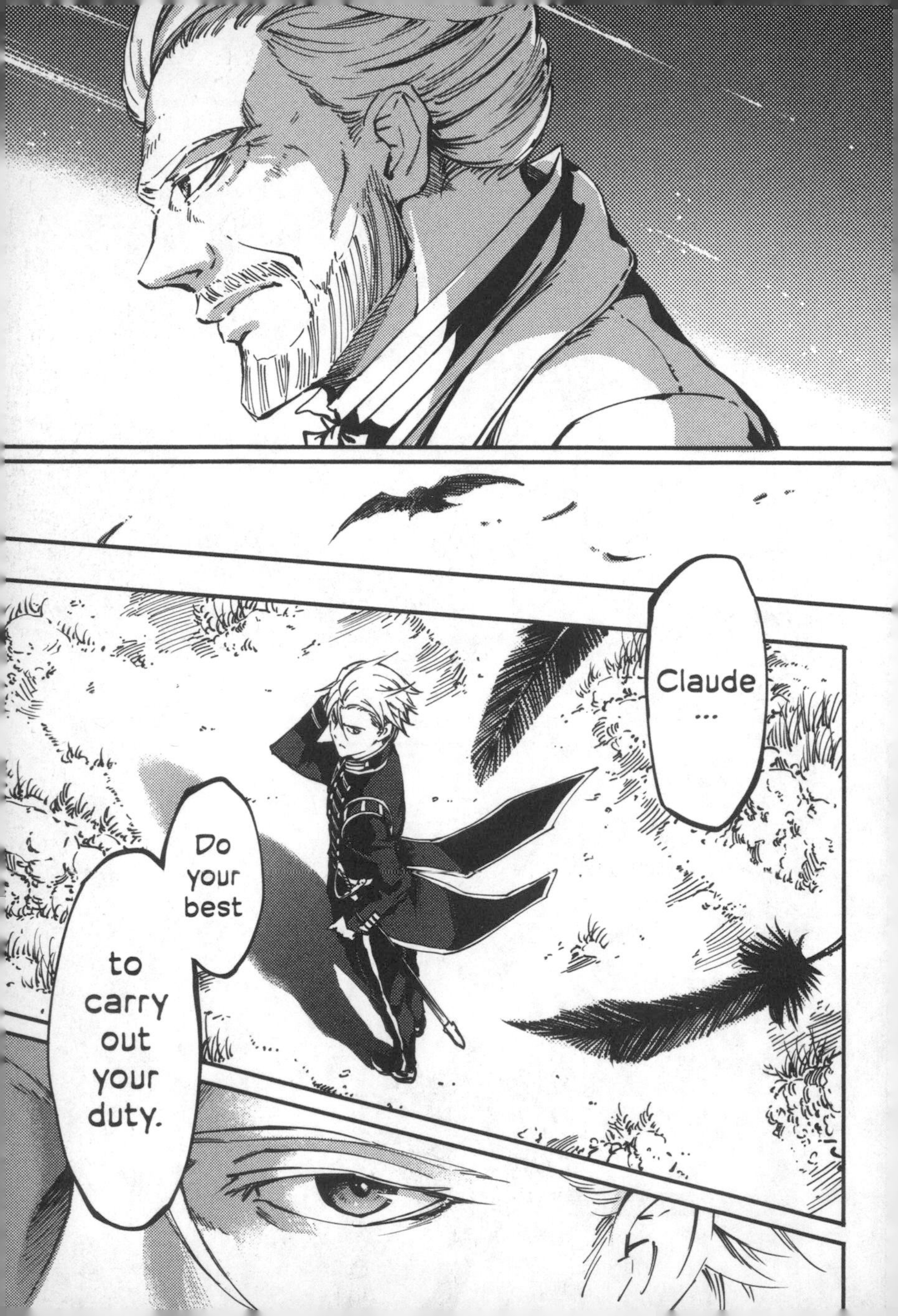
Claude ...
Do your best to carry out your duty.

To the Abandoned
Sacred Beasts

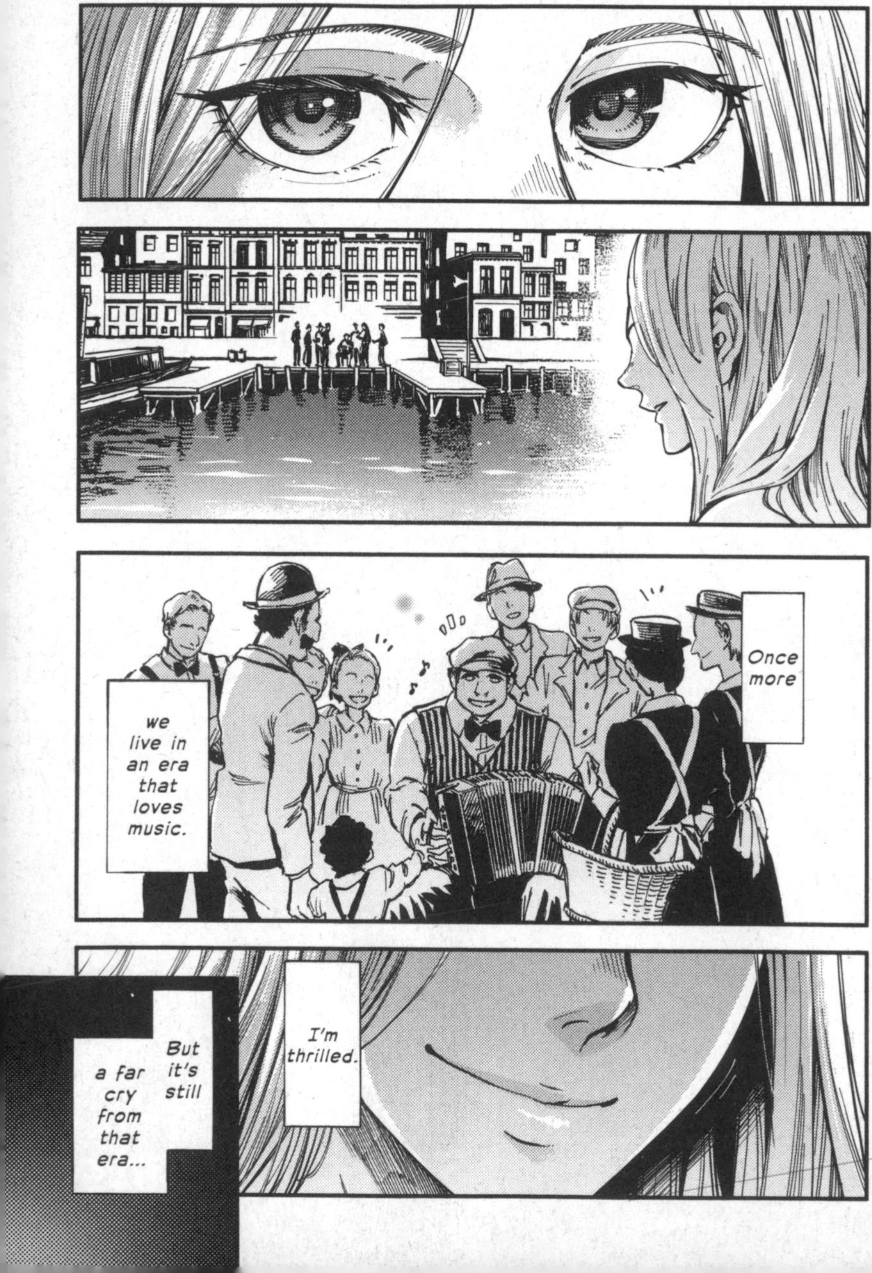
Once more
we live in an era that loves music.
I'm thrilled.
But it's still a far cry from that era...

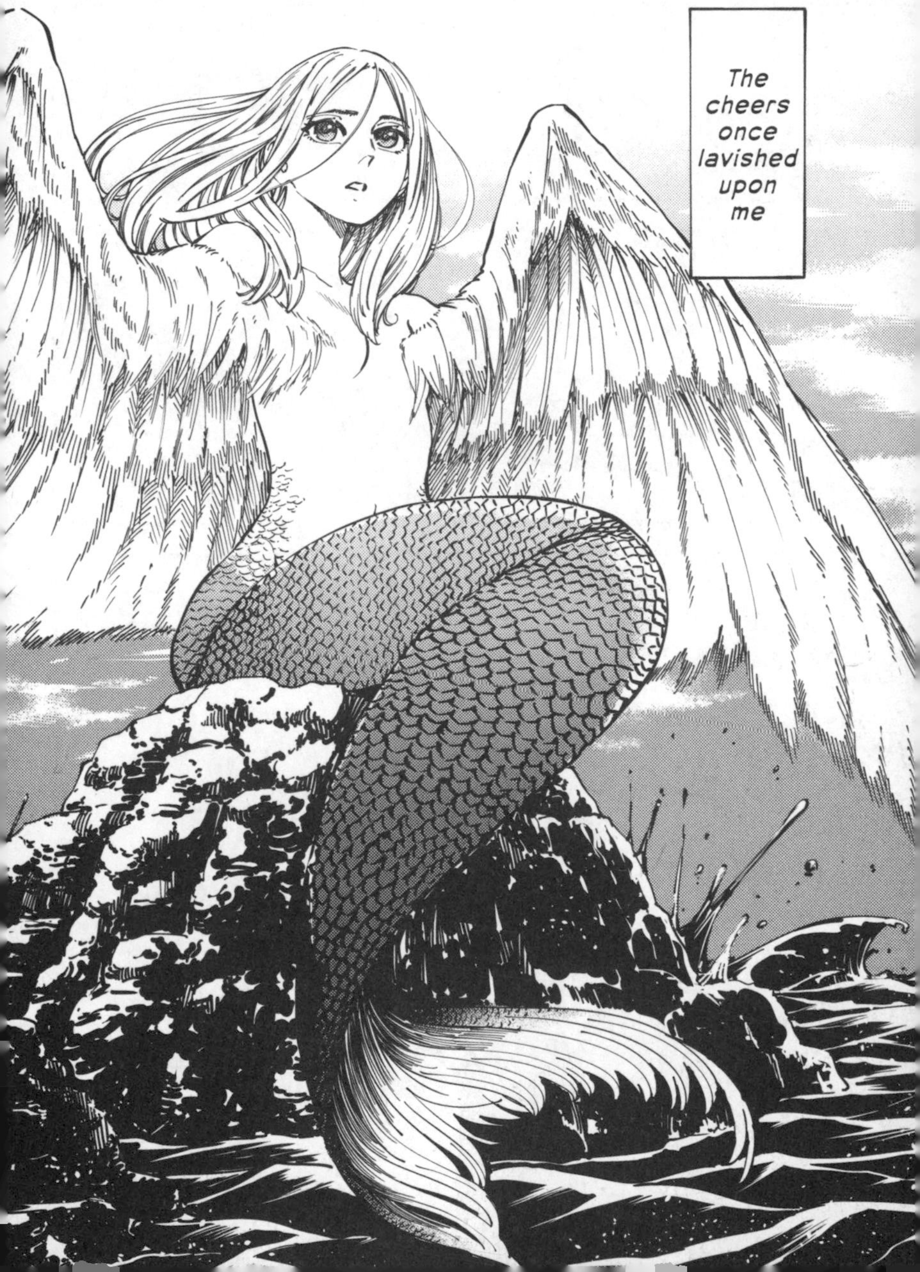
The cheers once lavished upon me

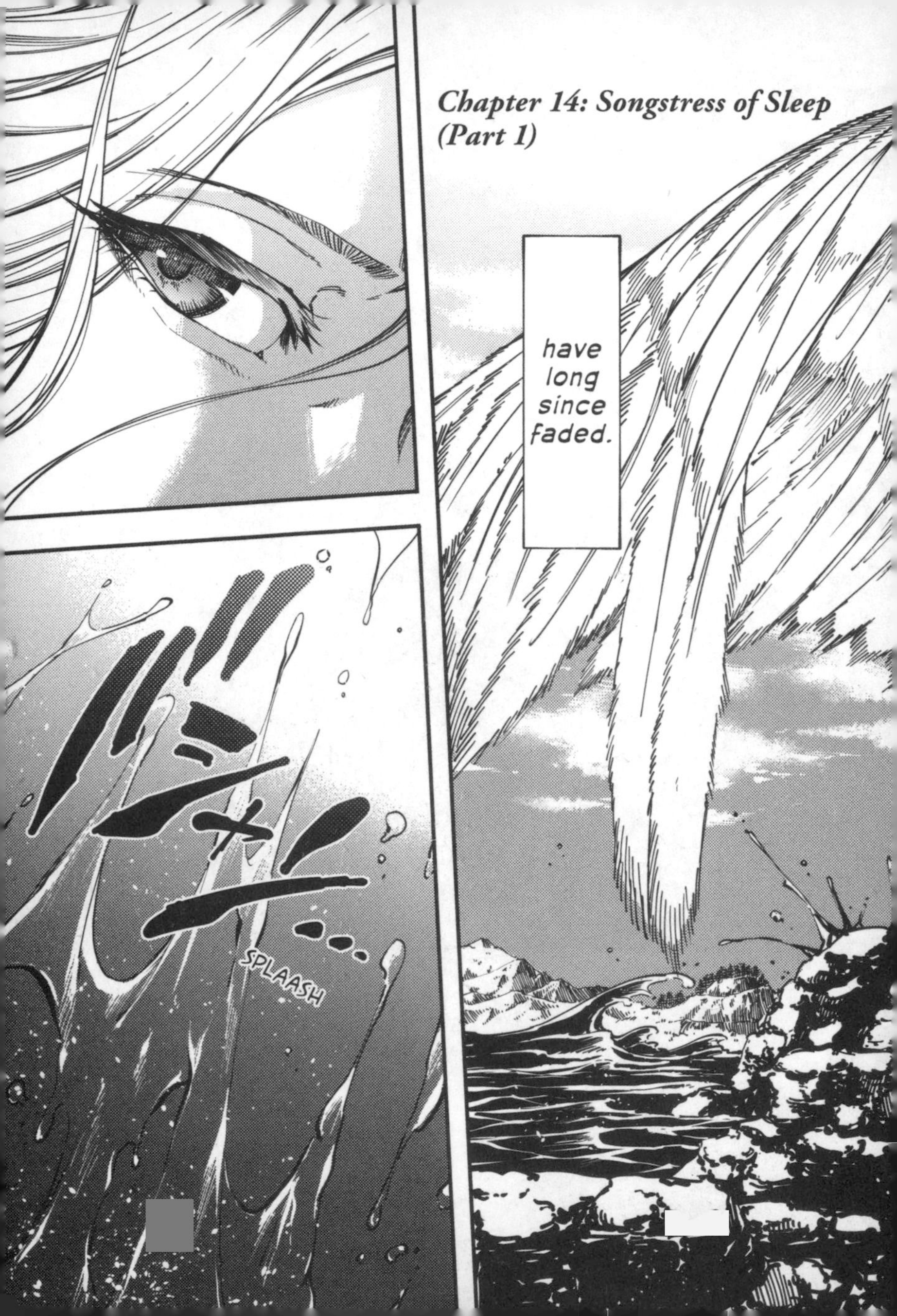
Chapter 14: Songstress of Sleep (Part 1)
have long since faded.
SPLAASH

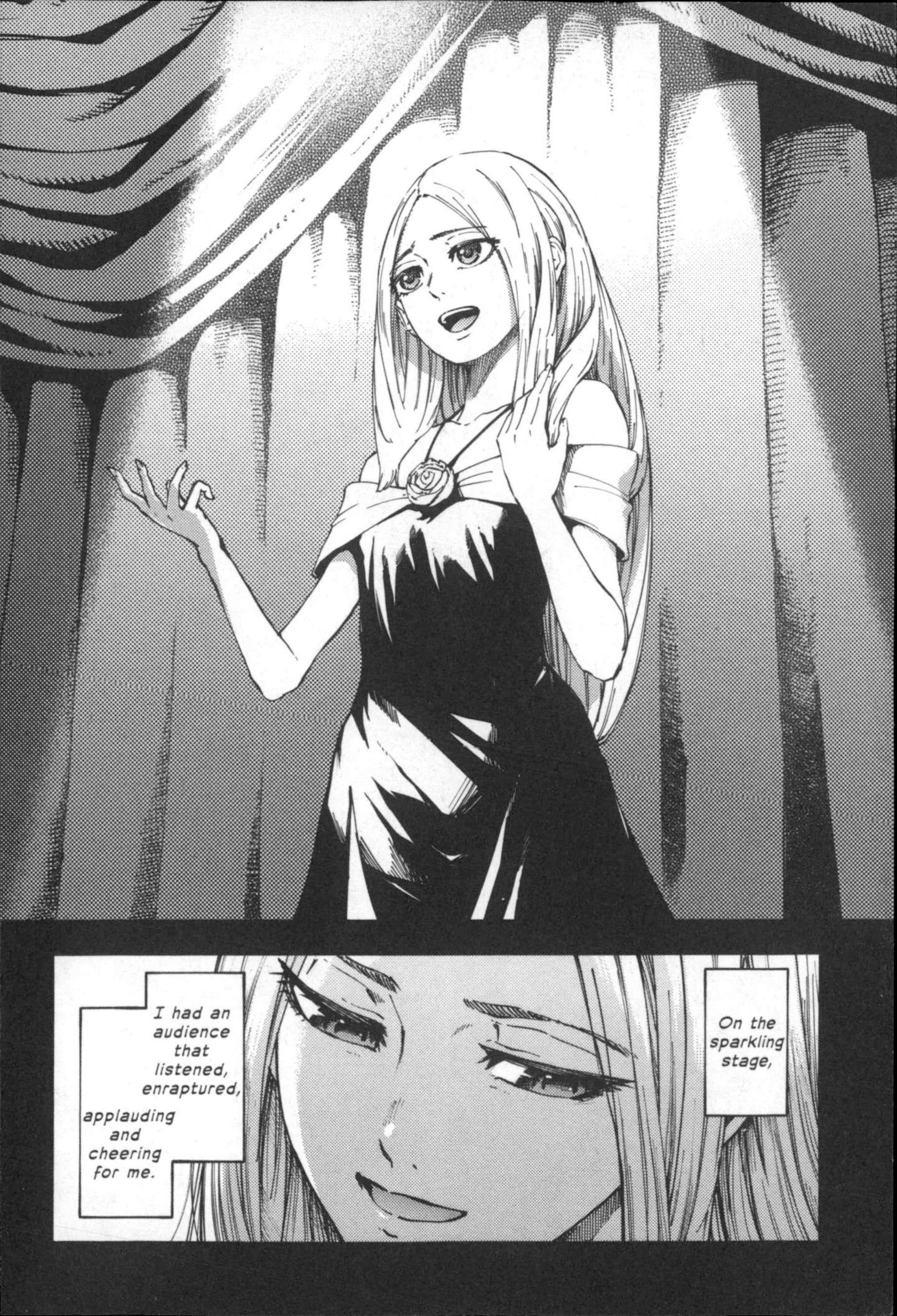
On the sparkling stage,
I had an audience that listened, enraptured, applauding and cheering for me.

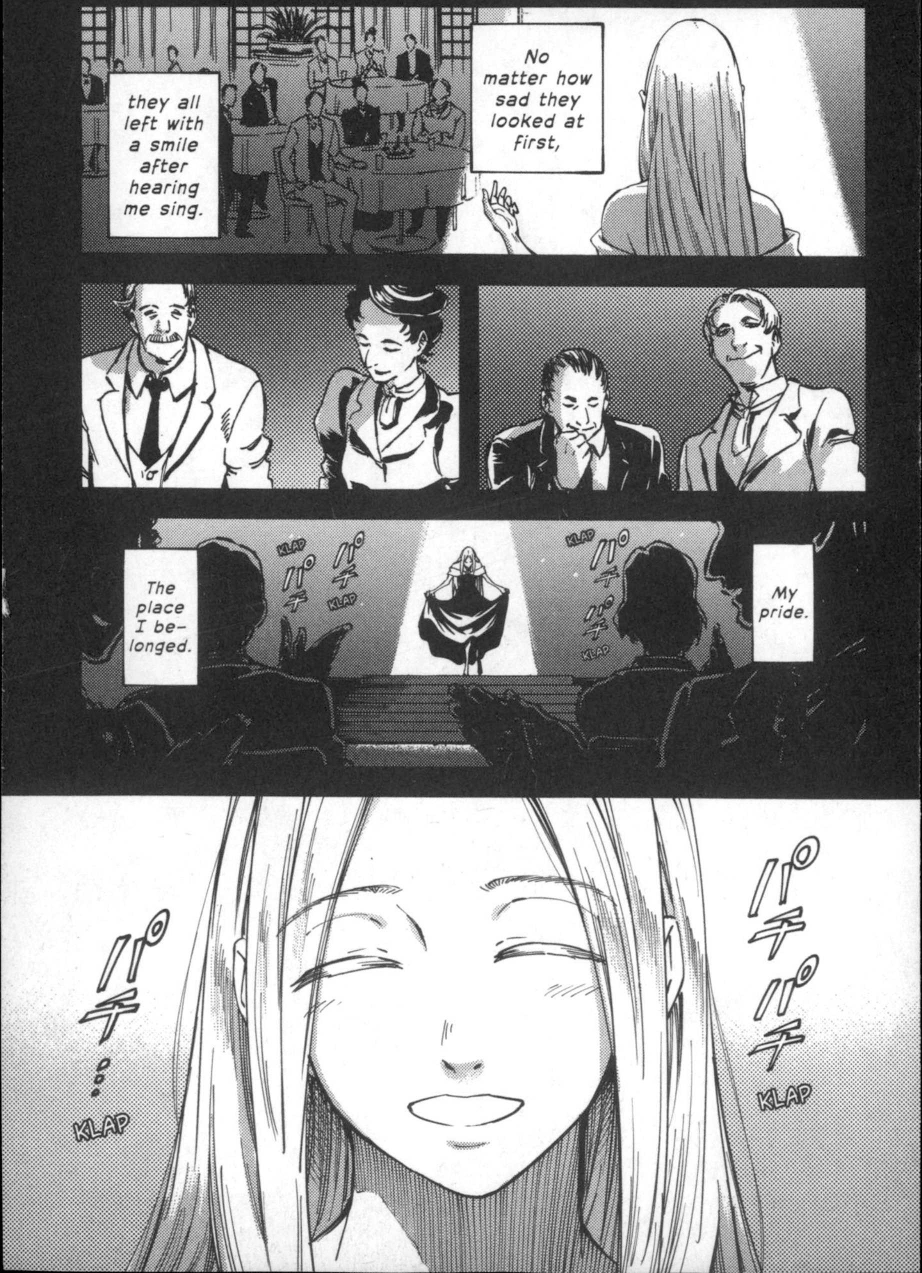

No matter how sad they looked at first,
they all left with a smile after hearing me sing.
My pride.
KLAP
パチパチ
KLAP
KLAP
パチ
パチ
KLAP
The place I be-longed.
パチパチ
KLAP
パチ…
KLAP

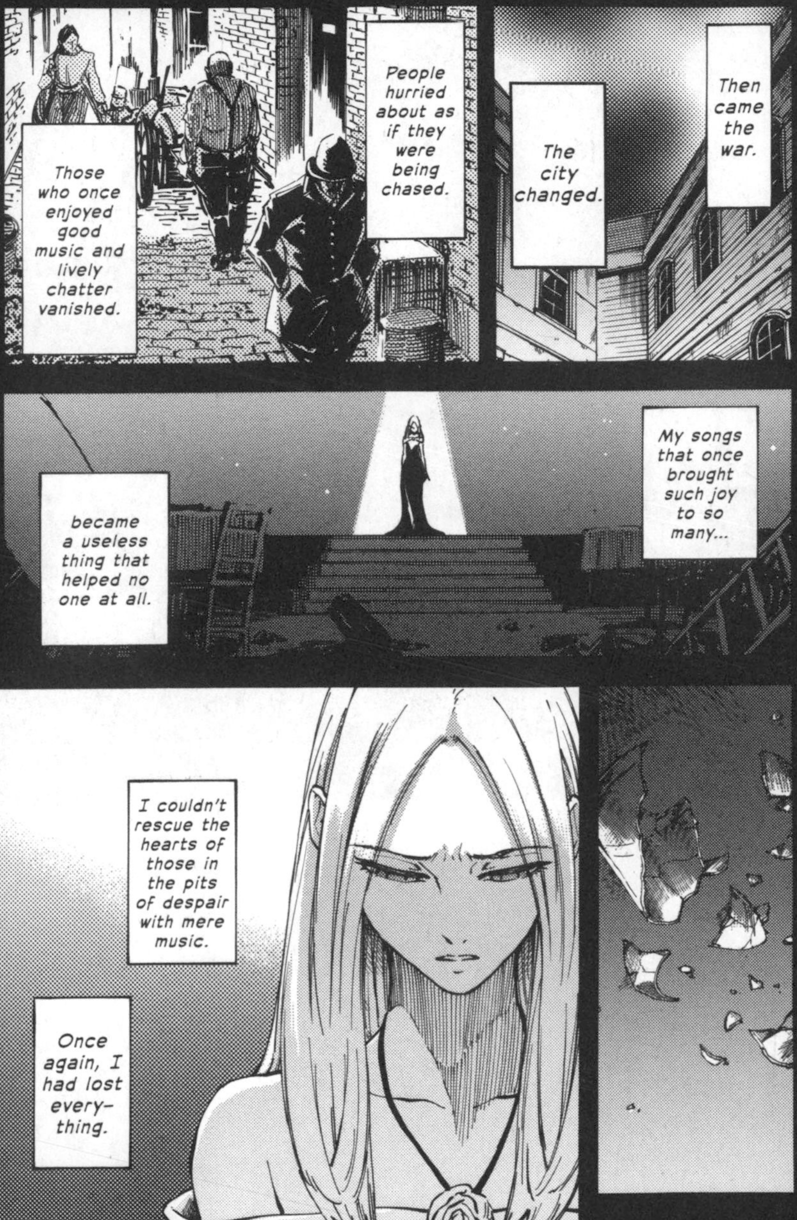
Then came the war.
The city changed.
People hurried about as if they were being chased.
Those who once enjoyed good music and lively chatter vanished.
My songs that once brought such joy to so many...
became a useless thing that helped no one at all.
I couldn't rescue the hearts of those in the pits of despair with mere music.
Once again, I had lost every-thing.

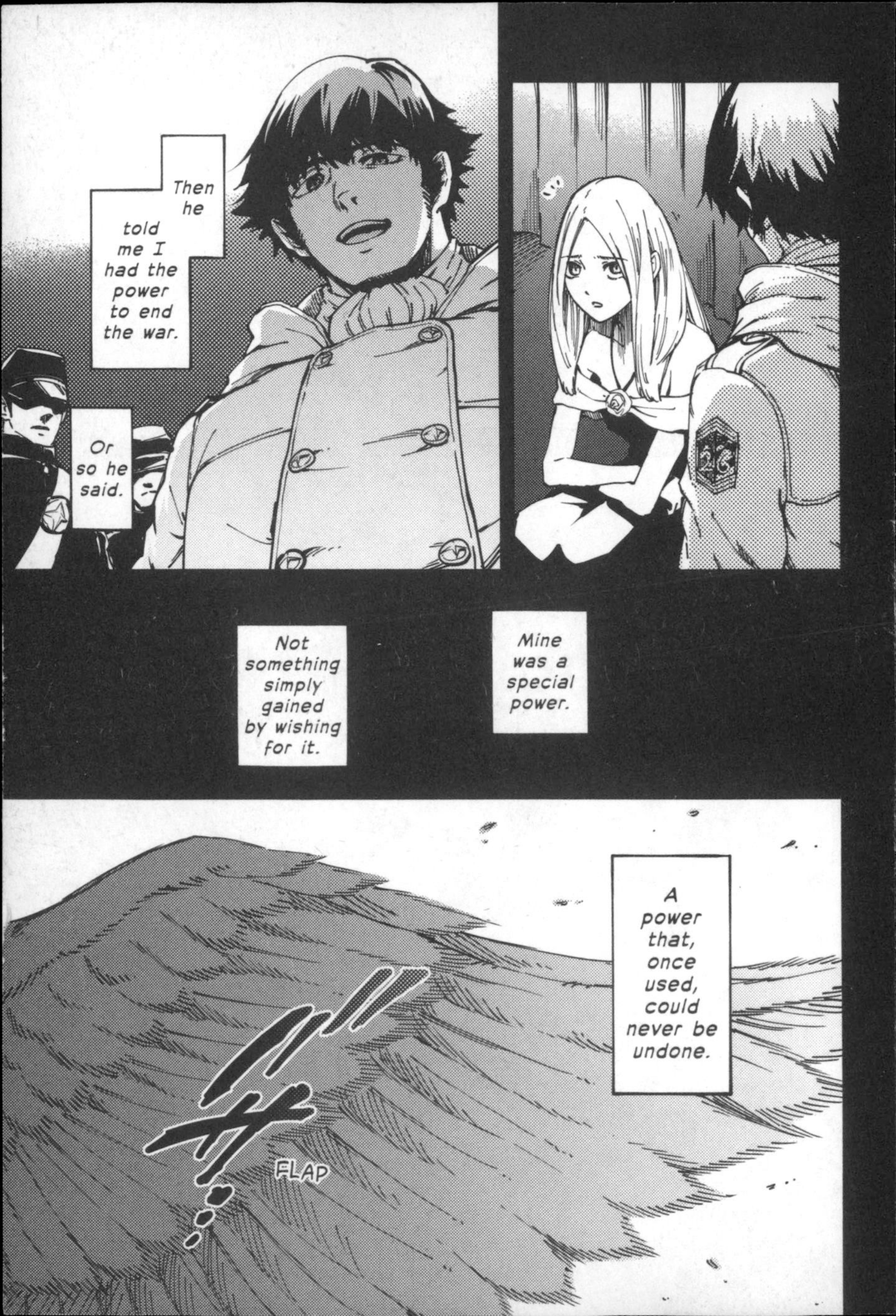
Then he told me I had the power to end the war.
Or so he said.
Mine was a special power.
Not something simply gained by wishing for it.
A power that, once used, could never be undone.
FLAP

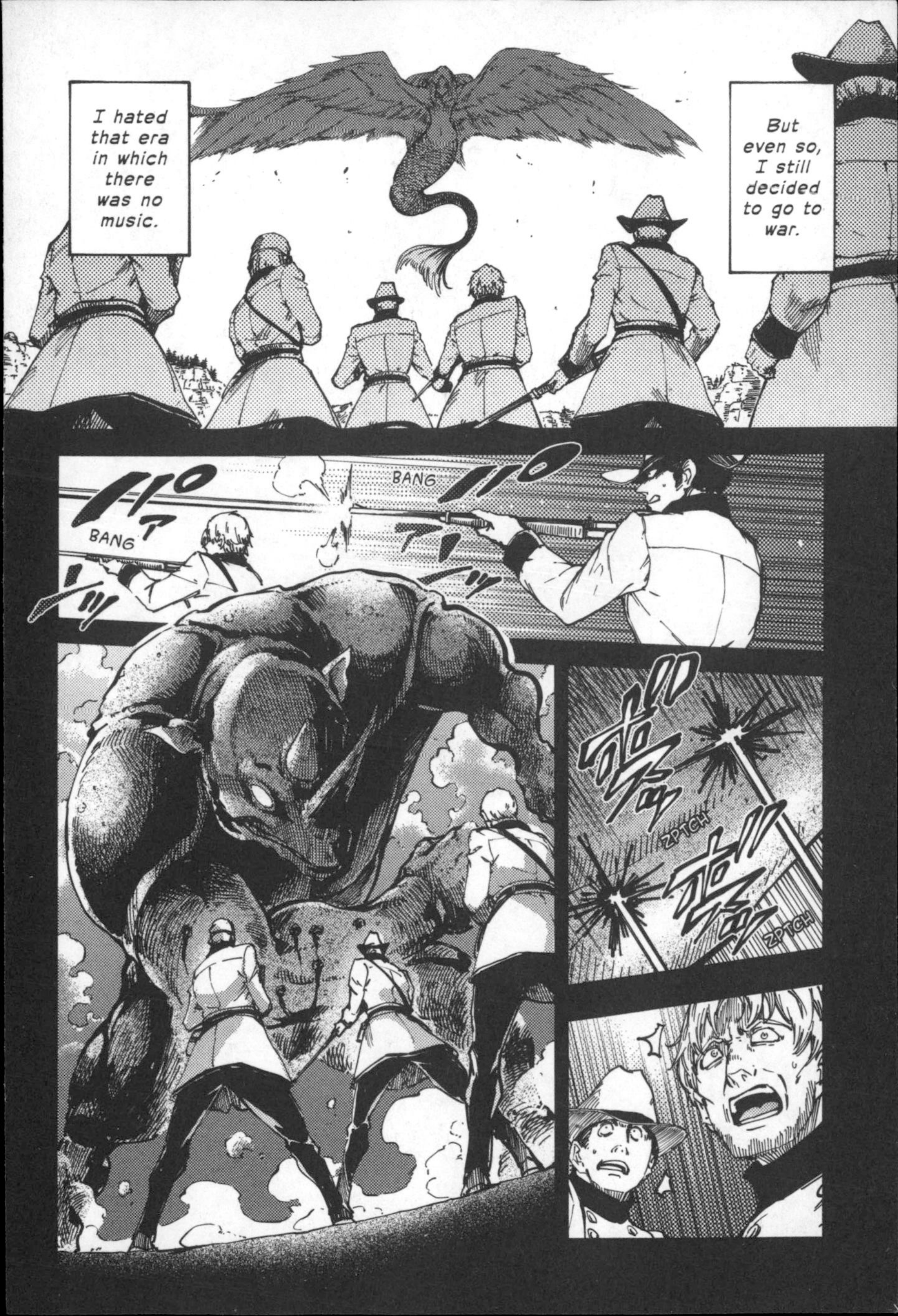
I hated that era in which there was no music.
But even so, I still decided to go to war.
BANG
BANG
ZPTCH
ZPTCH

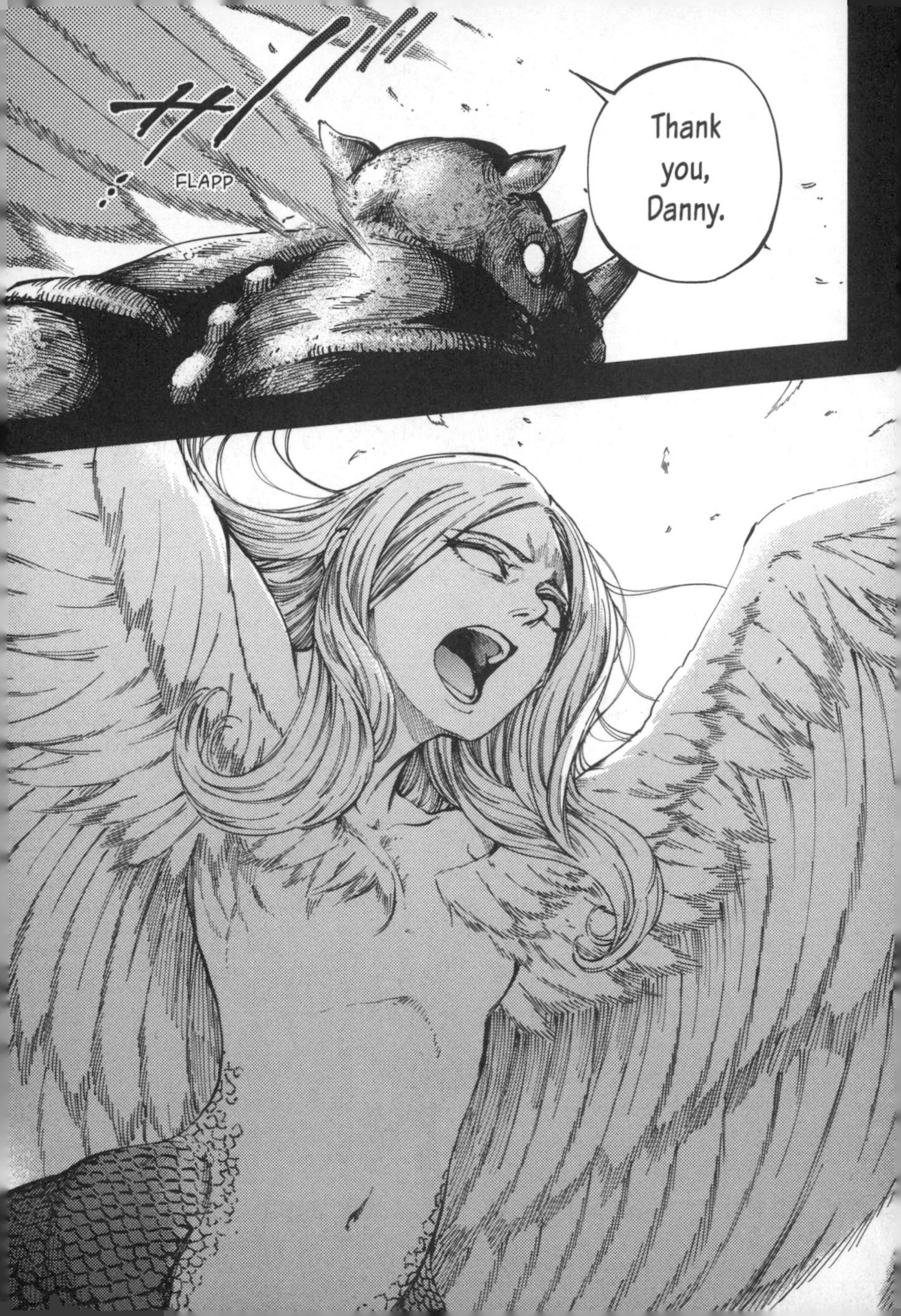
Thank you, Danny.
FLAPP

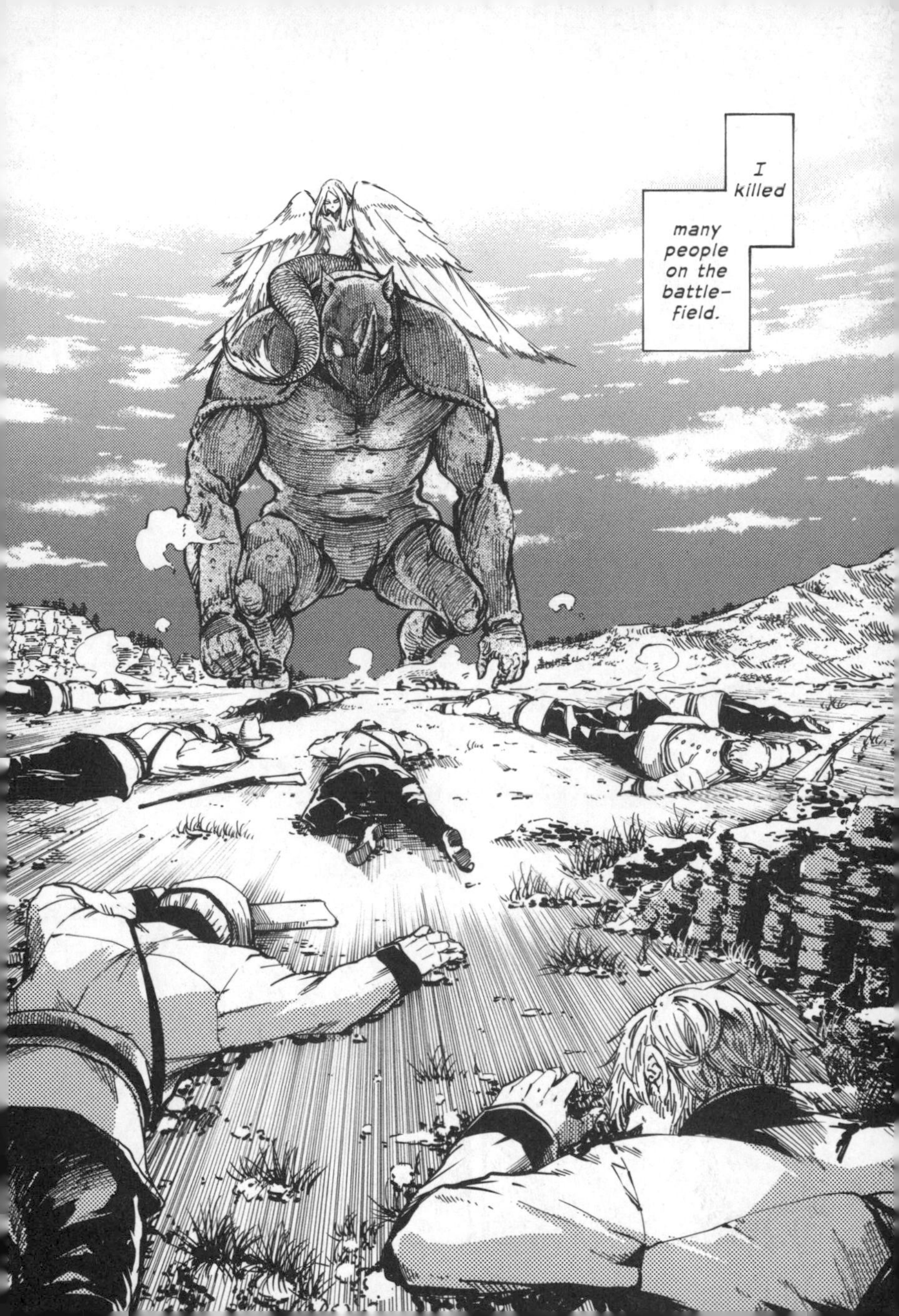
I killed many people on the battle-field.

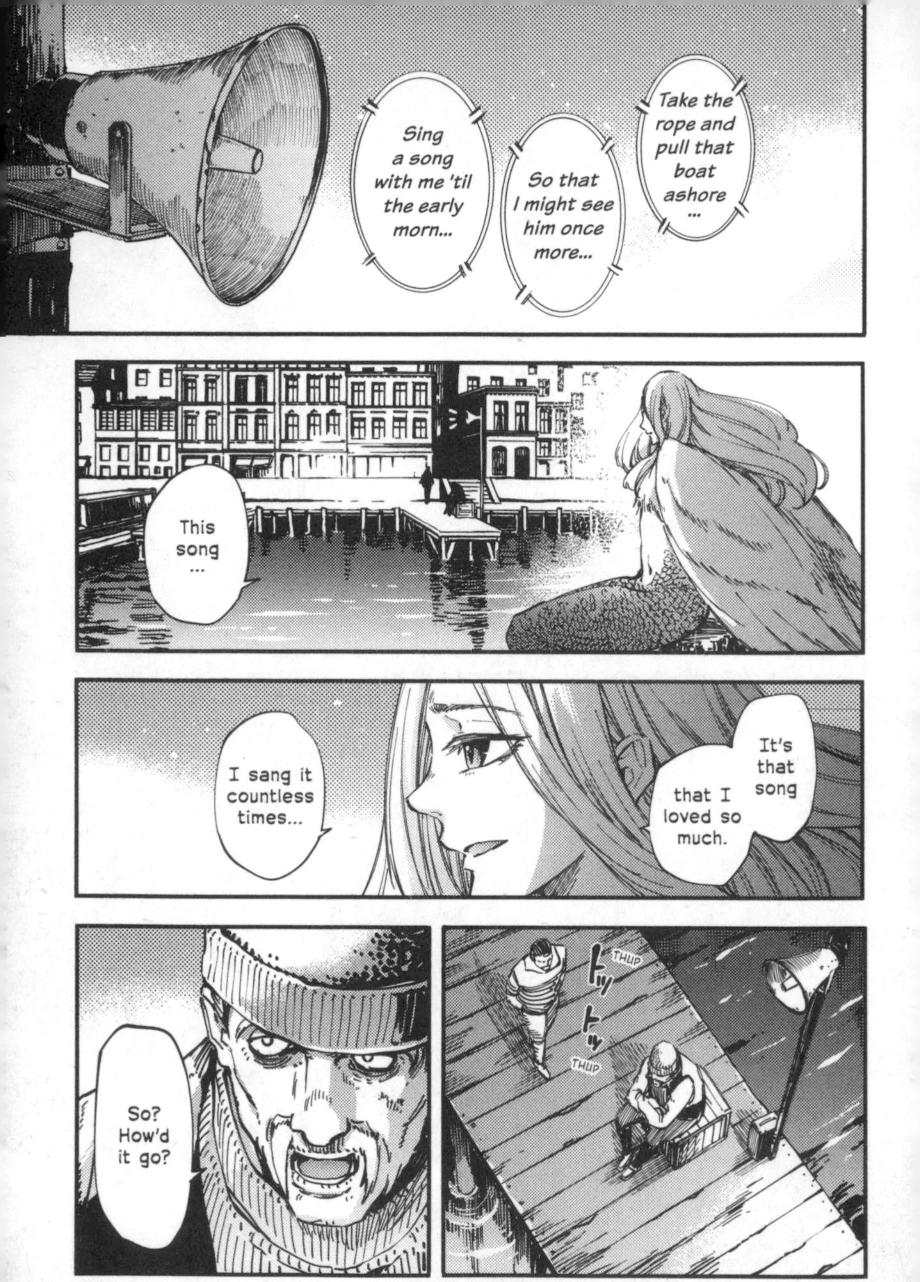
Take the rope and pull that boat ashore ...
So that I might see him once more...
Sing a song with me 'til the early morn...
This song ...
It's that song that I loved so much.
I sang it countless times...
ドッ THUP
ドッ THUP
So? How'd it go?

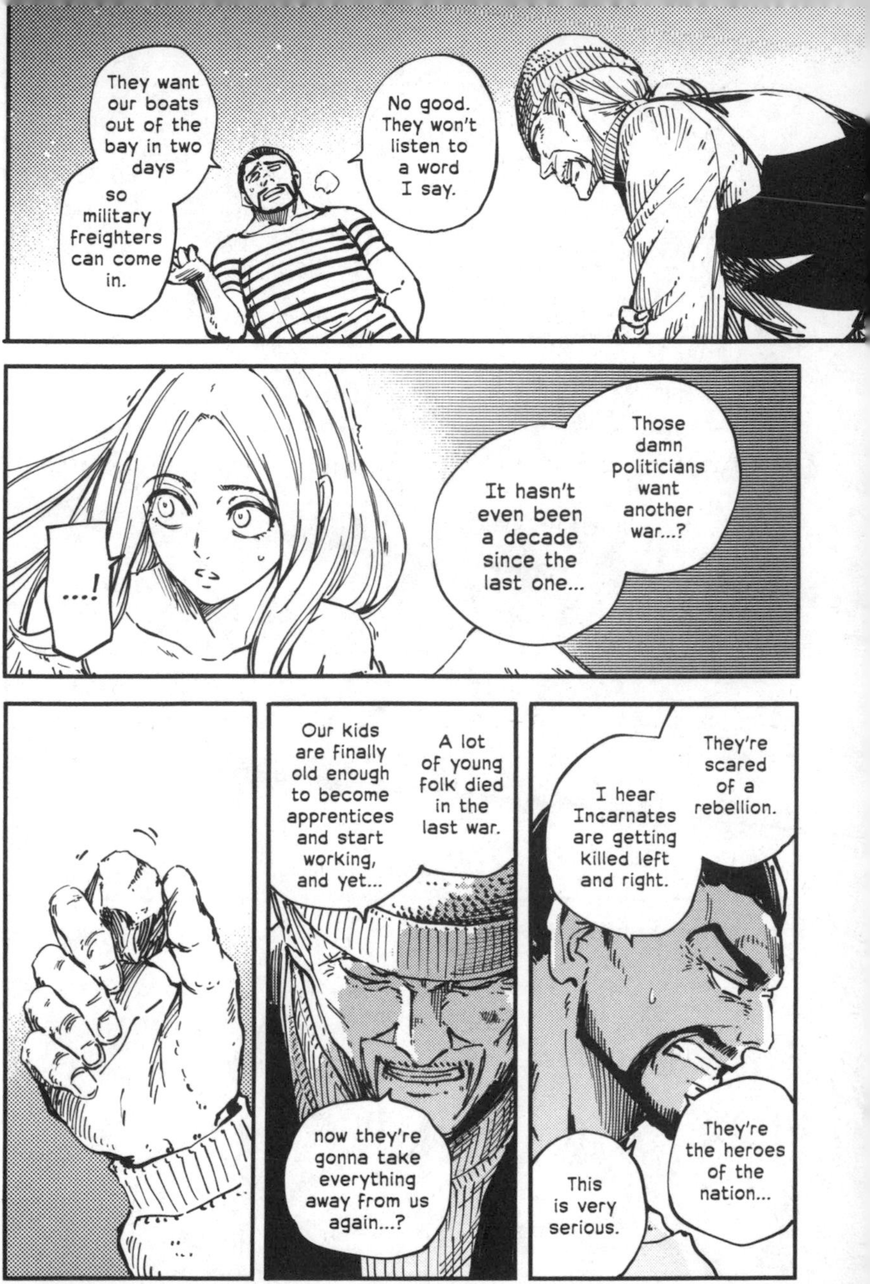
No good. They won't listen to a word I say.
They want our boats out of the bay in two days
so military freighters can come in.
Those damn politicians want another war...?
It hasn't even been a decade since the last one...
...!
They're scared of a rebellion.
I hear Incarnates are getting killed left and right.
They're the heroes of the nation...
This is very serious.
A lot of young folk died in the last war.
Our kids are finally old enough to become apprentices and start working, and yet...
...
now they're gonna take everything away from us again...?
...

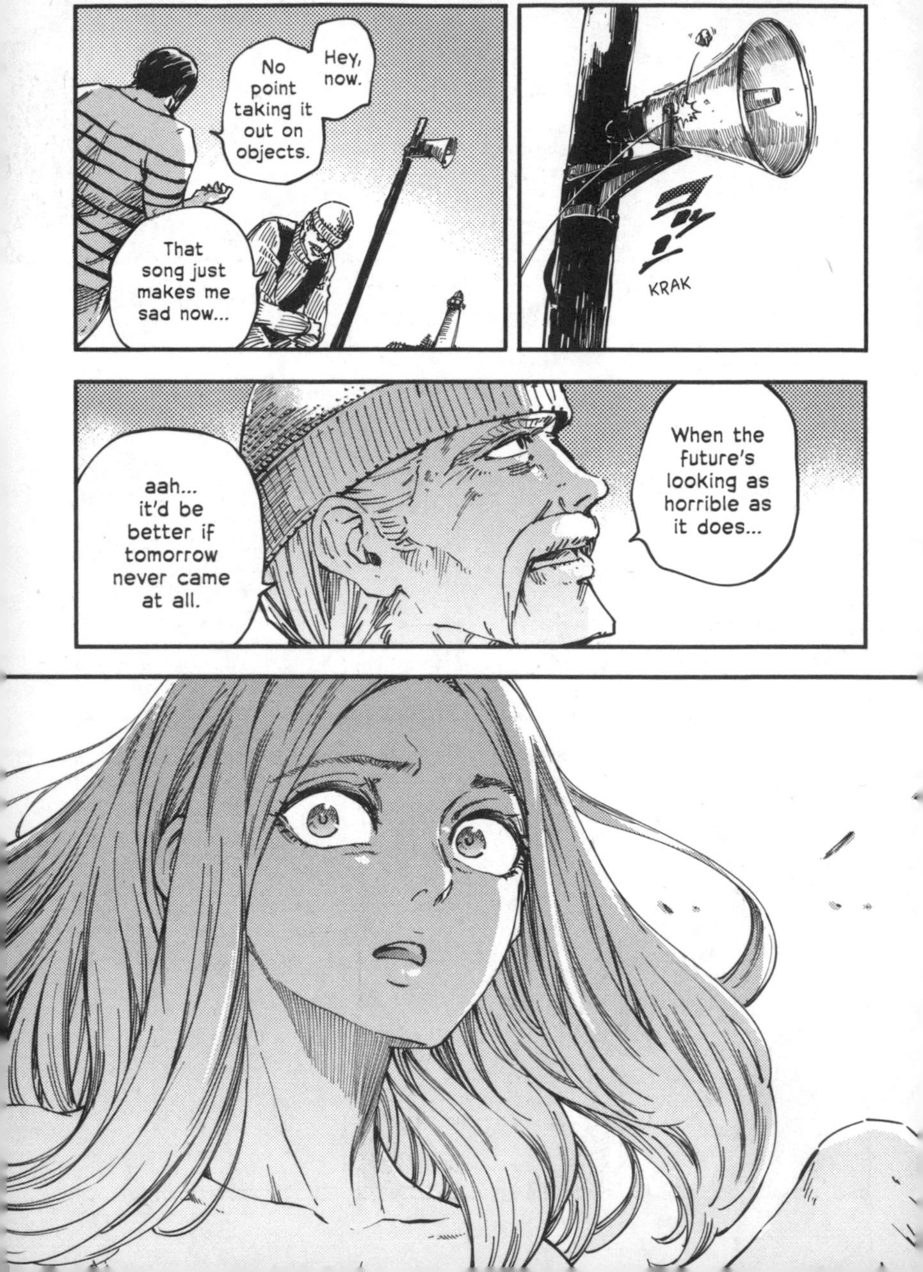
KRAK
Hey, now.
No point taking it out on objects.
That song just makes me sad now...
When the future's looking as horrible as it does...
aah... it'd be better if tomorrow never came at all.

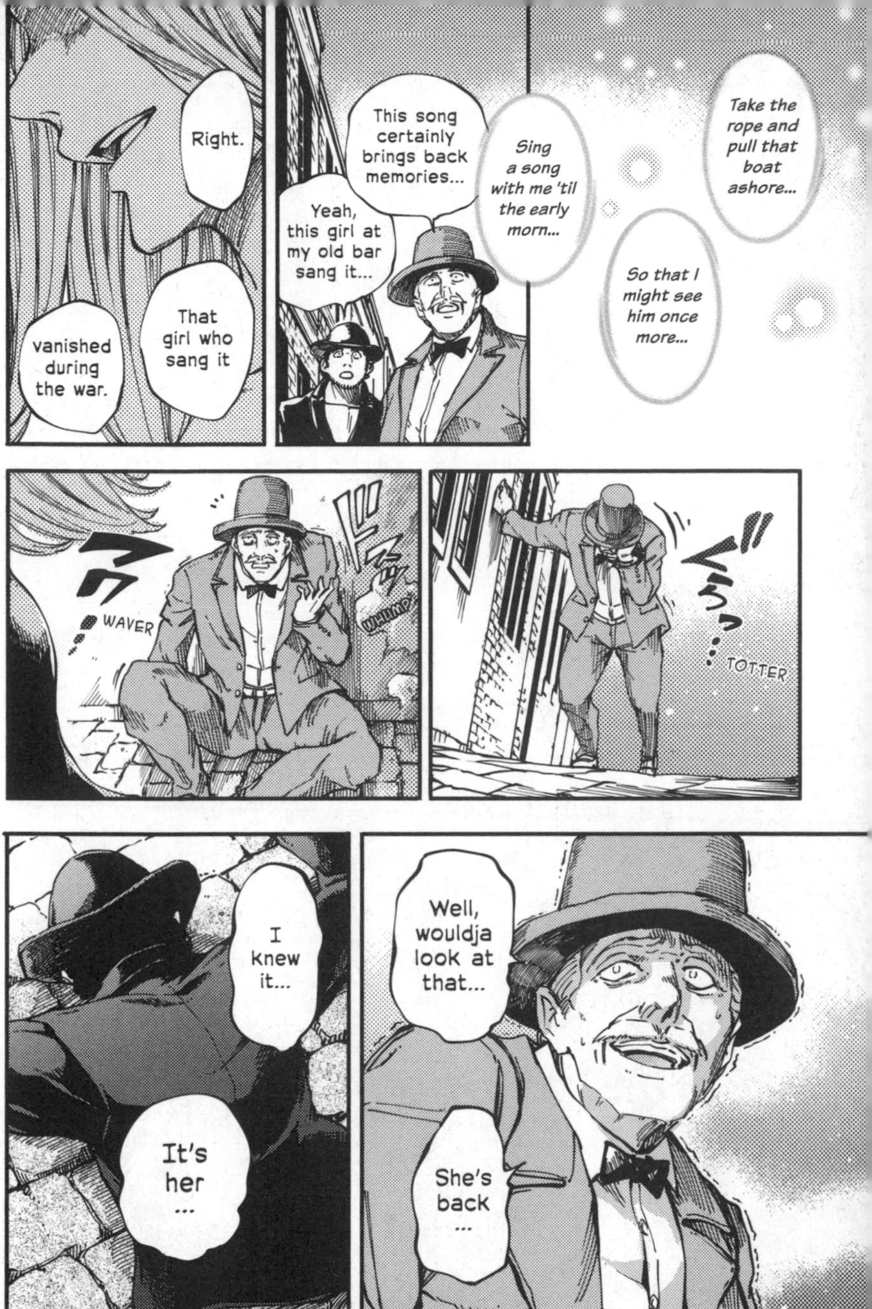
Take the rope and pull that boat ashore...
Sing a song with me 'til the early morn...
So that I might see him once more...
This song certainly brings back memories...
Yeah, this girl at my old bar sang it...
Right.
That girl who sang it
vanished during the war.
TOTTER
WHUMP
WAVER
Well, wouldja look at that...
She's back ...
I knew it...
It's her ...

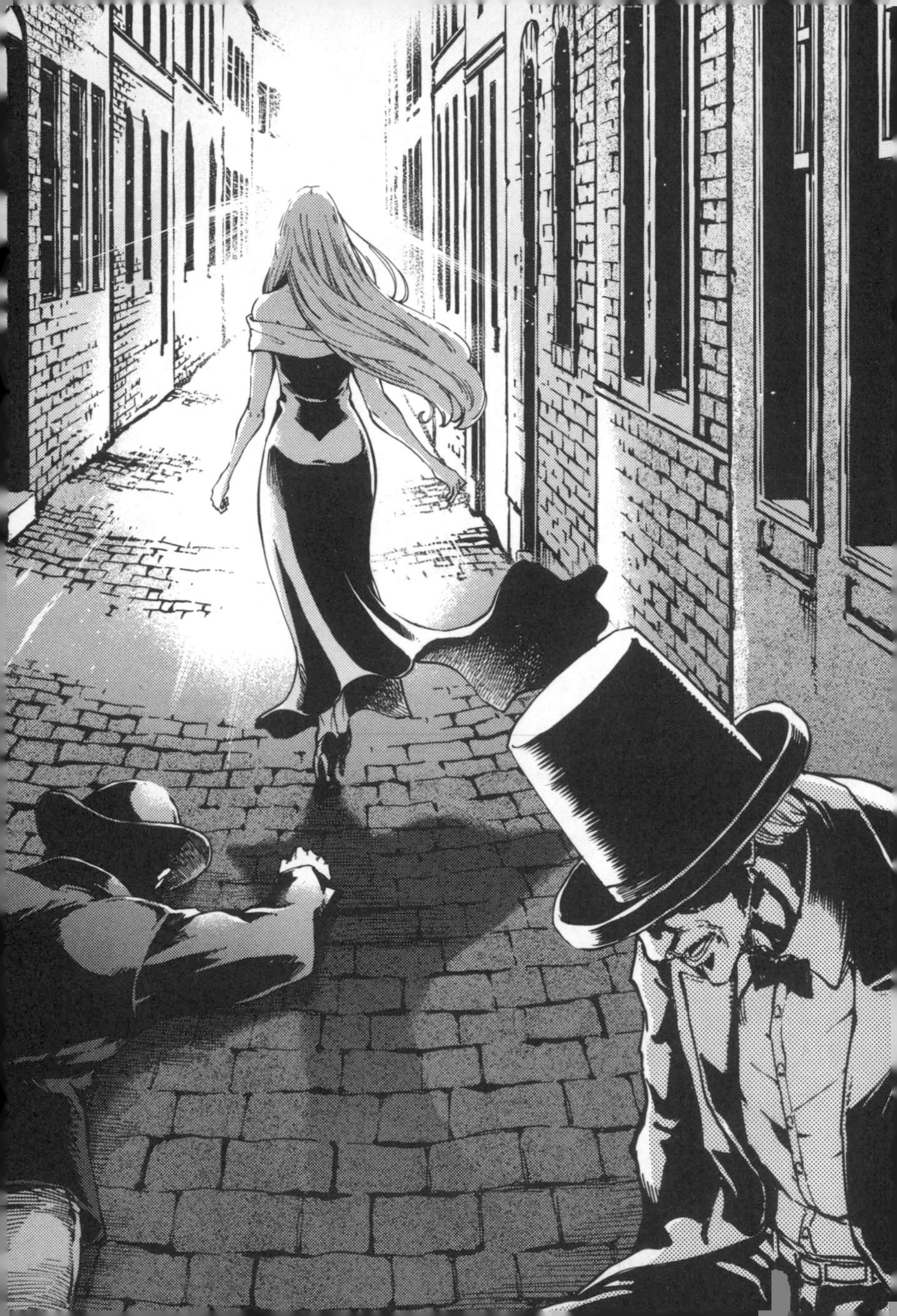

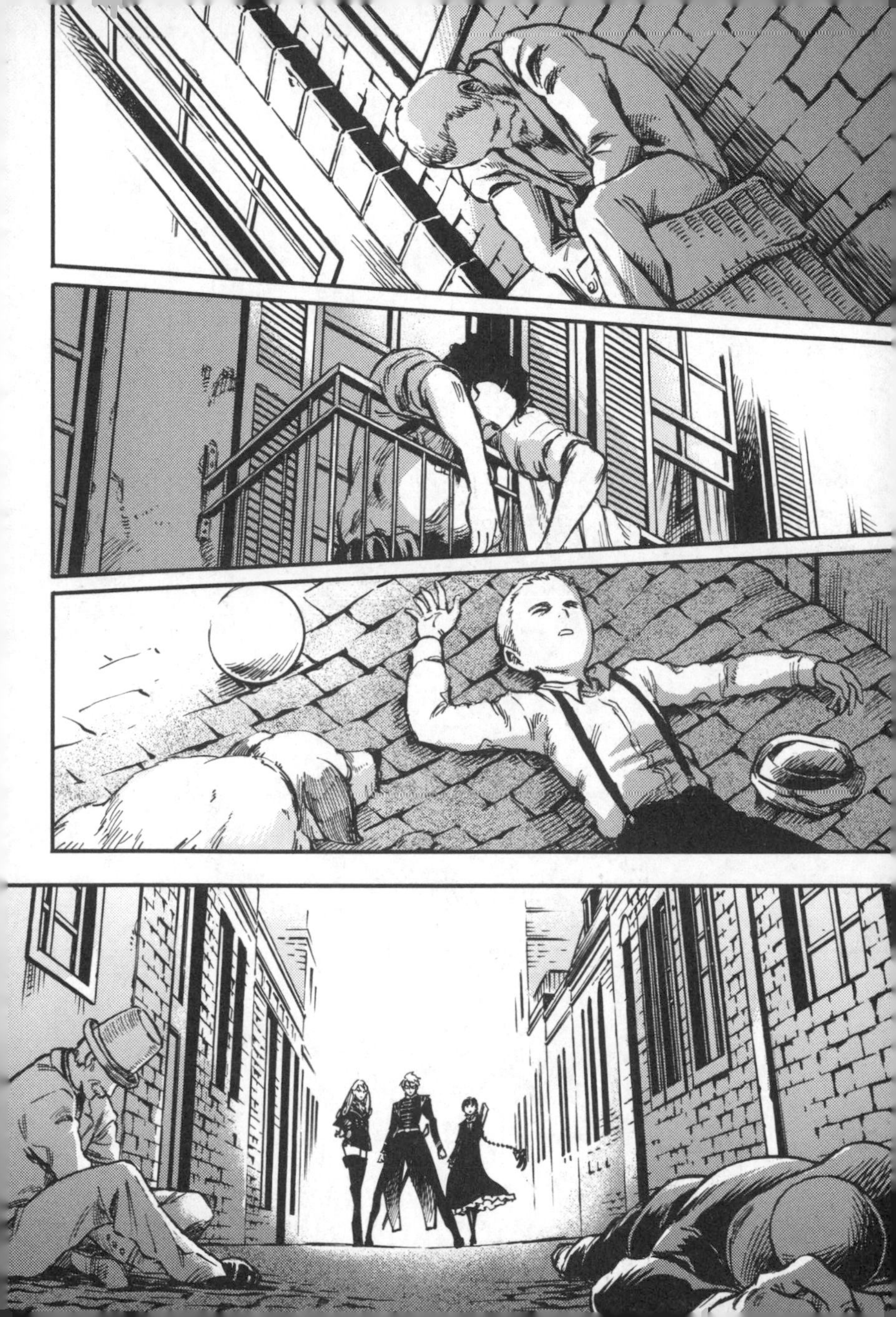

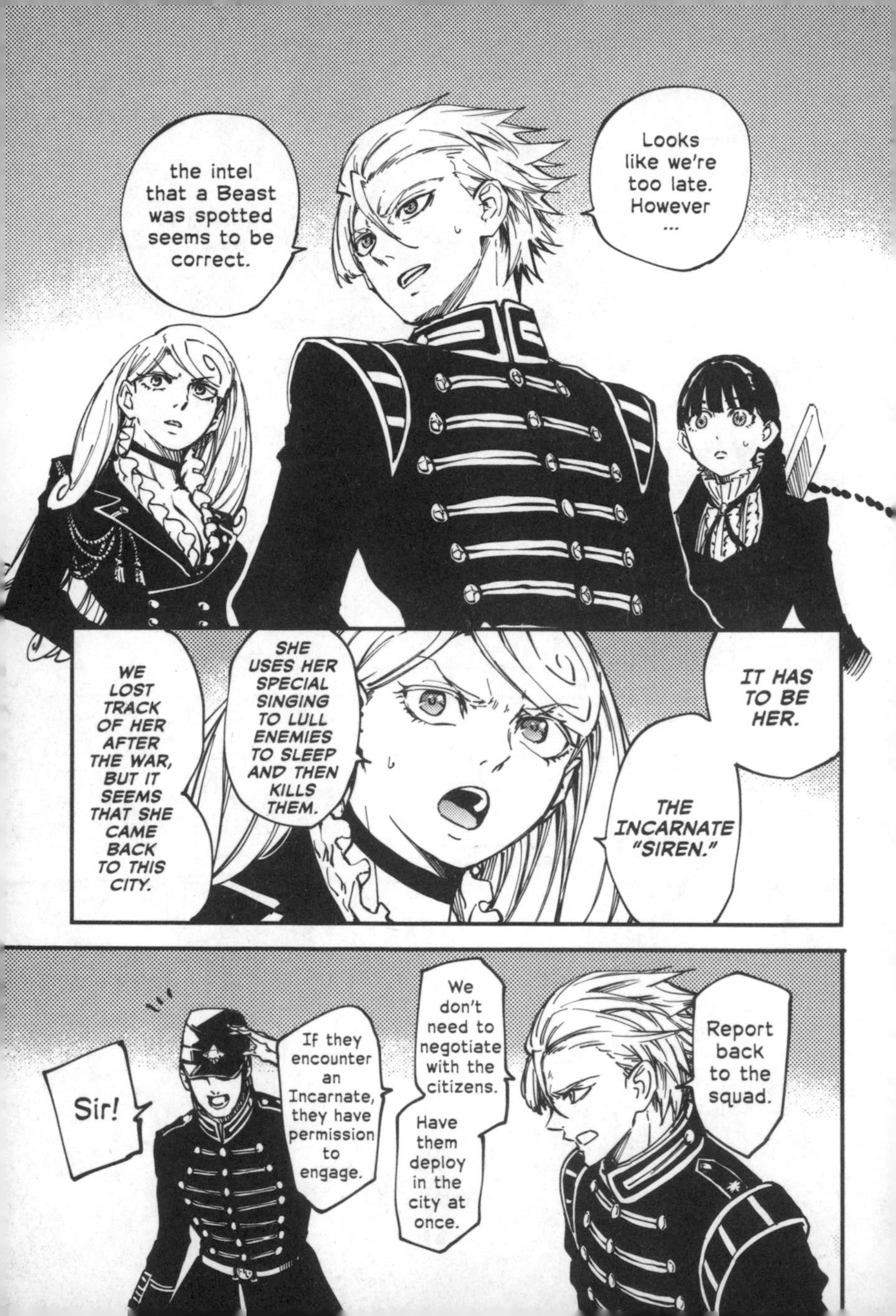
Looks like we're too late. However ...
the intel that a Beast was spotted seems to be correct.
IT HAS TO BE HER.
THE INCARNATE "SIREN."
SHE USES HER SPECIAL SINGING TO LULL ENEMIES TO SLEEP AND THEN KILLS THEM.
WE LOST TRACK OF HER AFTER THE WAR, BUT IT SEEMS THAT SHE CAME BACK TO THIS CITY.
Report back to the squad.
We don't need to negotiate with the citizens.
Have them deploy in the city at once.
If they encounter an Incarnate, they have permission to engage.
Sir!

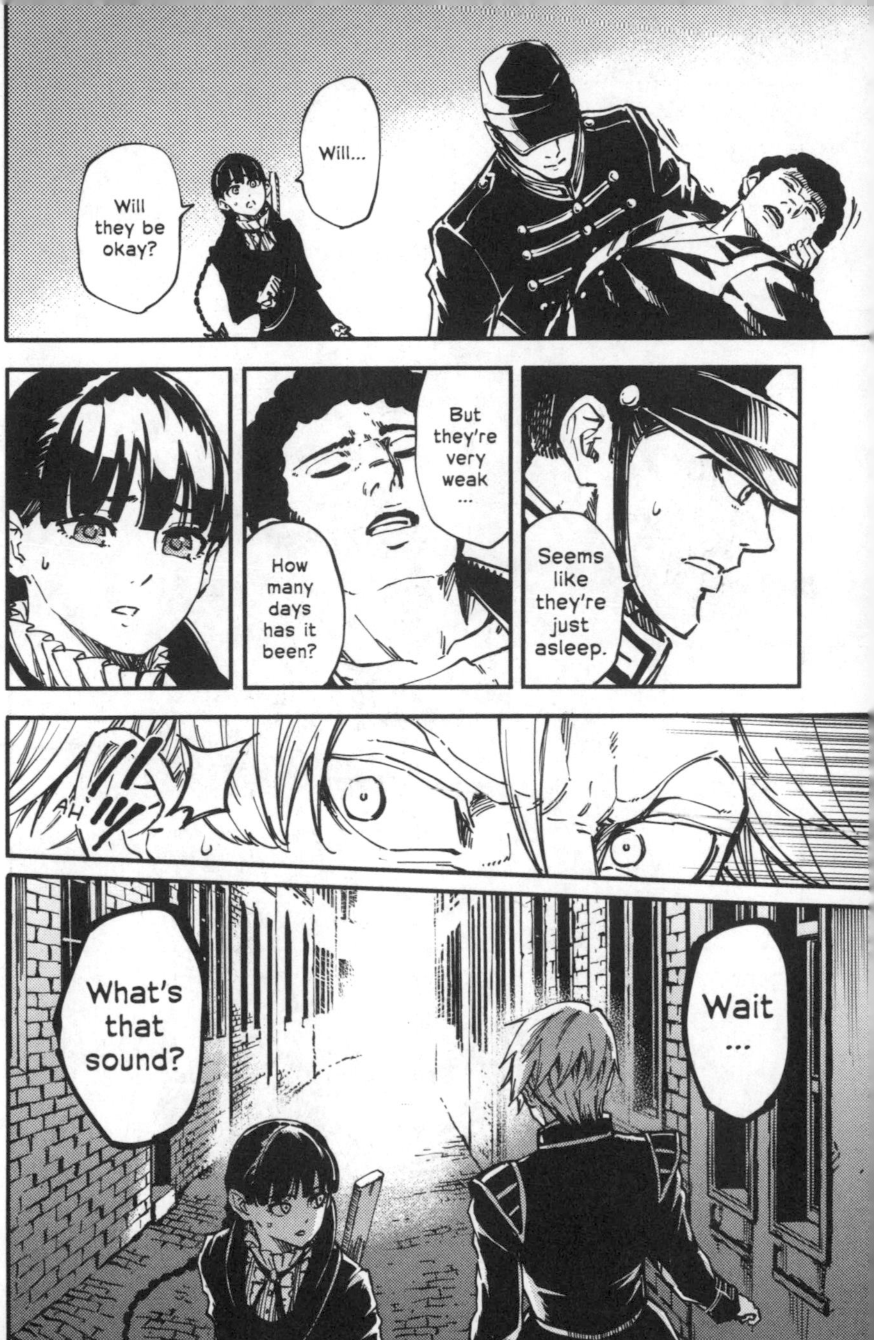
Will...
Will they be okay?
Seems like they're just asleep.
But they're very weak ...
How many days has it been?
AH
Wait ...
What's that sound?

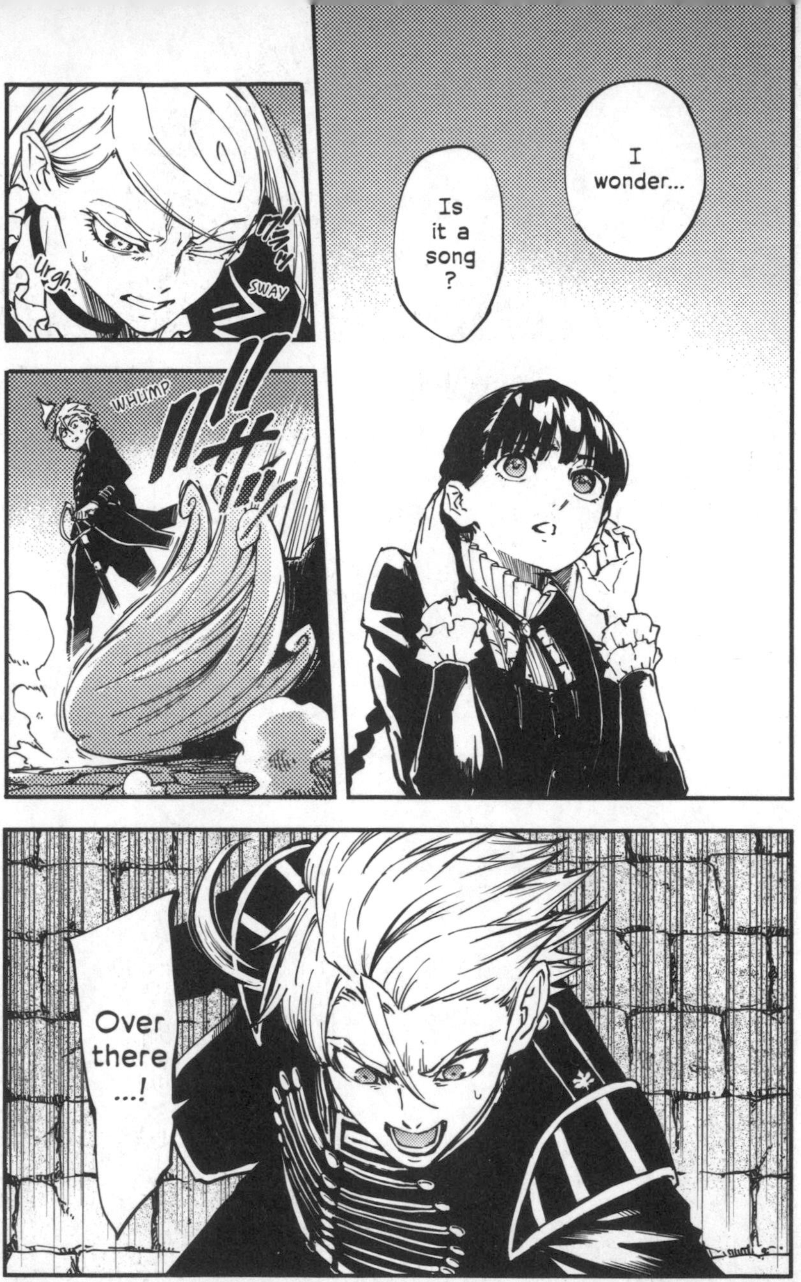
I wonder...
Is it a song?
Urgh...
SWAY
WHUMP
Over there ...!

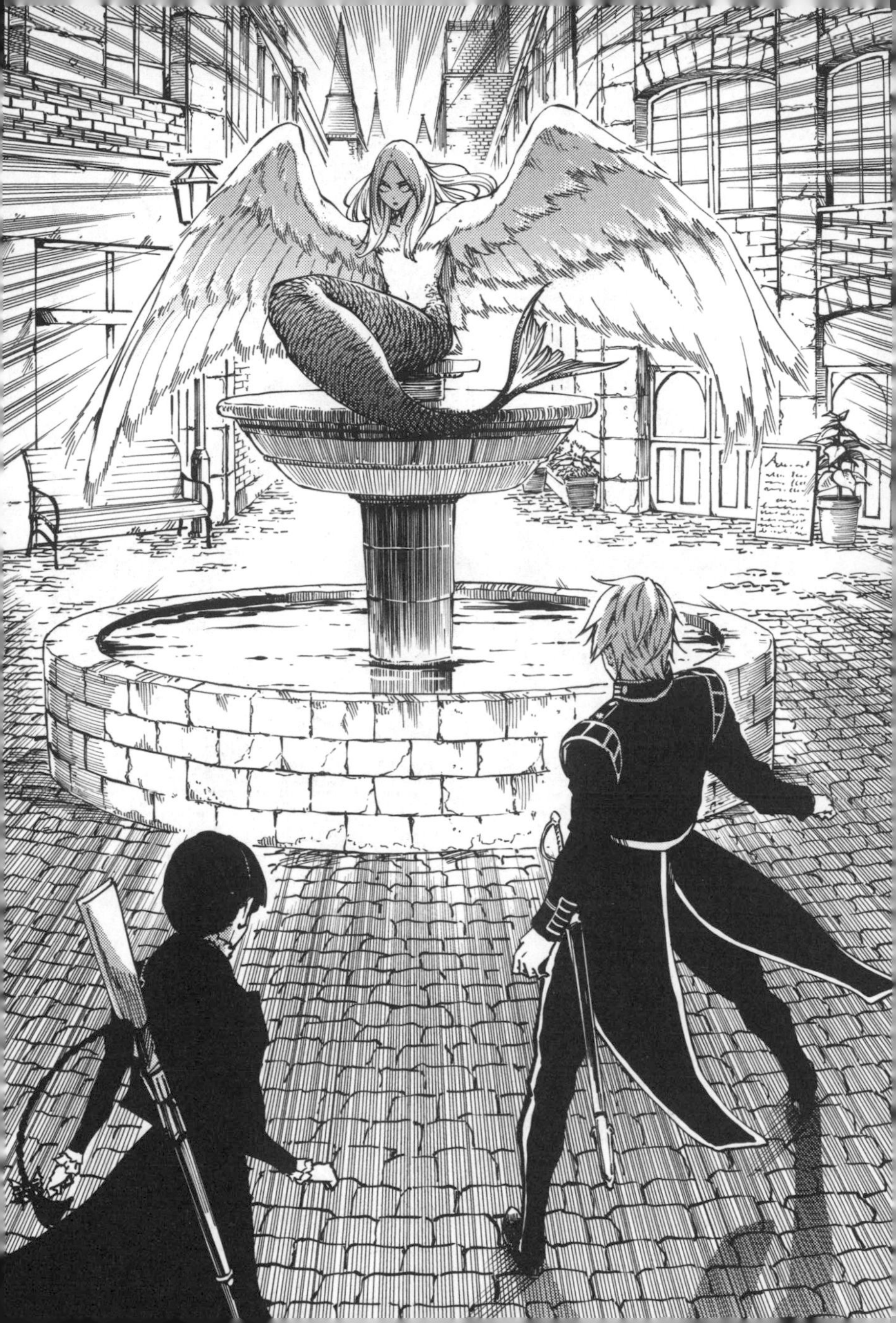

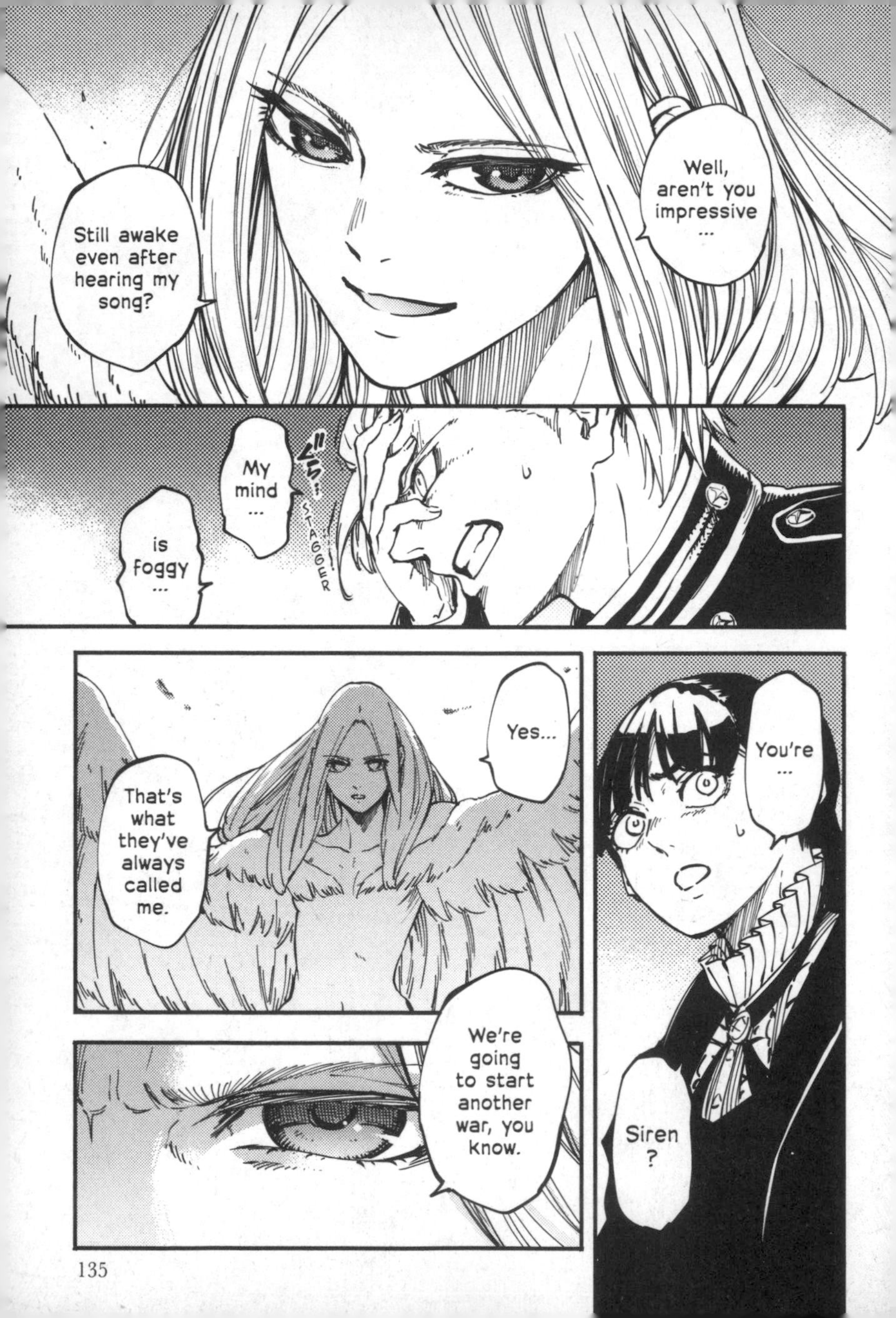
Well, aren't you impressive ...
Still awake even after hearing my song?
My mind ...
STAGGER
is foggy ...
You're ...
Siren ?
Yes...
That's what they've always called me.
We're going to start another war, you know.

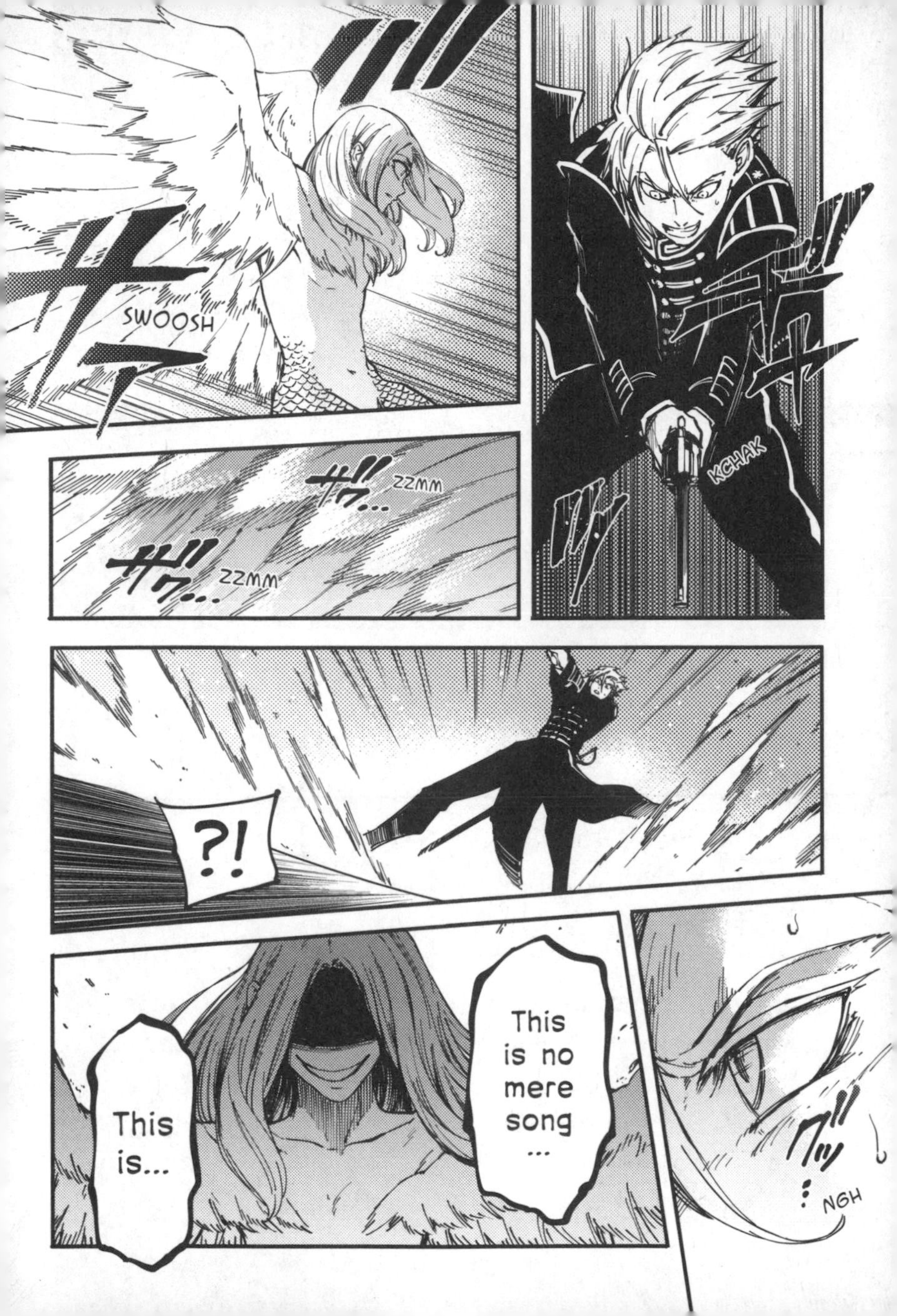
KCHAK
SWOOSH
ZZMM
ZZMM
?!
NGH
This is no mere song...
This is...

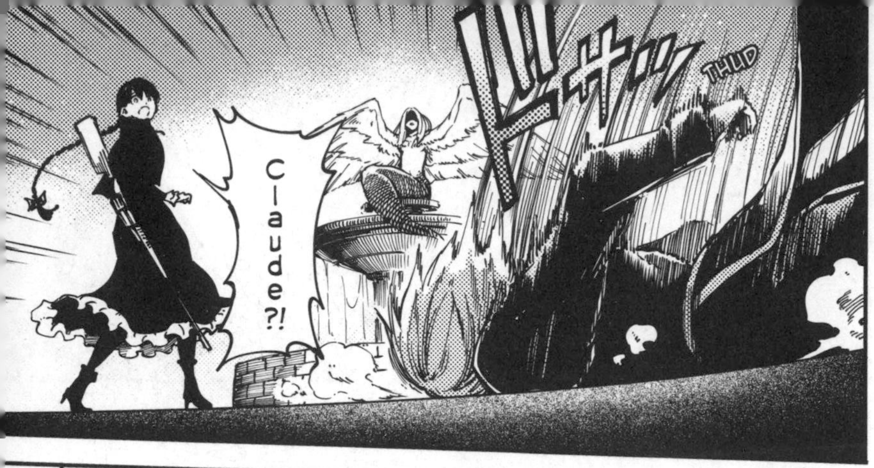
ドサッ
THUD
Claude?!

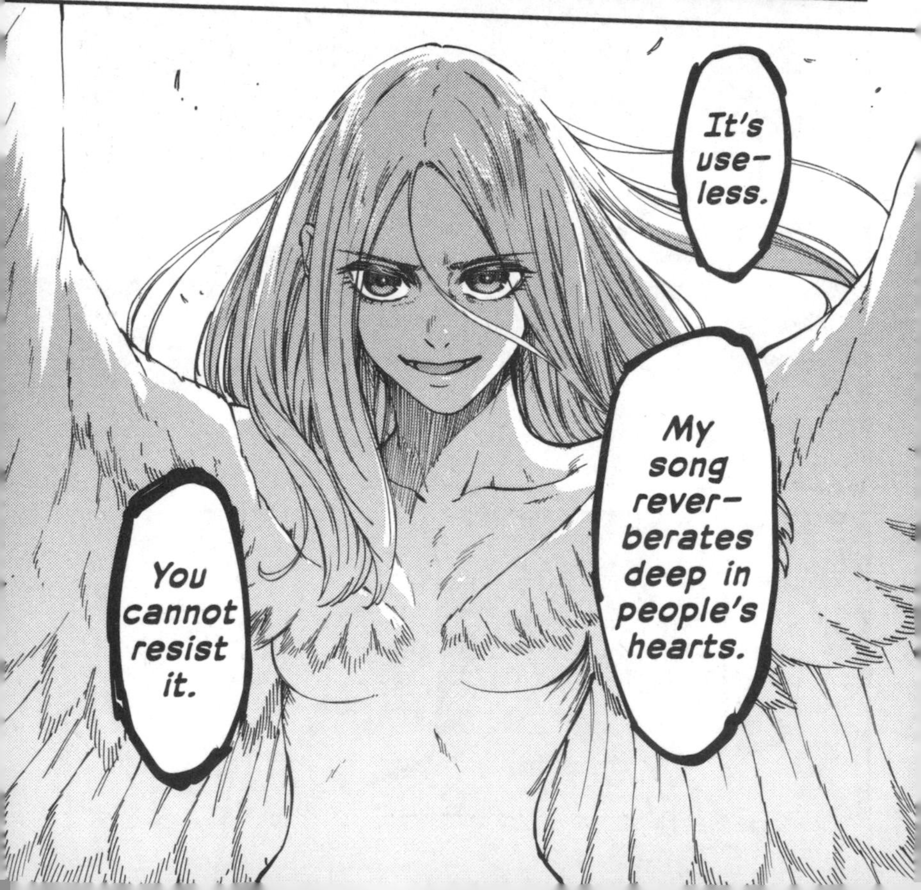
It's use-less.
My song rever-berates deep in people's hearts.
You cannot resist it.

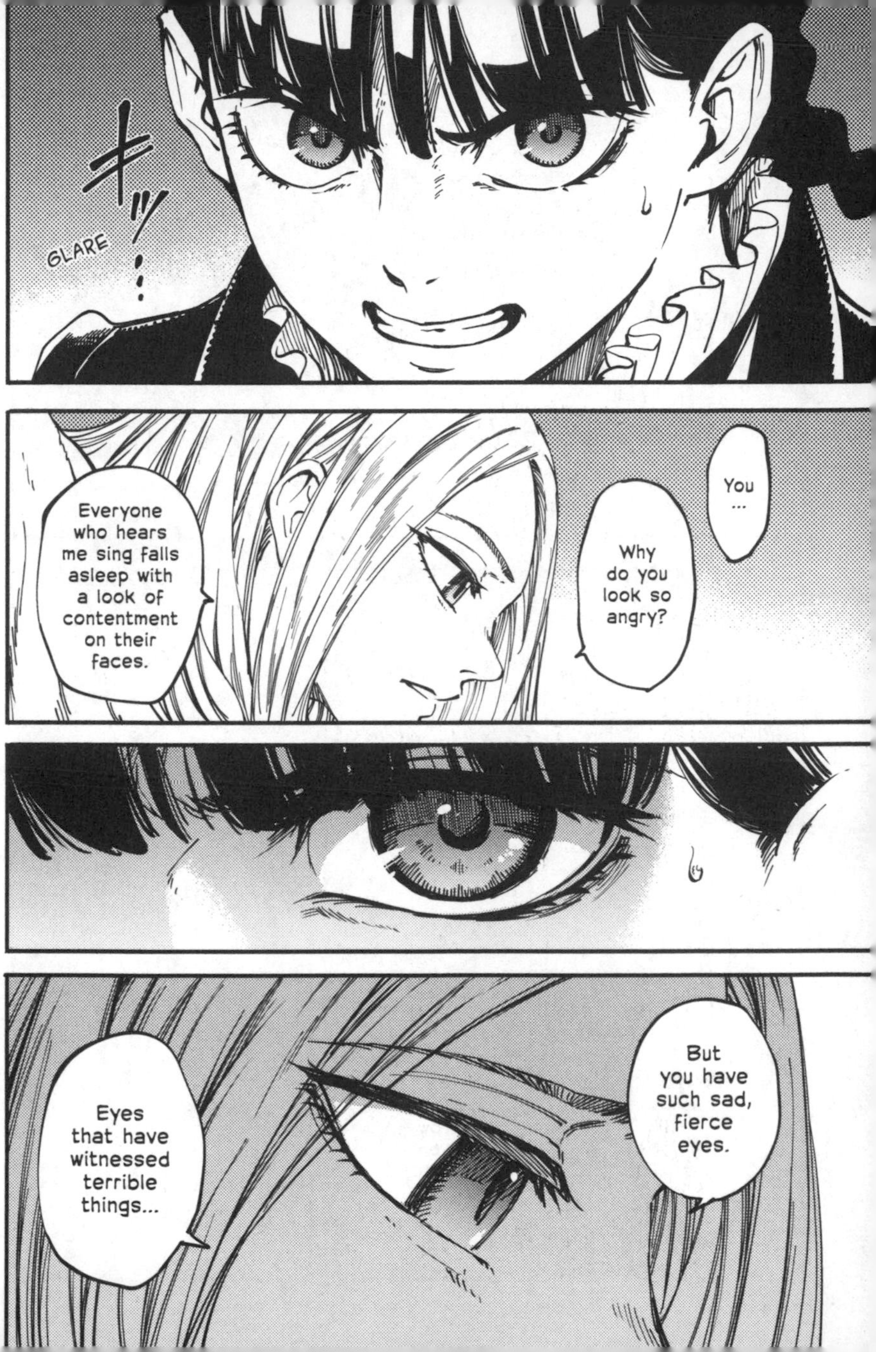

GLARE
You ...
Why do you look so angry?
Everyone who hears me sing falls asleep with a look of contentment on their faces.
But you have such sad, fierce eyes.
Eyes that have witnessed terrible things...

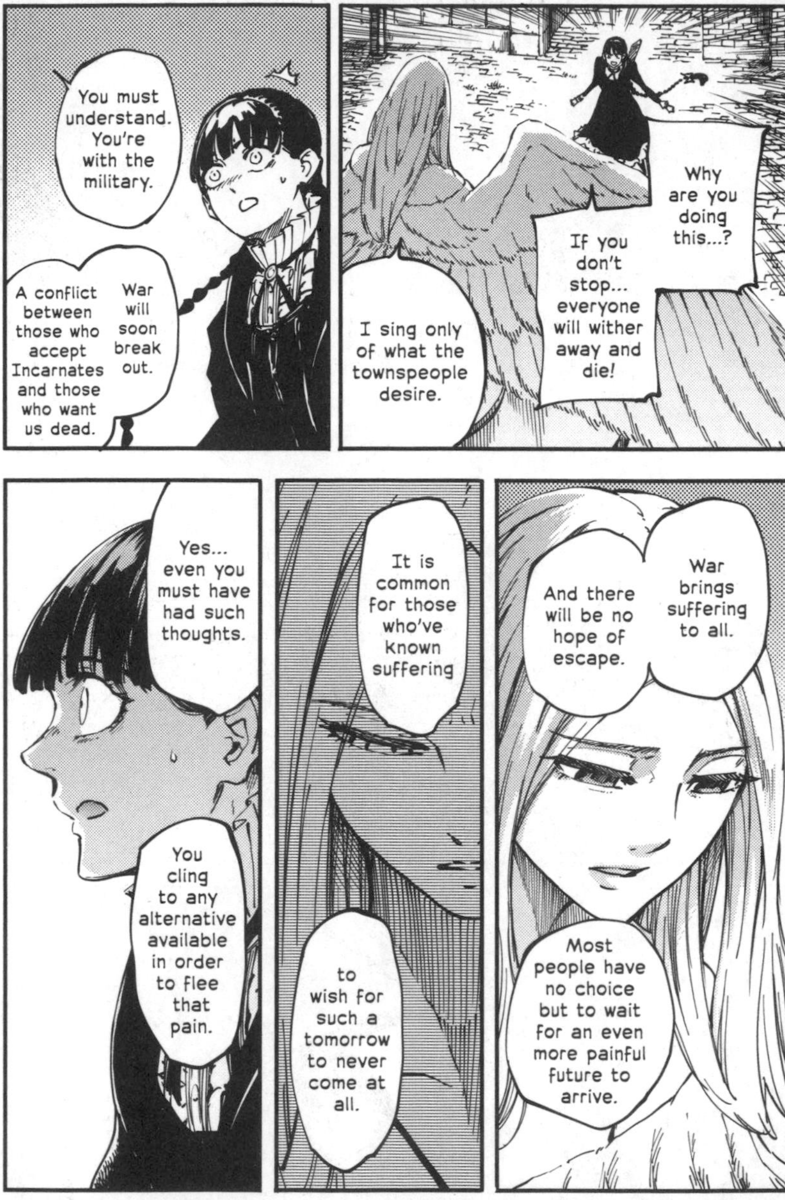

Why are you doing this...?
If you don't stop... everyone will wither away and die!
I sing only of what the townspeople desire.
You must understand. You're with the military.
War will soon break out.
A conflict between those who accept Incarnates and those who want us dead.
War brings suffering to all.
And there will be no hope of escape.
Most people have no choice but to wait for an even more painful future to arrive.
It is common for those who've known suffering
to wish for such a tomorrow to never come at all.
Yes... even you must have had such thoughts.
You cling to any alternative available in order to flee that pain.

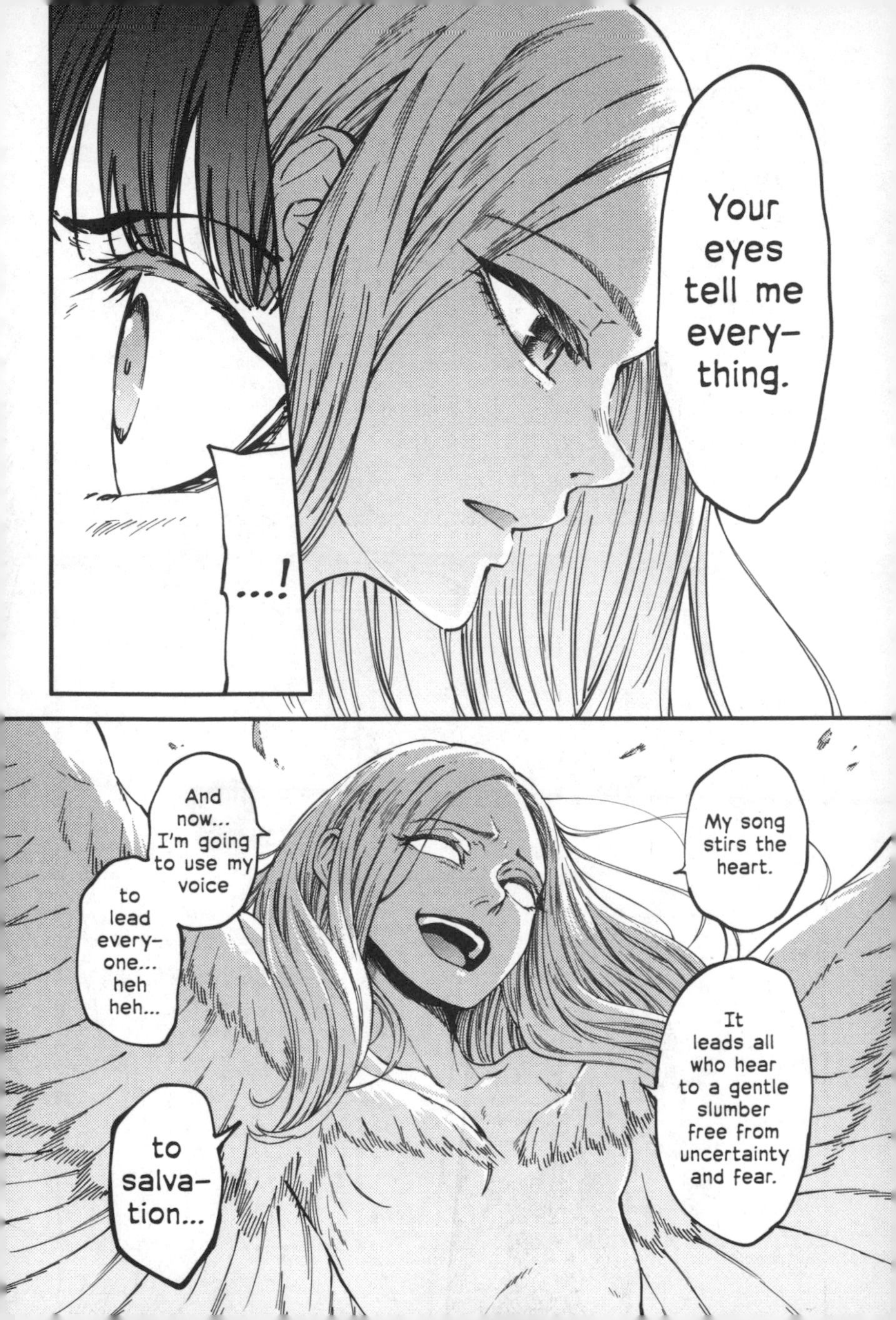
Your eyes tell me every-thing.
...!
My song stirs the heart.
It leads all who hear to a gentle slumber free from uncertainty and fear.
And now... I'm going to use my voice
to lead every-one... heh heh...
to salva-tion...

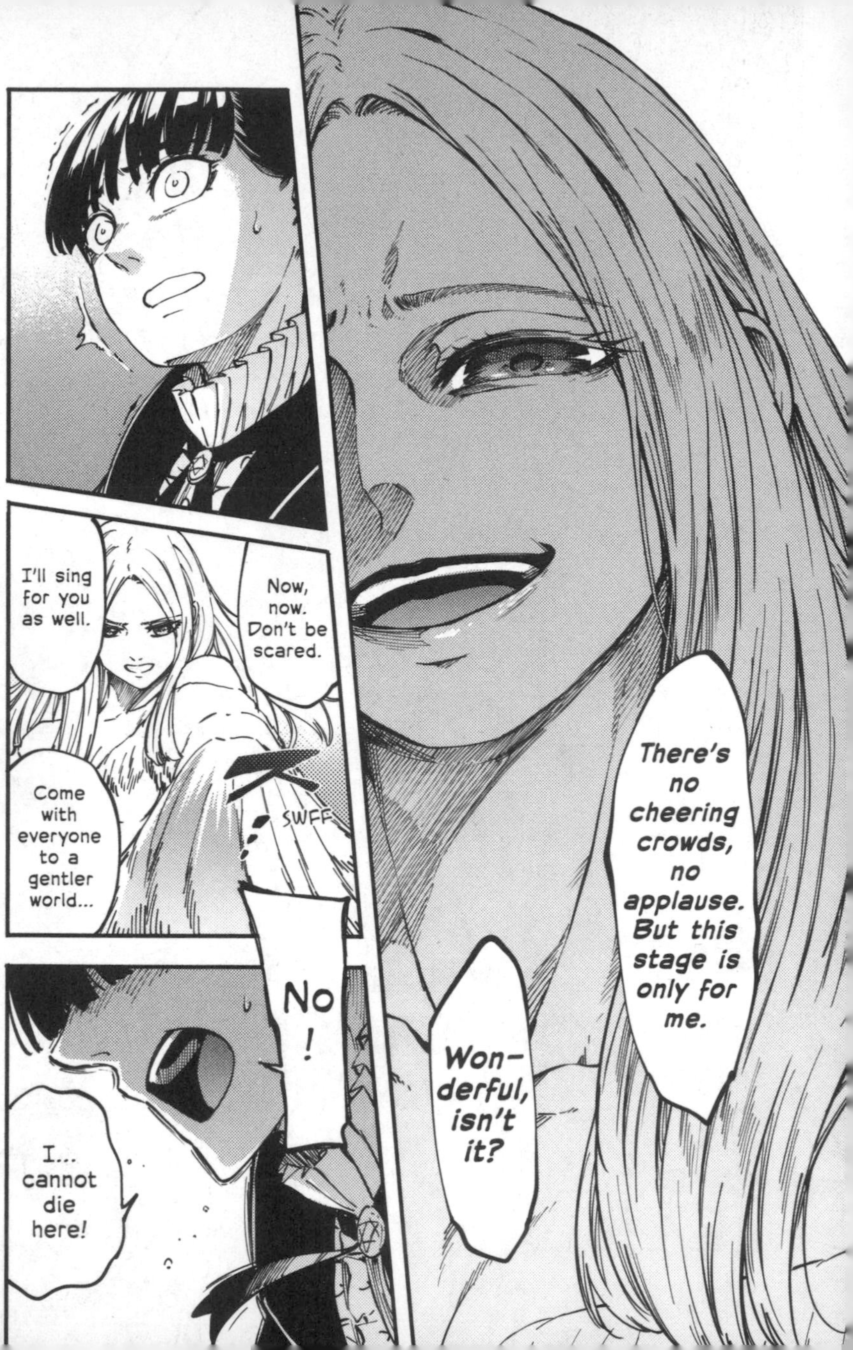
There's no cheering crowds, no applause. But this stage is only for me.
Wonderful, isn't it?
Now, now. Don't be scared.
I'll sing for you as well.
Come with everyone to a gentler world...
SWFF
No!
I... cannot die here!

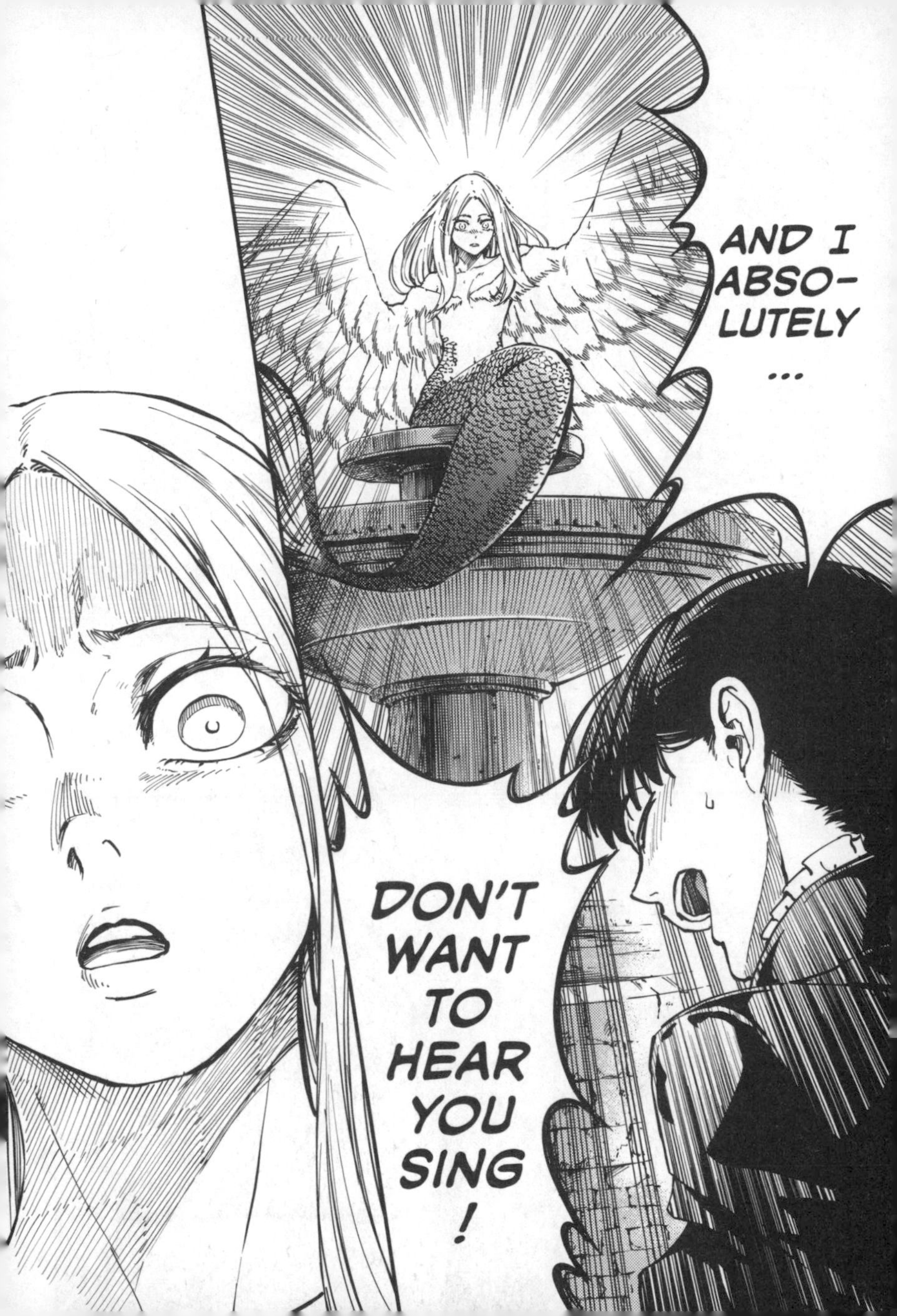
AND I ABSO-LUTELY ...
DON'T WANT TO HEAR YOU SING !

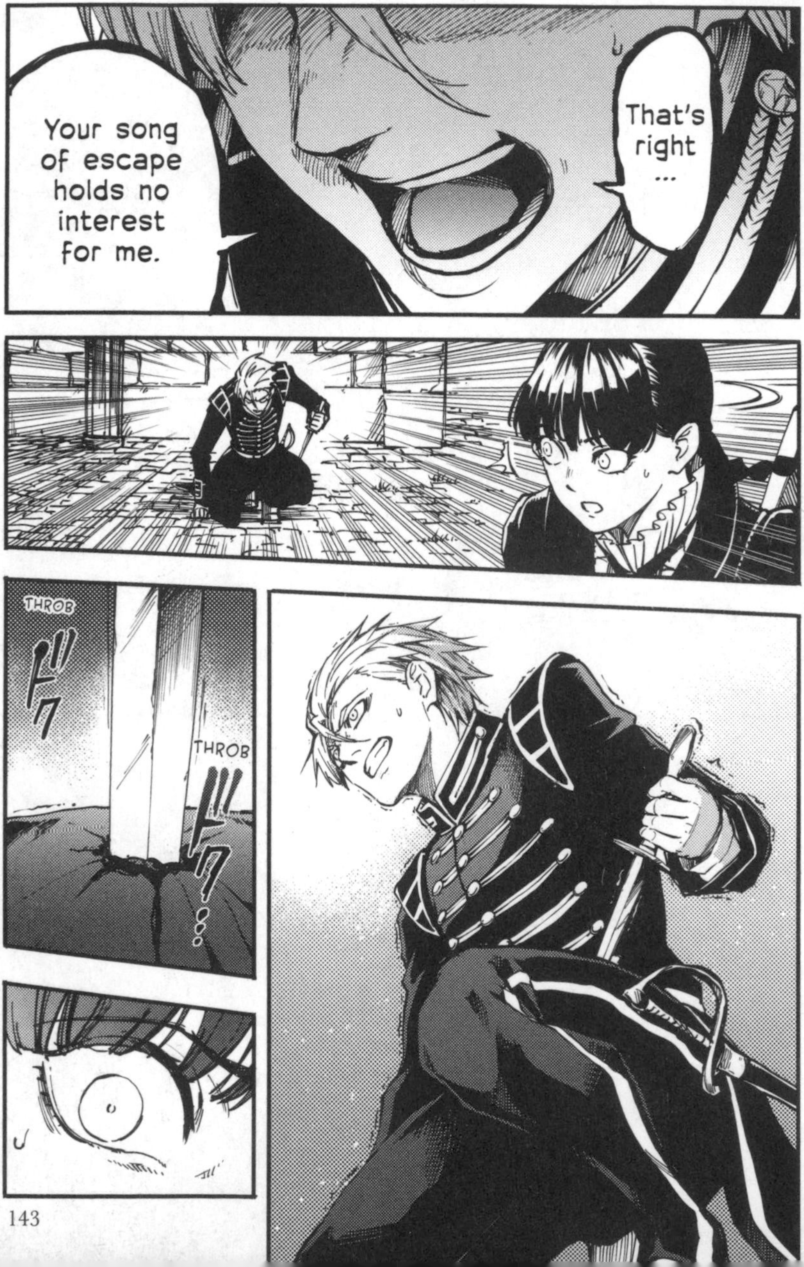
That's right ...
Your song of escape holds no interest for me.
THROB
ドク
THROB
ドク…

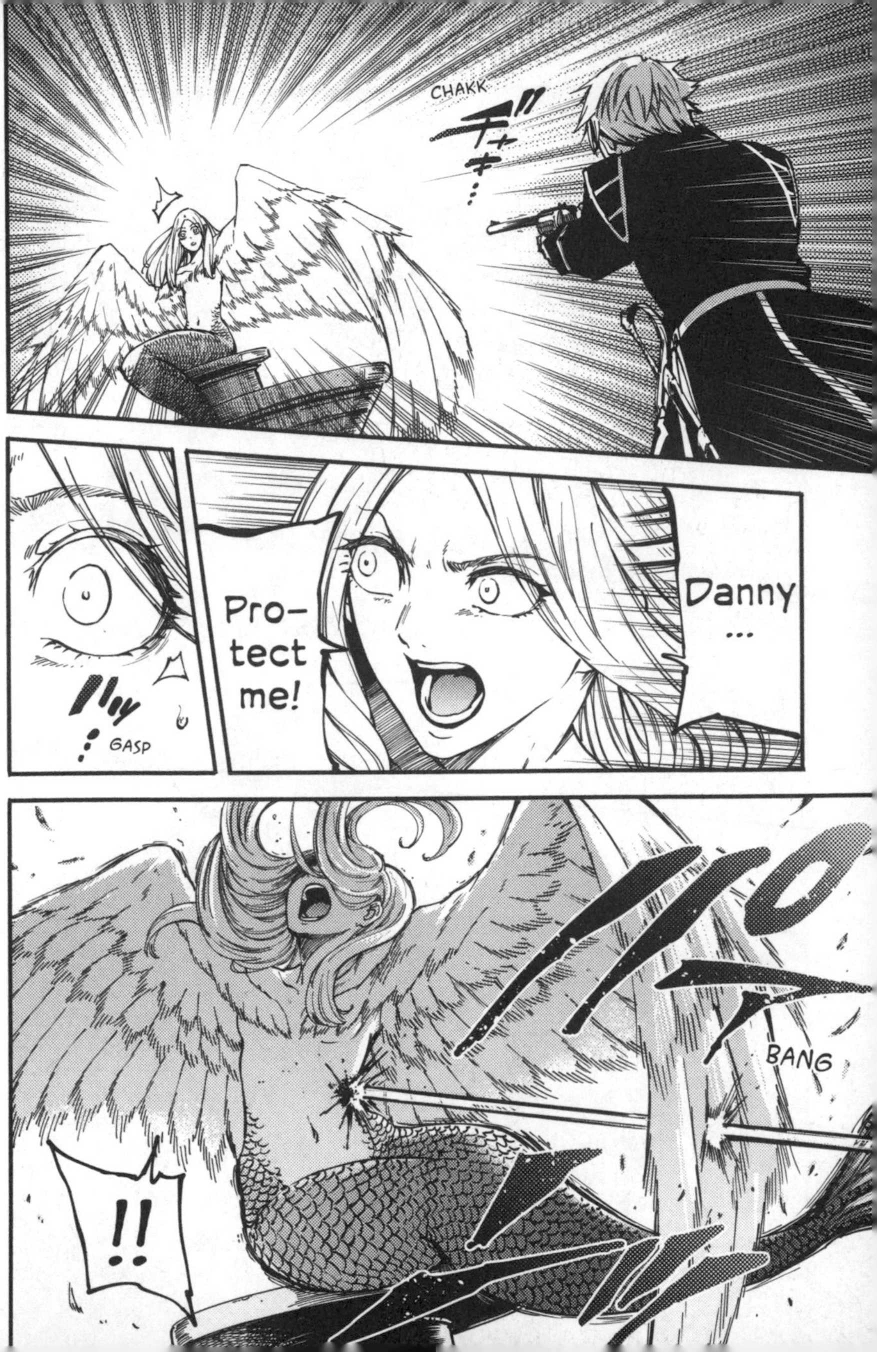
CHAKK
Danny ...
Pro-tect me!
GASP
BANG
!!

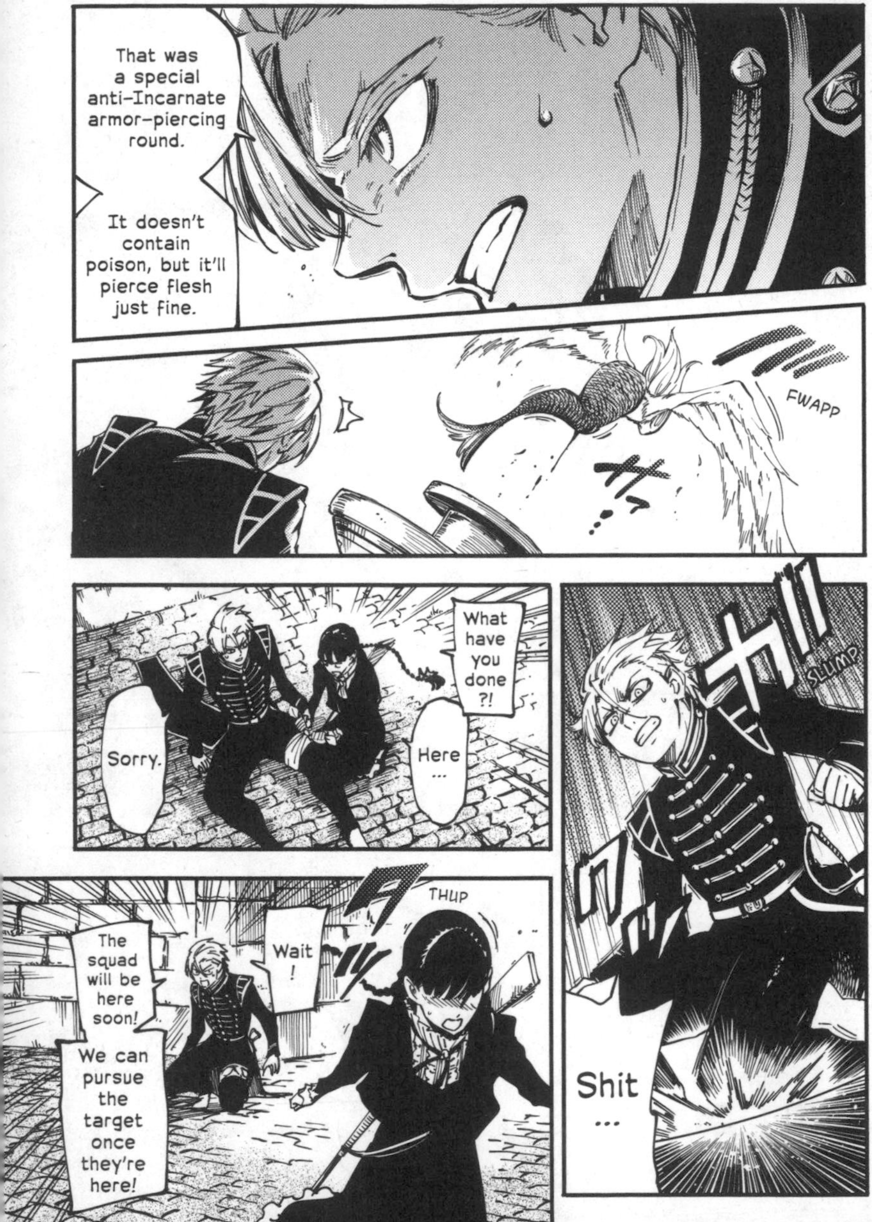
That was a special anti-Incarnate armor-piercing round.
It doesn't contain poison, but it'll pierce flesh just fine.
FWAPP
SLUMP
Shit ...
What have you done?!
Here ...
Sorry.
THUP
Wait!
The squad will be here soon!
We can pursue the target once they're here!

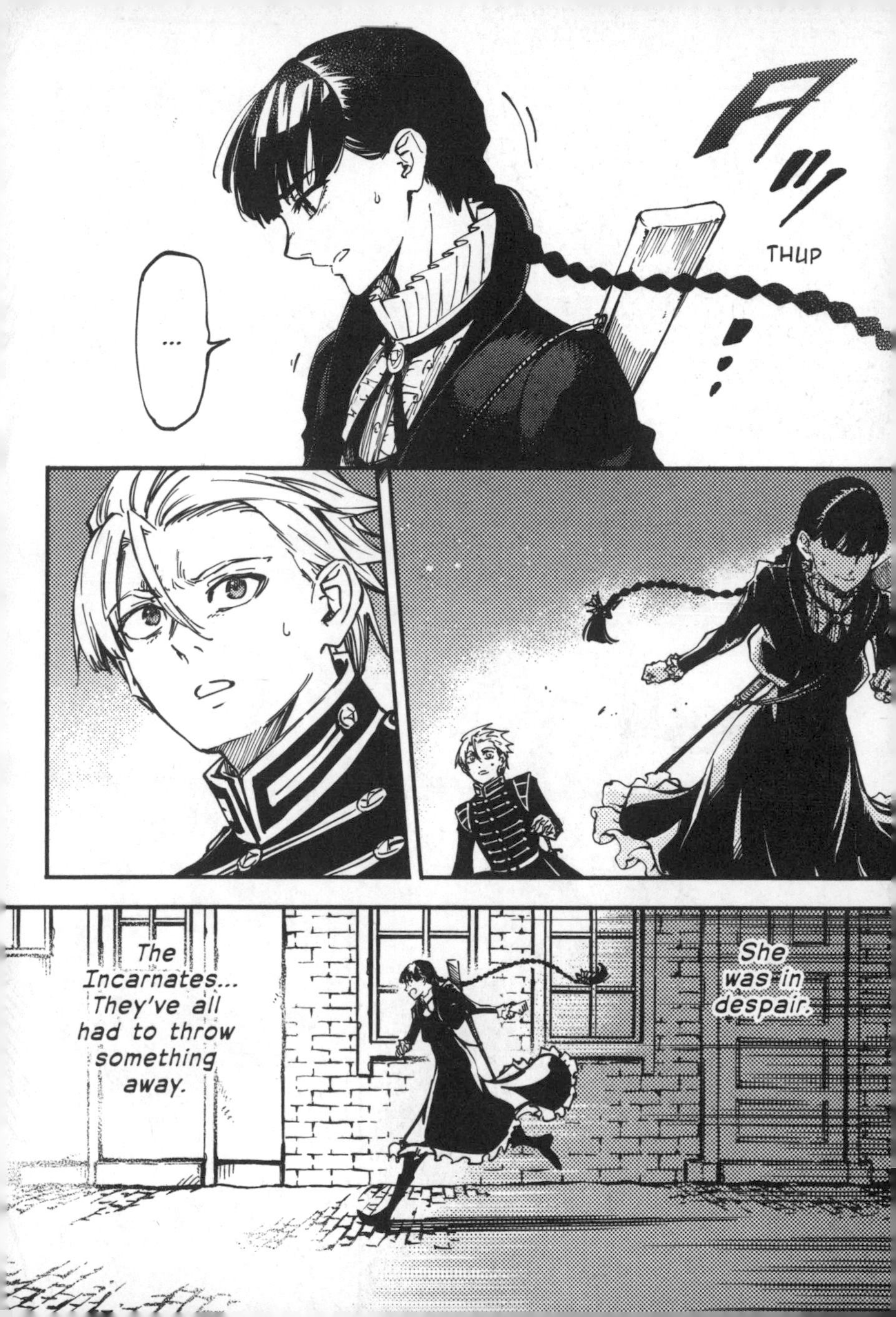
THUP
...
She was in despair.
The Incarnates... They've all had to throw something away.

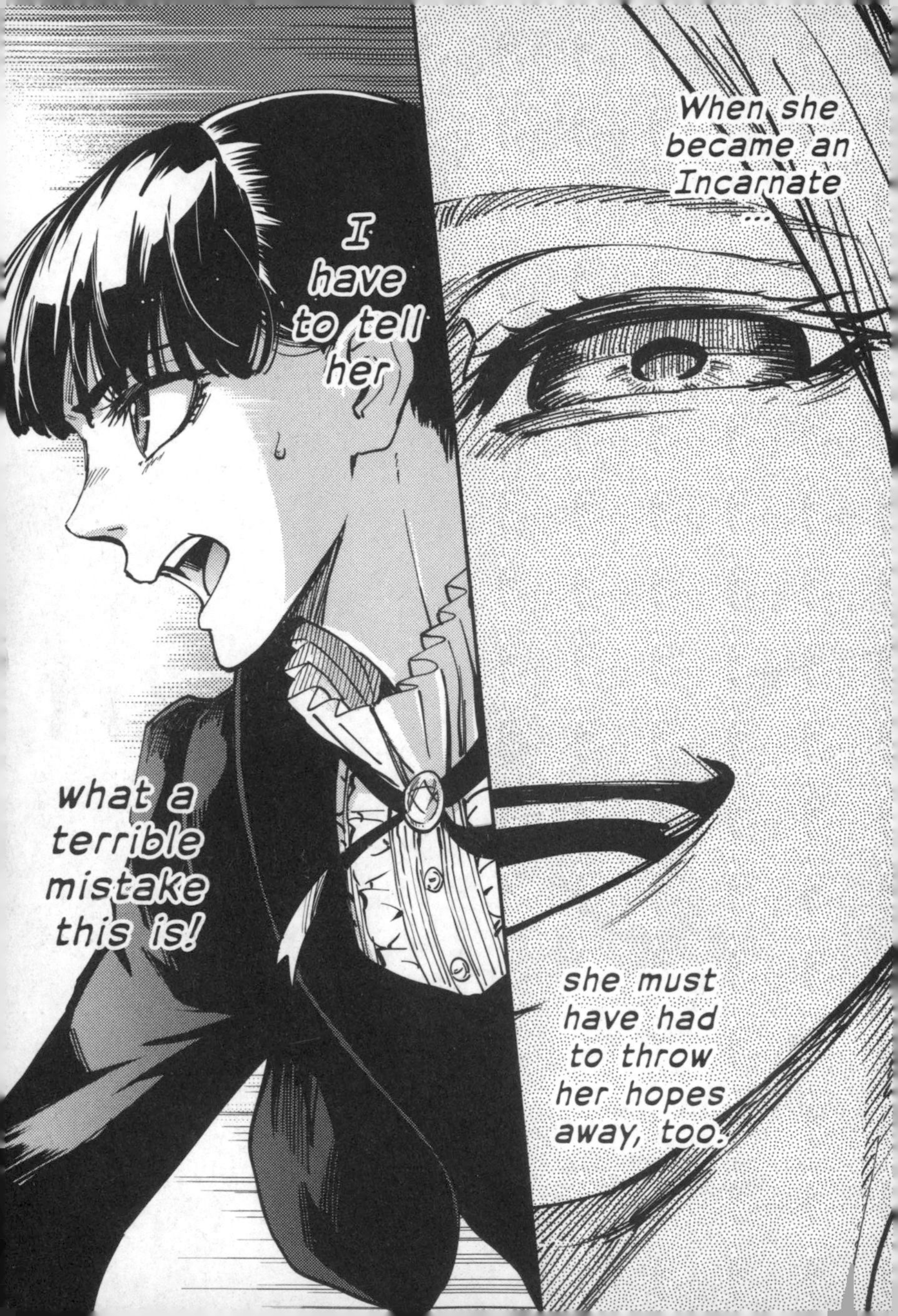
When she became an Incarnate ...
I have to tell her
what a terrible mistake this is!
she must have had to throw her hopes away, too.

To the Abandoned
Sacred Beasts

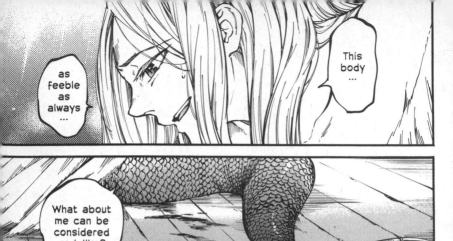

This body...

as feeble as always...

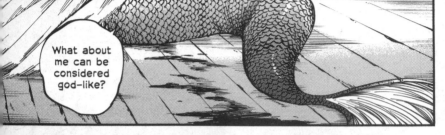

What about me can be considered god-like?

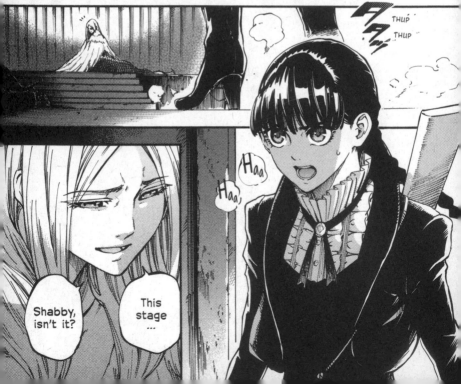

THUP THUP

Haa

Haa

Shabby, isn't it?

This stage...

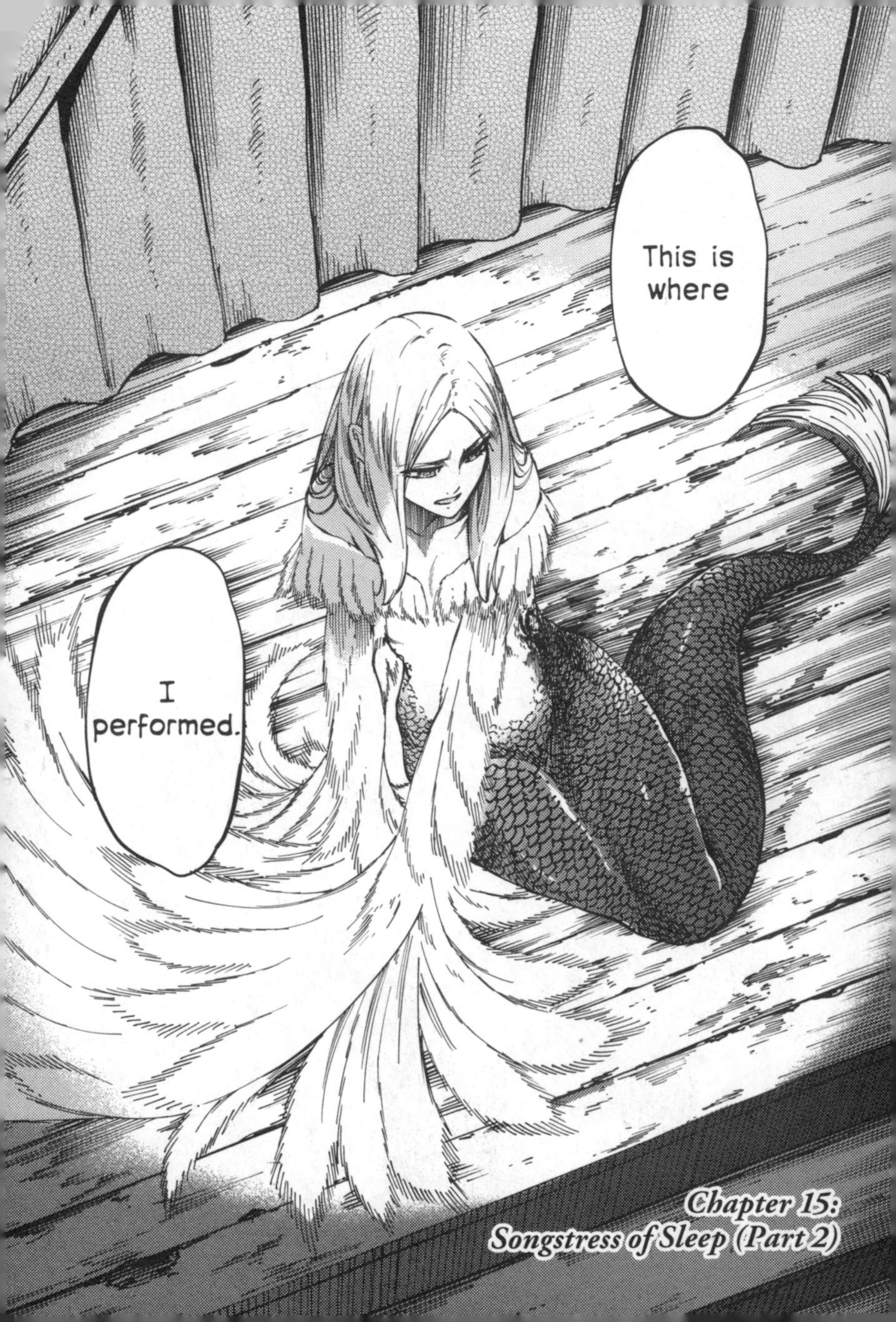
This is where
I performed.
Chapter 15:
Songstress of Sleep (Part 2)

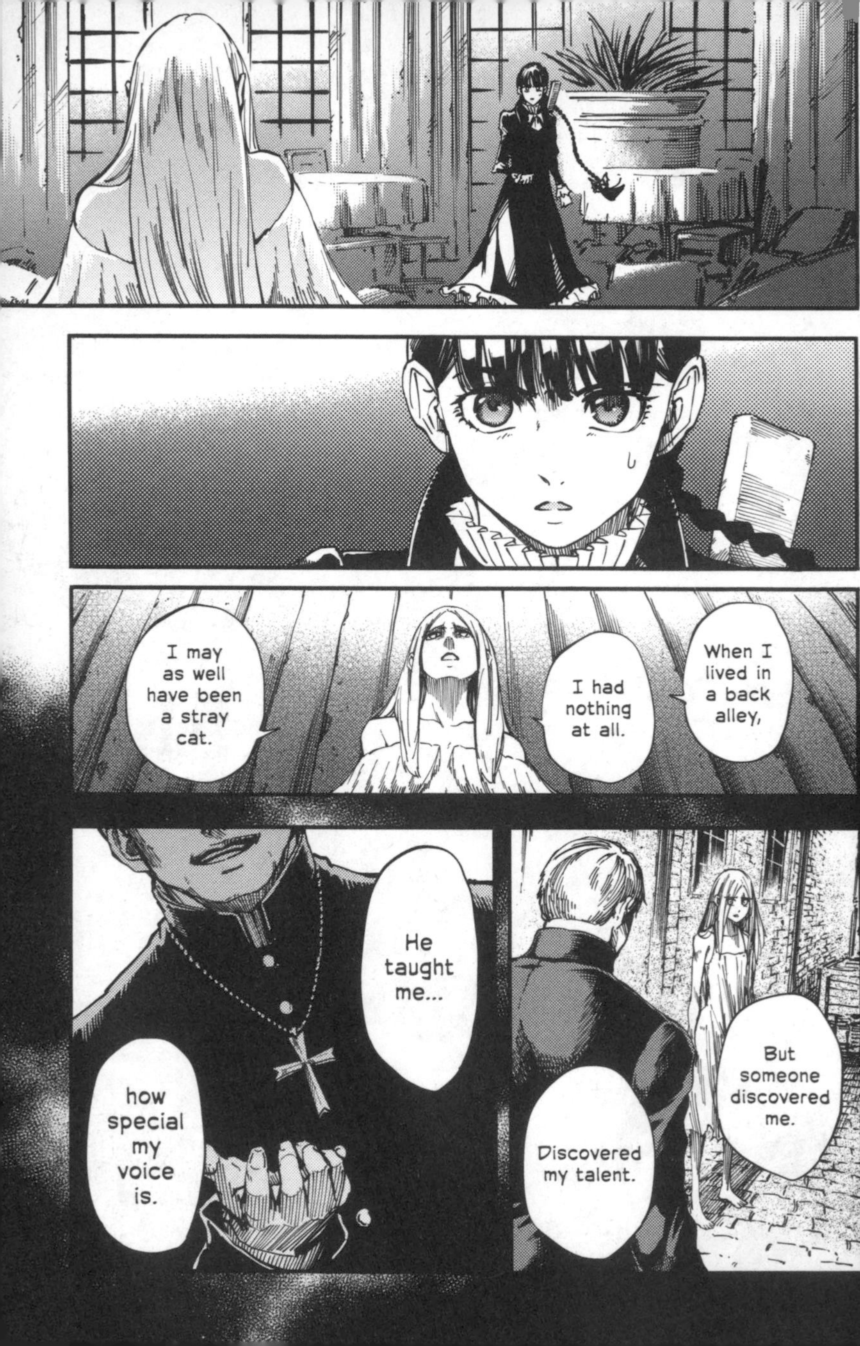
When I lived in a back alley,
I had nothing at all.
I may as well have been a stray cat.
But someone discovered me.
Discovered my talent.
He taught me...
how special my voice is.

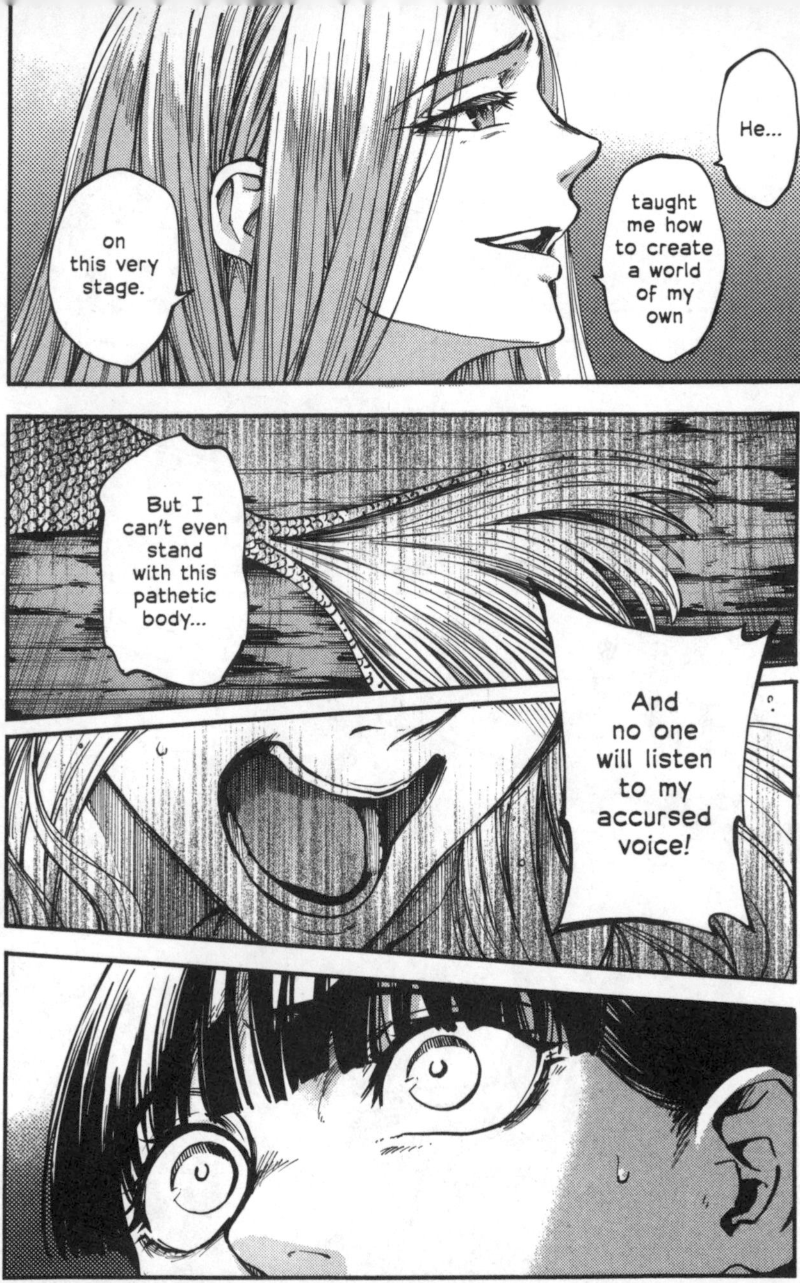
He...
taught me how to create a world of my own
on this very stage.
But I can't even stand with this pathetic body...
And no one will listen to my accursed voice!

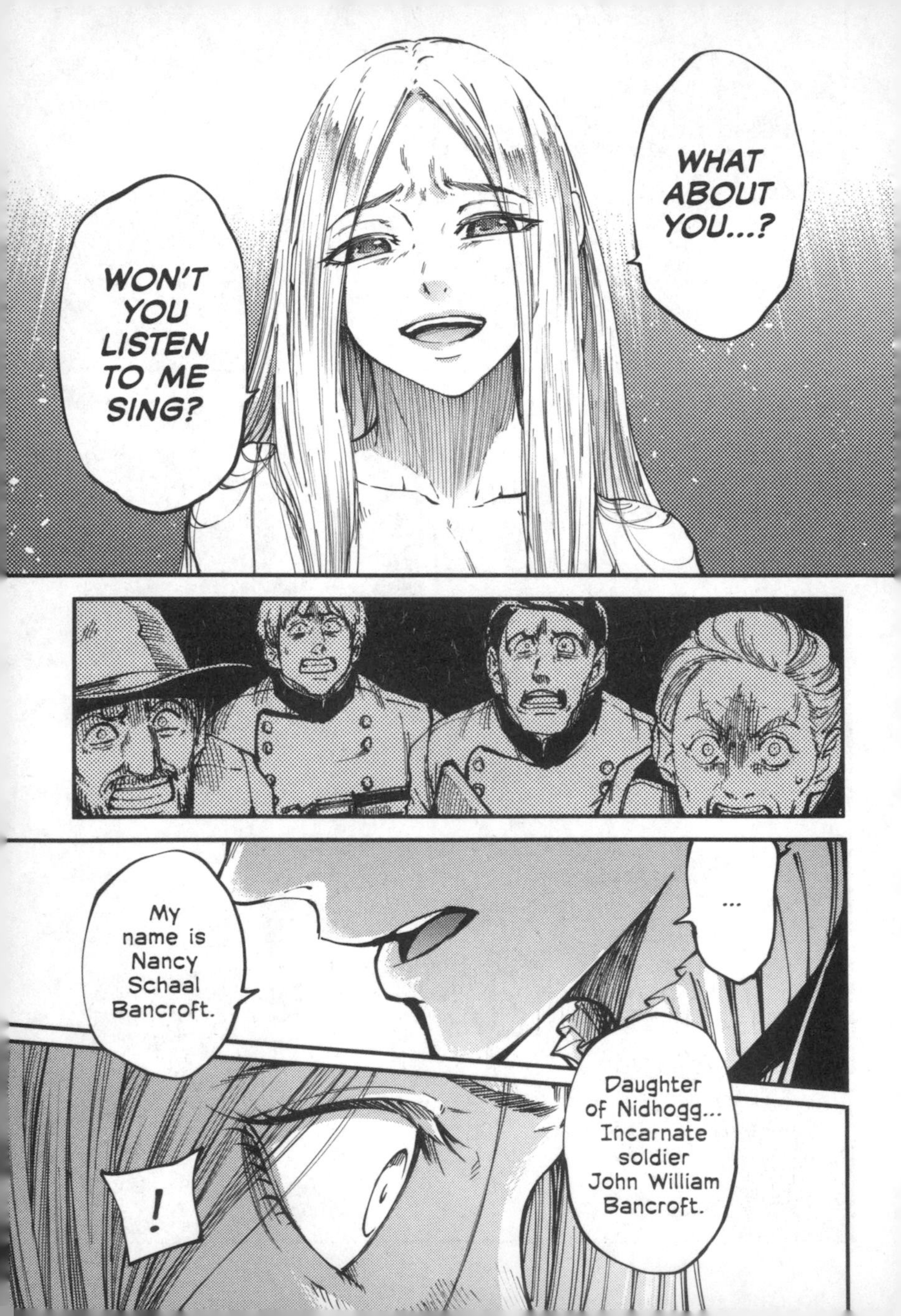
WHAT ABOUT YOU...?
WON'T YOU LISTEN TO ME SING?
...
My name is Nancy Schaal Bancroft.
Daughter of Nidhogg... Incarnate soldier John William Bancroft.
!

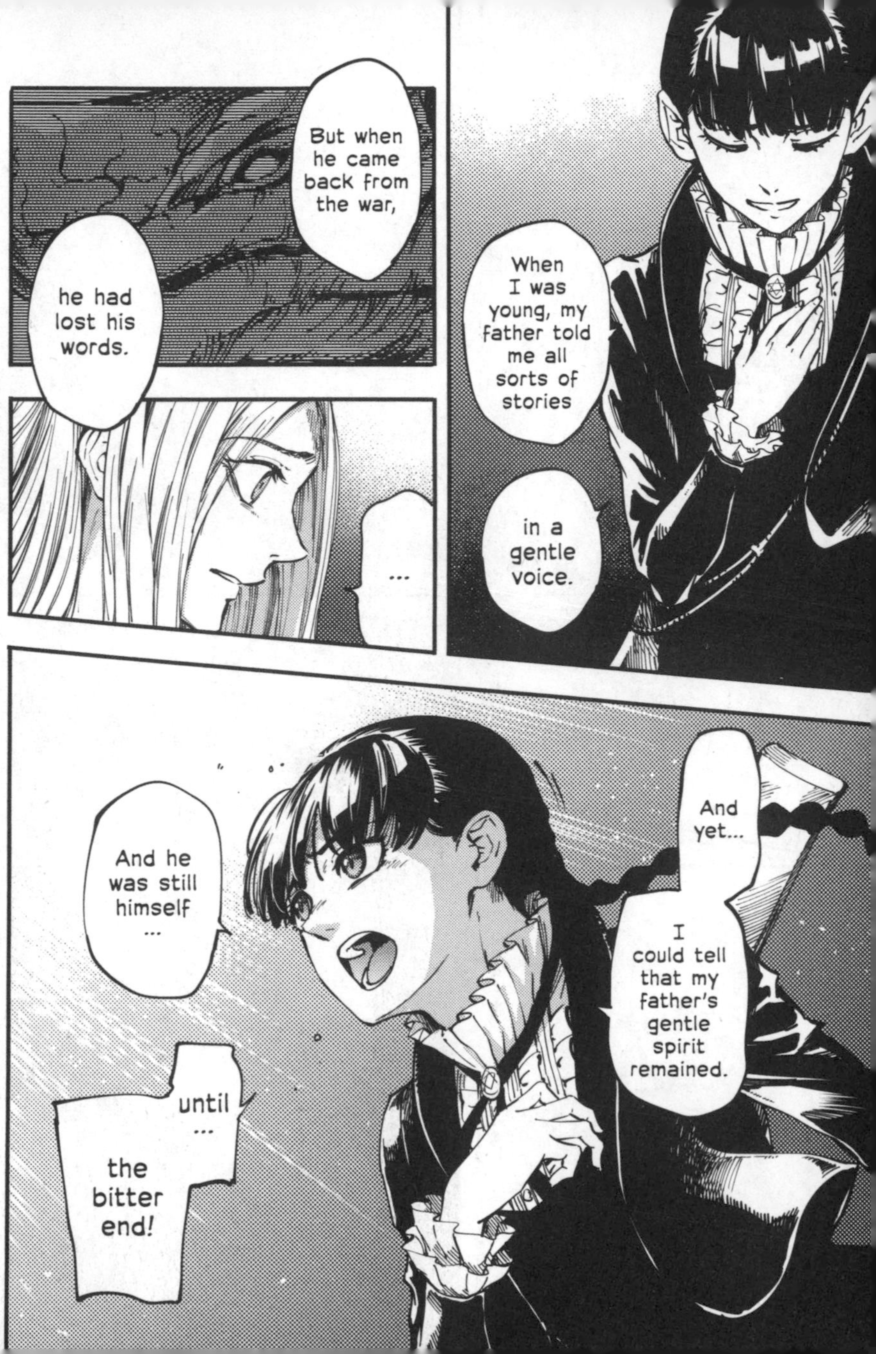
When I was young, my father told me all sorts of stories
in a gentle voice.
But when he came back from the war,
he had lost his words.
...
And yet...
I could tell that my father's gentle spirit remained.
And he was still himself ...
until ... the bitter end!

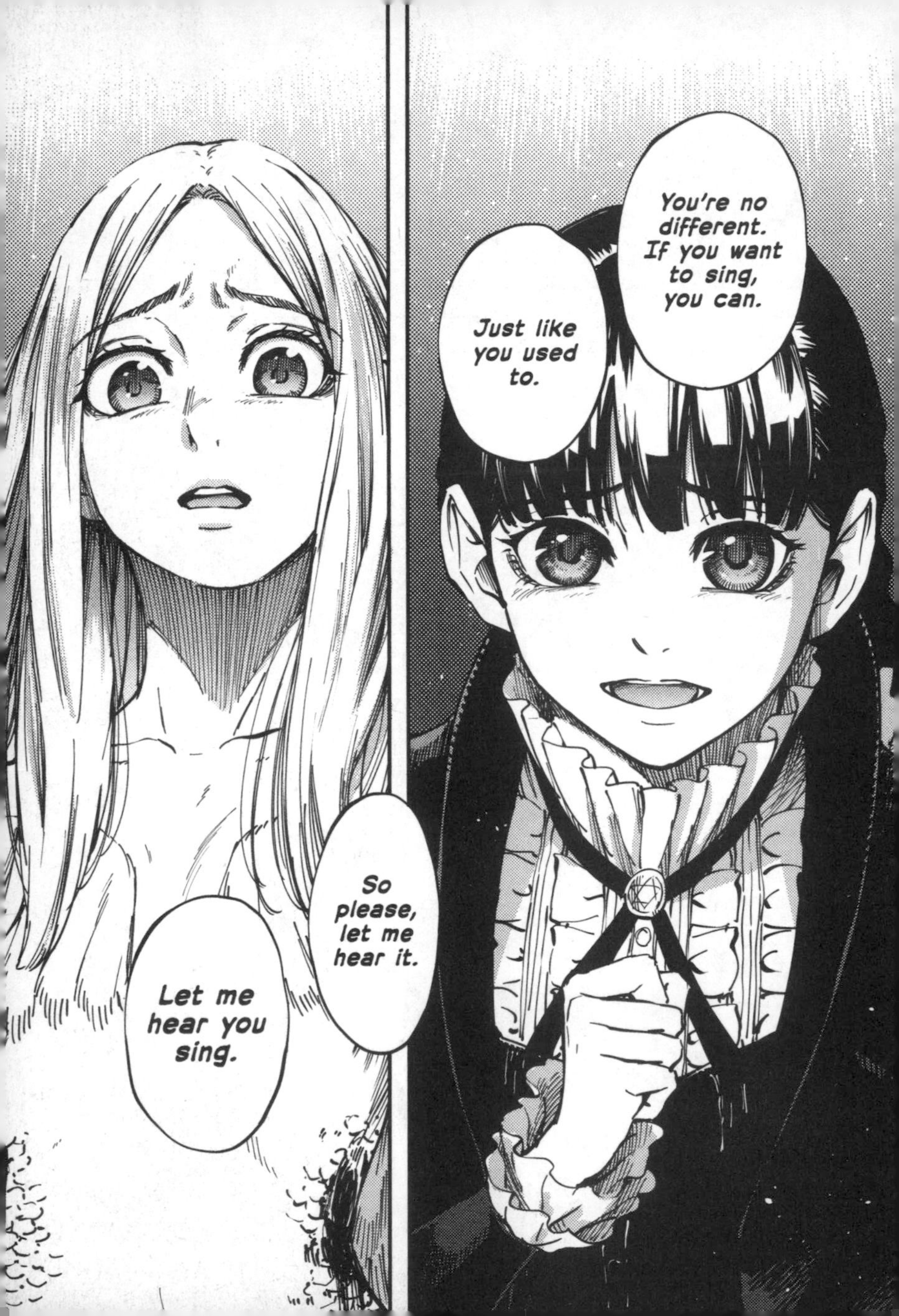
You're no different. If you want to sing, you can.
Just like you used to.
So please, let me hear it.
Let me hear you sing.

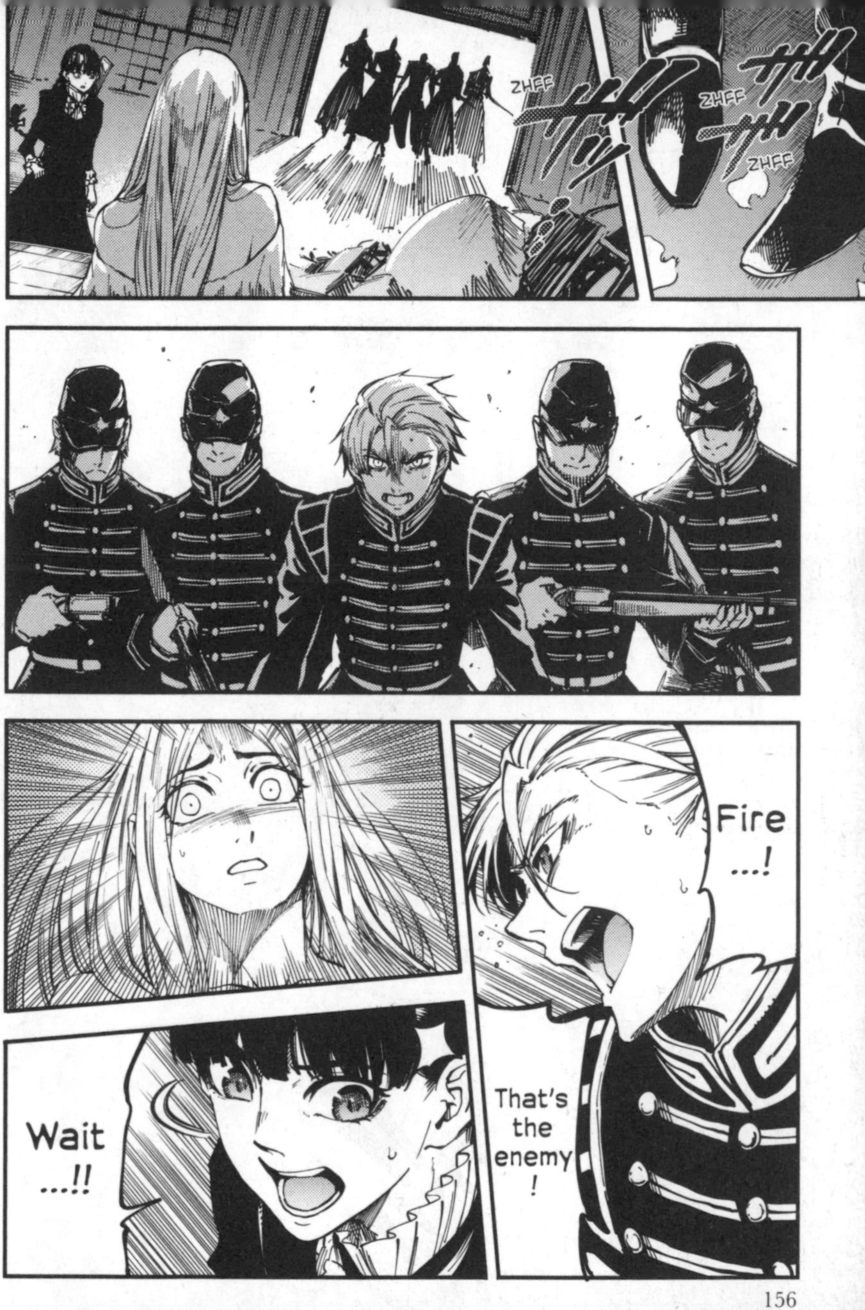
ZHFF
ZHFF
ZHFF
Fire ...!
That's the enemy!
Wait ...!!

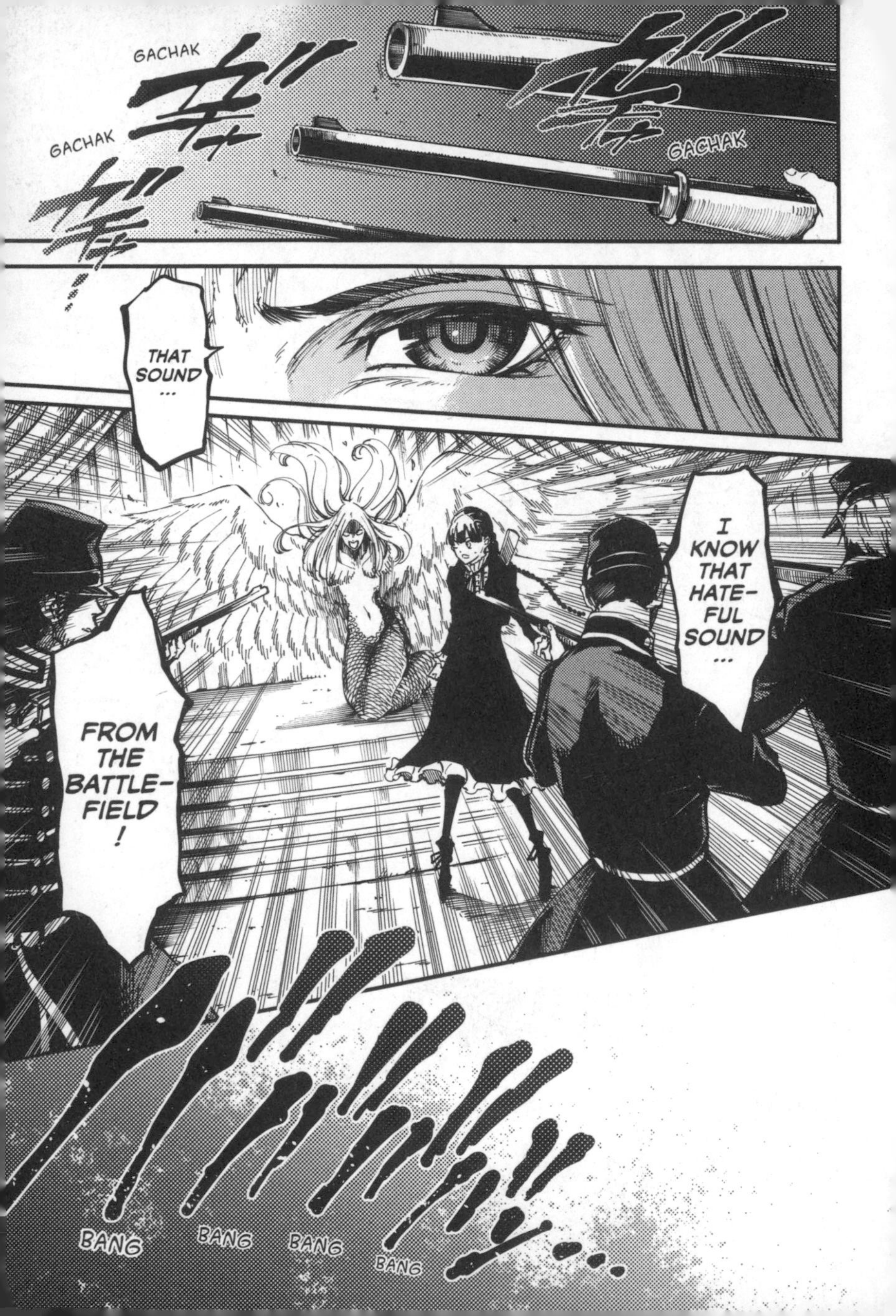
GACHAK
GACHAK
GACHAK
THAT SOUND ...
I KNOW THAT HATE-FUL SOUND ...
FROM THE BATTLE-FIELD!
BANG
BANG
BANG
BANG

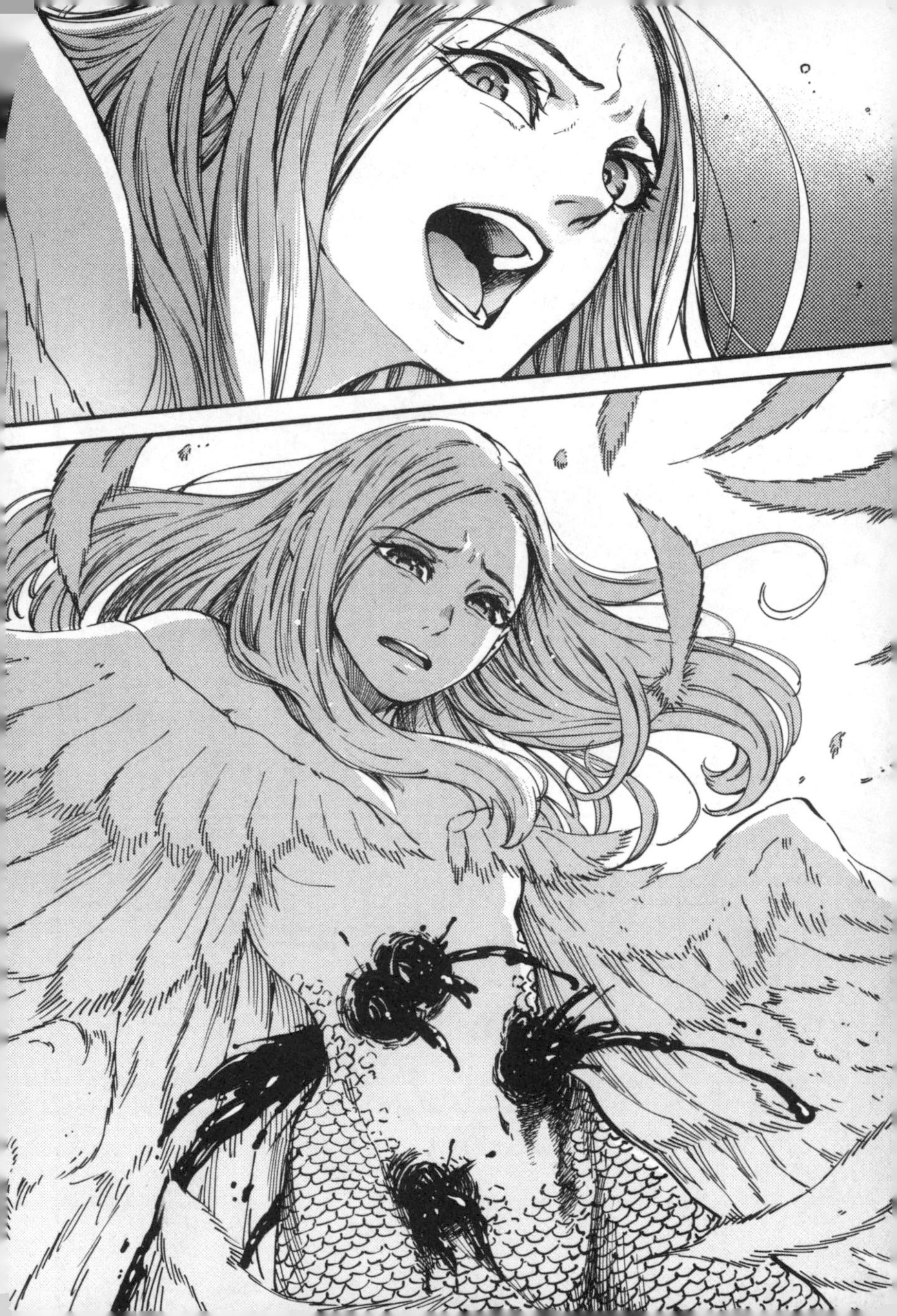

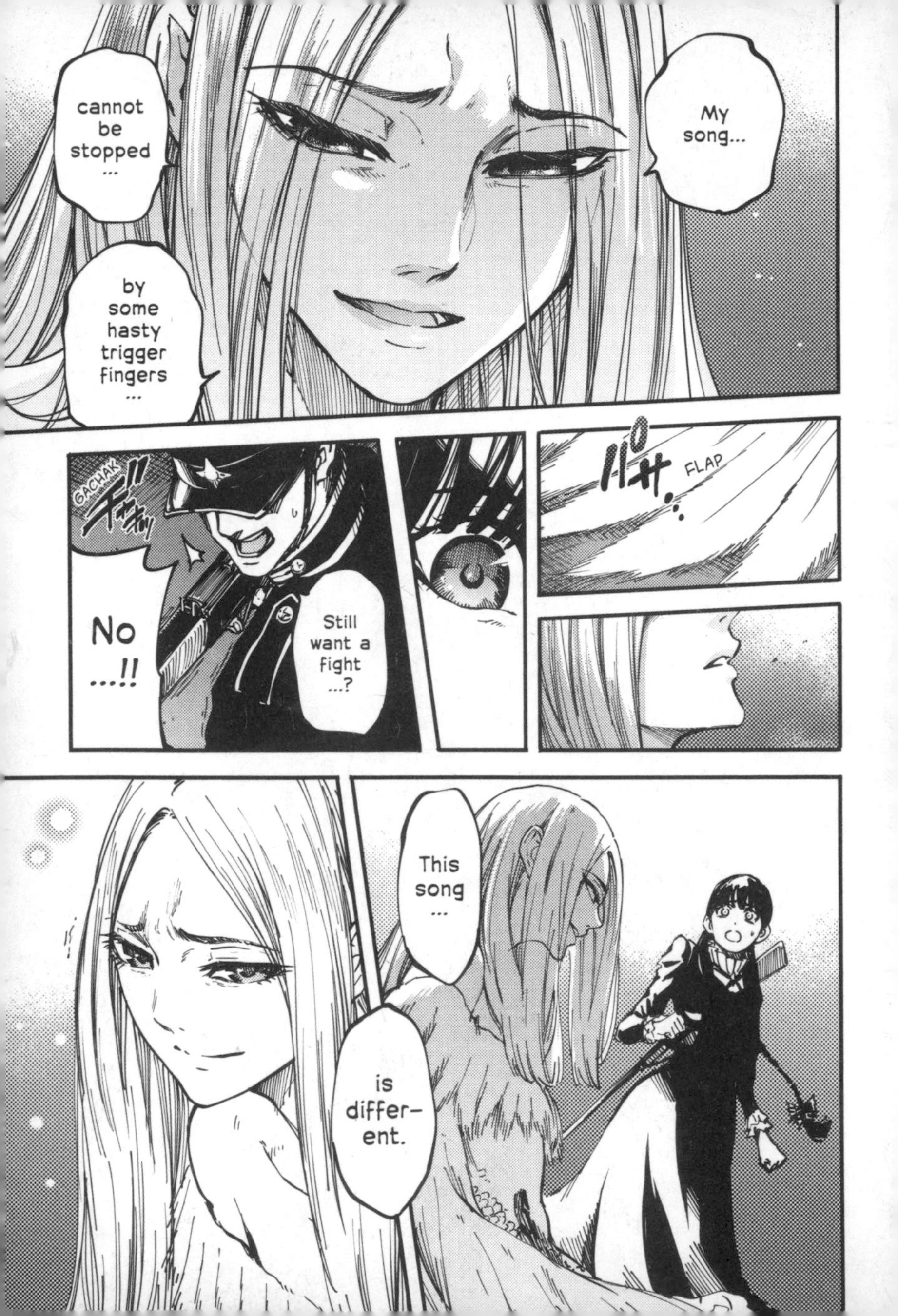
My song...
cannot be stopped ...
by some hasty trigger fingers ...
FLAP
Still want a fight ...?
GACHAK
No ...!!
This song ...
is differ- ent.

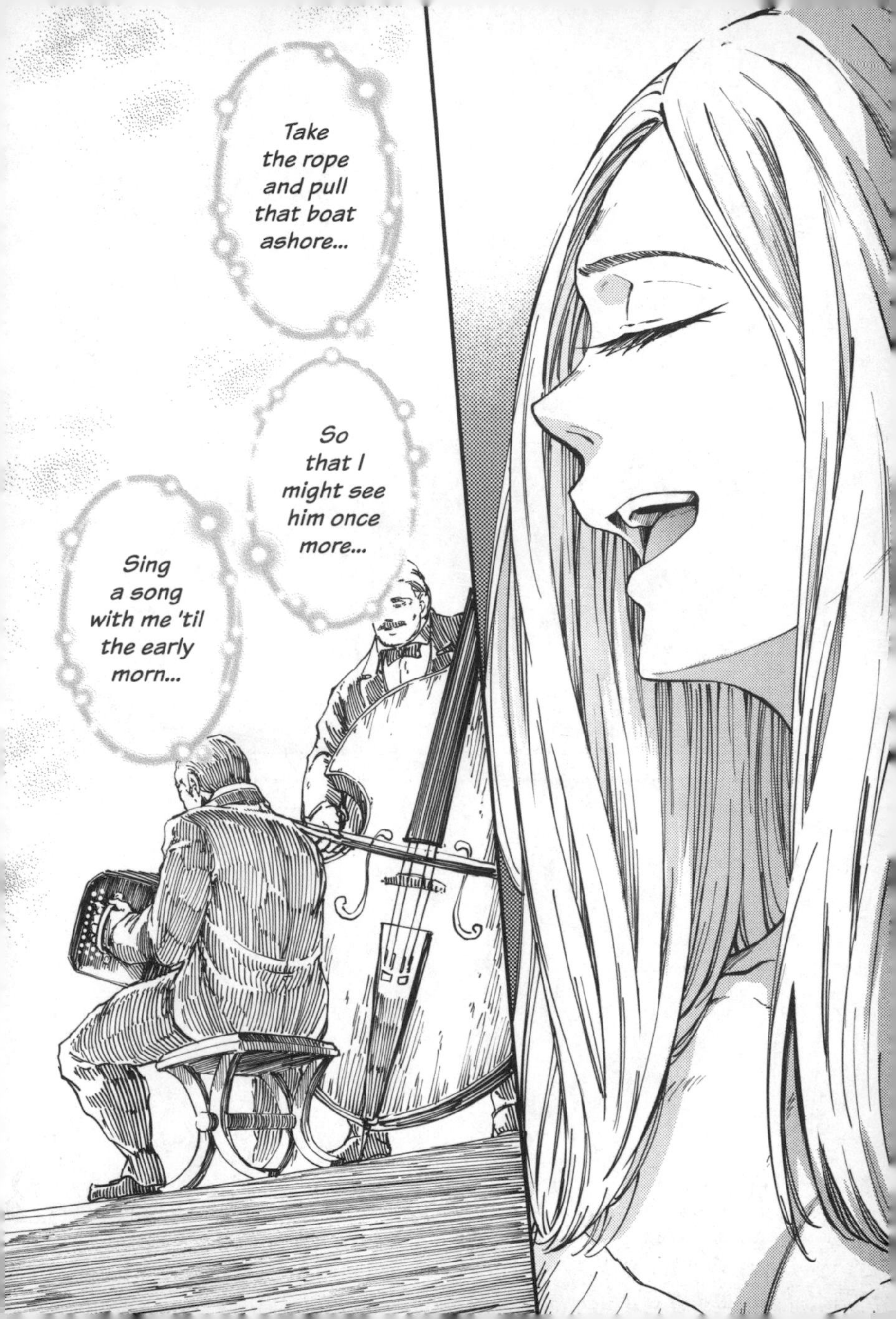
Take the rope and pull that boat ashore...
So that I might see him once more...
Sing a song with me 'til the early morn...

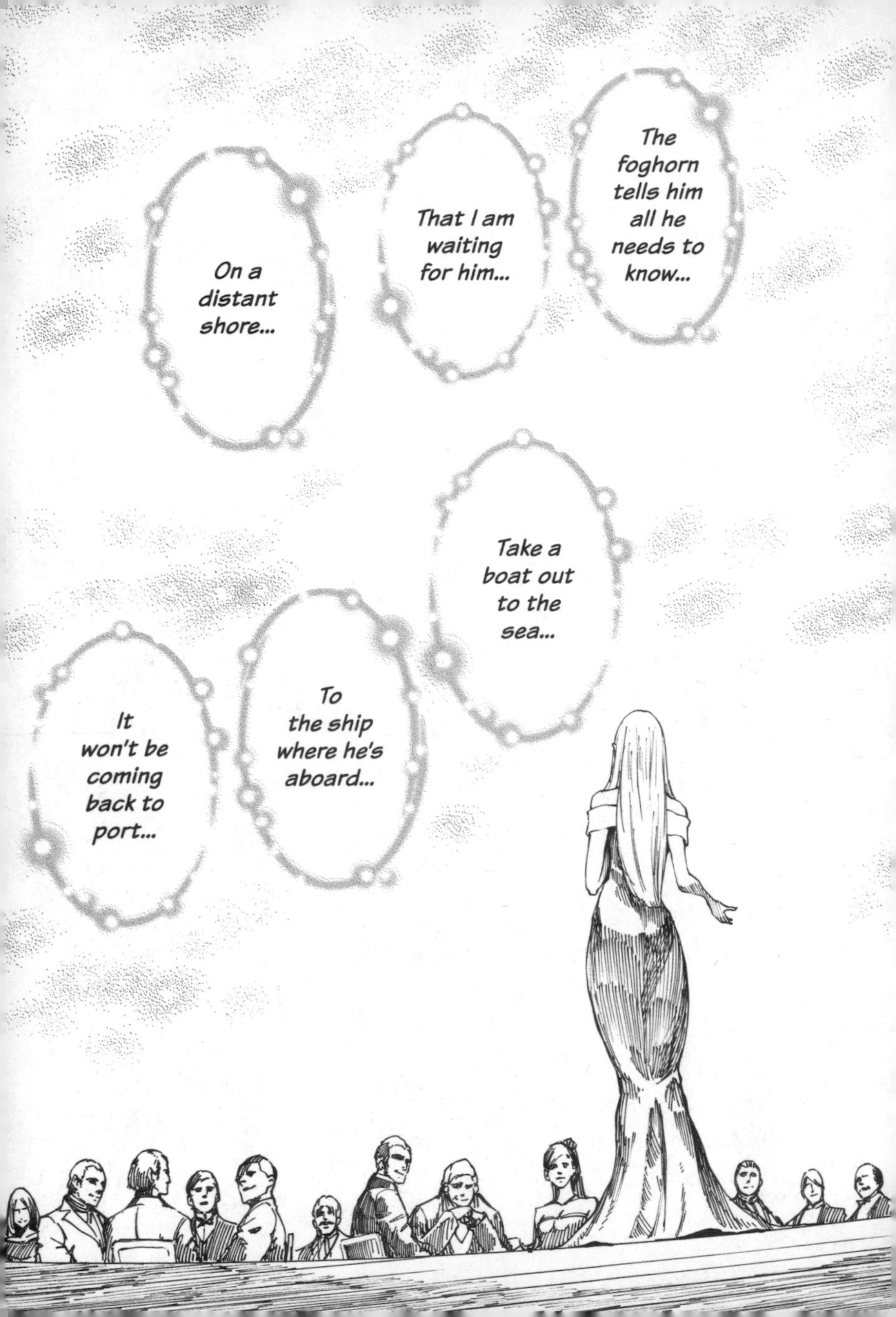
The foghorn tells him all he needs to know...
That I am waiting for him...
On a distant shore...
Take a boat out to the sea...
To the ship where he's aboard...
It won't be coming back to port...

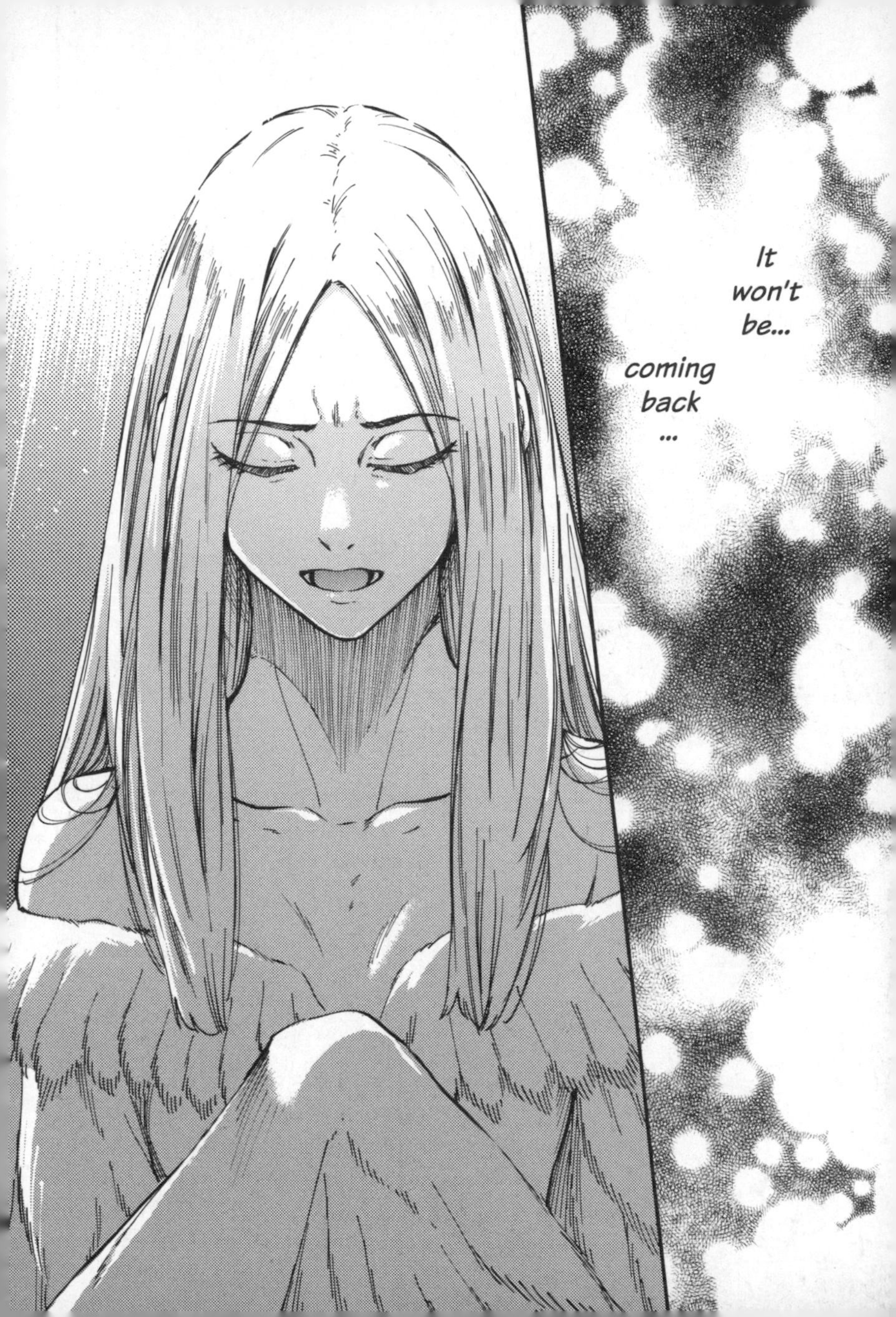
It won't be...
coming back ...

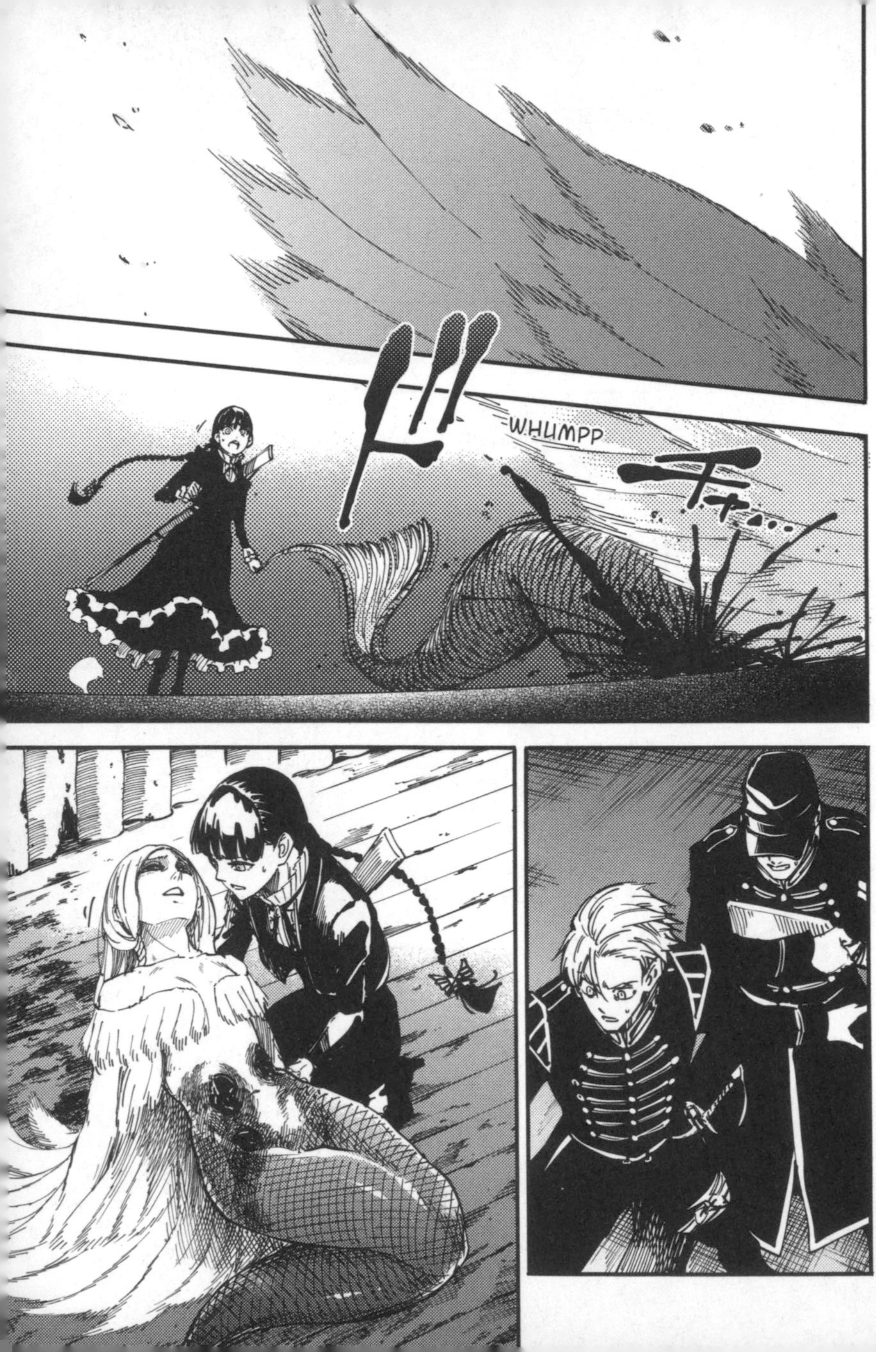
ドチャ...
WHUMPP

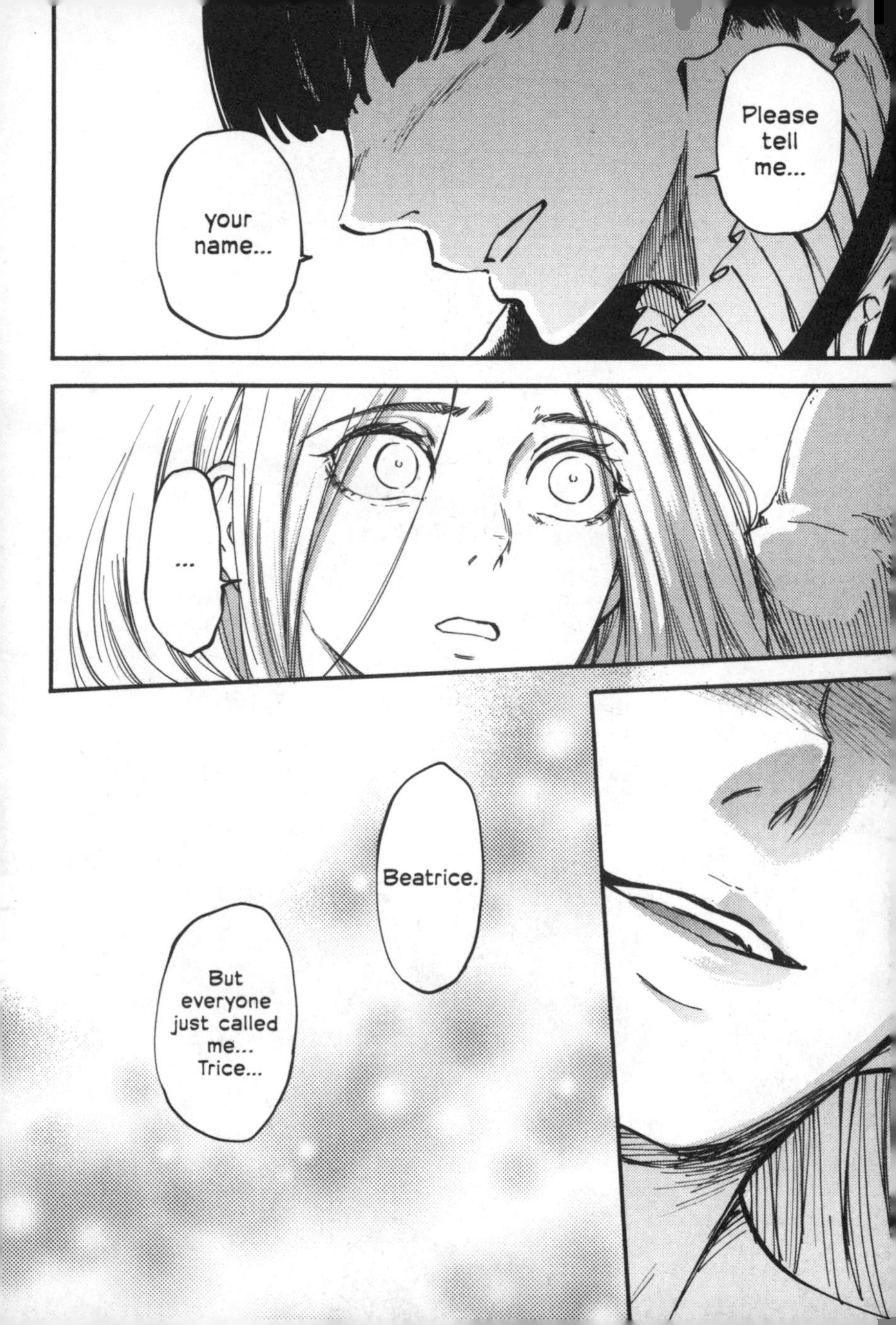
Please tell me...
your name...
...
Beatrice.
But everyone just called me... Trice...

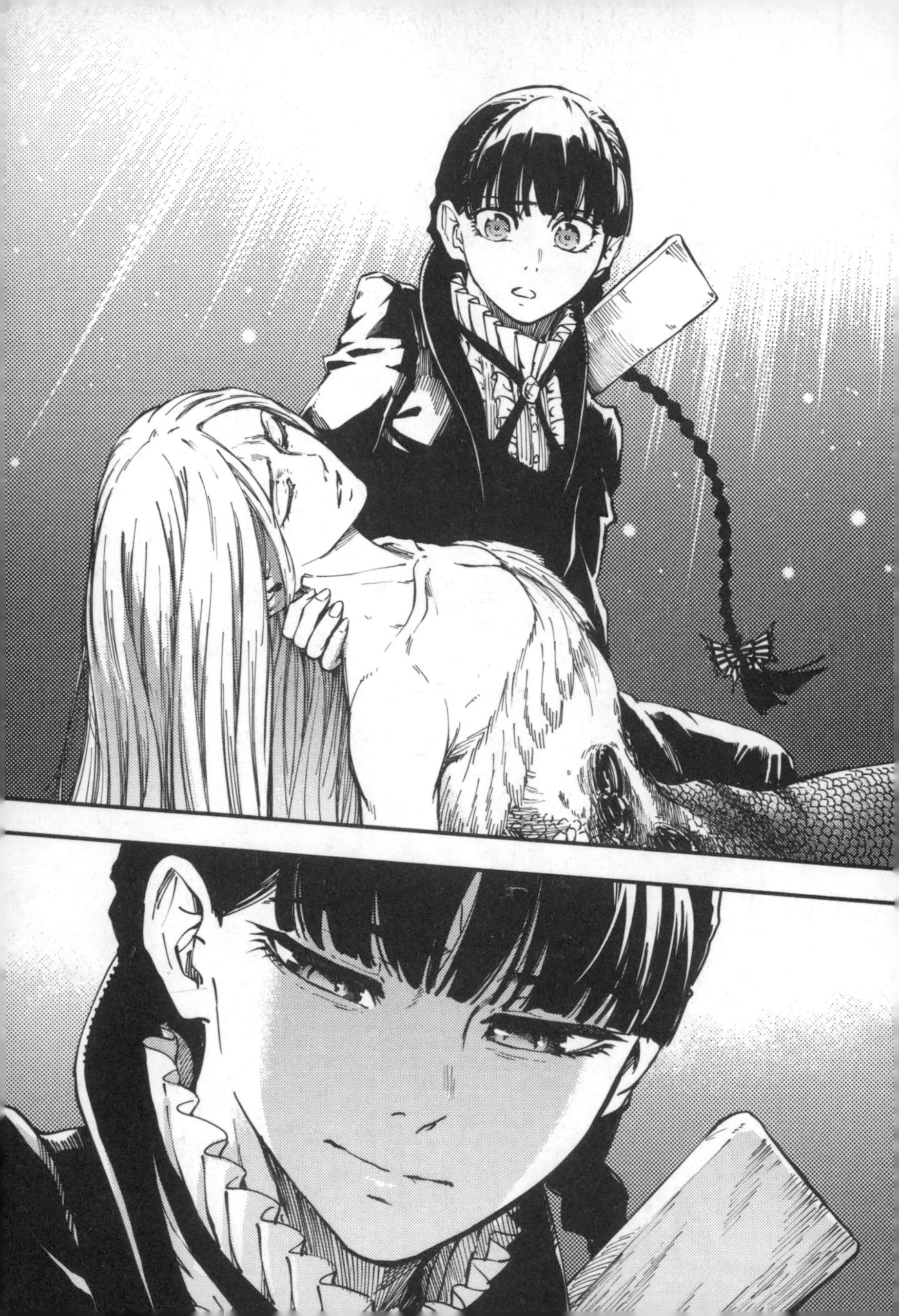

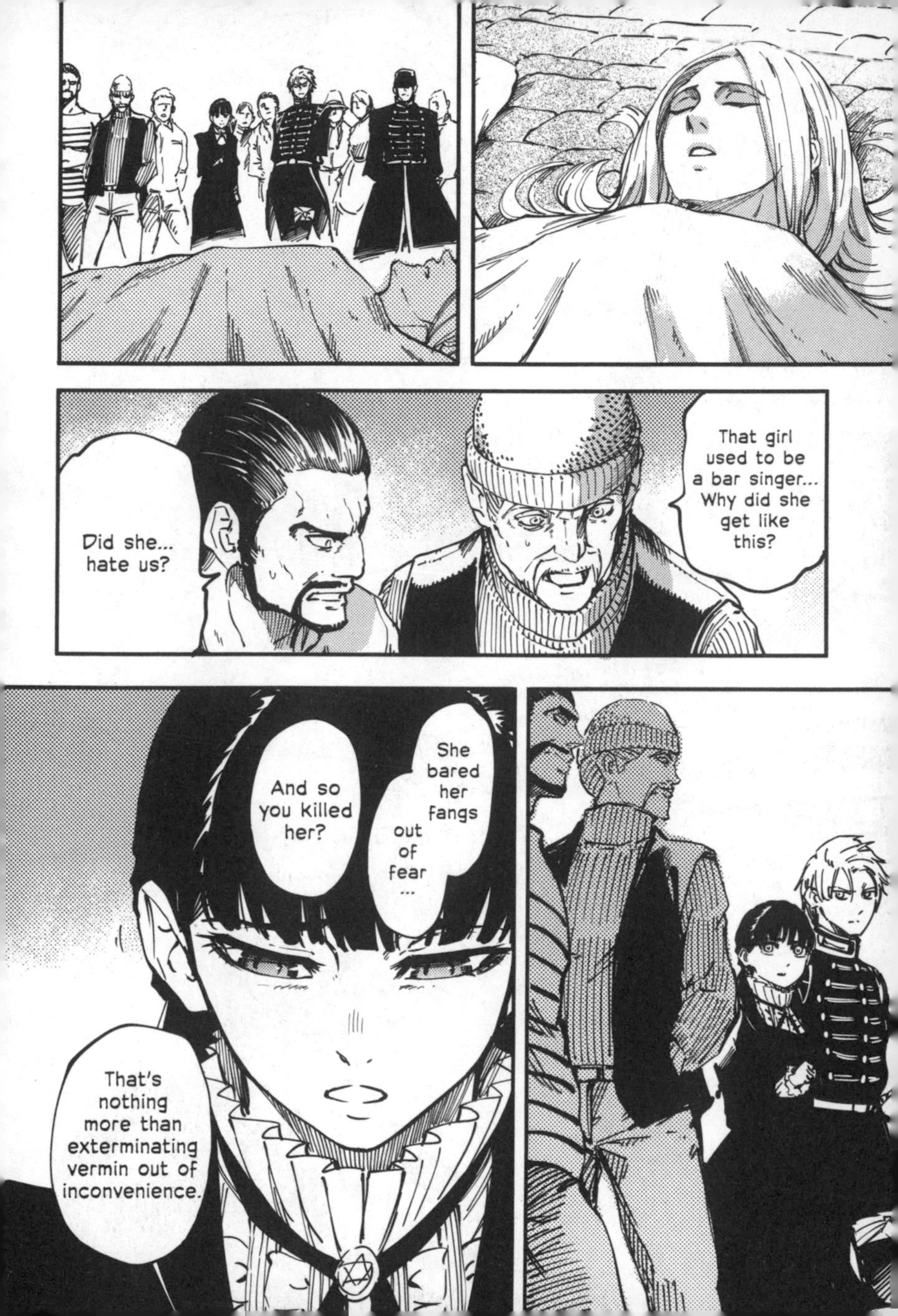
That girl used to be a bar singer... Why did she get like this?
Did she... hate us?
She bared her fangs out of fear...
And so you killed her?
That's nothing more than exterminating vermin out of inconvenience.

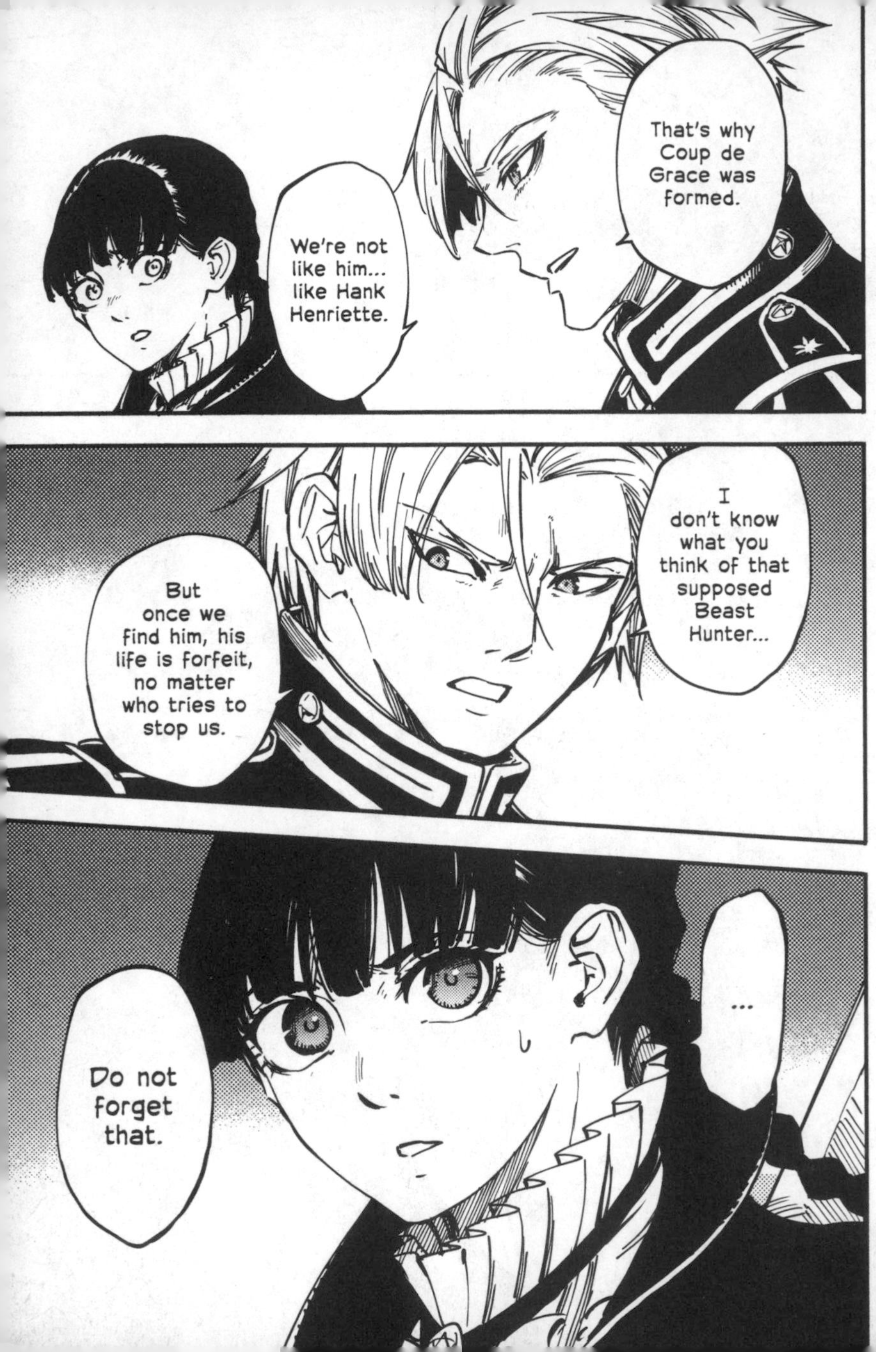
That's why Coup de Grace was formed.
We're not like him... like Hank Henriette.
I don't know what you think of that supposed Beast Hunter...
But once we find him, his life is forfeit, no matter who tries to stop us.
...
Do not forget that.

To the Abandoned
Sacred Beasts

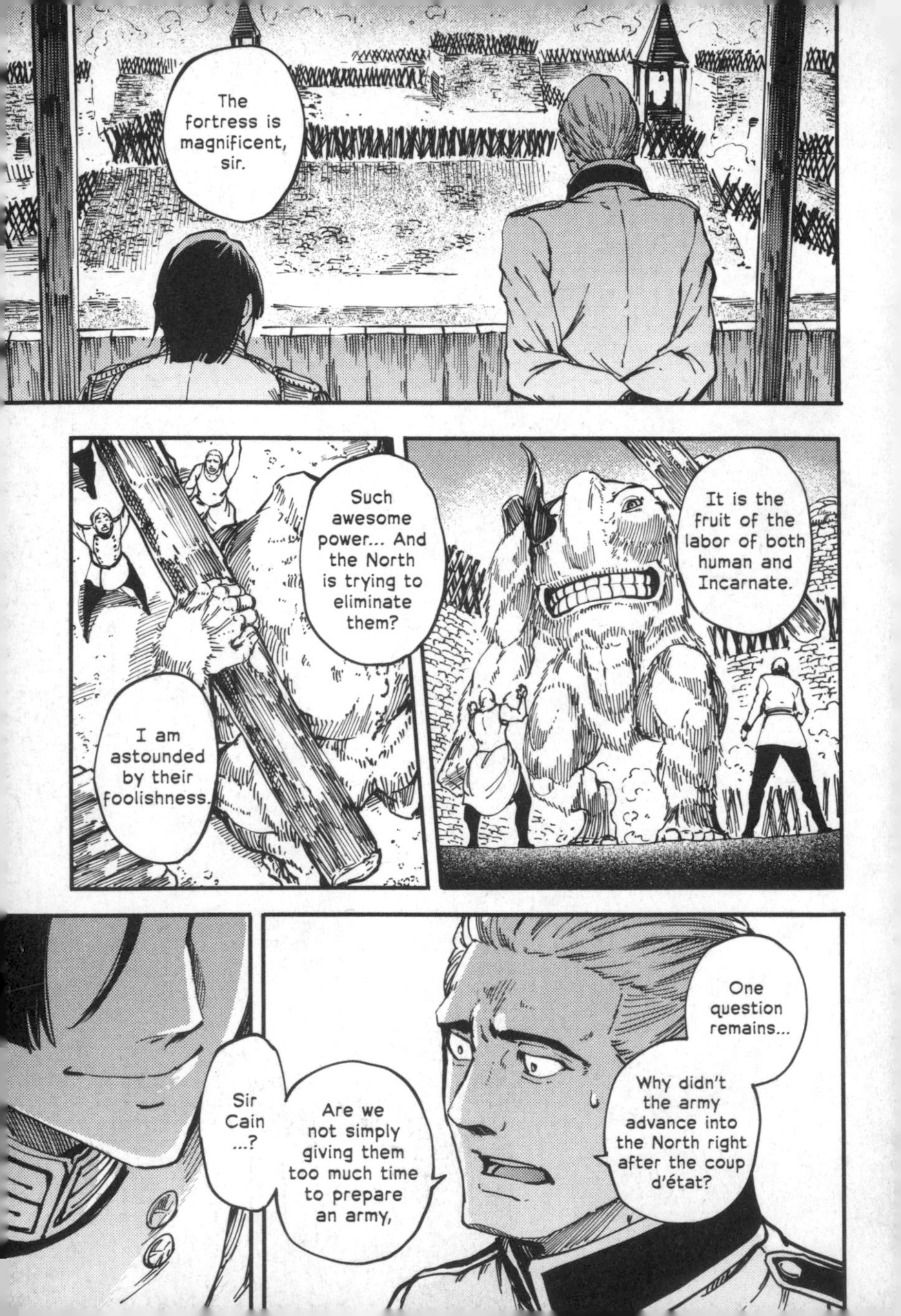
The fortress is magnificent, sir.
It is the fruit of the labor of both human and Incarnate.
Such awesome power... And the North is trying to eliminate them?
I am astounded by their foolishness.
One question remains...
Why didn't the army advance into the North right after the coup d'état?
Are we not simply giving them too much time to prepare an army,
Sir Cain ...?

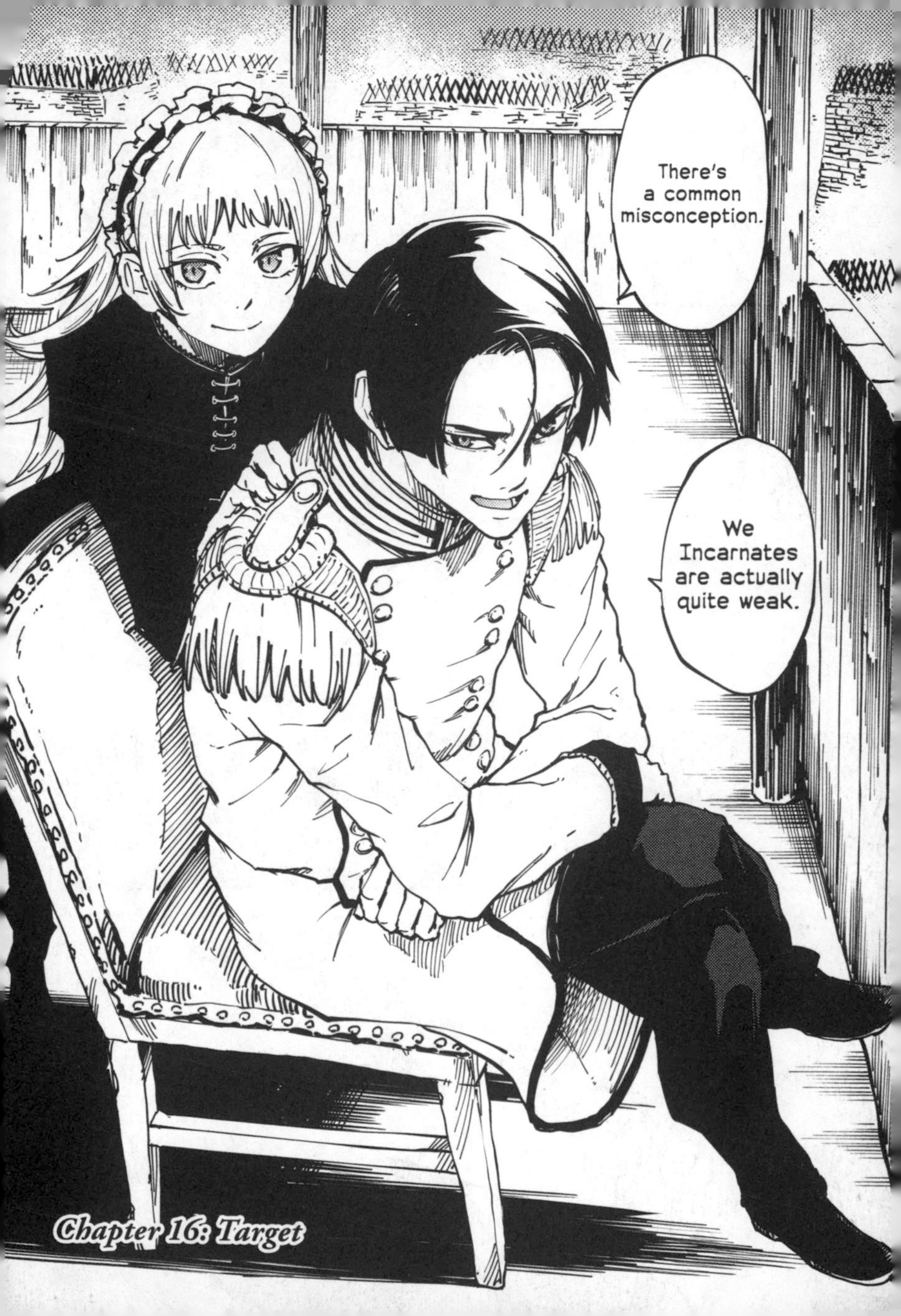
There's a common misconception.
We Incarnates are actually quite weak.
Chapter 16: Target

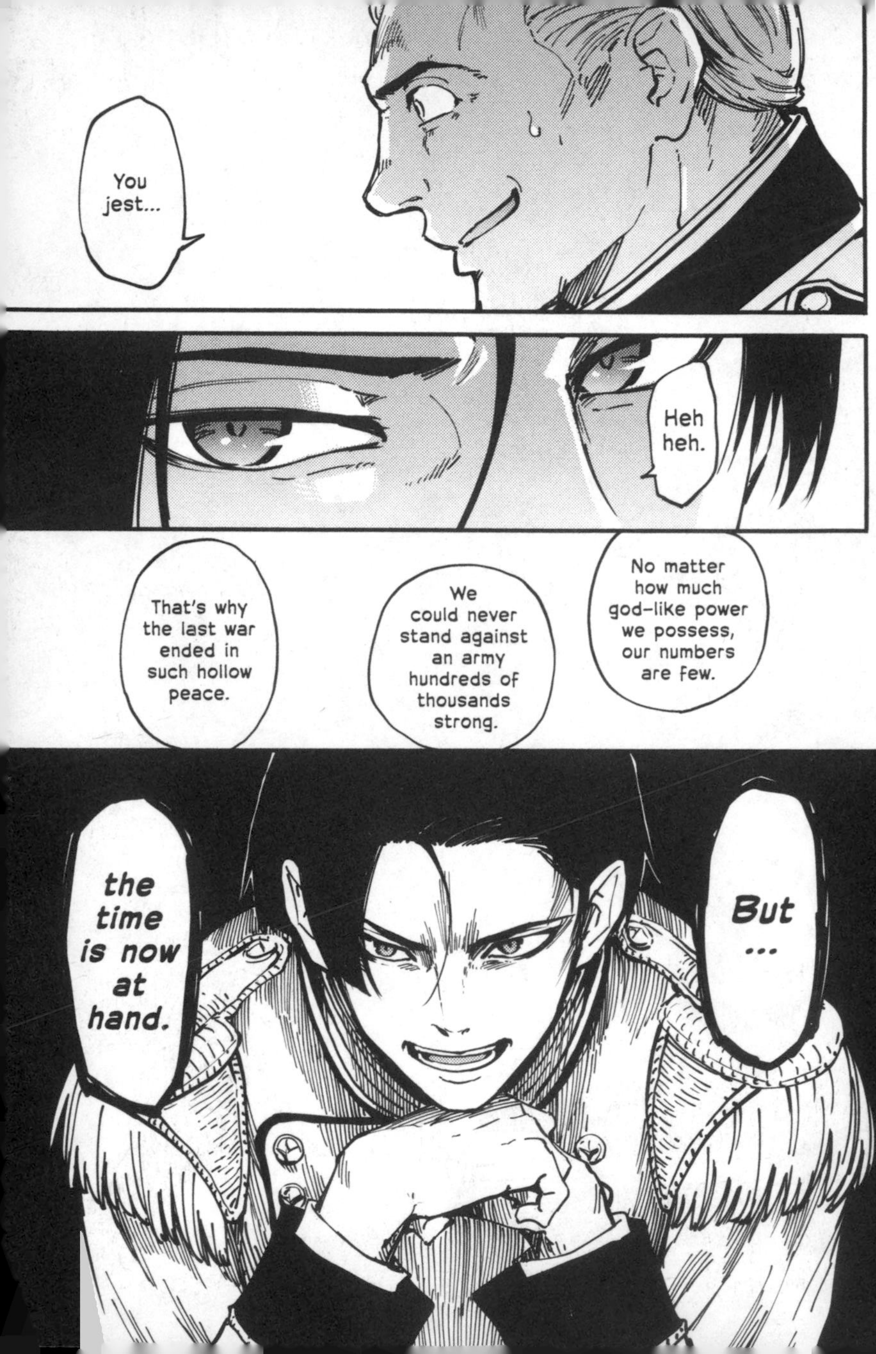
You jest...
Heh heh.
No matter how much god-like power we possess, our numbers are few.
We could never stand against an army hundreds of thousands strong.
That's why the last war ended in such hollow peace.
But...
the time is now at hand.

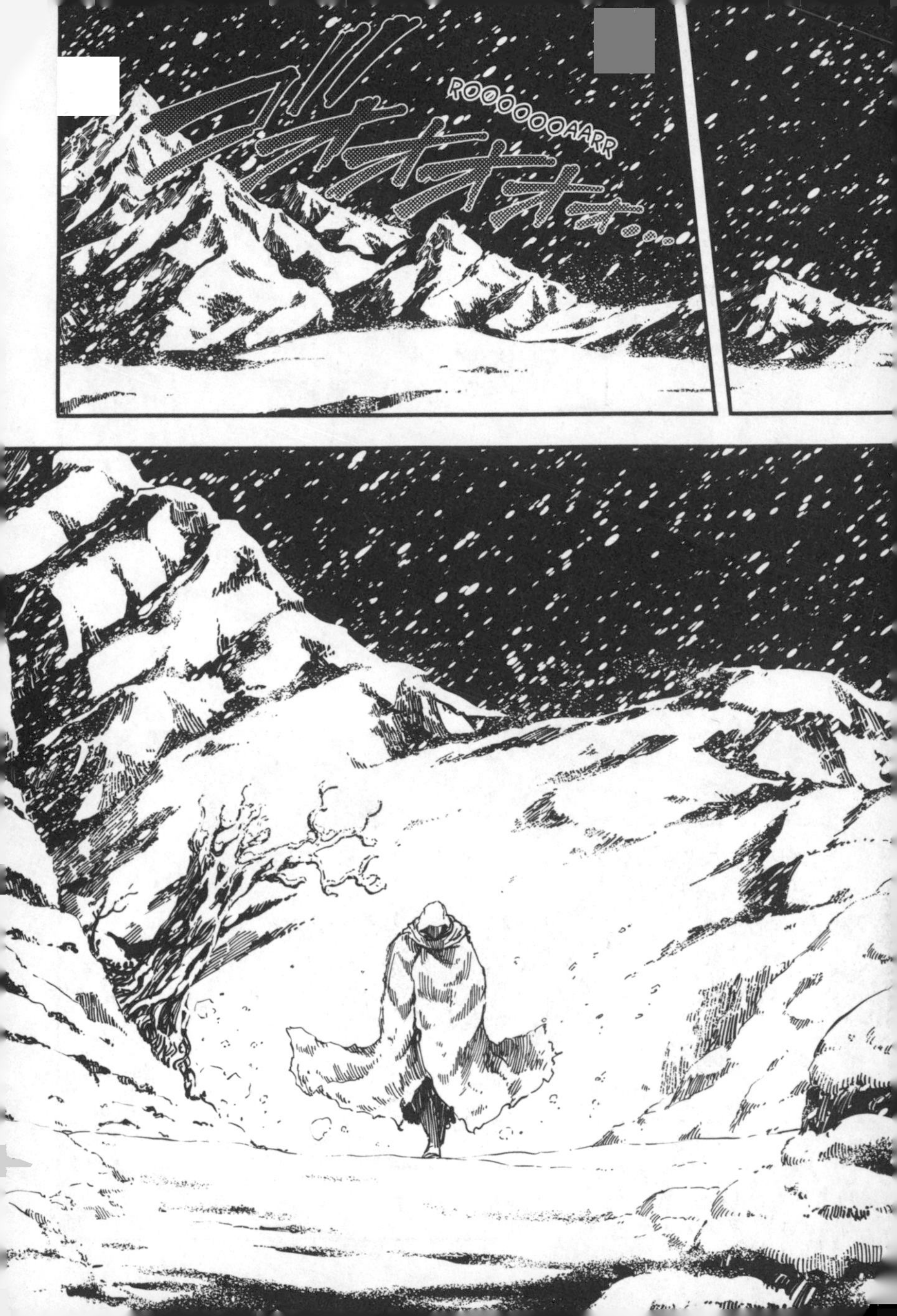
ROOOOOOAARR

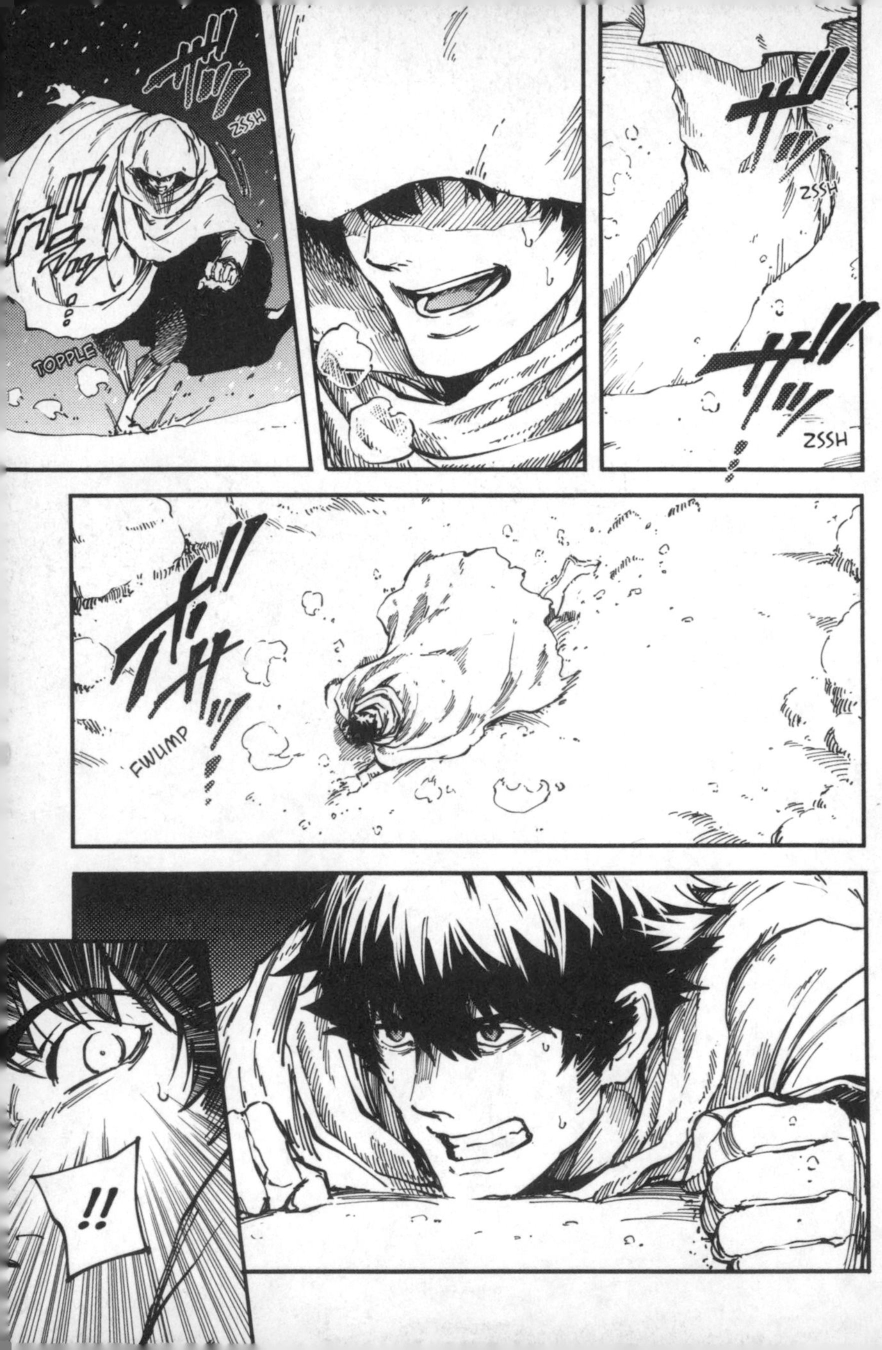
ZSSH
ZSSH
ZSSH
TOPPLE
FWUMP
!!

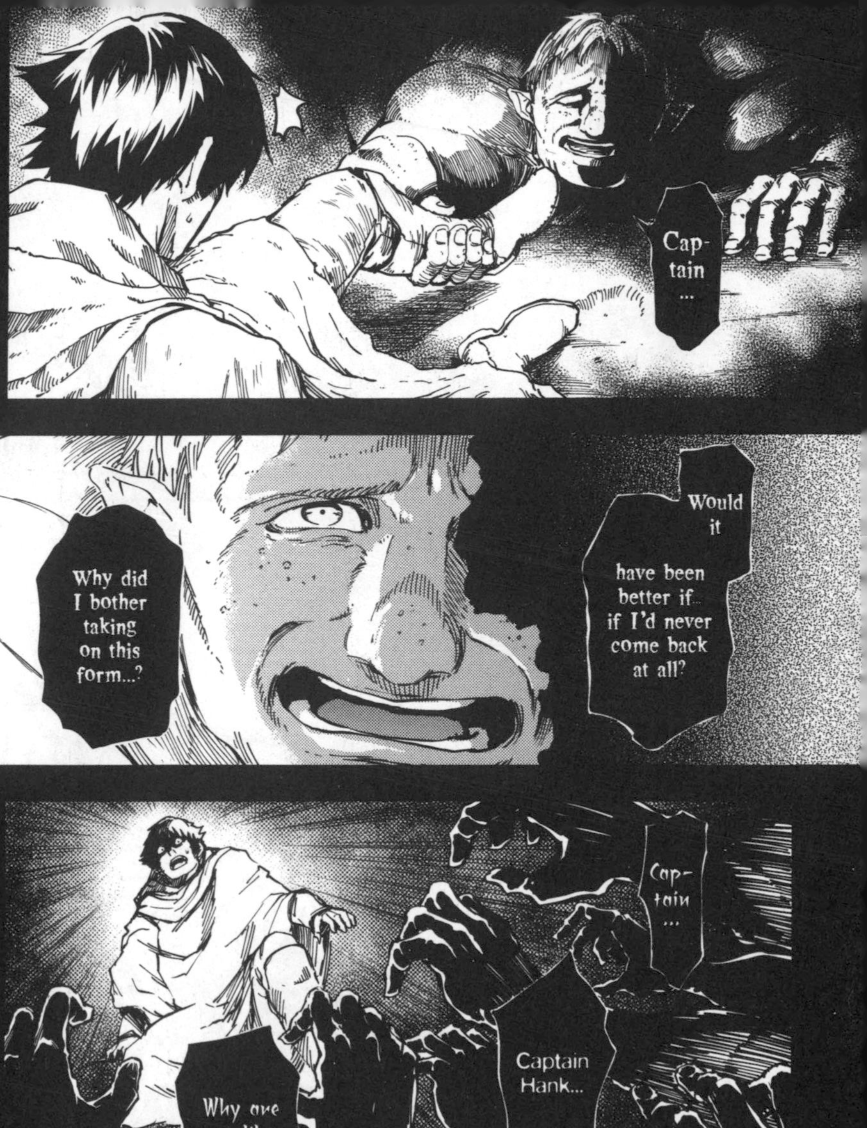
Cap-tain ...
Would it have been better if... if I'd never come back at all?
Why did I bother taking on this form...?
Cap-tain ...
Captain Hank...
Why are we like this...

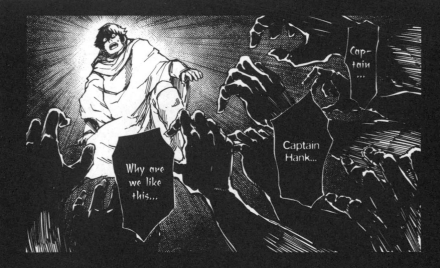

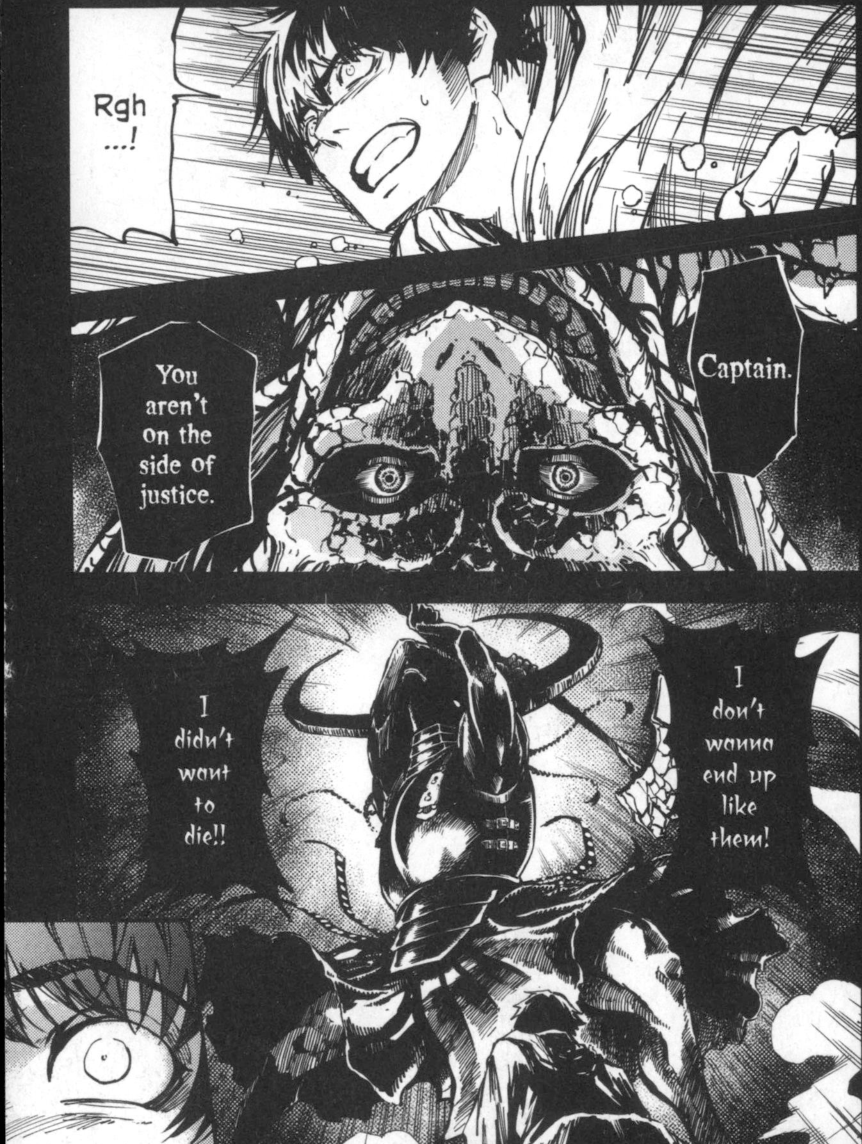
Rgh ...!
Captain.
You aren't on the side of justice.
I don't wanna end up like them!
I didn't want to die!!

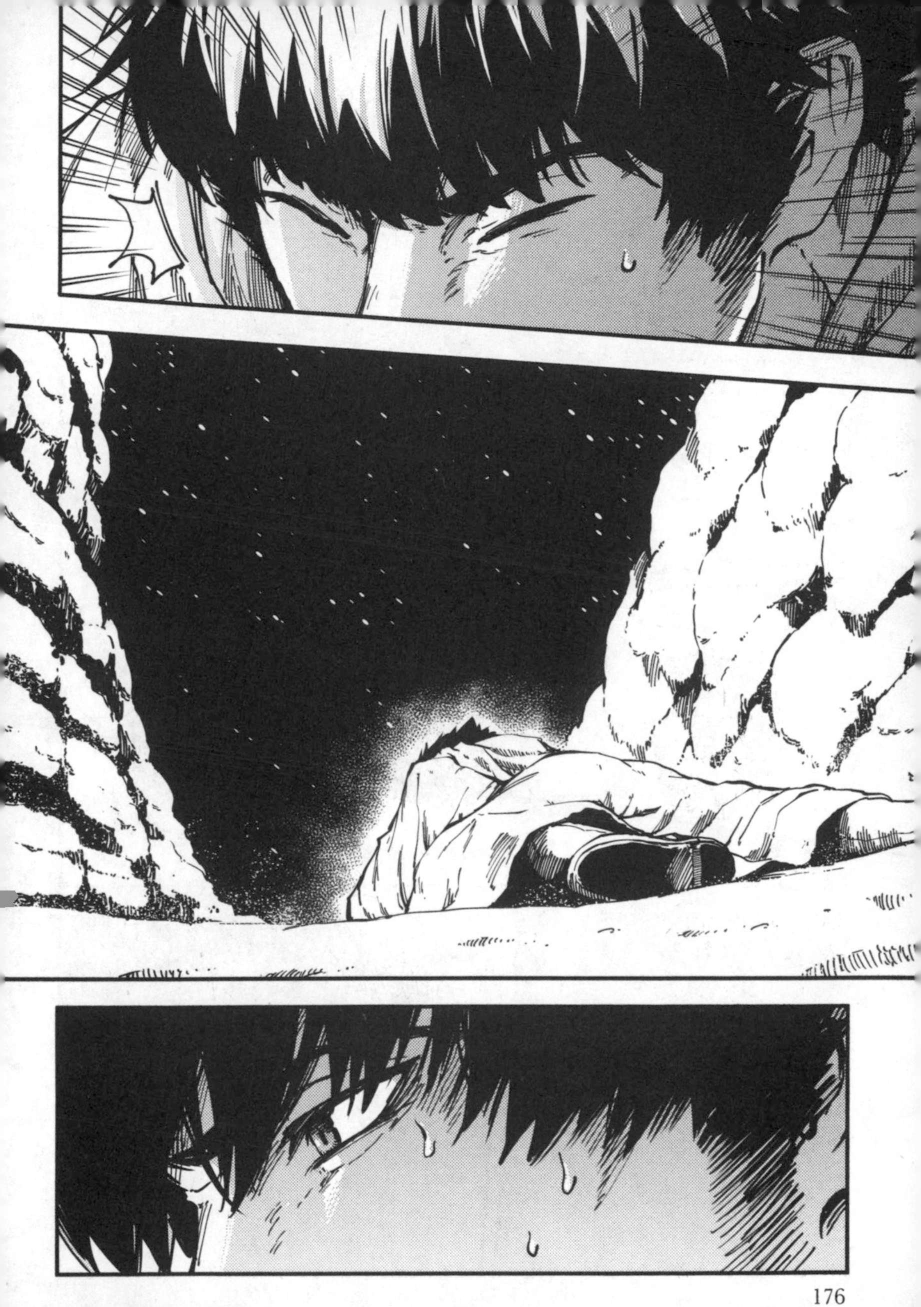

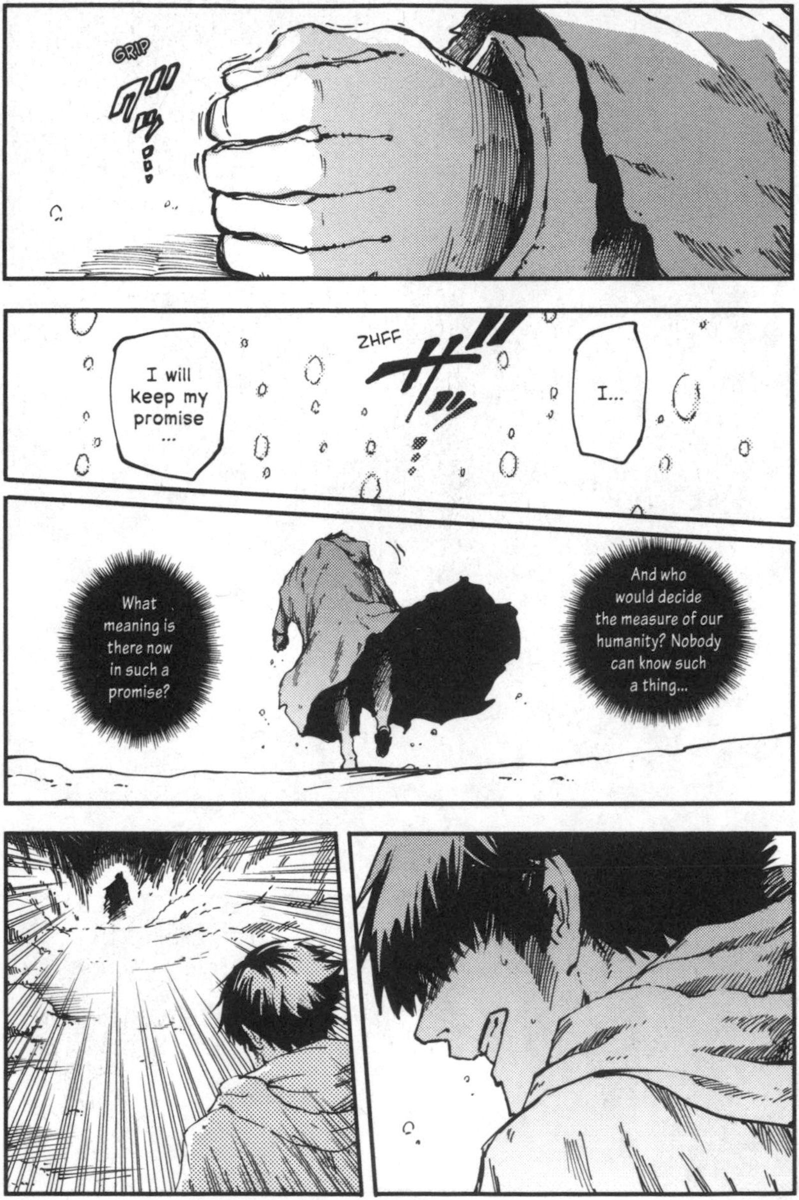
GRIP
I...
ZHFF
I will keep my promise ...
And who would decide the measure of our humanity? Nobody can know such a thing...
What meaning is there now in such a promise?

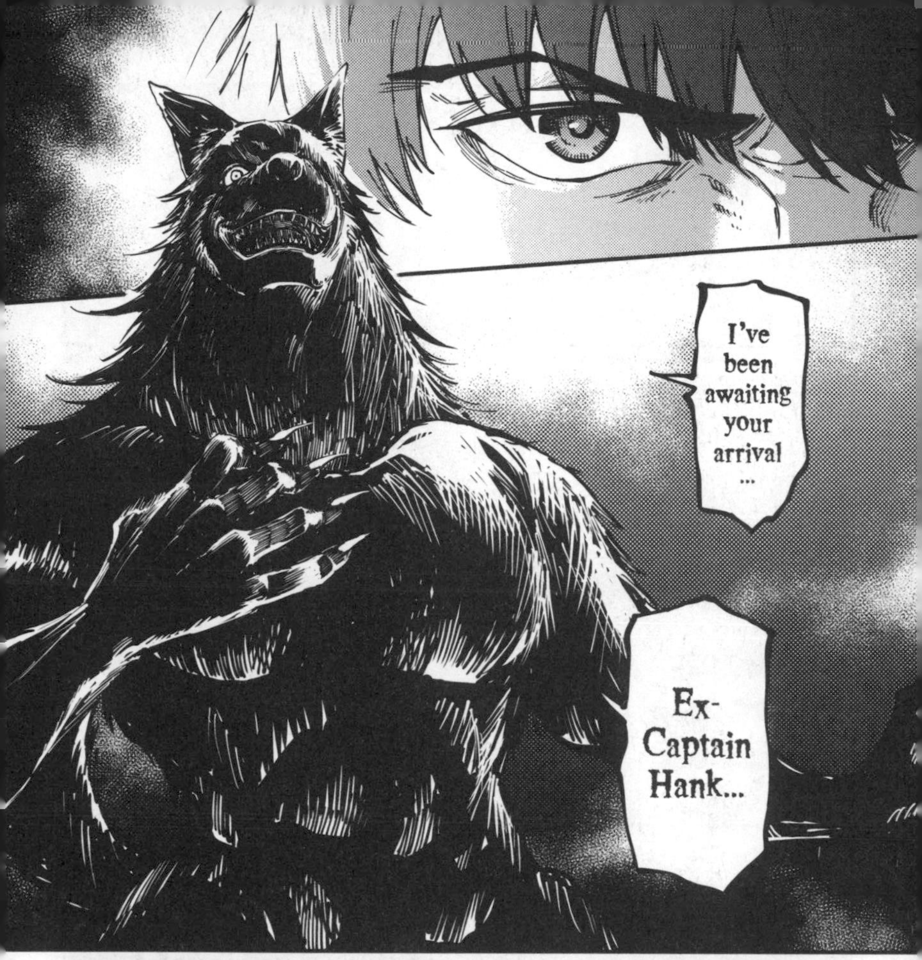
I've been awaiting your arrival ...
Ex-Captain Hank...

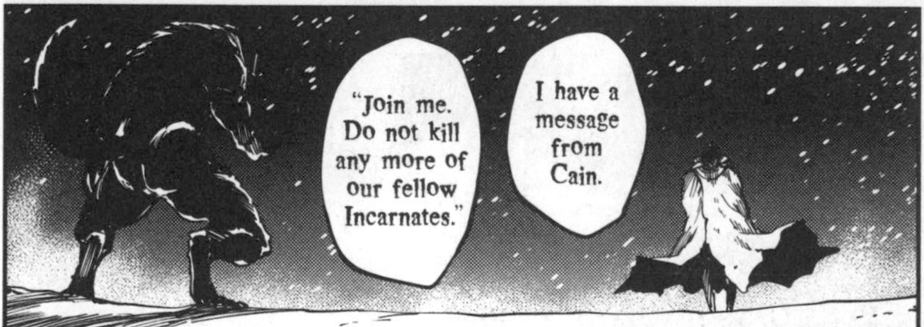
I have a message from Cain.
"Join me. Do not kill any more of our fellow Incarnates."

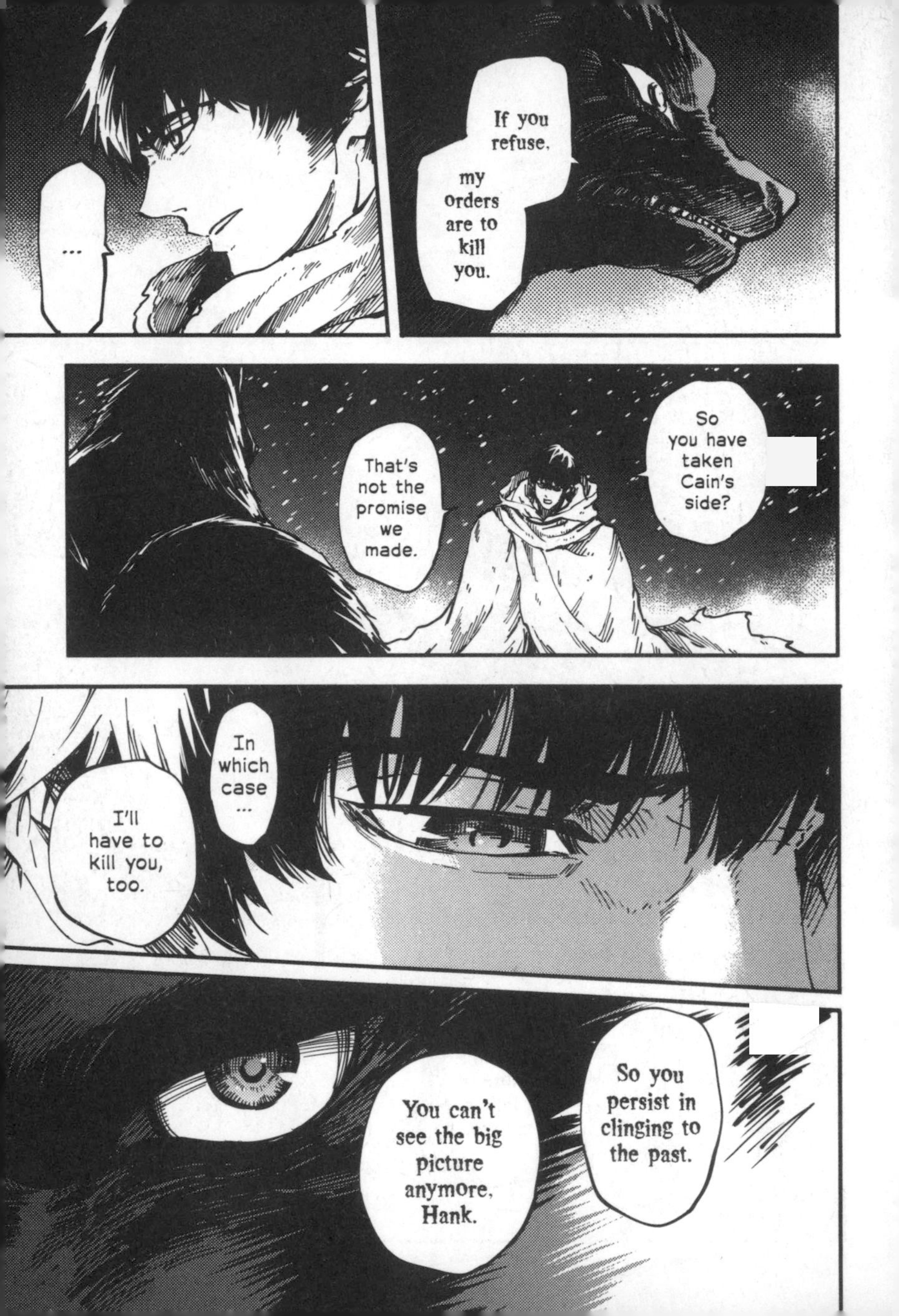
If you refuse, my orders are to kill you.
...
So you have taken Cain's side?
That's not the promise we made.
In which case ...
I'll have to kill you, too.
So you persist in clinging to the past.
You can't see the big picture anymore, Hank.

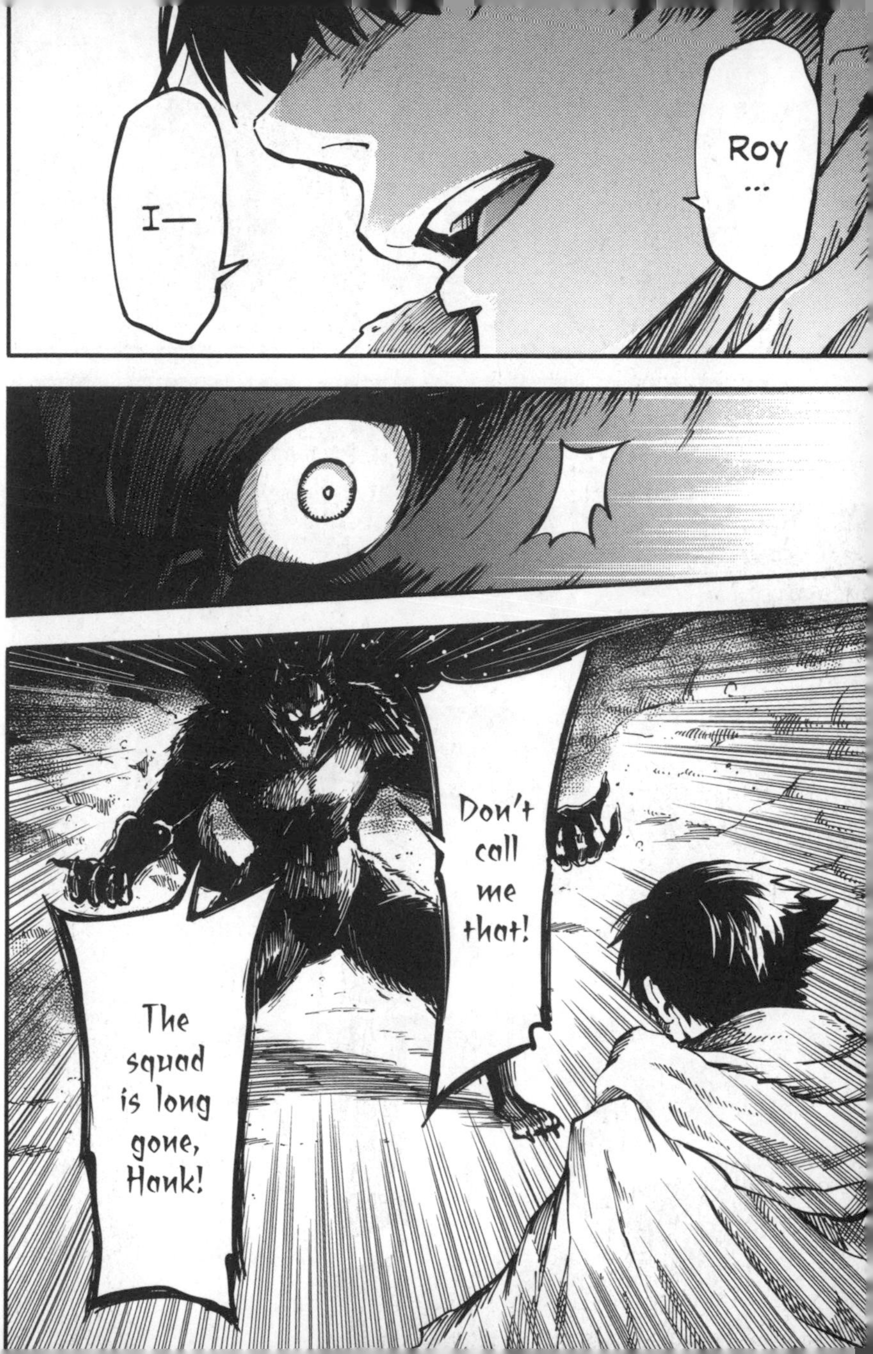
Roy ...
I—
Don't call me that!
The squad is long gone, Hank!

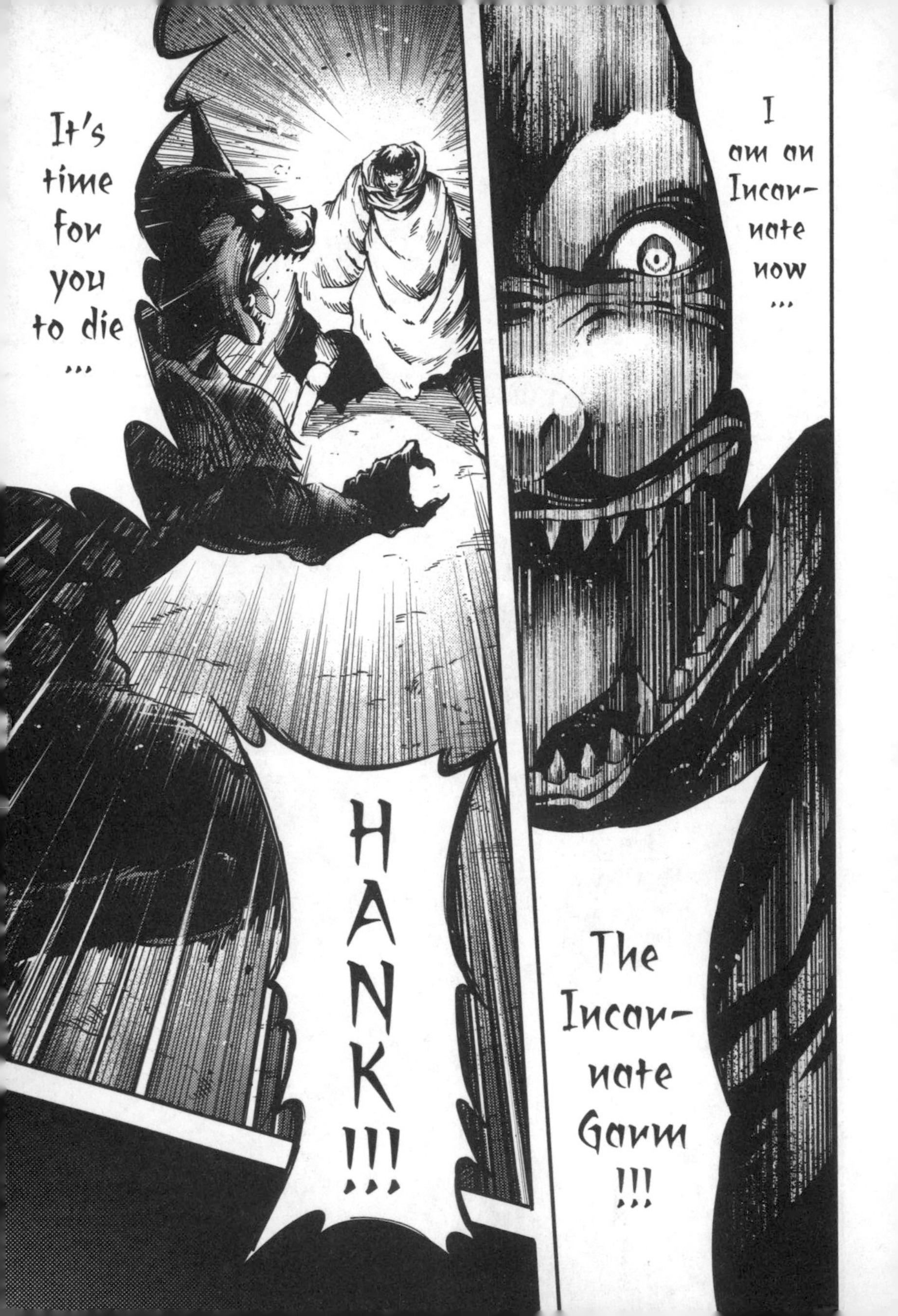
I am an Incarnate now ...
The Incarnate Garm !!!
It's time for you to die ...
HANK!!!

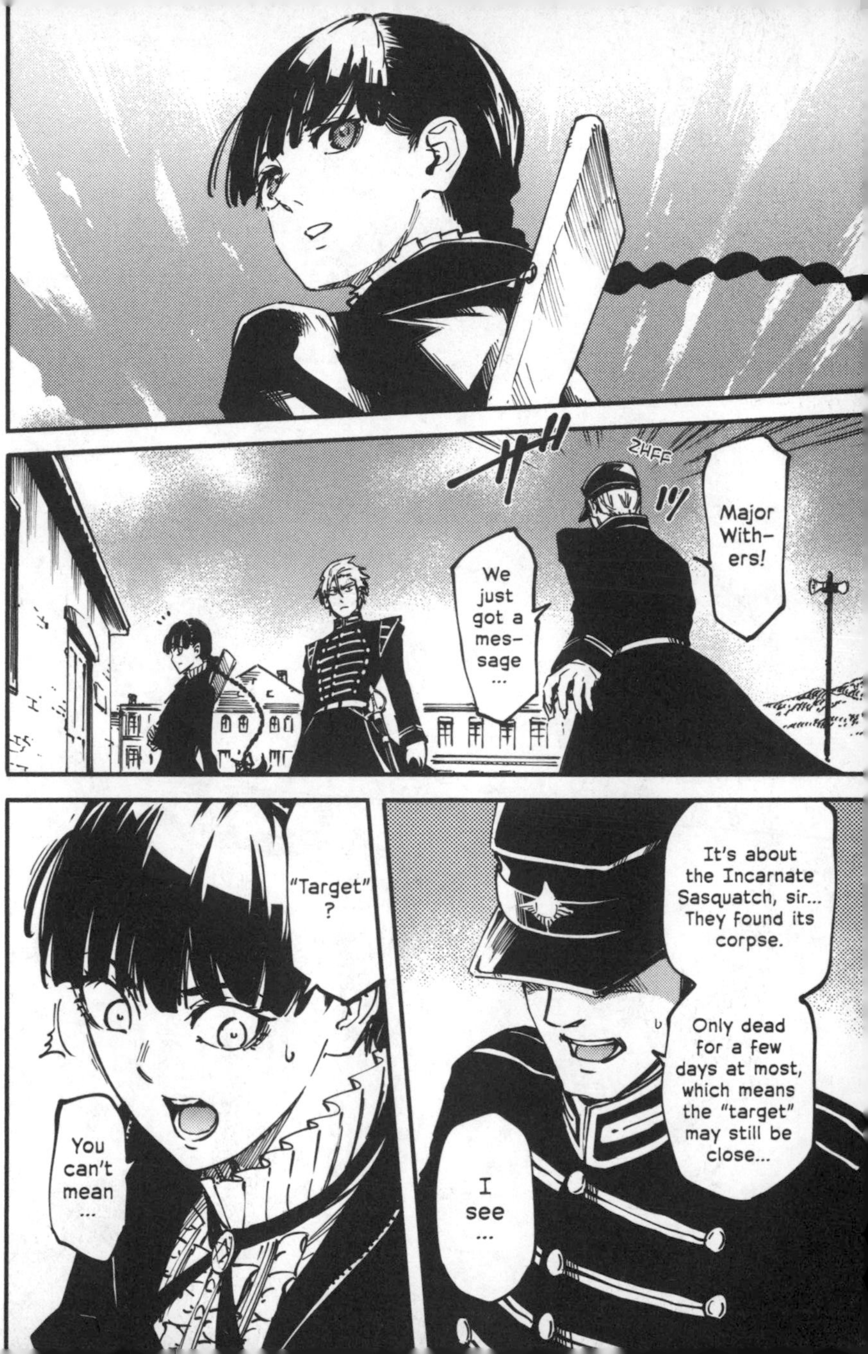
ZHFF
Major Withers!
We just got a message...
It's about the Incarnate Sasquatch, sir... They found its corpse.
Only dead for a few days at most, which means the "target" may still be close...
I see...
"Target"?
You can't mean...

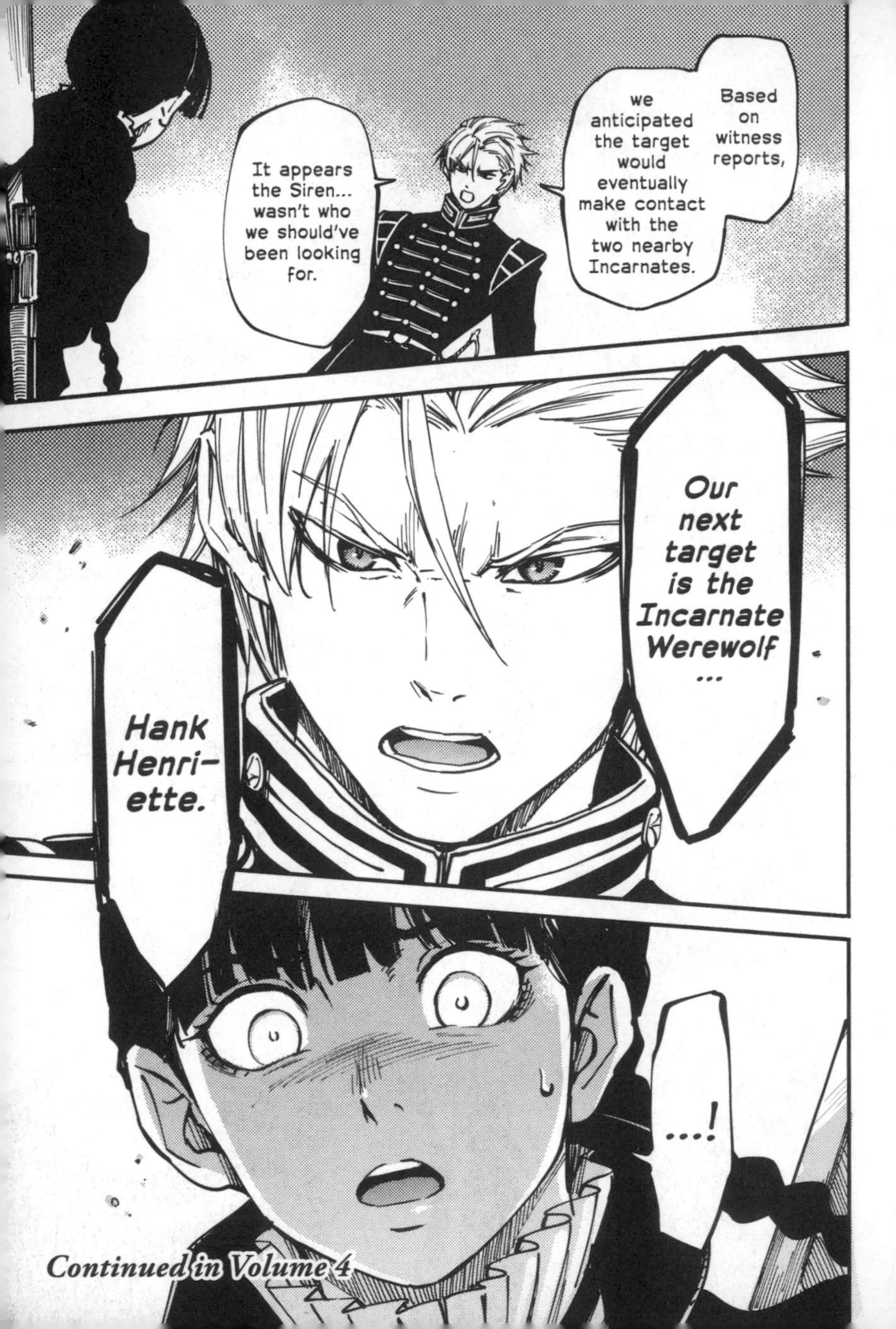
Based on witness reports, we anticipated the target would eventually make contact with the two nearby Incarnates.
It appears the Siren... wasn't who we should've been looking for.
Our next target is the Incarnate Werewolf...
Hank Henri-ette.
...!
Continued in Volume 4

Encyclopedia Entries

file no. 9 | *Incarnate Nidhogg*

Height: 98 ft.

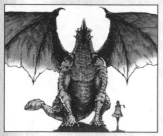

An undying dragon who witnessed the end and survived.

Gifted with a powerful, resilient body and inexhaustible life energy, the Nidhogg also possesses bullet-deflecting scales and muscular mobility far surpassing what its massive frame would suggest. Its total strength ranks among the highest of any Incarnate, making it the Northern forces' secret weapon.

In open engagements, the Nidhogg's overwhelming defensive and destructive capabilities could shatter battle regiments, and its wings, small considering its massive frame, allow for short-term flight.

Its life-force far surpasses that of other Incarnates. On several occasions, the Incarnate has survived battles that left both armies in shambles.

If the Nidhogg has any weakness, it's an abnormal hunger. It requires vast amounts of food to maintain its incredible mobility and life-force, but one theory suggests there is also a latent desire that drives it to consume so much.

file no. 10 | *Incarnate Siren*

Height: 8 ft.

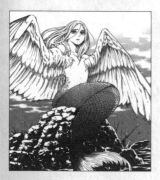

A winged mermaid that lures seafarers with song.

A strange creature with the arms of a bird and a lower body resembling that of a fish, the Siren lulls its foes into a deathly slumber with the power of song.

Contrary to their grand appearance, the Siren's wings are incapable of providing steady flight; at best, they allow the Siren to hover for brief periods of time when traveling on land. Its heavily muscled lower body impedes flight, but enables astonishingly fast underwater movement in return.

The Siren's greatest strength, its "song," is created not by using its voice, but by vibrating its wings. Exactly how this sonic assault affects its victims is unclear, but it appears to directly affect the brain and nervous system, dulling the senses and eventually inducing a state similar to a swoon.

Although the Siren's song can cause devastating results over a wide area, its frail body is among the weakest of all the Incarnates, and a single gunshot can be fatal. For this reason, it is advisable to pair the Siren with a defensively-oriented Incarnate when on the battlefield, where it can be exposed to the line of fire.

Sacred Beasts

file no. 11 | *Incarnate Sasquatch*

Height: 11½ ft.

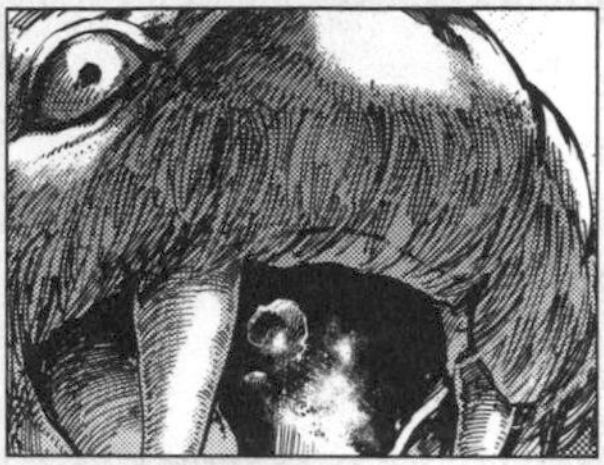

A supremely powerful demi-human who lurks deep in the mountains.

Highly suited to covert operations in mountainous regions, the Sasquatch's well-balanced muscles and human feet make advancing through rugged terrain easy, while its bristly coat of fur provides protection from gunfire.

In addition, the Sasquatch's subdermal fat layer provides excellent resistance to cold temperatures and allows for long periods of solo activity without support or supplies. The thickness of this fat layer can widely fluctuate, with the Sasquatch's weight sometimes shrinking in half following a particularly long operation.

Making use of these characteristics, the Sasquatch was frequently deployed as a stealth solo agent in mountainous regions to crush enemy reconnaissance forces and detachments. In spite of its exceptional ability to work covertly, it nonetheless left rare traces of its presence in the snowy mountainous regions. While its massive feet kept it from sinking into deep snowdrifts, it left behind footprints that were clearly not human. Those who came across these footprints imagined a creature of even greater size than the Sasquatch was, which planted seeds of terror in onlookers.

file no. 12 | *Rivulet Wood*

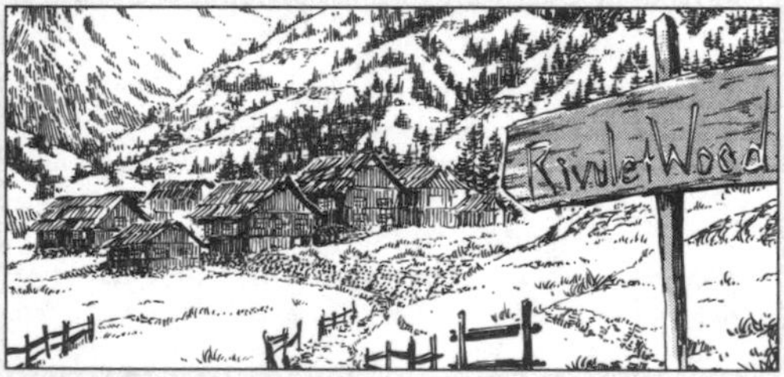
Rivulet Wood

A poor village nestled deep within a ravine.

A small village on a small stretch of flatland ensconced in sheer cliffs and deep valleys, Rivulet Wood was once a popular resting place for those braving the treacherous mountain passes during the wild frontier days. Following the discovery of alternate routes through the pass, however, the town's inhabitants have been forced to eke out a meager agrarian existence from what little arable land there is.

Within the village are the remains of a disproportionately large church building, built with donations from travelers wishing for a safe journey, but which became too much for the villagers to maintain on their own. Records show that outsiders ran an orphanage within the abandoned church at one point, but it's since been boarded up.

In recent years, war and lack of jobs have forced the village's younger population to leave, and Rivulet Wood is quietly slipping into decline.

file no. **13** | *Port Gulf*

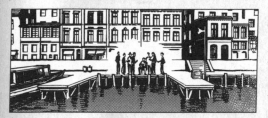

A port town whose glory has faded.

Blessed with natural features perfectly suited for a marine port, Port Gulf was a populous fishing village since time immemorial. Following the modernization of shipbuilding and the use of ships for material transportation, the town rapidly expanded into a hub for intercity transport.

During the Civil War, Port Gulf became a Patria Union base and a target for the Southern forces which wrought destruction on the town. Already struggling to recover after the end of the war, the city was dealt another blow by the development of rail networks across the country. Its geographic placement was already inconvenient, and so Port Gulf was forced to watch as the majority of its intercity traffic was stolen away by more convenient rail service.

With its population of sailors nearly wiped out from the war and the town's former glory all but lost, Port Gulf is slowly returning to its humble days as a quiet fishing hamlet.

file no. **14** | *Patria*

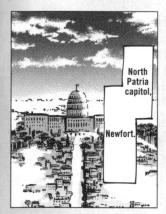

North Patria capitol, Newfort.

A young nation rocked by war.

Patria is a democratic republic created by colonists of the Patrian continent who achieved independence from the Old World roughly 100 years ago.

The well-industrialized North and the natural resource-rich South are divided by a vast, undeveloped plains region. Numerous economic disagreements with the Northern central government eventually led several Southern regions to form a confederation, marking the beginning of a long civil war between the Northern Union of Patria, where the capitol of Newfort stands, and the Southern Confederation of Patria.

Relations between North and South have normalized following the end of the war, but both sides continue to use their own systems of governance. The Incarnates brought the Civil War to an end, but the country's wounds run deep. Both sides continue to struggle with poverty and inequality resulting from the conflict, and the underlying causes of the war remain unresolved. Even now, the embers yet burn.

Sacred Beasts Encyclopedia Entries

file no. 15 | *Northern Union of Patria*

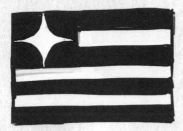

The vainglorious leader of the young nation.

Colonization of the Patrian continent started on the northeast coast, making the Northern region the oldest and most storied. This is where the heart of Patria's political economy beats, and the coastal regions are dotted with large port cities that serve as windows to foreign countries.

The North has many aristocrats descended from leaders who profited from the early colonists and moguls of industry who built their fortunes in the new land, both of which command wealth unlike anyone else in the world. Industrial titans seek to expand growth even further by monopolizing domestic demand through protective trade practices. However, the North depends almost entirely on the South for coal, iron, textiles and other recently discovered resources, with profits between the two sides remaining mutually exclusive.

file no. 16 | *Southern Confederation of Patria*

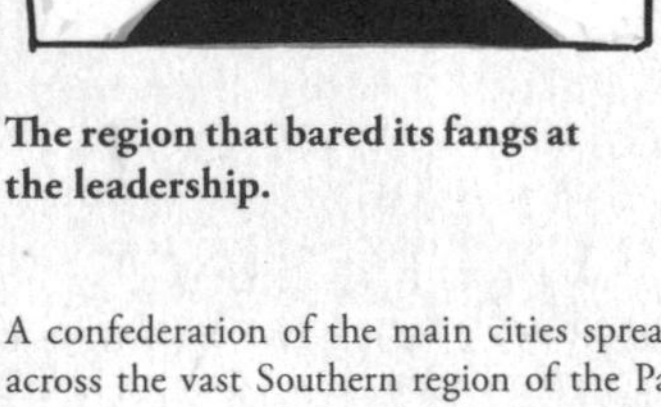

The region that bared its fangs at the leadership.

A confederation of the main cities spread across the vast Southern region of the Patrian continent, the South boasts bountiful natural resources and high populations, thriving agricultural and mining industries, and numerous large cities throughout the inner and coastal regions.

Southern business owners sought free trade with the Old World in order to increase exports of its vast stores of natural resources, but this led to an ideological conflict with the North. By the time war broke out, while the South was technologically disadvantaged, their superior access to resources allowed them to hold the upper hand until the appearance of the North's Incarnates.

The Incarnates' unbelievable strength turned the tides in an instant, and the resulting ceasefire left a sense of bitterness and resentment in part of the populace, some of whom would later join the Free Nation of New Patria, located in the western section of the continent.

file no. 17 | *Free Nation of New Patria*

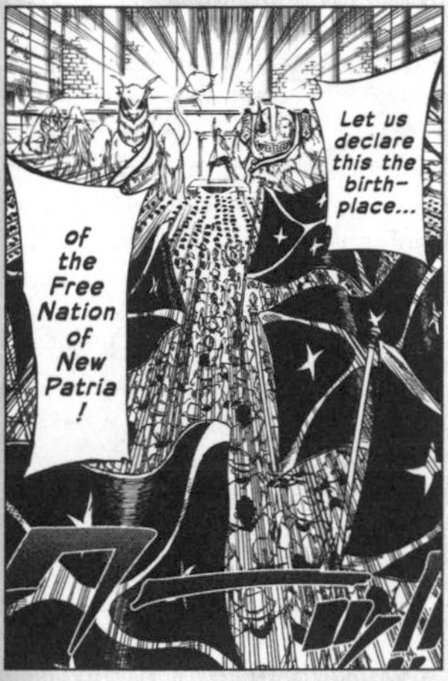
Let us declare this the birth-place...
of the Free Nation of New Patria!

A utopia for humans and Incarnates.

A rebel force comprised primarily of people disappointed in the way the Civil War ended in peace, New Patria seeks to overthrow Patria's government, and is rapidly expanding throughout the continent's western expanses.

With a core force of surviving Incarnates led by former Incarnate Squad Lieutenant Cain Madhouse, New Patria's military forces have been further bolstered by former soldiers of the Northern and Southern armies who had nowhere to go after the war ended. Their numbers are weak when compared to the military of the Northern Union of Patria, but the presence of Incarnates poses a definite threat. The Incarnates garner respect as tragic heroes and are spared the persecution they would face elsewhere.

Despite calling itself a nation, neither the Northern Union nor the weakened Southern Confederation acknowledge New Patria's sovereignty.

file no. 18 | *Incarnate Extermination Squad, Coup de Grace*

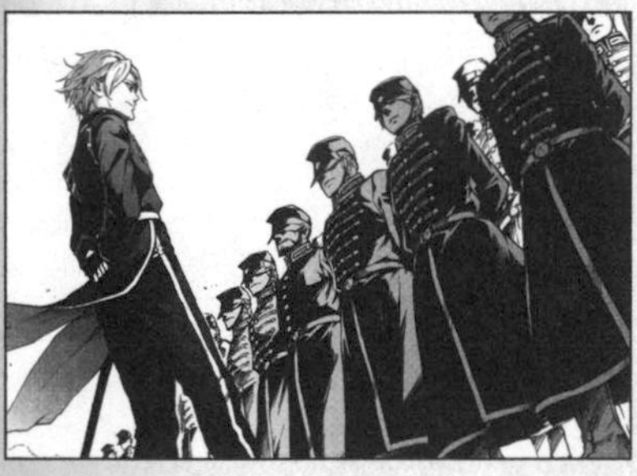

A human squadron created to hunt down Incarnates.

A squadron formed by Northern Patria's government to hunt down the remaining Incarnates, Coup de Grace's members number around 30 strong, and are backed up in their mission by reserve and support units.

Coup de Grace was ostensibly formed in response to public outcry against Incarnates following the widespread destruction in the aftermath of the Whitechurch Incident, but its true purpose is to whittle away reverence for Incarnates and thin their numbers in preparation for the coming battle against New Patria.

Formed around a core of young, elite Union Military talent and outfitted with special equipment specifically designed for anti-Incarnate combat, Coup de Grace exists as a unique entity within the Union forces and does not have a unit number.

True to its name, the intent of the squadron is to deliver a swift and merciful death to the heroes-turned-Beasts.

Sacred Beasts Encyclopedia Entries

file no. **19** | *Rotary Machine Cannon*

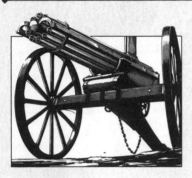

A superweapon that generates a deluge of bullets.

A special weapon prepared for Coup de Grace capable of firing a rapid succession of anti-Incarnate armor-piercing rounds through its rotating barrels.

Based on an anti-infantry weapon developed towards the end of the Civil War, its heaviness makes moving and rotating the cannon difficult, which, when combined with its limited range, makes it all but impossible to strike a target without first luring it directly in front of the barrels.

The machine cannon used by Coup de Grace has been modified to be more powerful in combat with Incarnates as well as altered to make it somewhat lighter. These changes have proven effective, allowing the cannon fire to pierce durable Incarnate skin and armor. The cannon is also able to be disassembled into smaller parts for transport, making it ideally suited to a squadron that must travel to various regions in order to fell Incarnates.

To the
Abandoned
Sacred
Beasts

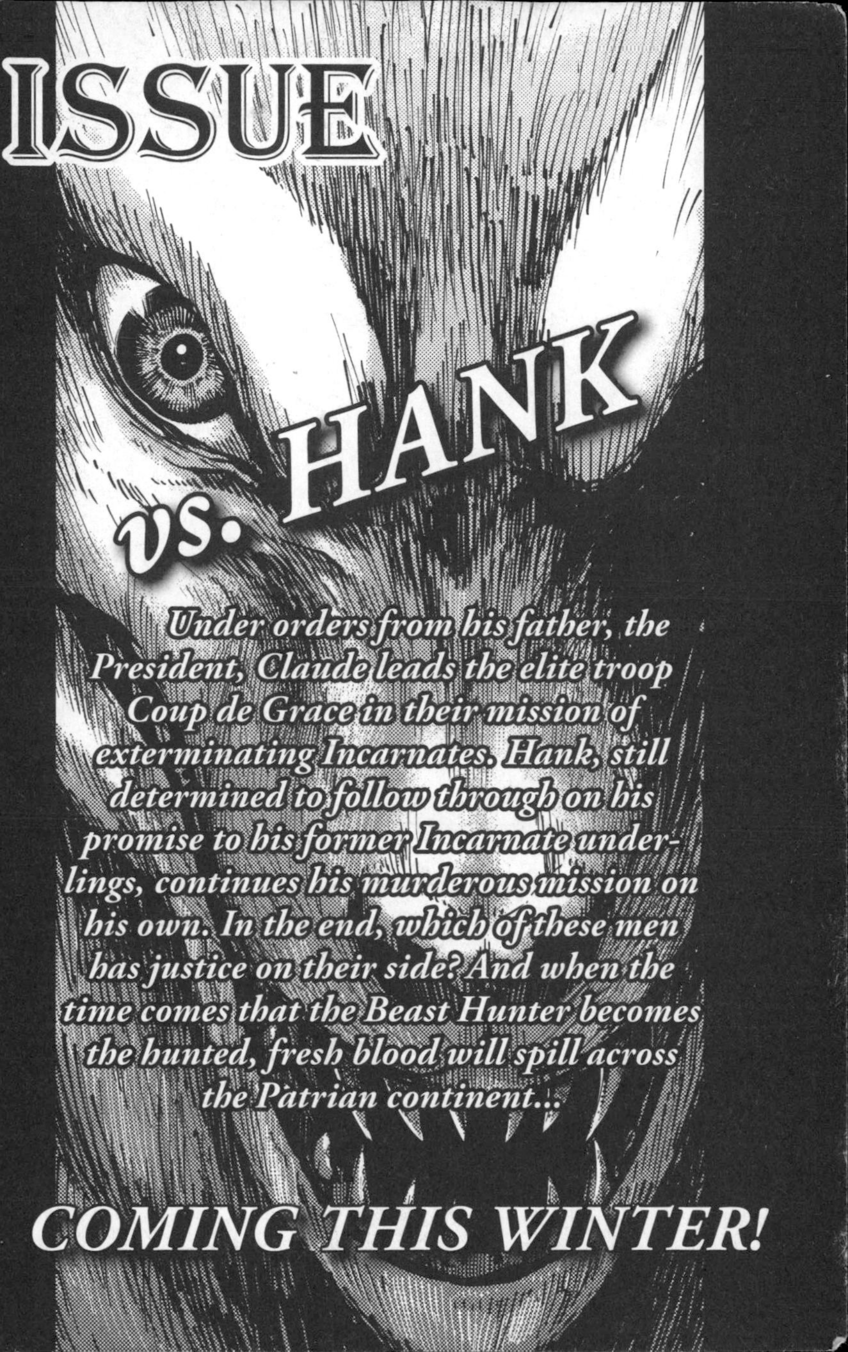
ISSUE
vs. HANK
Under orders from his father, the President, Claude leads the elite troop Coup de Grace in their mission of exterminating Incarnates. Hank, still determined to follow through on his promise to his former Incarnate underlings, continues his murderous mission on his own. In the end, which of these men has justice on their side? And when the time comes that the Beast Hunter becomes the hunted, fresh blood will spill across the Patrian continent...
COMING THIS WINTER!

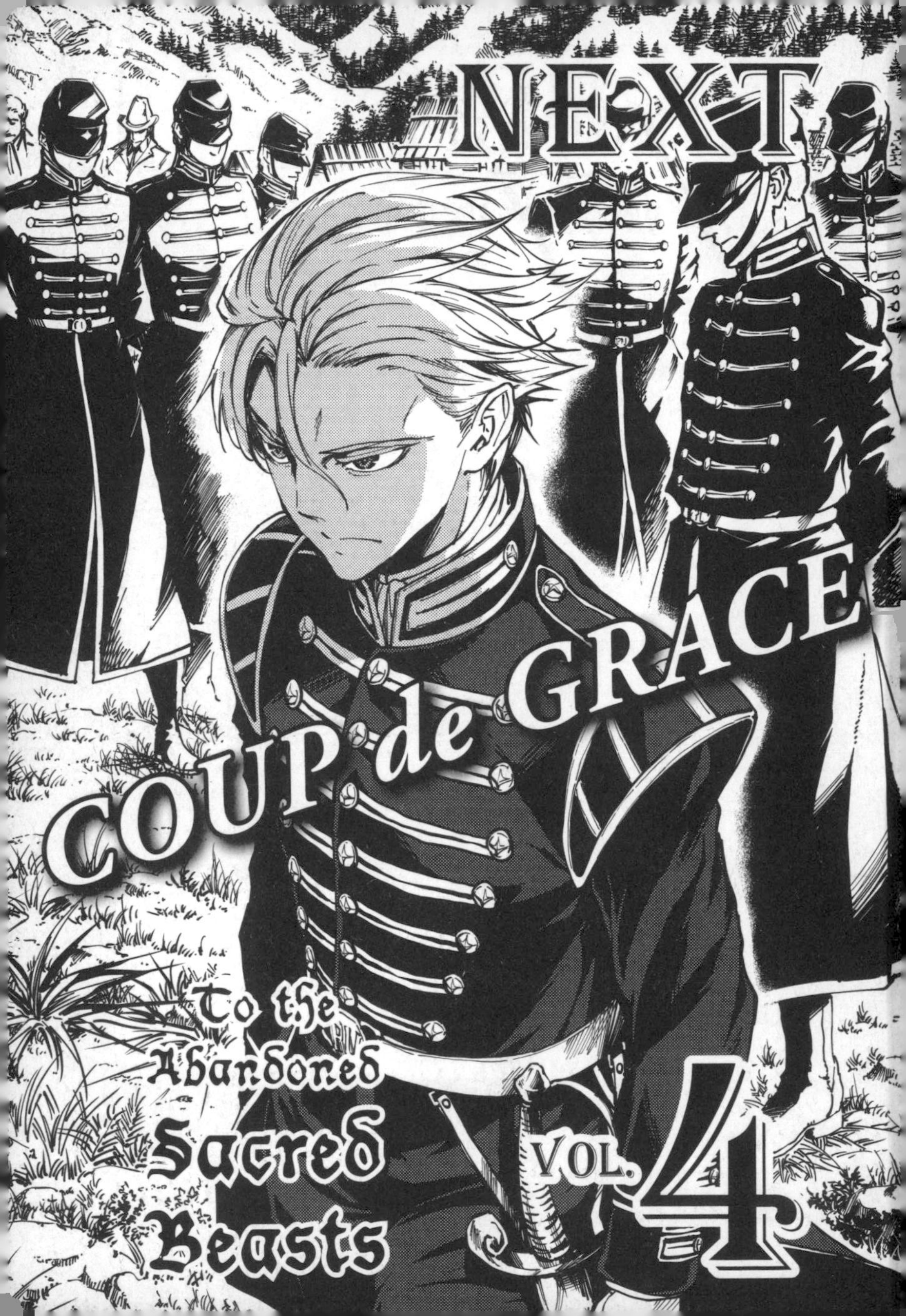
NEXT
COUP de GRACE
To the Abandoned Sacred Beasts
VOL. 4

To the Abandoned Sacred Beasts
Volume 3

Translation: Jason Moses
Production: Grace Lu
Anthony Quintessenza

First published in Japan in 2015 by Kodansha, Ltd., Tokyo
Publication rights for this English edition arranged through Kodansha, Ltd., Tokyo
English language version produced by Vertical, Inc.

Translation provided by Vertical Comics, 2016
Published by Vertical Comics, an imprint of Vertical, Inc., New York

Originally published in Japanese as *Katsute Kami Datta Kemono-tachi e 3* by Kodansha, Ltd.
Katsute Kami Datta Kemono-tachi e first serialized in *Bessatsu Shonen Magazine*, Kodansha, Ltd., 2014-

ISBN: 978-1-942993-64-3

Manufactured in Canada

First Edition

Vertical, Inc.
451 Park Avenue South
7th Floor
New York, NY 10016
www.vertical-comics.com

Vertical books are distributed through Penguin-Random House Publisher Services.